PREPARING
FOR
MINISTRY

PREPARING
FOR
MINISTRY

A PRACTICAL GUIDE TO THEOLOGICAL FIELD EDUCATION

GEORGE M. HILLMAN JR.
EDITOR

Preparing for Ministry: A Practical Guide to Theological Field Education

© 2008 by George M. Hillman Jr.

Published by Kregel Publications, a division of Kregel, Inc., P.O. Box 2607, Grand Rapids, MI 49501.

Library of Congress Cataloging-in-Publication Data
Preparing for ministry : a practical guide to theological field education /
[edited] by George M. Hillman Jr.
    p. cm.
  Includes bibliographical references (pp. 359–66).
 1. Pastoral theology–Fieldwork. 2. Clergy–Training of. I. Hillman, George M.
  BV4164.5.P74 2008
  230.071'1–dc22

                      2008036366

ISBN 978-0-8254-2757-2

Printed in the United States of America
08 09 10 11 12 / 5 4 3 2 1

To our mentors, the pioneers of field education

who blazed the trail that we inherited

Contents

Preface

As I write this, I am flying from Tampa back to my home in Dallas. I am not returning from a week at the beach enjoying the gorgeous sun and sand, however. Instead, I am returning from spending two days with our seminary students who are serving at churches in the Tampa area. While I missed out on the ocean views on this trip (maybe next time), I am taking back something even better. I am taking back once again a reminder of why I love my job so much. I am a field educator at a seminary, and I am returning from the field and from talking face-to-face with students who are serving Christ in their various ministry settings.

Looking back on my own seminary education, I know firsthand how life-changing a great internship can be. My own field education experience literally altered the course of my life. Now as the "internship guy" on a seminary campus, I get to watch that same level of discovery, uncertainty, stretching, wonder, and praise seep through my students' lives as they involve themselves in the wonderful messiness of ministry. I (as well as everyone who contributed to this book) am passionate about student development. A field education internship is not busywork or cheap labor but is instead a fundamental element in the intentional development of a future ministry leader. A great internship experience can place a student in an environment where God can work through him or her in the lives of other people and (more importantly in many ways) where God can work in the student's own life to develop calling, character, and competencies.

The Birth of a Book

The birth of this book took place during an evening conversation in a Dallas hotel lobby as twenty-two members of the Evangelical Association of Theological Field Educators (EATFE) gathered for our annual meeting.[1] Many of us discussed how there were very limited resources currently available that addressed ministerial internships from an evangelical perspective or that dealt with some of the new realities of theological education. We talked about how we wished there was a resource that we could give to churches

---

1. Originally started in 1983 as a caucus organization in the larger ecumenical Association for Theological Field Education (ATFE), EATFE is a professional field education organization representing a wide variety of denominational and nondenominational Bible colleges, seminaries, training centers, and nonprofit organizations. Information about both ATFE and EATFE can be found at www.atfe.org.

and organizations that were looking for information on how to either start or improve their own internship program. We also reminisced on our own entry into the world of field education and how all of us had to learn our jobs by trial and error. Most of us were ministers who had entered the academic world by a variety of paths. How we all wished that there had been a new field educator's how-to manual to guide our ignorance.

Out of that initial discussion, we collectively decided to cooperate on a ministry preparation book. The purpose of this book is to provide a resource for ministry students, church leaders, nonprofit organization leaders, and Bible college and seminary professors that addresses many of the questions they pose when either participating in or organizing a formal internship program. We felt that a collaborative book would best represent current thought in evangelical theological schools and could address a wide audience.

The men and women who are contributors to this book are some of my dearest friends in ministry. I came out of the pastorate into the academic world as a field educator at a major seminary, and many of these individuals were my literal lifeline that first year as I tried to figure out my job in the strange world of academia. While many of us see each other only once a year, we have that type of instant connection that dear friends have.

A Word About Vocabulary

One of the challenges in editing this book is the lack of a common vocabulary among Bible colleges and seminaries when it comes to what we do as a ministry and a profession. The technical term for what we do as professional educators is *field education*, since it is literally education that takes place in the field of vocational service instead of in the classroom. However, there is a wide variety of terms our schools use to describe our programs: *internship, practicum, residency, apprenticeship, practical training, pastoral training, mentored ministry,* and so on. While we have chosen the term *field education* in both the title of the book and in most of the chapters, please feel free to substitute the word on your campus that identifies the ministerial training that takes place on the field instead of in the classroom.

Different schools also use various terms for the person who works with the student intern during an internship. Some schools use the word *mentor.* Other schools use the word *supervisor* or *coach.* We have chosen the word *mentor* because we think it communicates a warmer feel than *supervisor* or *coach.* What takes place in an internship is more than an employee-employer relationship. Real mentoring (which will be discussed in greater detail in the book) is the goal regardless of the term used. Again, you may substitute your school's term for this person throughout the book.

Throughout the book we will be speaking about the relationship between the mentor and the student. Nevertheless, in our almost exclusive use of the term *mentor* for clarity's sake, we do not want to exclude others who may be involved in the internship process. Depending on the setting and the requirements, the student intern may have a lay committee or advisory council involved in the process as well. For example, I ask students on our campus to have four "ministry consultants" in addition to their mentor. The number of people and the role of these people vary greatly depending on the school and denomination. In those settings where such a group is required, a group of laypeople (usually but not always) work alongside the on-site mentor in providing feedback, guidance, assessment, and prayer support throughout the internship. If you are reading this book as a member of such a supervisory group, please know that many of the items that are specifically addressed to the mentor can easily be applied to you as well. Although you may not have as much time with the student as the mentor, you are still a valuable member of the team.

The Umbrella of Spiritual Transformation

Formal theological education is about much more than reading books, listening to lectures, and taking tests. While there is always a very vital cognitive part to any educational process, theological education is far more than just intellectual growth or competency development. At the heart of theological education is the heart of the student. The heart of leadership is the leader's heart.

A student can have an engaging personality, but personality will only get that student so far in ministry without the development of the heart. A student can be a driven person with a very clear vision of the future, but that student can easily drive off the road without the foundation of the spiritual life. A student can be passionate about what he or she is doing, but those passions also can blind the student who lacks the light of spiritual insight. A student can be the smartest person in the class, but good grades will never make up for a lack of spiritual formation.[2]

I hate writing these words, but nothing surprises me anymore when I hear about fallen leaders. Talented pastors misuse their power. Eloquent speakers drown in pornography. Creative artists have affairs. Energetic ministers neglect their own families. Loving counselors step over respectable boundaries. Wise administrators mismanage money. Showcase couples get divorced. High school student leaders in the youth group get pregnant. Energetic clergy members run themselves to emotional burnout and physical neglect. The classic seven deadly sins of pride, envy, gluttony, lust, anger, greed, and sloth are, unfortunately, very active in the church today.

Being (spiritual transformation and character) always must precede doing (tasks and skills). Everything in leadership must be grounded in the idea of spiritual transformation and character. In both 1 Timothy 3:1–13 and Titus 1:5–9, the focus is primarily on character qualifications for spiritual

---

2. Stephen Graves and Thomas Addington, *A Case for Character: Authentic Living in Your Workplace* (Nashville: Broadman & Holman, 1998), xiii; Henry Cloud, *Integrity: The Courage to Meet the Demands of Reality* (New York: Collins, 2006), 8.

leaders. Leadership development is about the whole person, not just the *how-to* of leadership. In reality the *how-to* part is much easier than spiritual and character development. A good internship and mentoring relationship can create healthy leaders of spiritual substance and character. The internship should direct the student to examine his or her spiritual life in order to discover the integrity blind spots and encourage the student to begin dealing with the issue before it becomes a serious problem later.

While it may not be specifically said in a chapter, everything you will read in this book is under the overall umbrella of spiritual transformation. The contributors of this book are not interested in developing hollow men and women who look good on the outside but lack Christlikeness on the inside. We are not interested in training leaders and administrators who lack integrity. We are interested in developing godly servant leaders, men and women who will change the world by being useful vessels of the Holy Spirit in their churches and organizations. This growth in spiritual development and personal integrity can be the most important aspect of an internship and a mentoring relationship.

To remind the reader of this foundation, we have asked each contributor to begin his or her chapter with a relevant Scripture verse and to end his or her chapter with a prayer of transformation. So as you read even the "mundane" aspects of field education administration, please understand that every aspect is there to contribute to the spiritual transformation of the student's life. Our prayer is that an environment will be created in the internship in which the Holy Spirit can transform the student (and maybe even the mentor) from the inside out.

—George M. Hillman Jr.

Contributors

Harley Atkinson is chair and professor of Christian education at Toccoa Falls College in Toccoa, Georgia.

Joye Baker is adjunct professor of Christian education and women's adviser in Christian education at Dallas Theological Seminary in Dallas, Texas.

Luke Bobo is the former assistant dean for training ministries at Covenant Theological Seminary in St. Louis, Missouri.

Thomas Fuller is director of ministry leadership development, placement, and assessment at Beeson Divinity School in Birmingham, Alabama.

Nelson Grimm is associate professor of applied theology and the director of field education at Northeastern Seminary in Rochester, New York.

Dipa Hart is assistant director of spiritual formation and leadership at Dallas Theological Seminary in Dallas, Texas.

George M. Hillman Jr. is associate professor of spiritual formation and leadership at Dallas Theological Seminary in Dallas, Texas.

Tara Hornbacker is associate professor of ministry formation at Bethany Theological Seminary in Richmond, Indiana.

Walter Kime is associate professor of field education at Ashland Theological Seminary in Ashland, Ohio.

Katherine Kyte is assistant director of mentored ministry at Gordon-Conwell Theological Seminary in South Hamilton, Massachusetts.

Doran McCarty is the former executive director of seminary extension of the Southern Baptist Seminaries and is a former professor at Midwestern Baptist Theological Seminary and Golden Gate Theological Seminary.

Don Payne is associate dean and assistant professor of theology and ministry at Denver Seminary in Denver, Colorado.

Paul Pettit is director of spiritual formation at Dallas Theological Seminary in Dallas, Texas.

Jeff Sanders is associate dean for relationship education at Bethel University in St. Paul, Minnesota.

Mary Sanders is associate director of personal and professional formation at Bethel Seminary in St. Paul, Minnesota.

Phillip Sell is associate professor of pastoral theology and director of supervised ministries at Trinity Evangelical Divinity School in Deerfield, Illinois.

Daryl Smith is associate professor of mentored ministry and Christian leadership at Asbury Theological Seminary (Florida campus) in Orlando, Florida.

William Torgesen is assistant professor of pastoral studies at Moody Bible Institute in Chicago, Illinois.

Timothy Witmer is professor of practical theology at Westminster Theological Seminary in Philadelphia, Pennsylvania.

PART 1

Purposes of Field Education

Vocational Discernment
Ministry Skill Competence
Theological Reflection
Cultural Awareness

Chapter 1

Field Education and Vocational Discernment

NELSON GRIMM

Having gifts that differ according to the grace given to us, let us use them: if prophecy, in proportion to our faith; if service, in our serving; the one who teaches, in his teaching; the one who exhorts, in his exhortation; the one who contributes, in generosity; the one who leads, with zeal; the one who does acts of mercy, with cheerfulness. (Rom. 12:6–8)

God continues to call people to himself. He invites people to receive his grace, to become his disciples, and to fulfill their created place in his kingdom. Earnest Christians have always attempted to sort out God's will for their lives and have concluded that a life well lived involves faithfully following God's leading. People have discovered that thriving in life means to live a life consistent with who God created them to be.

I will never forget the joy expressed when a student told me, "Field education changed my life!" She used her field education assignment to explore ministry options and found a perfect fit. In many ways, field education is a chance to test-drive ministry and to gain the insight necessary to make good decisions.

The reflective nature of field education provides an excellent opportunity for men and women to consider how God has gifted and graced them for life and how they can prepare themselves for effective service within God's kingdom. The vocational discernment process involves asking the right questions. How is the student unique? How has God shaped the student for life? What are the student's abilities and strengths? What experiences has the student had that have been most rewarding? What societal needs challenge the student's heart the most? Furthermore, the reflective process may help one to recognize unresolved disappointments or hurts that need healing.

The supportive environment of seminary encourages students to appraise their gifts, interests, and abilities and to design meaningful learning goals. As students are able to test-drive ministry, they are better able to confirm their sense of fit with their anticipated vocation. A goal of field education is to provide opportunities for seminarians to develop their professional understanding and competence in ministry, while supervised in the practice of ministry. A desired outcome is a greater vocational clarity and confidence.

For some students, field education involves doing something new. Perhaps they will preach a sermon for the first time, lead a small group, or visit someone in the hospital. For others, field education is not about doing something new but about doing something in a new way. I recall a student who had been a pastor for many years before coming to seminary. When he came to talk about what he would do as his assignment, he indicated that he had done it all, that his twenty-plus years of pastoral ministry provided him with all sorts of experiences.

I agreed with his assessment. He had experienced the wide range of pastoral responsibilities, so I challenged him to think of what he could do in a new way. He chose to work on his preaching and designed a rigorous program including soliciting feedback from parishioners and videotaping sermons, which he reviewed later with his mentor. Within weeks, parishioners were commenting on how much his preaching had changed. He moved away from overuse of particular words and awkward mannerisms. He improved his eye contact with people and structured his sermons more simply. Whether a student is very new to ministry or brings multiple years of experience, field education provides the opportunity for exploration and growth.

Understanding Self

Vocational discernment requires a clear understanding of who the student is and how God has gifted the student. God uses a student's interests and abilities, joys and desires to invite that student into his service to the world. We are not all the same. A student can use his or her field education experiences to explore what it is that makes that student unique. Every student was created with a particular set of interests and skills and has been shaped by events and circumstances. This wonderful blend of elements becomes the context of life.

Alongside these elements of life are the needs of the world. Where these two intersect will largely define a student's particular vocation. Frederick Buechner famously puts it this way:

> There are all kinds of voices calling you to all different kinds of work, and the problem is to find out which is the voice of God rather than of society, say, or the Superego, or Self-Interest. By and large a good rule for finding out is this. The kind of work God usually calls you to is the kind of work (a) that you really need to do and (b) that the world needs to have done. If you really get a kick out of your work, you've presumably met requirement (a), but if your work is writing TV deodorant commercials, the chances are you've missed requirement (b). On the other hand, if your work is being a doctor in a leper colony, you probably met requirement (b), but if most of the time you're bored and depressed by it, the chances are you have not only bypassed (a) but probably aren't helping your patients much either. Neither the hair shirt nor the soft berth will do. The place God calls you is the place where your deep gladness and the world's deep hunger meet.[1]

Revisit Sense of Call

Students should use the field education experience to revisit their original sense of call, to reconnect with their initial images of ministry, and to sharpen their focus on the future. Students can begin the process by recalling the circumstances surrounding the first time they consciously determined that they were going into professional ministry. Some questions that help with this exploration are the following: What was happening in the student's life at that time? Who did the student first tell about his or her decision? What was the person's reaction to the news? How did the student tell his or her family? What attracted the student most to the idea? How has the student's early experiences in ministry differed from his or her expectations? Let the student look for patterns or recurring themes. How has the student's sense of call evolved or matured since his or her earliest inclination? What new thing has God been teaching the student about himself or herself and his or her place in God's kingdom?

While in many ways the call to ministry goes beyond one's ability to comprehend completely, there are elements within the call itself that are knowable. As students revisit their initial sense of calling, they can also consider how God has called others into his service. In what ways does a student's call resemble biblical patterns of God working in the lives of people? A student might identify with the dramatic, surprising call of Paul, who fell to the ground in the brilliance of God's presence. Paul's call to

---

1. Frederick Buechner, *Wishful Thinking: A Theological ABC* (New York: Harper & Row, 1973), 118.

God's service was unmistakable. It was the defining moment of Paul's life. There are those today who testify to this type of life-changing experience. They have had some sort of divine encounter that has carved certainty and assurance into the very core of their beings.

Yet, many students spend years trying to sort out God's call. Sometimes a student may respond to God's call with multiple questions or even resistance. The student may be like Moses (without the excitement of the burning bush), who carried on a debate with God, listing all the reasons why God should look for a more qualified leader. It is easy for students to identify their limitations (others can see them as well). However, God's grace and mercy are abundantly able to transform one's weaknesses into dimensions of life that bring glory to his name. It is natural for people to have a sense of wonder and amazement at God's call to salvation. Furthermore, it is healthy to have some sense of unworthiness when being called to Christian service.

After all, as Paul reminds us in 2 Corinthians 12:7–10, it is God's grace that makes all of us competent to serve:

> So to keep me from being too elated by the surpassing greatness of the revelations, a thorn was given me in the flesh, a messenger of Satan to harass me, to keep me from being too elated. Three times I pleaded with the Lord about this, that it should leave me. But he said to me, "My grace is sufficient for you, for my power is made perfect in weakness." Therefore I will boast all the more gladly of my weaknesses, so that the power of Christ may rest upon me. For the sake of Christ, then, I am content with weaknesses, insults, hardships, persecutions, and calamities. For when I am weak, then I am strong.

In addition to these common types or patterns of calling, biblical scholar John Polhill identifies the community, the misdirected, and the redefined call.[2]

Community Call

Polhill reminds his readers of the role of the church in Timothy's calling and the importance of the community of believers in helping people discern the will of God. There are occasions when others, for reasons perhaps unknown to them, impose their own will on the life of another. I have seen this especially among individuals who live with deep regret themselves and have overextended themselves upon others as a way of compensation. However, it is a central responsibility of the church to affirm the presence of

---

2. John Polhill, "Toward a Biblical View of Call," in *Preparing for Christian Ministry: An Evangelical Approach*, ed. David P. Gushee and Walter C. Jackson (Grand Rapids: Baker, 1996), 65–79.

the gifts and graces needed for ministry and to confirm the call of God upon the life of a person. As will be seen later in detail, students need to be open to how the Lord may use others to guide them in their discernment and to assist them to mature in faith.

Misdirected Call

Polhill serves students well by noting that sometimes students can misinterpret God's call. He recalls the account of a man healed by Jesus in Mark 5:1–20. The man immediately concluded that he should become Christ's disciple and go along with Jesus from town to town. Jesus told him to go to his own home and community and serve him there. As Polhill writes,

> Sometimes people have a powerful spiritual experience that convinces them that God is calling them into a fulltime ministry, yet later discover that God is calling them to greater commitment in their present life situation. On occasion, I have talked with seminary students who have reevaluated their call and have determined this was the case with them. Returning home, they have served in lay positions in their home churches with a renewed sense of commitment. Theirs, however, are no less significant a call than those called to career ministries.[3]

Redefined Call

A number of seminary students experience a redefining of their call while in seminary. They may have come to seminary with a particular sense of direction and, like Stephen and Philip, realize a new focus for their lives. For some, this happens as they develop a clearer self-understanding. Students may see their gifts and graces for ministry more completely. Other students may come to have a better understanding of the nature of ministry. In either case, it results in a more informed decision and a better work environment fit. For many, if not most, this maturing process continues throughout life as they grow in their understanding of who they are and in response to the world in which they live.

What Has God Created?

After a student has revisited his or her sense of call, the student should continue this vocational discernment process by asking good questions about who he or she is and how God has created him or her. Students can list the experiences they have had and note the defining moments when they discovered something new about themselves. In doing this, students need to be sure not to limit their thinking to only their employment history but to include their volunteering experiences as well. Students should take note of

---

3. Ibid., 78.

those occasions that brought the greatest joy or satisfaction. What were the circumstances surrounding the event or accomplishment? What was it about that activity or achievement that made it so memorable? What patterns or themes do students see as they review the past? Students might also consider what experiences created the greatest anxiety. The presence of anxiety, in and of itself, may not be a red flag. Anxiety may simply indicate that greater information or experience is required.

Identify Heroes

Another way to increase self-understanding is to identify a student's heroes. Consider the people that the student admires most and the characteristics and qualities that make them instrumental people in the student's life. What makes them unique? How do they live out their giftedness? As a student identifies the characteristics he or she admires most in others, realize that the student is making a statement regarding the things valued most in life. While the student's heroes may exhibit these traits to a greater degree, the qualities are present within the student's life as well.

Students can do a personal inventory, exploring the ways that they have lived out the qualities that they have seen in their heroes. With this in hand, students can take some time and write down ideas regarding ways to foster growth in these identified areas. What would it take for the student to live out these qualities to a greater degree? What changes would he or she need to make for these characteristics to have an increasingly important place in life? What does this information tell the student about the person he or she is, and how does this insight influence the way the student does ministry?

Formal Assessment Tools

Many seminaries provide some sort of formal assessment opportunities that allow students to get another perspective on their spiritual giftedness and personality preferences.[4] Utilizing well-developed personality measures can be a very informative and productive way of gaining self-understanding and insight. Some programs offer the services of psychologists or other personnel who utilize assessment tools such as the following.[5]

California Psychological Inventory

California Psychological Inventory is designed to help people better understand their strengths and opportunities for development. A large variety of scales target areas of life such as interpersonal behavior, social and personal values, cognitive needs and performance, and personal and work-related characteristics.

---

4. A more detailed discussion of two additional assessment tools not discussed in this chapter (Clifton StrengthsFinder and IDAK Career Match) is found in chapter 17, "Comparing Natural Talent Inventories for Use in Field Education."

5. The following information was adapted from test publishers' descriptions.

Strong Interest Inventory

Strong Interest Inventory can provide students with an in-depth assessment of their interest among a broad range of occupations. The instrument helps individuals to understand their preferred work environment and seeks to describe preferred style of working, learning, risk-taking, and team participation.

Myers-Briggs Type Indicator

Myers-Briggs Type Indicator reflects personal preferences in four primary areas revolving around the following main questions: Does one prefer to focus on the inner or external world? When one makes decisions, does he or she value logic and consistency or does he or she look at the people involved and the unique circumstances? How does one prefer to gather information or form meaning? Does one prefer to get things decided and move on, or would one rather remain open to new possibilities and options?

Thomas-Kilmann Conflict Mode Instrument

Thomas-Kilmann Conflict Mode Instrument (TKI) is a tool for assessing how different conflict-handling modes, or styles, affect interpersonal and group dynamics and for learning how to select the most appropriate style for a given situation. The TKI offers a pragmatic, situational approach to conflict resolution and demonstrates how and when to use the five conflict-handling styles effectively.

Fundamental Interpersonal Relations Orientation-Behavior

Fundamental Interpersonal Relations Orientation-Behavior (FIRO-B) increases understanding of how an individual interacts with others at work and in his or her personal life. The assessment tool gathers insights into how personal preferences for inclusion, control, and affection can shape interactions with others.

16PF

16PF may assist by gathering information for general vocational guidance to help determine occupations for which the individual is best suited. The tool helps to assess normal-range measurement of anxiety, adjustment, and behavioral concerns. The 16PF considers five primary global factors: extraversion, anxiety, tough-mindedness, independence, and self-control.

Create a Time Line

A visual way of gaining a new perspective on life is to create a time line. A few years ago, I spent some time looking back over my life, identifying those defining moments in my personal development. While there are a variety of ways of developing a time-line chart, I used color-coded sticky notes to help me review how significant people and experiences of life have helped to shape me into the person I am today. I began by using one color to remind me of the events that have had the biggest impact upon my life.

I put these notes on poster board according to the year or period of my life. I have a section on the board that reminds me of my home life and college and seminary years and columns for the important circumstances that happened during each of my pastoral appointments and other major periods of my life. I identified both positive and negative experiences and included a word or phrase that described how I saw God at work in my life. Similarly, I used a different color sticky note to represent significant people and included words or phrases that reflected how God used them to shape my life.

The process gave me a new perspective on life.[6] The act of systematically reflecting on the events of life helped to show me how God has been at work in ways I had not previously seen or had forgotten. Furthermore, I developed a new appreciation for God's gift of people. Family, friends, pastors, teachers, members of my congregations, and many others who have added to my self-understanding have blessed me.

A very significant result of the process was the clarification of personal values and character traits. As I reflected on the events of life, I was able to see patterns of decision making and recurring ways of relating to people. It reminded me of the specific ways that God has gifted and prepared me for ministry, as well as areas in my life that needed to be developed. An additional benefit of the process was a sharper focus on the future. I came away with a fresh understanding of the past and found new energy for my next chapter in life.

Terry Walling has developed a very helpful list of assumptions that underlie this type of life processing. These assumptions include the following:

1. When Christ calls a believer, he intends to develop the believer to his or her full potential.

2. Each believer is individually responsible for his or her own development, as opposed to a spouse, pastor, or church leader.

3. God continually develops believers. Spiritual renewal and formation habits shape believers to be more effective.

4. Every believer operates from a set of convictions from the past and uses these to provide guidance into the future.[7]

---

6. For more on how to develop a personal time line, see materials by J. Robert Clinton, *Leadership Emergence Theory* (Altadena, CA: Barnabas Resources, 1989); John Trent, *Life Mapping* (Colorado Springs: WaterBrook, 1998); and Terry Walling, "Perspective Time Line," in *Focused Living Resource Kit*, ed. Terry B. Walling (Anaheim: ChurchSmart Resources, 1996).

7. Walling, "Perspective Time Line," 14.

The Role of Community

The Christian community plays a vital role in developing vocational clarity within a person's life. Students come to know themselves within the context of their community. Other people help students to learn about their strengths, weaknesses, temperament, personality, and worldview. While it is possible for the community to complicate the process of self-discovery, as individuals from time to time may impose their own expectations on students; healthy communities provide an invaluable source of wisdom and support for vocational exploration. Feedback from mentors and lay advisory committees can result in life-changing vocational discovery and can provide confidence-building confirmation.

Students need people to help interpret how others are receiving their ministry. For pastors, this often means having a pastor/parish relationship committee (or some other group) to serve as a sounding board and to provide insight into congregational life and concerns. Communication builds community; therefore as people spend time together, communication lines remain open and can avert the potential of built-up frustration. Likewise, students need to have some group to fulfill this role for them. For students, it may be the pastor/parish relationship committee, personnel committee, or board of elders. By letting a student's church family know of his or her sense of call, the student expands the circle of support and encouragement.

The church has an important role in confirming an individual's call to ministry. Ben Campbell Johnson has an excellent chapter on the role of community in clarifying vocational formation. He identifies the irreplaceable value of the reflections of a friend, group(s), and the congregation for the person seeking spiritual discernment. Johnson draws upon the insights of Elizabeth Liebert, who suggests the following steps:

1. Form a clear question for discernment. It is important to be as clear and specific as possible.

2. Pray with an eye turned toward God rather than the transient things of earth. Ask others to pray. Pray until you desire God's will more than your own.

3. Gather appropriate information about the issues. What issues surround the specific issues being considered? Whom does it affect and how? What does Scripture have to say about the issues? What does the Christian community—past and present—say about the concern? What life lessons relate to this issue? What do other people and the culture around you say?

4. List the pros and cons of the issue and pray through them. Here the process of discernment goes beyond standard ways of analyzing data. As you bring these items before God in prayer, pay attention to how

you feel about them. Be alert to possible feelings of anger, apathy, fear, happiness, or peace.

5. Make the decision that seems best. Often at this stage of discernment, the choice has become obvious. If it has not, have the courage to make the decision that has the most evidence, both internal and external, in its favor.

6. Bring the decision back to God in prayer. This time, pray from the perspective of having made the decision. This way of prayer permits you to "live" into the decision and to discover how it fits your life in Christ.

7. Live with your decision for several days or weeks before acting on it. Living into the decision provides space to see how you really feel about it. Are you embracing the decision, or is it making you feel uneasy?

8. Look for inner peace and freedom. The peace of God signals confirmation. Peace is one of the important dialects in the language of God. Ignatius of Loyola emphasized peace as a sign of God's presence and affirmation.

9. Follow your call step-by-step. Do not expect to see the end from the beginning. Learn the ways of God and the assistance of God as you go. Keep a sense of humor and a sense of trust. When your sense of humor is faltering—trust. When your trust is shaky—draw on your sense of humor.[8]

Some field education programs ask students to form a lay advisory committee to help support and guide the student while he or she is involved in the field education program. This group of three to five persons provides a supportive environment for the student to lay out his or her goals for the semester. The student may use this group to share his or her spiritual journey and hopes and dreams for the future. As a spirit of mutuality develops, I encourage students to revisit their earliest sense of call and to recall the events surrounding this awareness. There are great benefits from recounting how this sense of God's leading has emerged. Most generally, students are able to express their questions and find prayerful support within the group.

Students need to let others know of their interest and look for those who are involved in that area of ministry. I remember thinking that God

---

8. Ben Campbell Johnson, *Hearing God's Call: Ways of Discernment for Laity and Clergy* (Grand Rapids: Eerdmans, 2002), 85–86.

was calling me to become a hospital chaplain when I was in college. I called three major hospitals in the area and arranged interviews with the chaplains at each facility. The chaplains welcomed me and gave me tours of their hospitals. I asked them questions about what they did during a typical day and what they liked most and least about their work. I also asked them how they got their job and what suggestions they would have for someone interested in becoming a chaplain. I found each person to be helpful and affirming, and the interviewing process was very informative.

In addition, the chaplains introduced me to their own professional organizations and gave me copies of recent journals. They told me about the certification process and the specialized training that was required in addition to seminary. The process was extremely valuable and served as a template for my exploration of other areas of ministry.

Explore One's Options

Fortunately, God continues to call and prepare men and women for pastoral leadership. While the local church remains the centerpiece of God's strategic plan for reaching the world with the gospel, the way we do church is changing. Ministry options are expanding, and there are more opportunities for Christian service than ever before. Larger churches are creating part-time or full-time ministry positions that target such areas as community development, communication, equipping, and strategic planning. These areas are in addition to those that provide leadership for age-level ministries, celebrative arts, membership care, evangelism, and church planting.

Some churches have expanded their ministries to include social service ministries and counseling. Others have added child-care ministries, preschools, after-school programs, or even well-developed elementary and secondary schools. Still other congregations are looking for ways to provide care for the growing senior population and have active ministries designed for this constituency. The school's field education director should be aware of the variety of specialized ministries in the area churches.

Beyond the local church, there are ministry needs in schools, hospitals, children's homes, and nursing homes, in addition to jails and prisons. An interesting development in recent years has been the addition of chaplains within a commercial or industrial setting. While some corporations are beginning to appreciate the benefit that chaplains bring to their employees, there are still only limited industrial or marketplace chaplaincy opportunities across the country. A growing number of companies are providing the services of a chaplain to their employees as a part of their employee benefits package.

It is important to consider one's cultural preference for ministry. Certainly people can and do adapt to a wide variety of ministry environments. However, it is likely that some cultural contexts will fit more comfortably than others will. Some of the variables may relate to geographic location.

A few years ago, I was considering an invitation to be the pastor of a church in a college town on the West Coast. While the size of the community was similar to where I was serving as a pastor in the East, there were enough differences in perspective on processing decisions in the life of the church and the pace of life that I decided to stay in New York. I quickly learned that there is a difference between an opportunity and a calling and that it is important to consider culture when making important decisions.

Sometimes the issues are not regional differences but relate more to the size of the community. Rural and urban churches and communities are clearly different. A pastor feeling at home in village ministry may feel distant from urban issues or the other way around. Whatever the size and regional location of the community, it is important that the pastor feels able to relate to the people in a meaningful way. Sometimes God blesses a person by introducing him or her to ministry contexts that go beyond what the person has experienced.

Kenneth Moe makes a helpful observation:

> Culture shock is not the fault of the pastor, who has no control over the existing ethos of the parish. But to do effective ministry, the pastor must enter the world of the parishioners who are being served. . . . You must accept without judgment the reality of life as it is lived in the place where your ministry is grounded and meet the people where they are.[9]

Develop a Personal Growth Plan

While a student has been intentional about gaining a new understanding of his or her strengths and preferences, it is likely that the student also has identified some behaviors that may occasionally complicate his or her life. While one generally tries to lead with his or her strengths and build ministry around the things the student does well, sometimes self-defeating patterns of behaviors emerge.

Pastoral consultant Roy Oswald suggests that a person identify those patterns of behavior that got him or her into difficulty in the past. Oswald distinguishes between weaknesses and self-defeating behavior. Pastors can use their weaknesses to their advantage; after all, did not Paul declare that God often uses our weaknesses to bring glory to his name?

Self-defeating behaviors, however, serve no one well. Oswald uses the illustration of becoming extremely angry when under pressure and observes that "flying off the handle" only results in diminished respect from parishioners. Oswald suggests trying to learn from mistakes by noting specific patterns. Asking the following questions will be helpful in this process:

- Where in the past has one found himself or herself backed into the same old corners?
- What situations continually de-energize the person?

---

9. Kenneth Alan Moe, *The Pastor's Survival Manual* (Bethesda, MD: Alban, 1995), 12.

- Under what conditions does the person usually tighten up and become defensive?
- What things does the person usually put off or postpone that get him or her in trouble over the long run?
- What types of people (age, gender, physical characteristics, attitudes, behaviors, etc.) challenge the person the most?
- Where does the person feel inadequate, unskilled, or undertrained?
- What are the time and places that evoke the person's anger?[10]

A student may want to share what he or she has learned about self-defeating patterns of behavior with his or her mentor or peer reflection group at the seminary.[11] A student can identify two or three changes he or she can make that will result in the greatest personal growth. In some cases, it might be helpful to consider this as an agenda item for further counseling or spiritual direction.

Take Care

Seminary is stressful. Students have huge amounts of material to read and comprehend, there are assignments and deadlines, and often there are work and family concerns that need their attention. In addition to these concerns, students also may be sorting out vocational identity issues. While there is a certain amount of excitement and energy that comes with new experiences, that excitement generates additional stress. Students need to plan to take better care of themselves during these days of transition. Remember, the healthier one is, the more effective one can be in ministry.

When students are under a lot of stress, they can easily struggle with a loss of perception. Trying to keep all the plates spinning may cloud one's view of reality. The world may not be as fearful as he or she has imagined. The opposition may not be as overwhelming as it seemed at first. One may simply not be able to process all the data coming at him or her as well as one would like. Furthermore, when a person is dealing with stress, he or she has a tendency to lose sight of options. Fortunately, there are usually more alternatives than one realizes!

I recall that one of the questions I had to answer for my doctoral comprehensive exams dealt with the physiological effects of stress. Just remembering that experience makes my muscles tense up! Stress is a powerful agent, and while small amounts of stress are helpful to keep us on task, persistently large levels of stress will literally wear us out. Although a well-developed discussion of the physiological effects of stress go beyond the scope of this chapter, it would be helpful to note some of the ways to care for one's self during stressful situations.

---

10. Roy M. Oswald, *New Beginnings: A Pastorate Start Up Workbook* (Bethesda, MD: Alban, 1993), 57.

11. See chapter 10, "Building Biblical Community in Theological Education," for more information on peer groups.

A key to health is learning how to cope well with the stresses of life and the effects of burnout. Both students and mentors need to be intentional about fostering physical, emotional, and spiritual health. Here are some suggestions that can help.[12]

Remember Your Identity!

There is an immeasurable sense of calmness in recalling that a person is a child of God! The God who created and sustains the world loves us. We have been bought with a price! We are more valuable than any amount of silver or gold. Linger with God!

Keep Up with the Spiritual Disciplines

Plan a retreat to give a chance to experience silence in the midst of a chaotic world. For some, this retreat may mean an hour home alone. Hopefully, however, a person can carve out even more time (at least occasionally) for prayer, silence, and reflection. Read the Scriptures, study the biographies of biblical and early church leaders. Use a journal to help process thoughts. Explore the Psalms.

Sort Out Values and Review Gifts

As we have considered earlier, a tremendous value comes from taking inventory of how God has gifted and is preparing one for ministry. Revisit the time line. Take some time to look back over the journey, acknowledge the progress made. Do not take the growth experienced for granted.

Check Expectations

Are a person's expectations reasonable? The Bible provides us with some background information into the lives of Moses, David, and Paul (just to name a few) and illustrates how people spent years in preparation before launching into public leadership. Is the time line for ministry development realistic?

Develop Friendships with People Outside of One's Congregation

I have observed how many leaders, in their passion to advance the church, have inadvertently narrowed their circle of friends. Concentrating one's support (sometimes exclusively) from within his or her congregation creates a vulnerability to stress and magnifies the personal turmoil if the person's relationship to his or her congregation changes. Broaden the circle of friends and stay connected to the people who care.

Find a Hobby—Twelve Months a Year

Hobbies serve as a cognitive eraser; they help wipe the slate clean. The

---

12. For additional information, see James E. Hightower Jr. and W. Craig Gilliam, *A Time for Change? Revisioning Your Call* (Bethesda, MD: Alban, 2000); and Roy M. Oswald, *Clergy Self-Care: Finding a Balance for Effective Ministry* (Herndon, VA: Alban, 1991).

temporary distraction of hobbies provides a healthy release from the anxieties of transition. One who does not already have a hobby may need to help to find one that stimulates his or her imagination and creativity.

Remember That Action Builds Morale

Take some incremental steps toward healthy change or resolution. Sometimes the stress becomes so great that people feel paralyzed to act. Acting upon what one knows rebuilds confidence and rekindles personal energy.

Maintain Health

The demands upon a person's body grow during times of transition. Stay in touch with a physician. Healthy eating and appropriate exercise habits help to lower stress and strengthen immune systems. Listen to music and enjoy the arts. Cultivating creativity can help lower anxiety. Take time to appreciate God's creative beauty.

Putting It All Together

Gather the data described above and organize it in a way that is convenient. I like putting the information in a notebook. We have

- reviewed one's sense of call and identified personal strengths;
- explored the biblical patterns of how God worked and is working in one's life;
- systematically reflected upon one's ministry experiences;
- gained insight from a variety of personality and/or interest inventories;
- developed a personal time line that highlights the defining moments and the significant people in one's life;
- shared one's impressions with others and considered their responses; and, most importantly,
- prayed.

Take a break and remember that God is not in a hurry. Allow some time for the heart and mind to synthesize the material gathered. Be confident that the Holy Spirit has been involved in the process long before one ever considered vocational ministry. God has been equipping students for this moment. Students have a vast range of experiences and abilities that are preparing them for this next step.

Ask God for courage! Students may very likely be stepping out of their comfort zone. Exploring new ministry options will challenge students in new ways. I remember my first hospital field education internship. I had gone through the steps listed above and felt certain that hospital ministry was my calling. After a brief orientation, I was assigned to the intensive care unit and waiting room. On my first visit, I could see from a distance that the waiting room was nearly full. The closer I came to the room, the more anxious I became. Just as I came to the open door, I froze and walked past the room. I went down the hall, turned around, and tried again.

The second time was no better than the first! This time, I went to a quiet spot in the lobby area and had a conversation with God. I knew that God had called me to vocational ministry and that this internship was part of God's training process. However, I knew that I was stuck and that I would have no impact on the lives of others if I stayed out in the hall. I needed the empowering presence of God to cross over the threshold to get over my fears and go into the waiting room. I went back to the waiting room; however this time, I entered the room and introduced myself to the first person I met. Immediately, my anxiety lessened and I began to connect with hurting people in a way that brought glory to God.

Vocational discernment and vocational formation develop as students move forward using all the insight they currently have. One's level of insight increases with experience and obedience to what he or she knows. I had more understanding after my fourth quarter of clinical pastoral education than I had that fearful morning during my first quarter. Students can gather data, pray, and seek the counsel of others, but it takes learning by doing to connect all the dots. Sometimes discernment comes only as students move forward, walking in the light of what they know. Just as automatic doors only open as people approach the building, often the clarity students seek comes only as they move into new experiences. Students can utilize field education to test-drive a variety of ministry opportunities. In doing so, students are not alone; peers, mentors, and field education faculty are there to help. Students should take advantage of the supportive environment of seminary to move into new rooms of life and service to the glory of God!

Prayer of Transformation

Father, may the light of Christ illuminate our hearts and minds and guide us into his fullness. May the love of Christ bring healing to the brokenness places of life. May the joy of Christ empower and encourage us in our calling. May the peace of Christ keep us centered upon him throughout all the changes of life. Amen.

Reflection Questions

1. Review how the following leaders in the Bible experienced their call to ministry. Were their experiences somehow similar to yours? If so, how?

    a. Moses (Exod. 3:1–4:17)
    b. Gideon (Judg. 6:11–24)
    c. Samuel (1 Sam. 3:1–21)
    d. Isaiah (Isa. 6:1–13)
    e. Jeremiah (Jer. 1:4–10)
    f. Amos (Amos 7:10–17)
    g. The disciples (Matt. 4:18–20; Mark 3:13–19)
    h. Paul (Acts 9:1–20; 16:6–10)
    i. Peter (Acts 10:17–20; 12:7–8)
    j. Philip (Acts 8:26)

2. How does your sense of call differ from the call of God given to all Christians? How has your sense of call developed over the years? Have you shared your sense of calling with others? If so, what was that experience like? In what ways is your local church affirming your sense of call?

3. Frederick Buechner makes the observation, "There are all kinds of voices calling you to all different kinds of work, and the problem is to find out which is the voice of God rather than of society, say, or the Superego, or Self-Interest. By and large a good rule for finding out is this. The kind of work God usually calls you to is the kind of work (a) that you need most to do and (b) that the world most needs to have done."[13] Which world need seems most urgent to you? Which world need challenges your heart the most?

4. What do you see as your gifts for ministry? How are these gifts being used in ministry already? What ministry experiences are the most rewarding? What gifts do others recognize in you? In what ways are you seeking to develop your latent gifts?

---

13. Buechner, *Wishful Thinking*, 118.

Further Reading

Brouwer, Douglas. *What Am I Supposed to Do with My Life?* Grand Rapids: Eerdmans, 2006.

Cullinan, Alice. *Sorting It Out: Discerning God's Call to Ministry.* Valley Forge, PA: Judson Press, 1999.

Guinness, Os. *Rising to the Call.* Nashville: W Publishing Group, 2003.

Hightower, James E., Jr., and W. Craig Gilliam. *A Time For Change? Revisioning Your Call.* Herndon, MD: Alban, 2000.

Johnson, Ben Campbell. *Hearing God's Call: Ways of Discernment for Laity and Clergy.* Grand Rapids: Eerdmans, 2002.

Palmer, Parker. *Let Your Life Speak.* San Francisco: Jossey-Bass, 2000.

Smith, Gordon T. *Courage and Calling.* Downers Grove, IL: InterVarsity Press, 1999.

Chapter 2

Field Education and Ministry Skill Competence

TIMOTHY WITMER

And David shepherded them with integrity of heart;
with skillful hands he led them. (Ps. 78:72 NIV)

Bill recently graduated from a fine seminary with an outstanding grade point average and bright prospects for his future. However, on arriving at his first parish, one of the most respected members of the church passed away. Bill's first responsibility: to officiate at Mrs. Mitchell's funeral. The problem? Bill did not have a clue as to exactly what he should *do*. The result was an unmitigated disaster. Bill began to question his call to the ministry, and the congregation began to question their call to Bill!

Integrity and Skills

In the process of ministerial formation, the development of "competency" is generally considered to be directly related to what students will eventually *do* in ministry. Therefore, it is concerned with the development of ministry *skills*. The verse noted above identifies Shepherd-King David as someone who "shepherded them with integrity of heart; with skillful hands he led them." At the outset of this chapter, it must be reinforced that for the individual preparing for ministry, "competence" in skill can never be divorced from "integrity of heart." The individual who serves God effectively is one whose service flows from love for Christ and love for the sheep for whom Christ died. After all, David, the shepherd-king, was a man "after God's own heart." When the disgraced apostle Peter was reinstated to his place of service, his threefold affirmation of love for the Master was the foundation for the threefold commission to feed the Lord's "sheep" (John 21:15–17).

The biblical view of ministerial formation must be holistic. An early American example of this commitment to comprehensive ministerial formation was the Log College in Neshaminy, Pennsylvania, founded by William Tennant, who was succeeded by his son, Gilbert. On one of George Whitefield's many visits to Philadelphia, he visited the Log College and heard Gilbert preach. Of this experience, Whitefield said, "He convinced me more and more that we can preach the gospel of Christ no further than we have experienced the power of it in our own hearts."[1] All effective competence in ministry must be empowered by the risen Christ through his indwelling Spirit.

In a largely academic approach to theological education, this needs to be reinforced at every turn. As Leith Anderson has written in *A Church for the Twenty-first Century*, "Traditional seminary education is designed to train research theologians who are to become parish practitioners. Probably they are adequately equipped for neither."[2] Robert Banks has warned that the current model of theological education emphasizes "*knowing*, at the expense of *doing and being*" and that "the professional school model now dominates, and this continues to ignore the *being* of the student, to exalt professionalism over calling and vocation."[3] It is crucial, therefore, that the development of competence in ministry be built on the foundation of growth in Christlike character through a vital walk with the Good Shepherd. When this element is missing, mere "hired hands" are the result (see John 10:12–13).

Having said this, the development of "skillful hands" is an important element of ministerial preparation if one is to lead God's people effectively. This chapter will provide a "how-to" approach to the development of ministry competencies. For the purposes of this chapter, the terms *ministry competence* or *competency* and *ministry skill* will be used interchangeably. The aspect of competency development is extremely important since church search committees or mission agencies who call individuals to positions of leadership should have confidence that candidates not only "know their stuff" but also know "what to do."

God's people are truly blessed when their leaders are not only mature in Christ but also competent in fulfilling their calling. It was also said of David

---

1. Archibald Alexander, *The Log College* (London: Banner of Truth Trust, 1968), 30.

2. Leith Anderson, *A Church for the Twenty-first Century* (Minneapolis: Bethany House, 1992), 46.

3. Robert Banks, *Reenvisioning Theological Education: Exploring a Missional Alternative to Current Models* (Grand Rapids: Eerdmans, 1999), 135.

that "everything that the king did pleased all the people" (2 Sam. 3:36). This reveals the wisdom in practice that God gave to David for carrying out his responsibilities as the shepherd-king of Israel. Ideally, the development of ministry skill is nothing less than the growth of wisdom in practice for students and must be an important part of any institution's program that hopes to be effective in preparing individuals for ministry.

Field Education and Competency

There is a sense in which the development of competence in ministry is what field education is all about. It is only in the field of the local church or other ministry site that a student can get the opportunity to develop skills for ministry with the guidance of an experienced mentor. This is certainly the model that is clearly evident in the Scriptures. Models of biblical, mentor-based leadership training include such familiar teams as Moses and Joshua, Elijah and Elisha, and Paul and Timothy. Of course, the most vivid example is that of our Lord and his disciples, who are identified as those who were "with him" (Mark 3:14). Their training was in the villages, the desert, the hills, and with diverse peoples, from a woman condemned for adultery to the highest civil and religious officials in the land. This was truly field education at its best. It is undoubtedly for this reason that institutions accredited for the Master of Divinity degree by the Association of Theological Schools are required to include a practical field education experience in their programs.[4]

The importance of training in ministry competence in the field is not unlike the approach found in other professional disciplines. Schoolteachers are required to spend time student teaching, and prospective physicians work countless hours in internships and residencies, sharpening their skills as they shadow veteran practitioners. This is where the knowledge gained in the classroom moves into hands-on training so that the student will be ready to move into his or her respective practice. For the ministerial student, this experience in practical training in competency is crucial in helping confirm gifts and calling to a lifetime of ministry.

For this reason, it is important to urge students to get involved in such experiences early in their degree program. In the educational field, we have all heard horror stories about prospective schoolteachers who complete their academic requirements only to discover when doing their student teaching in *the last* year of their program that they absolutely hate the classroom! Because engagement in mentor-based training in ministry competence is an important ingredient in confirming a student's gifts and calling, it should be planned to begin sooner rather than later in the degree program.

Prerequisites for Effective Competency Development

Before getting to the actual process of mentoring ministry competence,

---

4. The Association of Theological Schools, "Degree Program Standards," http://www .ats.edu/accrediting/standards/DegreeStandards.pdf.

there are three preliminary questions that must be addressed: What ministry competencies should be developed? Who should do the mentoring? Where is the best setting for competency development? Without the foundation provided by the answers to these questions, effective development of competence in ministry will be compromised. The how-to question will be outlined in greater detail in the next section, where a suggested process for developing competence in ministry is presented.

What Ministry Competencies Should Be Developed?

In order to be effective in developing competence in ministry, it is crucial to understand exactly *what* skills we are hoping the student will be able to *do*. There are different factors involved in answering this question. It is important for the institution's field education director to develop a list of competencies to provide guidance to the student and the mentor on the field. In developing such a list, everyone should take into account the basic *biblical* ministry competencies.

Another consideration in answering the "what" of training in ministry competence is to include requirements of the institution's ecclesiastical constituencies. Wherever possible, there should be an effort to coordinate the institution's field education competency requirements with those of the church. However, there must be flexibility in the development of such a list as it is impossible for the list to reflect the competencies needed for *every* aspect of ministry preparation. It is wise to make this a *recommended* and not a *required* list of competencies, which gives flexibility in tailoring the experience to the student as well as to the particular needs of the ministry site. For instance, while the core competencies for a church planter would be similar to those preparing for an established church ministry, there will be some important variations that could be included for a student hoping to move toward planting a church. Again, as in the medical field, some attention must be given to specialization in ministry skills. This reinforces the flexibility that is desirable in developing a list of recommended learning activities for the student.

Since it is unlikely the student will be able to complete all of the recommended learning activities concurrently, it is important for the mentor to work closely with the student to identify which of the activities will be the focus of the current experience. As noted above, flexibility to include elements that might be requested by the student due to his or her perceived professional ministry objective should be allowed. Research has shown that adult learners want to take part in setting their program of development.[5] This fosters ownership in the process and motivation for the tasks at hand. In any case, collaboration between student and mentor is important to set

---

5. For a thorough discussion of the distinctive elements of andragogy (adult education), see Malcolm Knowles, *The Modern Practice of Adult Education: From Pedagogy to Andragogy* (River Grove, IL: Follett, 1980).

the ministry skills to be engaged together with the time frame within which it is to be accomplished.

The development of such a list is an important guide for the mentor on-site as well because there can be a tension between the concrete ministry needs of what the *church* needs and what the *student* needs in order to gain a broad exposure to ministry competencies. Except for such a guide, students might spend all of their field education in youth or children's ministry and never have exposure to other competencies needed for effective pastoral ministry among adults, such as preaching and visitation. Therefore, it is important to provide mentors with a guide that provides the outline of competencies necessary for effective ministry. Figure 2.1 provides a sample listing of recommended learning activities. The list follows a "shepherding" motif as it focuses on providing competencies desirable for pastors.

Figure 2.1. Recommended Learning Activities

Walking with the Chief Shepherd
- ❑ Review spiritual formation issues
- ❑ Review biblical character qualifications (1 Tim. 3; Titus 1)
- ❑ Review family life issues

Feeding God's Flock
- ❑ Questions about preaching with mentor
- ❑ Log 10 to 20 preaching opportunities outside of seminary classroom, including at least 5 with mentor evaluation
- ❑ Log 10 to 20 teaching opportunities, which can include Sunday school, youth group, etc.

Leading God's Flock
Administration
- ❑ Attend 3 session (or board) meetings
- ❑ Attend 2 deacons' meetings
- ❑ Attend 2 church committee meetings
- ❑ Attend 1 congregational meeting
- ❑ Attend 2 presbytery meetings
- ❑ Read the Westminster Standards, Book of Church Order Rules of Government section or comparable ecclesiastical standards and discuss with mentor

Worship
- ❑ Lead worship at least 5 times
- ❑ Observe 1 funeral service
- ❑ Observe 1 wedding service

❑ Observe 1 baptismal service
❑ Observe 1 Communion service

Ministry
❑ Discuss the church's philosophy of ministry with mentor
❑ Lead a specific ministry of the church
❑ Evangelism
❑ Discuss the church's outreach strategy with mentor
❑ Participate in some aspect of the church's outreach
❑ Make 3 evangelistic calls with mentor or experienced trainer

Protecting God's Flock
Shepherding
❑ Discuss the church's shepherding plan with mentor
❑ Participate in the church's shepherding plan under the guidance of mentor

Visiting
❑ Visit 3 church members with mentor
❑ Visit 3 hospital patients with mentor
❑ Visit 2 nursing home residents

Counseling
❑ Sit in on one complete counseling case

Disciplining
❑ Read denominational Book of Discipline and discuss with mentor and discuss an actual case (at the prerogative and discretion of mentor)

Notice that the list begins with spiritual formation, character qualifications, and family life issues. These are foundational matters and should be reviewed regularly together with the mentor. Other competencies reflect the biblical picture of ministry practice. There are other matters that could be included and certainly should be discussed, such as managing a schedule in ministry among others. The list is not intended to be exhaustive but merely to provide a basic form that can then be molded to meet the needs of the student, ministry setting, and ecclesial constituency.

Who Should Guide the Development of Competence in Ministry?

The answer to this question is the key to the whole endeavor of field education and is covered thoroughly in another chapter. However, it is important to highlight at least three characteristics of the individual who is effective in mentoring ministry competence.

Mentors Effective in Ministry Competence

First, the *mentor* must be competent in ministry. The old saying "practice makes perfect" sounds good, but it is better expressed in the words "perfect practice makes perfect." The obvious point is that it is possible to learn something improperly, and key factors in students' practice are the models and mentors to whom they look. The example of the newly ordained pastor being assigned a funeral in his first months is my story, except that the departed member had not only requested that I officiate but also that another retired minister "assist" me.

In the seminary classroom I was well taught in the victory of Christ over death and the hope of the resurrection, but there were several practical matters to which I had not been introduced. Such things as how to plan a funeral service, how to write a funeral message, how and when to minister to the bereaved family, how to interact with the funeral director, and even where to stand at the graveside service were all matters left to me to figure out. This seasoned pastor who assisted me had conducted hundreds of funerals, while this was my first. Being able to work with this godly and experienced pastor enabled me to do my part well. I learned much, not only from my frantic phone calls, but also by observing a truly competent minister and shepherd interact with the bereaved and lead his part of the service (mostly from memory, by the way!). Once again, it was not merely his competence in ministry that impacted me but his maturity and godliness. What a wonderful privilege to be able to connect students with such experienced mentors *before* they engage in their first postseminary calling.

An early example of such a competent, godly model was Joseph Bellamy, who mentored more than a hundred men for ministry in the Congregational Church in New England before the days of the theological seminary (between 1742 and 1790). It was said that he

> required them to write dissertations on the several subjects which had occupied their attention; and afterwards, sermons on those points of doctrine which he deemed most important; and finally, sermons on such experimental and practical topics as they might choose to select. *He was particularly earnest in inculcating the importance of a high tone of spiritual feeling, as an element of ministerial character and success.* His students are said to have formed the very highest idea of his talents and character, and, in some instances, to have regarded him with a veneration bordering well nigh upon idolatry.[6]

Bellamy was a man who was committed to the holistic approach to ministerial formation. Having said that mentors must be competent, it is important to add that they will never be perfect. Looking for perfection in a mentor is like looking for perfection anywhere else this side of heaven: it

---

6. William Sprague, *Annals of the American Pulpit* (New York: Carter and Brothers, 1859), 1:405–6; emphasis added.

does not exist! Given that no mentor is perfect, one who is *transparent* is very helpful since students can learn as much from another's mistakes and short-comings as from their strengths, if they are willing to share them. However, it is important in looking for individuals who mentor ministry competence that there be a track record of effectiveness in ministry that can be imparted to the student.

Mentors with Time to Mentor

Second, the mentor must have the *time* to mentor students. The days of Joseph Bellamy were the days before American Protestantism borrowed the "academy" approach to ministerial education from the European univer-sity model in the eighteenth century. Prospective ministers were nurtured by experienced pastors, sometimes living in the homes of their ministry mentors. While this level of commitment from a mentor might be unreal-istic today, it is not unrealistic to expect a sincere investment of time and wisdom into the lives of the next generation of kingdom servants. However, not every minister has the passion, the patience, or the time for such an endeavor.

On the other hand, there are many who are willing to share their lives and ministries for this purpose. Paul reminded Timothy, "The things which you have heard from me in the presence of many witnesses, entrust these to faithful men who will be able to teach others also" (2 Tim. 2:2 NASB). As Paul wrote these words, he was modeling the very principle he was urging upon Timothy. He shared his life and ministry with Timothy and others, preparing them for fruitful ministries of their own. The committed ministry mentor embraces the opportunity to invest in "faithful men" for the sake of the church at large.

The actual process of introducing individuals to the wide array of minis-try skills takes time. It is best for everyone involved not to connect students with mentors who do not have the time needed for the complete process of competency development outlined below.

Mentors Who Love the Lord, Love Ministry, Love Students

Last, but not least, it must be clear that the mentor has a love for the Lord, for the ministry, and for ministerial students. Unfortunately, there are many who are cynical about the work of the ministry generally and about people in the church particularly. Because what students gain in these practical training times will impact them for life, it is best not to multiply such negative attitudes. On the other hand, love for the work of the ministry and for the people of God is often "caught" from as well as "taught" by mentors whose love for the Lord and his people is nothing less than contagious.

A Team Approach

In terms of the "who" of mentoring ministry competency, many have found it to be helpful to establish a lay committee that will also provide assistance in the process. These individuals should share the commitment to partner in the preparation of future leaders of the church. While responsibilities of such a team will vary, at the very least they should come alongside the mentor to provide assistance and alongside the student to provide encouragement and constructive feedback. There is more on this in the evaluation segment below.

Where Should Competency Development Occur?

The benefit of field education is that it is on-the-job experience. Many of us have had the experience of being in a hospital when a physician surrounded by eager residents enters the room. The experienced physician is helping the residents to gain experience and understanding with you as the guinea pig! Hospitals that partner with medical schools in providing such hands-on experience are called "teaching hospitals." These are institutions where resources are committed to such training and where the patients are informed that their physician will have "company" as he or she pokes and prods on his or her daily rounds.

When it comes to the matter of mentoring ministry competence, it is important that the local congregation hold such a commitment to equip future shepherds of God's flock. They must be willing not only to share the pastor as a mentor to future pastors but also to share their own lives. These congregations will undoubtedly hear some "bad" sermons and experience some awkward moments as a student occasionally fumbles with what to do or say next, but they will be blessed as they see individuals nurtured for a lifetime of ministry. In mentoring ministry competence, nothing is more encouraging than a local congregation that not only understands their role in this process but also is committed to it.

Why not develop a network of "teaching churches" that relate to seminaries the way "teaching hospitals" relate to medical schools?[7] An earlier paragraph spoke of the rounds medical students make with their teachers in teaching hospitals. Such an institution shares a mutual commitment with a particular medical school to equip future doctors. This requires great cooperation in the teaching hospital from staff and patients alike to afford students such a unique and practical training setting. "Teaching churches" are recognized as those that have made a clear commitment to a partnership with the seminary in preparing a new generation of ministers.

These churches must be willing to commit the time of pastor or mentor to the process and be open to being ministered to by someone "in training." Ideally, a teaching church would also be committed to enabling the student to complete internship requirements for ordination in their respective

---

7. Westminster Theological Seminary, "Teaching Churches Network," http://www.wts .edu/mentor/tcnetwork.html.

ecclesiastical constituency, thus providing a well-rounded training in ministry competence.

In considering the matter of the "where" of training in competence, the concept of specialization should also be kept in mind. It is helpful if the focus of the site reflects the aspirations of the student. For example, if someone senses the Lord calling him to plant a church, strive to place him with someone developing a church plant. Someone who senses a call to missions should be mentored by a veteran missionary. It is helpful in these circumstances for the field education director to develop a network of "strategic partnerships" with mission organizations and other ministries that are willing to come alongside students as they seek confirmation of gifts and calling in nonparish type ministry settings. While a complete match of every student's perceived professional ministry goal with a corresponding practitioner in that area is very hard work, it is another area in which field educators can strive to tailor the experience for the benefit of the students.

A Process for the Development of Competence in Ministry Skills

This section will focus on a practical, how-to process for the development of competence in ministry skills. After the mentors and sites have been identified and the competencies to be included have been agreed upon, how should one proceed with the process of developing ministry competencies in a student? The plan outlined in this chapter includes four basic steps of the mentoring process, seen from the perspective of the mentor:

- Instruction
- Demonstration
- Observation
- Evaluation

By way of overview, the first two (instruction and demonstration) are modeling elements; that is, these are elements in which the focus of the activity is on the mentor modeling the particular ministry skill to the student. The second two (observation and evaluation) are multiplying elements, since the competency modeled for the student is now being reproduced in his life as the mentor observes and evaluates. Progressive movement through the four steps requires the student's increasing participation in the ministry task while the mentor's involvement gradually decreases.

Modeling
Instruction

Instruction is the aspect of mentoring competency in which information is communicated to the student that he needs to know in order to accomplish the task successfully. This should include both macroinstruction and microinstruction. The macroelements of instruction would include the biblical and theological principles that support and direct this particular aspect of ministry. It is important for students to learn not only the "how-tos" of this competency but also the "why." It should not be assumed that this has been covered in the seminary classroom. If it has, there is still the importance of understanding this competency in the context of the ministry setting. The mentor should help the student make the connections between the theory and theology of ministry and its actual practice. The microelements of instruction should include many of the specific how-tos of competence in ministry skills.

There are many examples we could employ as we walk through this process, but let us use the example of a hospital visit. What might the instruction segment include? Beginning with the macroelements, answer the question of why this particular competency is important. Talk about the importance of the hospital visit as part of the pastor's shepherding ministry to the congregation. Remind the student that ministry is incarnational and that it is important that the minister demonstrate compassion for the parishioner by being "with" the person in time of need and that this is a very real expression of the Lord's concern in a time of trial.

After having talked about why this is important, move on to instruct the student in the microinstruction of how to complete a hospital visit. Not only should the mentor provide the student with a list of Bible passages that are preferable to read depending on the particular situation of the patient, but the mentor should encourage the student to search out and develop his own list of Scriptures and resources to use. Instruct the student as to the purpose and elements of the prayer for the sick. Strive to inform the student of as many practical matters as possible. Where should the student park? When should the student go? How often should the student go? How should the student interact with hospital staff? What does the student do if there are other people visiting when he arrives? How should the student relate to another patient if it is a semiprivate room? What should the student do when the hospital room door is closed? How long should the visit be? The mentor needs to give instructions as to what should and should not be done on a hospital visit.

While it is impossible to anticipate every question, as much information as possible should be provided before actually moving to the second modeling step of taking the student on a hospital visit. The mentor needs to be sure to allow time for the student to ask for clarification or to articulate questions, as the student might have particular concerns that the mentor might not have addressed.

Figure 2.2 illustrates a sample reflection activity, an important resource to develop alongside the list of recommended learning activities.[8] Reflection activity pages provide the student with opportunity to record key principles from the instruction step as well as questions, reflections, and best learning from the evaluation step.

---

8. A full listing of "Reflection Activities" correlating to the "Recommended Learning Activities" mentioned in this chapter can be found at www.wts.edu.

Figure 2.2 Sample Reflection Activity

Protect the Flock (Pastoral Care): Hospital Visitation

Hospital Visit #1: Observe

Date of visit: _____

Whom did you accompany on the visit?_____

_____

Condition of the patient: _____

_____

What did *your mentor* do during the visit? _____

_____

Observations: _____

_____

_____

_____

Discussion of the visit with your mentor: _____

_____

_____

_____

_____

Hospital Visit #2: Participate

Date of visit: _____

Whom did you accompany on the visit? _____

_____

Condition of the patient: _____

_____

What did *your mentor* do during the visit? _____

_____

What did *you* do during the visit? _____

_____

Observations: _____

_____

_____

_____

_____

Discussion of the visit with your mentor: _____

_____

_____

_____

Hospital Visit #3: Participate

Date of visit: _____

Whom did you accompany on the visit?_____

_____

Condition of the patient: _____

_____

What did *your mentor* do during the visit? _____

_____

What did *you* do during the visit? _____

_____

Observations: _____

_____

_____

_____

Discussion of the visit with your mentor: _____

_____

_____

_____

_____

Demonstration

The second modeling element in mentoring ministry competence is demonstration. All of the matters listed under "instruction" could be communicated in a classroom; but in the mentoring experience, the student actually accompanies the mentor in the ministry experience. Using our example, suppose the mentor takes the student on hospital visitation, where the practices discussed in the instruction step are actually demonstrated to the student. In this step, the model to be followed is presented. The mentor should be sure that the student understands that he is to observe on this visit. Be sure to let the hospital patient know the identity of the other visitor if he or she does not already know the student. In fact, it is preferable to call ahead and inform the patient in advance. While the mentor should be self-conscious to be a good example of what he is seeking to model to the student, the mentor must also "be true to self."

Having concluded the visit, the mentor should be certain to allow time for interaction about the experience. Back at the office or in the car, work through the elements of the visit that were discussed beforehand and reflect on each one. The mentor should model an openness that allows the student the opportunity to ask pointed and difficult questions. Encourage the student to ask any and every question that comes to mind. There may be issues that were not covered in the instruction segment that come to mind as a result of the visit. Mentor and student will undoubtedly have experienced a variation on some of the "things to expect" discussed beforehand.

There also may be areas in which the mentor could have been more effective. This is where the transparency of the mentor is crucial. The student must be allowed the prerogative to ask "challenging" questions. The mentor should not be threatened by this but should model humility and openness in reflecting on the experience. If the mentor could have done better or would have done something differently in hindsight, this should be part of the discussion. After all, this is important to model, given that the mentor will eventually provide constructive criticism to the student and will expect openness from him. The openness and transparency of the mentor will be an encouragement to the student to exhibit the same traits. This time of mutual reflection is often neglected but is absolutely crucial to maximize the effectiveness of the modeling stage of mentoring ministry competency.

Multiplying

Observation

After the mentor has provided sufficient instruction and allowed ample opportunity for the student to demonstrate a particular ministry skill, the mentor now observes the student actually engaged in the particular ministry practice. The mentor must have wisdom to know when the student is actually ready to participate in the ministry skill at hand. How is it possible to know if the student is ready? One of the best ways to know is to simply ask the student. Student anxiety can largely be relieved if the mentor takes the time to outline exactly what the student will be expected to do so that there are no surprises—though such surprises are often an education in themselves!

Using the example of the hospital visit, a good way to begin is to ease the student into the competency by asking him to participate in one element of the visit. This is a valuable way to proceed with ministry skills that have several parts or pieces. Perhaps the first time the student will read the Scriptures. On successive visits the mentor allows the student to take the lead gradually in the visit with the mentor moving more and more to the role of the observer. Eventually, the mentor allows the student to "carry the ball" for the entire visit, with the mentor being as much in the background as is practicable. The student should be allowed to assume as much responsibility in such tasks as is allowable by the congregation and ecclesial judicatory.

There will be those competencies in which a student will not be allowed to participate fully until ordination. On the list of recommended learning activities, students are allowed merely to observe several ministry practices. For example, officiating at weddings and Communion services are examples of competencies that the student will ordinarily not have opportunity to "practice." It is all the more important that these nonparticipatory ministry skills be demonstrated to the student and discussed in detail. Competencies restricted to ordained clergy vary from church to church and the list of recommended learning activities should be adjusted accordingly.

Evaluation

Evaluation is the second element in the multiplying phase and is perhaps the most important of the entire process. If there is an element of training in ministry competence that is left out, it is usually evaluation. This, however, is where the best learning takes place. This is where the mentor truly ministers to the student in helping him refine and improve ministry practice.[9]

Returning to the example of the hospital visit, it is best if the mentor refers to the specific matters discussed in the instruction phase as the visit is reviewed. Begin by asking for the student's perception of how the visit went. Ask the student to articulate areas in which the student thought he did well, and then ask for some things the student thought he could have done better. If the instruction phase was well done, there will probably be a close correlation between the student's perception of things and that of the mentor. When it comes time for the mentor to provide input, it is important to lead off with encouraging comments. It is a lot better to start with "That was a beautiful prayer" than to begin with something critical. In leading with encouragement, the foundation is being laid for the constructive criticism

---

9. A more detailed discussion on evaluation is found in chapter 11, "Assessment and Evaluation in Field Education."

that must inevitably follow. The mentor needs to be as specific as possible in letting the student know how the visit could have been improved ("Don't sit on the hospital bed!").

The mentor should pay attention not only to the student's ability to complete the task successfully but also to the student's attitude and emotional state in carrying out the particular ministry skill. Does the student have an attitude appropriate to the occasion? Is the student's pastoral heart and concern evident? With regard to the example of the hospital visit, does the student have an appropriate bedside manner? Is he too grave? Is he too giddy? The mentor should not hesitate to engage the student on these important matters. This touches upon the area of emotional intelligence, which has been shown to be a crucial matter in effective competence in ministry. The ability of the student to develop healthy relationships with people and demonstrate emotional maturity is an important and often ignored aspect of ministerial formation.

It is at this point that the student's "Reflection Activity" page should be accessed in order to make important notes on the experience just completed, including mentor feedback and areas for improvement. It is also in this step that the feedback of the support committee should be solicited if one has been formed to assist in the student's growth and development.

While certain ministry tasks require greater emphasis on one element than the others, each of the steps should be included. Another consideration is that each mentor has a natural tendency to neglect at least one or overemphasize another. One mentor might love the initial instruction step while another provides little or no instruction to a student in the particular ministry task. The wise mentor will evaluate his tendency and compensate accordingly. Also, the elements are not mutually exclusive but interdependent. There is a sense in which the whole experience is instruction. The evaluation phase is actually a form of instruction, which essentially begins a new mentoring cycle.

Conclusion

As we have seen, effective mentoring in ministry competence must be built on a holistic picture of ministerial formation beginning with issues of spiritual and character formation. Ministry competence must not be seen as an end in itself; it must be properly motivated by love for the Lord and for his flock. Gifted and willing mentors must be sought out, mentors who will invest their lives in future generations of those sensing a call to ministry. Churches and other ministry settings where students will be free to test their gifts and calling must be sought. These are places where they can gain sincere encouragement from their successes and strengths as well as constructive criticism in areas of weakness and inexperience. The four-step process for training in ministry competence should be kept in mind, making sure all four of the steps are included.

The advantage of such a process is that the student will come to an understanding, not only of his giftedness and strengths, but also of his weaknesses. No one is gifted for everything! This will help the student grow in wisdom in future ministry as the student identifies areas he needs to strengthen as well as areas where he will need to deploy the gifts of others to provide a well-balanced ministry to the flock he serves. Hopefully, the process will also give the student a template for developing others in ministry, as well as for ongoing evaluation of his own skills throughout a lifetime of ministry.

All of these things taken together will, by God's grace, advance the preparation of the student to be an effective servant in Christ's kingdom, a shepherd who out of integrity of heart serves the flock with skillful hands for his glory.

Prayer of Transformation

Almighty God, we thank you that because you are our Shepherd, we have everything that we need for life and godliness. We ask that you would please fill our hearts with the Spirit you have given so that in all we do we might have integrity of heart, loving you with full devotion. We also ask that our service would be the overflow of our love for you and that, as such, we would seek to do the very best we can according to the gifts you have given to us—that we would develop skillful hands to serve you. Help us to remember that when we are effective and fruitful that this is a gift from your hand. Help us also to remember that when we are weak and stumble and fall, it is that same hand that picks us up and encourages us to go on. Thank you for the forgiveness of our sins through the gift of your Son, our Good Shepherd, and for the joy of serving your flock. Amen.

Reflection Questions

1. Have you sought to find a place to improve your competence in ministry skills? What are your perceived strengths? Your perceived weaknesses?

2. Do you give adequate attention to spiritual, character, and family formation?

3. Does the field education experience in which you are engaged give you opportunity for training in the full spectrum of ministry skills, including those in which you perceive yourself to be weak and inexperienced?

4. Have you sought to coordinate the competencies of your program to the ordination requirements (if applicable) of your ecclesial judicatory?

5. Have you sought to find a mentor who will spend adequate time with you in your growth in competence in ministry?

6. Do you have a humble and teachable heart that is characterized by a willingness to receive not only encouragement but also constructive criticism?

Further Reading

Alexander, Archibald. *The Log College.* London: Banner of Truth Trust, 1968.

Brookfield, Stephen. *Understanding and Facilitating Adult Learning.* San Francisco: Jossey-Bass, 1986.

Engstrom, Ted, and Ron Jenson. *The Making of a Mentor: 9 Essential Characteristics of Influential Christian Leaders.* Waynesboro, GA: Authentic Media, 2005.

Stanley, Paul, and J. Robert Clinton. *Connecting: The Mentoring Relationships You Need to Succeed in Life.* Colorado Springs: NavPress, 1992.

Chapter 3

Field Education and Theological Reflection in an Evangelical Tradition

Don Payne

For it has seemed good to the Holy Spirit and to us. (Acts 15:28)

The church budget is in crisis. Contributions have dropped steadily as a result of layoffs at a large local employer. A sermon series on stewardship backfired, creating both guilt and resentment among many church members. The church board is now wrestling with whether to lay off the part-time youth pastor or reduce the missions budget.

On Thursday afternoon the mail arrives. The pastor sorts through the stack, wondering how to triage the unpayable bills and maintain an upright reputation for the church within the community. A rather inconspicuous envelope rises to the top of the stack and beckons to be opened. To the pastor's astonishment, it contains a substantial check made payable to the church for an amount equal to half of the church's annual budget. The pastor is stunned! It appears to be one of those uncanny, serendipitous gifts from God at just the last minute. Then the pastor reads the enclosed letter. It is from the daughter of a couple who were involved in the congregation years ago before moving to another state. They have recently passed away. Their daughter has never shown any interest in the Christian faith, but as executor of their estate she recalls her parents' affection for the church and wishes to honor their memory with a gift designated for new stained glass windows throughout the church building. What can the pastor do with such a "gift" in a time when the church can barely pay its bills? How does theology relate to the decisions and conversations now facing the pastor? What values and resources will inform this dilemma? Does theology even matter here?

This vignette represents the vast array of situations that those in ministry confront on a regular basis. Theological education intends to prepare people for faithful and sustainable ministry. Sadly, however, students who traverse the halls and curriculum worksheets of our institutions often realize that their educational experiences have not equipped them to navigate these minefields. Thus, they may resort to resources, approaches, and values that are surprisingly inconsistent with their theological convictions in their search for guidance that seems sensible.

Field education affords unique opportunities for learning to integrate theology with the practice of ministry. This integration is as challenging to achieve as it is popular to advertise. Yet, through the disciplined practice of theological reflection, field educators can facilitate a symbiosis between the faith that we confess and the faith that we practice. Two well-known writers on the subject, James Whitehead and Evelyn Whitehead, have described theological reflection as "the process of bringing to bear in the practical decisions of ministry the resources of Christian faith."[1] Their description reflects the driving motivation for theological reflection: that the core beliefs comprising our Christian identity should be enacted in the ministry practices (not merely the verbal messages) by which we perpetuate that identity in our personal and corporate Christian life.

The practice of theological reflection challenges our compartmentalized approach to faith in which we unwittingly conceptualize and verbalize far more than we live. Theological reflection is no panacea for compartmentalization, yet it constitutes an important, deliberate step toward the integration that sustains integrity in our faith. Since the practice of theological reflection swims upstream against a strong and relentless current of atomizing forces, it is a practice that must be quite intentionally taught, modeled, and engaged. Field education is not merely an ideal opportunity for theological reflection: it falls short of its purposes without it.

What Is Theological Reflection?

The Whiteheads' definition of theological reflection, "the process of bringing to bear in the practical decisions of ministry the resources of Christian faith," provides a helpful starting place.[2] Theological reflection both illuminates and shapes the vital intersection between what we profess and what we practice. However, from one tradition to the next, conclusions

---

1. James Whitehead and Evelyn Eaton Whitehead, *Method in Ministry: Theological Reflection and Christian Ministry*, rev. ed. (Lanham, MD: Sheed and Ward, 1995), ix.
2. Ibid.

vary concerning the content and task of theology. Furthermore, theology and the practice of ministry are related to each other in a variety of ways.

Models of Reflection

In some traditions, the "practice" category (including experiential factors) carries more weight. Likewise, theology is sometimes understood as the fluid, accumulated, and contextually bound conclusions of tradition. For example, Patricia O'Connell Killen and John de Beer highlight the role of experience by stating, "Theological reflection is the discipline of exploring individual and corporate experience in conversation with the wisdom of a religious heritage."[3] John Patton recognizes a sort of bidirectional hermeneutic between faith and practice when he observes, "Christian ministry involves not only understanding what we do in the light of our faith, but also understanding our faith in the light of what we do."[4] Similarly, William Pyle recognizes the mutual influence of belief and practice but focuses on the outcome of integration through this process of mutual correction and clarification. He speaks of "the process of examining one's actions in order to identify the assumptions which are behind the actions, scrutinizing the accuracy and validity of the assumptions, and reconstituting these assumptions to include new insights, in order to make the assumptions more integrative of the experiences of reality."[5]

Ray Anderson takes the theological aspect of this integrative process a step further by suggesting the superordinate trajectory of God's work as that to which both belief and practice are accountable. He defines theological reflection as "the activity of the Christian and the church by which acts of ministry are critically and continually assessed in light of both revelation and reconciliation as God's true Word."[6] Where do these definitions leave us?

The Roman Catholic tradition, which has given extensive attention to the discipline of theological reflection, allots significant weight to tradition as a factor in discerning the path of faithfulness in the practice of ministry. Though some evangelicals may be tempted to dismiss Roman Catholic resources or approaches to theological reflection on this basis, it must be remembered that the authority Roman Catholics recognize in the *magisterium* does not attempt to address each and every issue that is confronted in daily life and ministry. Thoughtful Roman Catholics still wrestle with the

---

3. Patricia O'Connell Killen and John de Beer, *The Art of Theological Reflection* (New York: Crossroad, 1995), viii.

4. John Patton, *From Ministry to Theology: Pastoral Action and Reflection* (Decatur, GA: Journal of Pastoral Care Publications, 1995), 12.

5. William T. Pyle, "Theological Reflection," in *Experiencing Ministry Supervision: A Field-Based Approach*, ed. William T. Pyle and Mary Alice Seals (Nashville: Broadman & Holman, 1995), 110.

6. Ray S. Anderson, *The Shape of Practical Theology: Empowering Ministry with Theological Praxis* (Downers Grove, IL: InterVarsity Press, 2001), 55.

text of Scripture and seek to develop spiritual discernment for identifying paths of faithfulness in the midst of convoluted situations and menus of poor options. While evangelicals recognize a different weight of authority in tradition and appeal to other hermeneutical canons and resources, there is much to learn from the way Roman Catholic theological reflection respects the accumulated wisdom of God's people through the ages.

Numerous Protestant approaches to theological reflection highlight the role of culture, experience, and reason in theological reflection. This does not necessarily mean that Scripture and tradition are ignored or trivialized, though that is sometimes perceived to be the case. However, culture, experience, and reason are taken seriously as interpretive factors that shape the way Scripture and tradition function. Albert Outler's familiar methodological framework of Scripture, tradition, reason, and experience outlines components that many practitioners of theological reflection would accept, while differing about how those components relate to each other and which component is allowed to have functional control over the others.[7] Evangelicals typically would assert the preeminence of Scripture in that framework, even if it is admitted that tradition, reason, and experience have important hermeneutical roles.

Usefulness of Models

This chapter seeks to remedy two challenges that perpetually confront theological educators, especially those involved in field education. First, it is easier to establish the importance of theological reflection than to nurture it as a sustainable habit. Currently, theological reflection is often taught and practiced in ways that, though helpful, fit educational contexts better than ministry contexts. Thus, models for theological reflection in field education should be easily transferable to and useful within the ministry contexts that graduates enter, resulting in greater likelihood that they will continue to practice intentional and meaningful theological reflection on their own.

The second challenge is a bit more involved. Most of the well-known and widely used resources for theological reflection have emerged from outside evangelical theological traditions. These resources have given theological reflection credibility within academic cultures and have greatly enriched the practice. In most cases, these resources have been developed, understandably, with a desire to be highly accessible, minimally esoteric, and portable across traditions. This makes further sense because many in our congregations and seminaries reflect the increasing rate of denominational and theological transience. The lines between some theological traditions have blurred or softened, and in many instances we have learned to learn from each other. Democratic and pluralistic sensibilities have prompted us

---

7. Albert Outler, introduction to *The Works of John Wesley*, ed. Albert C. Outler (Nashville: Abingdon, 1984), 56ff.

to greater levels of respect for, or at least politeness toward, those of differing theological persuasions. These and other factors have understandably led us to affirm the importance of theological reflection while minimizing attention to the theology of those who are reflecting.

Hence, theological reflection is generally described as a process that transcends any particular theology. For example, Howard Stone and James Duke point out that their book, *How to Think Theologically*, "does not present a systematic theology or propose a one-and-only-one way of doing theology. It offers, instead, a framework in which to do ongoing theological reflection."[8] Their statement assumes that a framework or method for theological reflection can indeed function in isolation from theological commitments. This type of split ignores and even works against a core epistemological commitment that undergirds theological field education, in essence the interplay of method and content in our learning.[9] The usefulness and faithfulness of our theological reflection practices depend on models in which theology and method are organically linked.

The theological reflection constructs and practices suggested in broad-based, broadly aimed sources offer much that will benefit any practitioner of ministry. Yet, since the practice of theological reflection has such enormous potential to shape the character of ministry itself and, in turn, those who are shaped by that ministry, we must further explore the shape of a distinctively evangelical approach to theological reflection. To be sure, the varied models of theological reflection that are available have provided frameworks, resources, and stimuli for an evangelical model. Yet, Andrew Purves's observation about the field of pastoral theology (of which the discipline of theological reflection could be considered a part) is pertinent.

> The discipline has tended to organize around a psychological interpretation of human experience and to begin its so-called theological reflection from there. . . . the discipline has moved in a distinctly clinical, psychotherapeutic, or, more generally, social-scientific direction rather than a theological or doctrinal direction. There is no doubt that much has been learned from this shift, but it has also had two negative consequences. The first is the loss of Christology, soteriology, and the Christian doctrine of God in the pastoral theology and pastoral practice of the church. . . . The second, and a consequence of the first, is the tendency for pastoral work, when it lacks adequate theological foundation,

---

8. Howard Stone and James Duke, *How to Think Theologically*, 2nd ed. (Minneapolis: Fortress, 2006), vi.

9. Most field educators and directors will be familiar with Donald Schon, *The Reflective Practitioner: How Professionals Think in Action* (New York: Basic Books, 1983). Perhaps less widely used but no less vital for the epistemology of field education is Michael Polanyi, *The Tacit Dimension* (Gloucester, MA: Peter Smith, 1983).

to be given over to control by secular goals and techniques of care.[10]

The net effect of this provenance is that models of theological reflection can be concerned *with* God in a general manner without being constructed and directed *by* what is known *of* God. A consistently evangelical approach to theological reflection treats experience (in ministry as well as other domains) as an interpretive lens for knowledge of God rather than a primary source of knowledge of God. Evangelical theological reflection operates with a particular theology of revelation; what is revealed *of* God and *by* God controls the process of reflection *about* God and God's work in the world. Only thus can our processes or methods of theological reflection be both genuinely evangelical and "practical" for ministry.

An Evangelical Model

At this point the key word *evangelical* should be clarified. With the tapestry of influences that have shaped the definition of the word, especially since the Second World War in both North America and the United Kingdom, no particular tradition or ecclesiastical body can claim the right to define the term. David Bebbington suggests that conversionism, activism, biblicism, and crucicentrism "form a quadrilateral of priorities that is the basis of Evangelicalism."[11] Oliver Barclay adds "Christ-centered" to Bebbington's profile.[12] The combination of these five traits, along with the Reformation distinctives of *sola scriptura*, *sola gratia*, *sola fidei*, and *sola Christi*, will constitute a framework of theological values to focus our theological reflection model. The practice of theological reflection should embody as *praxis* some of the essential commitments widely and historically recognized as denoting "evangelical."[13]

Specifically, an evangelical approach to theological reflection must assume the Trinitarian nature of the God with whom we need to be reconciled, the reality of sin and its effects on the entire human experience, the centrality of the person and work of Jesus Christ for redemption, the authoritative role of Scripture as understood in light of Jesus Christ, the importance of faith in God's grace for navigating the unavoidable uncertainties

---

10. Andrew Purves, *Reconstructing Pastoral Theology: A Christological Foundation* (Louisville: Westminster, 2004), xiv.

11. David W. Bebbington, *Evangelicalism in Modern Britain: A History from the 1730s to the 1980s* (London: Unwin Hyman, 1989), 2–3.

12. Oliver Barclay, *Evangelicalism in Britain, 1935–1995: A Personal Sketch* (Leicester: InterVarsity Press, 1997), 10–11.

13. Anderson, *Shape of Practical Theology*, 47–48. I follow Anderson's understanding of praxis as "a particular form of action that should not be directly equated with the word *practice*. . . . [P]raxis denotes a form of action profoundly saturated with *meaning*, a form of action that is value-directed and theory-laden." He goes on to state, "When we speak of *praxis*, we are referring to a practical form of knowledge that generates actions through which the church community lives out its beliefs. . . . In a very real sense, belief is within the act itself. . . . Praxis, then, reveals theology in a very tangible form" (ibid.).

and hazards of ministry, and the eschatological promise of resurrection and renewal as the horizon that shapes our efforts in the present order.

Ray Anderson consolidates the dynamic thrust of these themes in his emphasis on "Christopraxis," which constitutes a useful criterion for an evangelical approach.[14] His explanation of theological reflection based on Christopraxis establishes important navigational bearings for the model that follows.

Theological reflection as a critical exercise leads to competence in ministry as the one who ministers unites both proclamation and practice in the truth of Jesus Christ. It is reflection not only on the nature of ministry from the perspective of biblical and theological truths but also on the nature of divine revelation from the perspective of its saving and reconciling intention in the lives of people.

It must be said also that theological reflection does not lead to new revelation, for God has spoken once and for all in the revelation of Jesus Christ, and Holy Scripture is the normative and infallible truth of that revelation. However, theological reflection takes note of the presence of the one who is revealed in his continuing ministry of reconciliation through the Holy Spirit. Theological reflection does not ask the question, What would Jesus do in this situation? because this question would imply his absence. Rather, it asks the question, Where is Jesus in this situation and what am I to do as a minister?[15]

This approach to integration is much more than conceptual. It is deeply evangelical in that it opens passageways for the power of the gospel to come alive in the practice of ministry with a full-orbed Christology as the integrative thread.

Purves suggests, "It is reasonable to expect that pastoral theology [and in our case, the practice of theological reflection] would in its own way express what Christians believe about God and the gospel of Jesus Christ."[16] As evangelical Christians we should expect methods of theological reflection that embody the character of our theological commitments, even with the variety of emphases that exists across our broad spectrum of traditions.[17]

The Practice of Evangelical Theological Reflection

Prerequisites

A method of theological reflection that is genuinely integrated with and empowered by our theological commitments must be marked by three features: sustainability, humility, and an action orientation.

---

14. Ibid., 54–56.

15. Ibid.

16. Purves, *Reconstructing Pastoral Theology*, xvii.

17. In the spirit of both Christian charity and educational cross-fertilization, our approaches to theological reflection can be enriched by an appreciation of how other denominations have pursued faithfulness. See W. David Buschart, *Exploring Protestant Traditions: An Invitation to Theological Hospitality* (Downers Grove, IL: InterVarsity Press, 2006).

Sustainability

Sustainable theological reflection depends on methods that are natural in one's ministerial habit long after formal education has been completed. Theological reflection must be taught and practiced from a well-integrated, intuitive, ministerial mind-set. It must become part of both who we are in ministry and how we interpret the world around us as ministers of the gospel. Thus, our methods must be simple and organic.

Humility

Our reflective practice must recognize that often in the current order, faithfulness cannot be determined with precision and certainty. That is to say, we minister in conditions that are so horribly broken by sin, directly and indirectly, that perfect decisions and absolute certainty that we have "done the right thing" often elude us. We face ethical "no-win" situations when providing moral guidance for people trapped between bonds of confidentiality and obligations to protect victims. We confront credibility dilemmas when forced to make personnel decisions based on information that would be inappropriate to release, when that information alone could justify our decisions in the public eye.

Thus, faithfulness cannot be determined by whether we are able to identify and implement "perfect" decisions in the ministry situations we face. When our methods of theological reflection are, even implicitly, propelled by the expectation and pressure to "get it all just right," we will have denied in practice a key evangelical tenet: that we are justified by God's grace alone. Rather, our methods of theological reflection must reflect and even point us back to God's grace through Jesus Christ as the only source of our freedom and peace when we must make decisions from a range of options that are far from perfect.

Action Orientation

The Whiteheads and others rightly emphasize that reflection upon ministry must empower ministry with accountable action steps, including contingency plans and follow-up plans.[18] All reflection must be undertaken with this expectation. In fact, genuinely evangelical theological reflection assumes that our triune God, as Truth, is personally and dynamically present in and through ministry (Heb. 4:12). This is the praxis envisioned in evangelical theological reflection. Theological reflection must affect the concrete ways in which we lead, listen, and love.

The Reflective Process: A Case Study

So, how might these commitments and assumptions take shape in an evangelical theological reflection model? The Whiteheads' three-stage approach of attending, asserting, and pastoral response breaks the process down into an accessible and helpful sequence of information gathering, analysis, and

---

18. Whitehead and Whitehead, *Method in Ministry*, 86ff.

action.[19] Their basic outline is to be commended with the qualification that in practice, the process may not always be quite so linear.

A Sample Ministry Incident

Utilizing a ministry incident or case study is probably the most recognizable exercise for teaching theological reflection.[20] The following ministry incident will provide an opportunity for theological reflection in a distinctively evangelical manner. Though this is an actual incident, some information has been changed for the sake of confidentiality.

Alise and Jon are a young couple who have visited Springdale Community Church for the past few weeks. A member of the pastoral staff contacted them by phone to thank them for visiting and to offer to answer any questions about the church they might have. They expressed interest in meeting to talk further. When the couple met with the pastor in a restaurant later that week, they unfolded the following story.

Both had become Christians during high school and have been active in church ever since. They were discipled fairly well in the basics of the faith and gradually grew into leadership roles. In their previous church, however, they became involuntary participants in an intense controversy between key church leaders. Long-standing friendships were shattered. Trust was broken by leadership. The results? Every sermon felt as if it was laced with hypocrisy. Worship felt hollow and contrived. Alise came to the point that she was not even able to go inside a church building without crying. They left the church not knowing whether they would ever be emotionally capable of attending church again.

After several months without attending church at all, they decided to try again but in another place. They like the services and the sermons but still find the experience incredibly difficult. Old memories are easily triggered. They are jaded about the possibility of ever being significantly involved again. Not only do they fear a repeat experience, but they fear the further disillusionment of discovering that the leaders of this congregation are flawed too. They know that perfect leaders are an illusion but feel that it is easier to maintain the illusion from a safe distance than risk the pain of experiencing another disappointment. Since they became Christians, God has worked in their lives in some ways that have marked them indelibly. Yet, they now find themselves angry at God for allowing such loss, confused at why the situations could not be resolved by seemingly godly people, and frustrated that the pain continues. Frankly, they admit, it was all they could do to even speak one-on-one with a pastor again. And they are skeptical about what the pastor might say even now in response to their story.

---

19. Ibid., 67–99.

20. See chapter 9, "The Use of Case Studies in Field Education," for examples of case studies.

A common ministry incident such as this one can lend itself to analysis from multiple angles, each of them important: psychologically, ecclesiastically, culturally, and theologically. Where should we begin our reflection process, and how should we proceed?

Two types of theological reflection may take place around an incident like this. For educational purposes, we might interact from a distance or abstractly in the context of a theological reflection seminar or mentoring session. The other type of reflection is that for which reflection in educational settings exists: when we actually find ourselves in such an occasion and must make decisions about what to say and do. In the ministry crucible, our theological reflection skills should be deeply embedded in our ministerial instincts. Hopefully, we have developed a habit of reflection that will operate in prayerful dependence on the Holy Spirit. The suggested steps that follow can be utilized in both educational settings and in the ministry moment.

Enlarge and Refine the View

A Christologically oriented theological reflection process can begin by asking questions (whether or not they are verbalized) that will illuminate the ways in which Christ's redemptive work is needed. Such questions may be broad in scope but specific to the incident in an attempt to gain a more nuanced picture of a situation and what is at issue as it is viewed against the backdrop of God's created intentions, the effects of sin, and the trajectory of redemption. This step can be compared to putting a light filter on a camera so that certain colors are accented.

In the incident with Alise and Jon, we could seek understanding by asking the following questions:

1. What might the concepts of forgiveness and redemption mean to them at this point in their lives?

2. What might account for the fact that they are still drawn toward the church in some manner, even with their wounds and misgivings?

3. Where is faith still in evidence in their lives?

Of course, much more information can and should be gained in order to clarify the situation and aid interpretation. A Christological approach to reflection on this scenario neither ignores nor trivializes that broader range of questions. It simply insists that the situation under examination cannot be rightly understood apart from criteria that are shaped by our theology! The process of gathering information is itself a theological act. Our theology shapes the questions we ask and the type of information we consider relevant to the decision(s) to be made.

In order to seek the fullest possible understanding of Alise and Jon's dilemma, the following additional questions also could be pursued:

1. What assumptions is the couple making, e.g., about truth, faith, community?

2. What is at risk for this couple that they may not see?

3. How do they understand or define the core problem?

4. What expectations do they have of your congregation and of God?

5. Behind their suspicions and wounds, where do points of openness exist in this couple?

6. What pastoral response is *not* likely to be helpful to them? Why?

Some of the best resources for theological reflection from both the Roman Catholic and broadly Protestant communities offer helpful suggestions for exploring the hidden personal and cultural dimensions of a ministry situation. These approaches can and should be utilized so that we do not unwittingly do damage by drawing premature conclusions.

Evangelicals' high view of scriptural authority makes it all too easy to quickly locate a passage of Scripture that seems to have implications for a ministry situation, run the situation through the grid of that text(s), and come to a rather premature conclusion. Such a strategy may have the look and feel of faithfulness while resulting in misguided or even disastrous decisions because important factors have been overlooked. Thus, it is advisable to begin the process of theological reflection with a disciplined examination of a situation in order to identify factors that may affect our interpretation and actions. Though it may seem counterintuitive and theologically suspect, the process should temporarily suspend drawing biblical and theological conclusions in order to help ensure due process in understanding the nature of the situation. The Whiteheads suggest that the "attending" phase examine the broader features of a ministry decision: cultural issues, personal implications and risks, complicating factors, and so on.[21]

Gathering information is an intensely personal act as well as a theological act. We bring not only our theological values but also our ecclesiastical backgrounds, personalities, wounds, and experiences of God's grace to the questions we ask and the interpretations we render. The informational step should illuminate not only the situation but ourselves as well. Healthy theological reflection will lead to bidirectional illumination, similar to what Calvin described in his well-known claim regarding the interconnectedness of knowing God and knowing ourselves.[22]

---

21. Whitehead and Whitehead, *Method in Ministry*, 67–74.
22. John Calvin, *Institutes of the Christian Religion*, trans. Ford Lewis Battles (Philadelphia: Westminster, 1960), 1.1.2.

Among the initial questions that should be asked of any incident is what type of decision is needed in this situation. With Alise and Jon, what challenges and options did the pastor face in the conversation, especially in the way it ended? What temptations were to be avoided and why? What possibilities could inform the pastor's response? In this instance it would not be uncommon for a pastor in this position to feel an internal pressure to somehow convince the couple that the church he or she represents is different from the church where the couple had the painful experience. Yet, as the pastor reflects theologically on the spot (asking some questions internally and others directly of the couple), there is an unusual opportunity to minister to them by helping them understand and process their experience. In this sense, collecting information is not merely a function of enhancing our own understanding for the sake of our reflection. It also allows those involved in the situation to do their own theological reflection.

After disciplined examination of the incident through both general and Christological lenses, the reflection process can move to more direct theological analysis.

Find Theological Focal Points

The distinctive theological move in this process involves specific questions that reflect our theological commitments. Though we work from a place of theological conviction, we also must take this step with humility, open to the prospect that the situation will test and refine our theology. This need not unnerve us as evangelicals since we recognize that at our best, we grasp God's truth only in part (1 Cor. 13:12). We are ever learning. God's truth does not change, but learning and formation can run in both directions.

How might our theology more directly shape the questions we ask so as to bring clarity of focus and lead to faithful decisions while remaining open to learning? Here are sample questions related to the situation with Alise and Jon:

1. What can we identify in God's creative and redemptive purposes that would help us form ideal goals for this situation (even if we realize that we may fall far short of those ideals)?

2. What aspects of personhood in God's image are involved or at risk in this situation? Where and how has this situation affected their sense of personhood in community?

3. In what other way(s) are the effects of sin evident?

4. Where or in what specific ways is forgiveness necessary? What steps and challenges might be involved in forgiveness? What might the fruit of forgiveness look like?

5. What would the incarnation and the resurrection imply for this situation?

6. What ministry do we need from the Holy Spirit in this situation?

How might these questions be answered in regard to Alise and Jon?

As we allow our own theology to be challenged, refined, and grown through this engagement, we might discover forgiveness as more layered or repetitive than we imagined. We may realize that silence and presence are more powerful than we expected because of the incarnation. How we speak about God's faithfulness might be reshaped as we realize that God meets us in our brokenness in unpredictable, yet consistently gracious ways without making everything "OK."

Identify Possibilities and Paths

The action component in theological reflection does not reduce the process to raw pragmatism. Rather, it reflects the theological belief that God acts decisively and redemptively in our lives, calling us into lives of engaged, obedient faith. Anyone in the trenches of ministry knows that at some point decisions must be made even if more information could be gathered and more analysis done. Even the most thorough, responsible, and theologically informed reflection process does not eliminate the element of risk and faith from acts of ministry. At what point and how do we connect our reflection process to our action steps?

First, we must realize that there is no absolute distinction between reflection and action. We are acting even as we reflect. Likewise, we should reflect as we act and after we act so that appropriate follow-up steps and midcourse corrections or adjustments can be made. A Christological reflection process involves the conviction that even as we listen to a person and observe a situation, God is working through our attentive presence. A genuinely evangelical reflection process also depends consciously on the ministry of the Spirit to grant discernment about how to join Christ's work in the moment.

The infinite variety in the ministry situations that we face suggests that there can be no formula for action that tidily resolves any and all problems. Yet, we can act both humbly and decisively in the freedom granted by the promise of Christ's active, redeeming presence in us through the Spirit. This provides confidence to take specific steps forward, knowing that we, too, need and can rely on God's forgiveness and redemption for our own shortcomings as we act. We can move forward with confidence that God mercifully uses even our flawed actions to touch lives, advance his work, and grow us in wisdom.

To take action is to look for possibilities and creative paths. It is to engage a ministry situation, whether firsthand or as an exercise, with the expectation that God will illuminate options that previously were unseen, that glimmers of hope will emerge, however slender and tenuous they may seem, and that God will meet our movements forward in faith, working out restoration in Christ through the power of the Holy Spirit. Jesus' repeated responses to halting, fearful, yet active faith have marked a path for us to follow in our own acts of faith when addressing some- times torturous ministry challenges and in our call to others to step forward in faith.

What might the action step look like for the pastor sitting across a restaurant table from Alise and Jon? Obviously, action must be based on a more thorough engagement with questions such as those suggested above. Yet, unlike a reflection exercise in which participants enjoy the luxury of working carefully and methodically through these steps, the pastor must be taking these steps in the moment. Still, a first and vital step is taken as the pastor listens to their story without attempting to explain, offer personal examples, teach, and either vindicate or vilify their former church. The pastor can be powerfully incarnational by entering their pain and standing at their side, not against a congregation or any individuals, but against the evil and brokenness that has devastated them. The pastor can bear witness that Jesus Christ is on their side against all that destroys people and the community of faith that (sometimes inhospitably) houses his Spirit.

Further, the pastor can verbalize permission for the couple to hurt as part of their healing. This is no mere psychological technique or develop- mental observation, but a profoundly theological act that acknowledges that wounds of any kind, and especially those to our person and our faith, rarely heal easily or instantaneously. We know this because of the depth and extent of Christ's suffering for the healing of our lives, as well by as the slow, progressive, and jagged nature of our transformation into his image. In many cases a pastor can speak words of grace that begin a healing process. This may even include the pastor seeking the couple's forgiveness on behalf of the church at large and offering to come alongside them to explore the shape of forgiveness with their previous congregation.

Clearly, Alise and Jon will make their own decisions about how to respond. The pastor has no ultimate control over the outcome. However, evangelical theological reflection is sustained by a relentless confidence in God's grace through Jesus Christ and, as such, can proceed without compul- sive slavery to outcomes. We can minister with the utmost of free sobriety and sober freedom. Genuinely evangelical theological reflection liberates us for action like no other theological framework.

Theological Reflection in Field Education

Actual ministry situations rarely lend themselves to a clean, linear process of reflection and response. Many situations are chaotic, unpredict- able, and hopelessly convoluted. A disciplined, structured process of theo- logical reflection can give students the necessary constructs and building blocks for reflecting well on ministry when in the trenches. However, the process for teaching and practicing theological reflection in our educational settings must take place in ways that are transferable to the complexity of actual ministry circumstances. How can these transferable approaches be cultivated?

Students must remember that while theological reflection models may have a linear appearance, good theological reflection can start at a variety of places. For example, a struggling Christian's questions about what forgiveness means when restoration is impossible provide an excellent starting point for reflection on the relational challenges behind the question. Theological reflection also may be prompted by the need to help a person or congregation process tragedy or trauma. A culture of theological reflection can be fostered by modeling such reflection in our preaching and teaching ministries. The most important factors are whether our reflection process is based on adequate information (the enlarged and refined view), whether our distinctive theological commitments are shaping what we look for, and whether we are allowing the experience of ministry to affirm and refine our current theological commitments.

As another chapter will explore, the use of case studies can be one of the most effective means of enriching our perceptions and honing our instincts so that in the actual practice of ministry we begin to see factors and raise questions that we would have missed otherwise. Another helpful means of teaching theological reflection in field education is to require students to look for integrative connections between their field education and the classroom-based courses they are taking during the same term. This can be done by asking each student to identify at the outset of the term at least one insight or bit of knowledge that she or he will be seeking from one or more courses in relation to the upcoming ministry field experience.

For example, perhaps a student enrolls in a course on the Minor Prophets during a field education experience that involves pastoral care in a hospice. How can meaningful theological reflection take place around those two, seemingly unrelated, experiences? When asked to identify the "hidden" intersections and paths between them, the student may reflect on what it means to care for those whose responses are outside his or her control (a phenomenon the prophets certainly faced!). A student taking a course on theological anthropology may want to reflect on the implications of bearing God's image for decisions that must be made about how to interpret and direct the energies of rowdy middle schoolers in a Tuesday evening youth group.

Theological reflection exercises can begin with a theological question and move to ministry issues it raises. It can begin with a thorny ministry problem followed by investigation into those resources that would speak to the problem. It can begin with an exciting but risky opportunity or a casual conversation. A variety of helpful pedagogies is available. Whatever methods are chosen, they should be simple, memorable, and help students craft questions that clearly emerge from their theology.

Conclusion

Theological reflection can be among the most difficult and rewarding aspects of a field education experience. The difficulty is often a result of the integrative nature of the practice. Integration may be a fashionable mantra in educational circles today, but it is by no means a simple task. Integration demands the interface of disciplines and experiences that do not ostensibly synchronize. Specialization and isolation become more and more inviting when they afford a sense of insulation from these questions that do not fit the structure of a discipline. Theological reflection forces us to engage the whole of life and ministry and put to the test our evangelical conviction that Christ is Lord of all.

Theological reflection is also difficult because it has an ambiguous and sometimes threatening role in a theological curriculum. On one hand, those in classical disciplines will often applaud the phrase because it offers a sense of reassurance that perhaps the practitioners care about theology after all! Yet, it utilizes an epistemology that recognizes the practice of ministry (an experiential type of factor) as an important hermeneutical criterion for understanding our theology. For evangelicals, who stand by the eternal and authoritative self-revelation of God in his incarnate and written Word, there should always be a healthy skepticism and reserve about how much weight experience carries in our belief systems. Still, faithful, evangelical theological reflection affords an opportunity to experience the "hermeneutical spiral" in real space and time.[23]

Why is theological reflection so crucial and so potentially rewarding? It is a crucible for discerning, following, and experiencing the power of the gospel in the raw, unfiltered realities of human life. Evangelical theological reflection takes place against the backdrop of being created in God's image, being horribly broken by sin, tasting the glory of God's redemptive touch, and being carried along by God's promise to restore all things. Theological reflection is far from the only thing we do in field education. Yet, without it the work of preparation for ministry shrinks to little more than the refinement of techniques that afford some temporary relief. Theological reflection is a living, pulsating means of staying connected to the source of eternal life in the practice of ministry, not merely on the pages of our textbooks.

---

23. Grant Osborne, *The Hermeneutical Spiral: A Comprehensive Introduction to Biblical Interpretation* (Downers Grove, IL: InterVarsity Press, 2006). Osborne's helpful paradigm recognizes that the task of applying our interpretations of Scripture to specific life situations can in turn clarify our interpretations.

Prayer of Transformation

Father, grant us the wisdom of your Spirit that we may know ways of faithfulness to Jesus among the myriad options we face and in the tragic brokenness of life. Let the light of the gospel penetrate the dark and hopeless situations in which we are often called to minister. In all our ministry decisions and approaches, may Jesus Christ be seen as the way to life where there seems to be no way, that you may be rightly trusted and praised by all through Christ our Lord. Amen.

Reflection Questions

1. What theological commitments from your own tradition would be important to incorporate into your theological reflection process? How would you frame questions based on those commitments?

2. Consider your current method of theological reflection with regard to its sustainability after your formal education. How can you more closely resemble the theological reflection opportunities that actually happen in ministry?

3. What was most and least helpful to you in learning to integrate your theology with your practice of ministry? What do your answers suggest about your current methods for teaching theological reflection to others?

4. In what ways has the practice of ministry shaped, refined, or challenged your theology? What have you learned about navigating the relationship between faithfulness to your convictions and a posture of teachability in the face of demanding ministry situations?

5. If you could tell someone only one thing about theological reflection and you knew the person would continue to follow your advice, what would it be? Why did you make the choice you made?

Further Reading

Anderson, Ray. *The Soul of Ministry: Forming Leaders for God's People.* Louisville: Westminster/John Knox, 1997.

Schon, Donald. *The Reflective Practitioner: How Professionals Think in Action.* New York: Basic Books, 1983.

Whitehead, James, and Evelyn Eaton Whitehead. *Method in Ministry: Theological Reflection and Christian Ministry.* Rev. ed. Lanham, MD: Sheed and Ward, 1995.

Chapter 4

Field Education and Cultural Awareness

DIPA HART

May the God who gives endurance and encouragement give you a
spirit of unity among yourselves as you follow Christ Jesus, so that
with one heart and mouth you may glorify the God and Father of
our Lord Jesus Christ. (Rom. 15:5–6 NIV)

Before one assumes this chapter is only for preparing students for the foreign mission field, please take a moment to observe the people around you. Applying the most recent census data, you should assume that one out of every five people you observe (20 percent) was not born in the United States. The United States Census Bureau estimates that by the year 2050, every other person residing here will be foreign born.[1] The implications for every ministry are substantial. Over the next forty years, every other person sitting in the pews will be attempting to integrate into American culture and will speak a language other than English in their homes. If that is not the demographic students see themselves ministering to in the future,

---

1. United States Census Bureau, "Projected Population of the United States, by Race and Hispanic Origin: 2000 to 2050," http://www.census.gov/ipc/www/usinterimproj/; and United States Census Bureau, "Summary of Fertility, Mortality, and Migration Assumptions by Race and Hispanic Origin: Lowest, Middle, and Highest Series, 1999 to 2100," http://www.census.gov/population/www/projections/natsum.html.

then they should consider how the following will impact their ministries: 50 percent of the people around church members, and even in the church, will be immigrants and their children will be seeking involvement in politics and a variety of social justice causes.[2]

The United States Census Bureau calculates such information to help the government and its entities to plan well for future growth and population changes. Shouldn't the body of Christ also be proactive and begin learning to minister well to our newest neighbors? How does this population shift affect theological education and the training of future ministers?

Churches today face the same dilemma the earliest churches did. Accepting someone from Nazareth as a religious leader, gathering to eat a meal with tax collectors and prostitutes, and working on a day for rest were social implications of the new religious teachings that challenged the entire Jewish nation to reconsider its purposes for societal structures. But when such radical change did not occur quickly, the earliest Christians became hidden until their numbers grew and became dangerously large to the power holders. Then, something radical did happen. The churches' leaders were unjustly accused of blasphemy and power hoarding and were subsequently executed without fair trial. Social challenges then began to multiply instead of decrease. Considering Gentiles as brothers and sharing meals with the uncircumcised were received as disgusting, putrid ideas brought on by the followers of Jesus.

However, the challenges are no less "putrid" to our American senses when we consider the implications of living with immigrants from underdeveloped countries whose cultures we do not value and languages we do not understand. The influx of immigrants begins to challenge our fabric of cultural values, such as the right to own a home with a white picket fence where only one family unit lives together.

Today, as the United States Congress struggles with how to manage both legal and illegal immigration, churches offer services in multiple languages through translators and even appoint multiple pastors for the different nationalities represented in their congregations. The few noteworthy churches leading the way in such church experiments have helped both first- and second-generation families worship together with the English-speaking community. Yet, would every church member even agree as to whether or not their church should minister to *those people* who might be illegally residing within the United States? Who is going to check their national identification cards? The hospitality team?

Whether the church or individual approves of it personally or politically, the culture and the demographics on the North American continent are integrating quickly. The student today, who will be a leader in the church tomorrow, must either be proactively prepared to impact the communities

---

2. Esther Wu, "Asians Finding a Place in the Political Process," *Dallas Morning News*, August 2, 2007.

of tomorrow with biblical truth, or face an inability to minister when the remotest parts of the world sit in the pews.[3] In America, few masters-level schools (including seminaries) offer formal classes to dialogue about race or cultural issues or challenge students during their educational activities to develop emotionally mature responses that reflect God and not just guilt for the sins of their forefathers. Unfortunately, few graduate schools (and seminaries) recognize the need for such conversations.

When students expect to enter cross-cultural or intercultural ministries, they will likely take courses to enhance their ability to communicate across cultures. Unfortunately, most other students do not seek out those classes or opportunities. In fact, few seminaries offer courses in cross-cultural or intercultural communication, practices, or patterns of conflict engagement. If anything is discussed about such issues, it is usually only embedded within the school's world missions courses.[4] Audience-centered applications and examples are taught in homiletics courses as a healthy preaching method, but usually these conversations revolve around teaching as it relates to gender and do not address racial or other intercultural issues within a congregation. Field education can become one of the places in a student's theological education where these issues can be given exposure and explored.

Today's Churches

Conflict of Cultures in Church

Congregations in America today can exacerbate cultural issues without even knowing it. For example, congregations usually divide up their ministries by age group or life stage and their services by worship style and language. The solution to differences has been individualization of services and classes based on likes, which unfortunately has resulted in separation within the church. Whereas individualization appears to facilitate easier ministry among some Westerners, it is worthwhile to consider whether such strategies are culturally sensitive.

First, ministries divided according to similarities are not accommodating to those whose entire family does not fit into the externally designated categories (language-specific services, for example). Second, non-Western cultures rarely separate families during services, and doing so may convey that the individualized experience is more valuable than the shared, community, or family experience. For example, take a simple value like the uninterrupted worship service, where mothers with young children are often secluded into crying rooms, and compare it with non-Western cultures that prefer to worship as a

---

3. While this chapter will deal with broader cultural issues, see also chapter 12, "Working with International Students in Field Education," for additional discussions on this topic.

4. Jack L. Seymour, "Perspectives on Diversity: Addressing and Embodying Diversity in Theological Education," in *ATS Folio: Diversity in Theological Education*, ed. Marsha Foster Boyd and William Myers (Pittsburgh: Association of Theological Schools, 2003), 7.

family unit and accept a crying infant as a normal, natural disruption. Such ministry structures and values were not created in churches to be ethnocentric, but today they do emanate an unwelcoming vibe to various ethnic groups with different cultural values that inform the structures of their lives.

Value discrepancies can be clearly seen when Christians who have lived predominately in the United States embrace an opportunity to travel overseas. They often return expressing a longing for the slower, simpler lifestyle of the other culture. In such comparisons, most are noting the difference in relational time versus the hectic pace of their own lives. Immigrants who come to the United States and expatriates who work overseas often struggle with this particular culture clash. Westerners value being on time and producing a product at the end of their day. Most other cultures value developing relationships over the logistics of events. Also, healthier relationships are not considered a measurable product to most Westerners, even though healthier relationships are desired.[5]

The common expectation for all immigrants is that they adjust to the American culture's time-sensitive values, and this may be a useful survival technique for an immigrant to remain employed. However, when a church demands timeliness of its parishioners, the non-Westernized immigrant will naturally feel his or her values are marginalized. When the immigrant desires in-home hospitality over the convenience of time, but the church provides opportunities for intermittent contact located primarily at the church, the immigrant's personhood is devalued. If these subtle value discrepancies are not addressed, they can disrupt the trust building process within a ministry.

For example, when a local church plant in Dallas began to minister across cultural boundaries to a refugee community, the church members' excitement waned as they encountered such cultural and logistical conflicts. Church members became frustrated at the nearly daily expectations within these new relationships that now took them into an impoverished community on more than an occasional visit and beyond the annual vacation Bible school. The refugees from the community, on the other hand, were frustrated because their children could not attend church without their parents' company, and the church leadership became strained due to the inability to start services on time. In hindsight it is no surprise that this church plant, along with over twenty other church plants in this East Dallas community, did not flourish due to a lack of knowledge about the refugee community it sought to minister to and of the individual nations represented.

Defining Missions

Church plants and missions departments alike are struggling to redefine what should be considered missions work. For example, some Caucasian American churches are considering what it means to include local ministry

---

5. See chapter 12, "Working with International Students in Field Education," for a more detailed discussion of cultural differences in values.

with international needs in their outreach visions. Some churches find it easier to employ overseas strategies here, yet challenges still remain when it comes to suspending the American value system on American soil. Sherwood Lingenfelter notes,

> Only by recognizing that cultural blindness is the rule, not the exception, and that our philosophies are our windows onto the world, can we free our fellowship and our theology from the bondage of our cultural philosophies and worldview. We must look through multiple windows if we are to genuinely apprehend the transforming power of the gospel and apply kingdom principles interculturally. Each believer sees through a glass, narrow and constraining, but together as disciples with differing perspectives, we can begin to comprehend the wider impact of the Scripture in a pluralistic world.[6]

However, some African-American churches tend to have the opposite problem. African-American churches have largely excelled in local ministry areas. Historically the local community has been their outreach focus because of the need for survival as a culture and community facing institutional slavery and racism.[7] Now, as they are challenged to engage in world missions actively, African-American churches struggle to overcome survival theology and to reconsider their role in global missions.[8]

It appears both Caucasian churches and African-American churches have a similar struggle in carrying out Jesus' plan in Acts 1:8:

> But you will receive power when the Holy Spirit has come upon you, and you will be my witnesses in Jerusalem and in all Judea and Samaria, and to the end of the earth.

The Caucasian church must learn to include the local community in its ministry vision and address its own Jerusalem, while the African-American church must consider how to include "the farthest parts of the earth" in its mission. Either way, they both must stretch their visions to include the needs of their immediate city and all of the world.

Division in Ethnic Churches

Ethnic churches structured around language or cultural similarities are not exempt from such sins of omission either. Take for example the issues

---

6. Sherwood G. Lingenfelter, *Transforming Culture: A Challenge for Christian Mission*, 2nd ed. (Grand Rapids: Baker, 1998), 21.

7. Clarence Shuler, *Winning the Race to Unity: Is Racial Reconciliation Really Working?* (Chicago: Moody, 2003), 83.

8. James Southerland, "African American Underrepresentation in Intercultural Missions: Perceptions of Black Missionaries and the Theology of Survival/Security" (Ph.D. diss., Trinity Evangelical Divinity School, 1988).

of societal class differences driving a wedge between middle- to upper-class Kenyan immigrants who were required to be educated to enter the United States, and recent Kenyan refugees who were relocated to America for survival and not held to such immigration standards. Can such a difference of class be overcome by common nationality? Can they exist in the same church?

The Gospel writers often recount the surprise and confusion of the disciples and the Pharisees when Jesus of Nazareth healed the unclean of society, such as the lepers and the demon-possessed, as often as he assisted members of the higher classes, such as the synagogue official's daughter and those at the already well-off wedding in Cana. Clearly Jesus would instruct these Kenyans to minister across classes; but in Dallas, there is little cross-pollination of educated immigrant communities and refugee communities because of such class and education discrepancies.

The Global Church: When Missionaries Succeed and Fail

Over the last decade, one of the most popular strategies among evangelical ministries has been to focus on that part of the world that contains the largest population of non-Christians. Known as the 10/40 Window, this area spans from 10 degrees to 40 degrees north of the equator, and stretches from North Africa across to China. Socioeconomic need and the lack of Christian resources were some of the original issues behind the creation of the 10/40 Window as a missions strategy. But even over these past ten years of strategic work, the 10/40 Window remains intact as the segment of the world with the fewest Christians.

The root issue was not a shortage of missionaries or lack of effort in the past or present. Interest continues to increase among present-day churches and ministries that have focused their prayers and sent workers and financial assistance to the fifty-six countries within the Window. No, the root issue for the last two thousand years stems from the inability of Christians to consistently overcome the cultural and religious barriers of these areas and provide a gospel that is contextually relevant and not steeped only in European or Westernized culture.

An example of cross-cultural success from outside the religious field can be read on a plaque in the San Diego Zoo, which recounts the history of how wildlife conservationists were able to overcome communication and religious hurdles in India to help save particular animals from extinction. Conservationists had little success in the beginning because their tactics were primarily focused on information dissemination—assuming that if the villagers knew more, they would logically act differently. However, after an initial failure to save the endangered species, conservationists adapted their message and began to explain the broader impact on societal life and nature through the vehicles of story, dance, and drama. Using such culturally adapted communication styles, they were able to communicate their message more accurately than they had previously with just information distribution.

Early efforts by missionaries in India resulted in causing Jesus to be either assimilated as another god into the Hindustani religion or to be considered the god brought by British imperialists to help dominate and manipulate them for financial gain. The few missionaries who experienced the fruit of their labor (such as William Carey) first found an audience among the lower socioeconomic classes because they chose to be immersed into the culture. Unfortunately, Christianity carries the stigma of being a Western, poor-man's religion, even though southern India claims a Christian lineage beginning with the apostle Thomas two thousand years ago.[9]

Overall, missionaries struggled to provide a contextualized Christianity grounded in Scripture that was both interactive with the various Indian subcultures and yet amenable to the original biblical meaning.[10] Throughout Asia and the 10/40 Window, people either approached Jesus of Nazareth as the *white* incarnation of the one true God or they absorbed Christianity's moral principles into their indigenous religions. This absorption can be seen in areas such as Buddhism's binding principles, known as the eight-fold path, or Hinduism's bhakti yoga, a personal and emotional approach to control sin in order to achieve salvation.

Five Imperatives for Educating Future Ministers

The limited impact of past missionary endeavors and the various issues plaguing local churches today should act as warnings for anyone involved in preparing themselves or others for Christian service. The following topics will require both theological and personal reflection so that institutions, educators, and students can develop well-informed, personalized internships that will effectively challenge the student and increase his or her effectiveness.

Seek Balanced Development

There are various approaches to addressing the areas for student development and, whereas there is not one correct approach, each approach has its benefits and blind spots. For example, students who prefer an exclusively Bible-centered approach might consider contextualization and interpersonal skills as superfluous to their primary goal of receiving a theological education. These students must be encouraged to consider the question, If the theological construct of sin and the fall has affected all of creation, then how would people's contextualization and interpersonal skills be affected? It logically follows, then, that we need to intentionally counteract sin's effects and reform our skills to reflect Christ. The apostle Paul's words assist the conversation by providing an example of desirability of these skills as he

---

9. Ralph P. Martin and Peter Davids, eds., *Dictionary of the Later New Testament and Its Developments* (Downers Grove, IL: InterVarsity Press, 1997), 1152.

10. Michael Pocock, Gailyn Van Rheenen, and Douglas McConnell, *The Changing Face of World Missions: Engaging Contemporary Issues and Trends* (Grand Rapids: Baker, 2002), 94–96.

probes Corinthian believers about their own preferences: "What do you wish? Shall I come to you with a rod, or with love and a spirit of gentleness?" (1 Cor. 4:21).

Other students with experience-centered or relational-centered approaches often become frustrated with a lack of emphasis on the "soft skills" and an overemphasis on knowledge learned apart from experience or relationships. For such students, Paul's subsequent warning in 1 Corinthians 10 regarding eating food offered to idols yields a helpful example of theology and experience interacting. Because the Corinthian belief system was formed out of experience, a syncretistic theology developed as the confused believers reconciled their view of God to their new experience. Paul spends a great deal of time correcting their behaviors and concludes his arguments in 1 Corinthians 15 with affirming and reciting the gospel because reforming their experiences will change their view of God.

Unbalanced student development will produce leaders who are unable to biblically analyze their experiences or to engage in meaningful conversation; as these leaders minister, they may cause newer believers to flee from their families and cultures and replicate again a great tragic fact of missions history: "that we have lost the thousand by the way we have won the one."[11] Thus, balanced development should maintain a continuous dialogue between experiences and relationships on the one hand and Scripture and theology on the other.

Discard Unbiblical Principles

Along with balanced development, it is important to understand past mistakes in cross-cultural and intercultural work. Because of the cultural imperialism that has characterized the majority of past missionary endeavors, local intercultural work and international missions strategies and outcomes will need to be regularly reevaluated for structurally unbiblical principles that bring God fame that is inconsistent with his character.

Scriptures have been manipulated for hundreds of years to proclaim lies about God's character and who is welcomed into his kingdom. The unbearable truth is that every race and nation is guilty of this sin. Hence the issues of biblically accurate contextualization and an integrated theological argument should be paramount to training leaders who desire both a sustainable ministry and impact in a globally revolving community. No denomination, race, ethnicity, or movement is without error in this area.

The Israelites in the Old Testament and Christians in the New Testament struggled with being kind to foreigners and treating them as citizens while not allowing their friends' pagan beliefs to influence their own lives. Thus, as we consider the fallen state of mankind, it is not an insult to acknowledge

---

11. Herbert Hoefer, "Rooted or Uprooted: The Necessity of Contextualization in Missions," *International Journal of Frontier Mission* 24, no. 3 (2007): 135.

our selfish and ethnocentric beliefs.[12] Unfortunately, American Christians often exchange healthy patriotism for ethnocentric behavior as we fuse our citizenship in heaven with our American citizenship. As North Americans who have been allotted privileges, we should be mindful of the writer of Hebrews' exhortation that not only is our citizenship in heaven, but our desire should be like those of our spiritual forefathers, who desired "a better country, that is, a heavenly one" (Heb. 11:16).

Acknowledge That Race Is an Issue

We agree that every ethnicity and race has equal access to the kingdom. But what happens when a woman notices a man of another race entering the same subway car? What causes domestic travelers to become concerned when they see a Middle Eastern person working in airport security? If I saw someone with a sign asking for help or a ride home and that person was not of my race, would I be less inclined to offer assistance than I would if someone of my own race needed help? How many of us would readily admit our fleshly reaction, or at the very least not attempt to disregard it as a "safety issue" more than a racial one?

The extent of our own depravity is not comfortable to discuss, but it is within our imaginations to at least consider. Yes, all ethnicities treat others differently—some treat others as neighbors, and some treat others with fear and contempt. The depravity of every culture should not be such a surprise. As trained theologians, the preparation to wisely critique cultures, institutions, and ourselves should become more instinctual as we actively resist such senseless hindrances to the gospel, not encouraging them in ignorance or becoming such hindrances ourselves! Letting God out of these self-made boxes, however, will require a few more suspensions of judgment and assumption.

With blatant instruction in Scripture regarding ethnic issues, coupled with North American equality legislation and religious freedom statutes, it is often difficult to identify various racial hindrances entrenched in our own American culture, let alone to discuss them freely without fear of retribution or the freedom to ask for clarity in areas of confusion. If we take a moment to be honest, whenever the discussion turns to race and ethnicity issues, everyone becomes uneasy, including most Christians. Such uncomfortable feelings need to become cues for students that an issue needs to be discussed and addressed, not cues that the topic needs to be avoided.

Recognize Misattribution

As mature believers, it is easy to *desire* racial and cultural unity, but we must be willing to consider whether the way we live our everyday lives

---

12. An ethnocentristic belief system assumes one culture is more valuable than another and requires the other culture to be forfeited in order for acceptance and assimilation to occur.

contradicts this desire. For example, fusing our Christian identities with our earthly nationalities may cause problems for missionaries who desire to be contextually relevant to their locations but have not yet defined their identities in Christ as separate from their native cultures. North American students who minister in their primary cultures generally would not consider the possibility that their Christian identities are tied to their national identities, not because of deliberate arrogance, but simply out of ignorance that an issue exists.

Take for example how some Christian Americans honor the godliness of the founding fathers of their country. To claim that the constitutional signatories were not of an evangelical Christian persuasion would be heresy in some arenas and furthermore would automatically earn this mistaken individual the description of being a liberal. However, take an African-American's viewpoint into consideration when forming such a description of the founding fathers, and the results might differ. The same founding fathers allowed the first Africans in America to be considered only two-thirds of a whole person and allowed slavery to exist until it became an economic battleground for control.[13] It is no wonder, then, that the celebration of independence is greater in African-American communities on Martin Luther King Jr. Day and on Juneteenth[14] than on July 4, where such a celebration might be considered an act of honoring those who legalized discrimination.

A contributing cause in conflict and misunderstanding is misattribution. Misattribution is ascribing meaning or motive to behavior based on one's culture.[15] Because cultural behaviors and values are so diverse, it is easy to see how misattribution can create an environment in which behaviors that are positive in one culture are viewed negatively by another culture. In the above example, both points of view ascribe meaning and value to independence celebrations based upon their respective cultures' experiences and interpretation of events.[16]

This is even more clearly seen when two nationalities from differing continents interact. For example, I am a naturalized American citizen. My family immigrated to Texas from India before my first birthday. My parents were not in favor of mixed-gender primary school projects and challenged my teachers frequently, much to my horror. During my college years, when I insisted on moving out of the dorms to live with another

---

13. Shuler, *Winning the Race to Unity*, 121, 132–40.

14. Juneteenth is a day that celebrates when Union soldiers arrived to broadcast the end of the Civil War two years after Abraham Lincoln's Emancipation Proclamation. Until then, Texas and other southern states continued to operate as if slavery were legal.

15. Patty Lane, *A Beginner's Guide to Crossing Cultures: Making Friends in a Multicultural World* (Downers Grove, IL: InterVarsity Press, 2002), 118.

16. Tony Evans, *Let's Get to Know Each Other: What White Christians Should Know About Black Christians* (Nashville: Thomas Nelson, 1995), 65; Curtiss Paul De Young, *United by Faith: The Multiracial Congregation as an Answer to the Problem of Race* (New York: Oxford University Press, 2003), 107, 111; Shuler, *Winning the Race to Unity*, 141.

single woman, they went as far as threatening to disown me, or at least to move into my apartment. In India, unmarried women are expected to live with family until they are married, regardless of their age or education level, otherwise they are considered loose women and a disgrace to the family name. From a cultural perspective, assimilation into another culture represents the death of one's heritage and identity.[17] Clearly, from my North American viewpoint, I was beginning to develop admirable independence and transition into adulthood; to my parents, however, my actions were not only rebellious and morally questionable, but a rejection of my cultural heritage.

This is why Christian identities should be evaluated judiciously with national and cultural issues underscored if we are to biblically assess how personal beliefs and values have been conditioned by previous personal, cultural, and national experiences. Such evaluation "reminds us of the limitations of our own understanding and helps us become more open to insights coming from the other culture."[18] Unfortunately, some Caucasian Christian churches and denominations have been silent on key social issues and, as a result, historically have been condemned for not initiating or endorsing the acceptance and celebration of other cultures. As immigration to the United States continues to rise, this requires attention because some churches still hesitate to become involved in intercultural relationships, even for the furthering of the gospel.[19]

Define Racism Appropriately

When my friend Cassie lived in Italy, cab drivers often attempted to speak English to her in order to guide her in describing the destination. However when shopping in Italy, Cassie often was left frustrated at having to pay different prices when the merchants spoke English to her. Yet after a few months, when her Italian improved and she could procure a better price for her purchases, Cassie began to welcome the different treatment her developing language skills were providing.

Which of Cassie's three interactions could be described as "racist" in nature? Dictionaries define racism without a negative connotation; the majority of definitions maintain racism assumes exterior attributes as predefining abilities. By that definition, if someone speaks to my friend in English while in Italy, it technically is racism because the person assumed her exterior attributes of blonde hair and blue eyes meant she had a limited grasp of the Italian language. Yet the taxi driver may not have assumed a superior attitude but simply was attempting to communicate more effectively.

---

17. Lane, *Beginner's Guide to Crossing Cultures*, 23.

18. Young-Il Kim, *Knowledge, Attitude and Experience: Ministry in the Cross-Cultural Context* (Nashville: Abingdon, 1992), 123.

19. Lane, *Beginner's Guide to Crossing Cultures*, 41.

Some definitions of racism, however, include a connotation of superiority of one race or culture over another. The interactions Cassie had while purchasing the same item at different prices characterize this definition because both scenarios highlight the Italian language as superior to the English language, resulting in a punitive effect for non-Italian speakers. However, with the help of a native Italian speaker, what tourist would complain about a better price on their souvenirs?

A potential way to circumvent such confusion over definitions is to leave political correctness behind and define racism more biblically as treating someone of another race or ethnic origin in a manner that causes harmful effects. Any action or thought can be perceived as racist based on the individual's motives and/or the harmful effects on the receiver of the action. In other words, believers should take responsibility for the effect of their actions and words, not just their motivations.

For those students new to the conversation on race issues, please note that saying one is "color-blind" is not a helpful statement when discussing racism. Instead of making one appear neutral, such a simplistic answer often will alienate others because it reduces the value of having a ethnic identity and the contributions each culture makes toward humanity and the body of Christ. Instead, statements highlighting God's creation of man in his image are helpful to starting more conversation. Consider the following responses:

- I have not experienced what you are describing; however, this experience appears to have a dehumanizing effect on you. Is this true?
- I often don't know what to say to that statement. Can you tell me more about what you are thinking and feeling?
- Even as a child of God, I have made thoughtless mistakes. Please help me understand what I am doing that is contributing to the problem.

As an individualistic American with inalienable rights, suspending rights is counterintuitive and feels counterproductive. But as Christians, being others-centered is what lies behind treating neighbors and enemies as oneself. Regardless of race and ethnicity, people may consider themselves more than willing to embrace cultural and nationality differences in others. Yet as a part of a globalizing culture, it is still appropriate to expect difficulty in adapting.

Field Education That Enlarges Cultural Awareness

Students who do not envision themselves in cross-cultural work, who do not see an immediate application apparent to their ministries, naturally will not select courses in ministering across cultures and religions. Students today, who have grown up in the new globalizing culture, also may not perceive a problem in their relational ability to communicate across racial and ethnic lines. However, for a fair assessment, institutions need to challenge the student's relational ability in a ministry setting and have their interactions analyzed by racially and ethnically different co-workers and friends. The challenge is for students to extend themselves beyond their own environment into relationships and experiences that differ from those in their own culture. This will also help expand the students' Christian view to a worldview that encompasses a kingdom vision.

As adult learners, students will internalize their internship and gain more wisdom if they are able to adapt institutional requirements and expectations to their specific needs and the context of their working environment. Preplanning meetings and proactive conversations early in the student's program will increase the student's ability to navigate the experience. This is why guiding a field education in a cross-cultural or intercultural setting is instrumental.

The following guidelines are not exhaustive. While planning cross-cultural or intercultural aspects of internships, each culture, each experience, and each student has unique attributes that need to be taken into account.

Field Selection

In tailoring internships to students' needs, one must start with identifying what activities would challenge a particular student's viewpoints or experiences. Activities that encourage relationships outside the seminarian's predominant culture will naturally challenge a student, but often this aspect of an overseas experience is overlooked if the student's ministerial dreams are not addressed as well.

Beyond the obvious experience of a short-term overseas mission trip, there are also local opportunities that can provide similar intercultural training closer to home if these experiences are intentionally designed. A student could work with immigrant communities where people are attempting to assimilate into the North American culture. Or a student could work with refugee communities that struggle both with assimilation and basic social issues such as finding a job, going to the grocery store, or providing clothing for their children. A student could also shadow a pastor for a few months and interact with a church of an ethnic or racial makeup other than the student's own. Imagine the benefit, however, if the experience could last for a full calendar year. A student could also assist an organization that encourages social responsibility to reduce inequalities and to promote justice for members of minority groups. Finally, a student already involved in a local church could research how that church could build bridges into its culturally diverse community, and help the church create sustainable relationships with the community.[20]

---

20. Some of these are contextualized adaptations from Michael Anthony, ed., *Introducing Christian Education: Foundations for the Twenty-first Century* (Grand Rapids: Baker, 2001).

Preparation and Planning

Every cross-cultural experience will produce confusion as to how a student should "be himself" or "be herself" in a new environment. Institutions should ask students then to begin by researching a well-known subject matter—themselves. They must be able to articulate and identify their Christian identities and articulate their life stories in a manner that reflects comprehension of how God authored their lives. This will be vital as the student ministers in a culturally diverse setting and invites individuals from these cultures to assess the student's cultural awareness and cultural engagement.

Any culture a student is attempting to enter should be researched thoroughly as well so that the complexities of the social, historical, political, and religious relationships are understood. A good book on the people group and subject should be helpful to the student. In this process, institutions should help students not to assume that if the language is familiar, then the culture will be too. Sharing ethnicities and knowing a few phrases may be endearing, but it will not reduce the basic disillusionment of not knowing how to interact with an unfamiliar culture. Quality research will help the institution and the student to select or design experiences that will maximize student development.

Experiences should be regularly, if not daily, debriefed on the field by a qualified mentor who is either a seasoned missionary or someone skilled at cross-cultural relationships. Coaching by such an experienced mentor will allow the student to initially identify personal misattributions, and to respond immediately to feedback as well as become pockets of familiar interactions that will aid in easing culture shock. Experiences designed to capitalize on interaction through required debriefs will naturally provide fertile ground for character growth.

Duration and Depth

Cross-cultural experiences should be as lengthy as needed to accomplish both awareness of and exposure to a different culture by the particular student. They should also provide adequate interaction with the culture, as well as enough solitude for reflection. Events included should also be interactive enough to distinguish diversity between this culture and the student's home culture. The entire experience should allow ample time and opportunity for the student to cultivate appreciation for the unique expressions and creativity encountered. Hence, enough duration and depth can be measured by asking the question, How will this experience challenge a student's understanding of God's sovereignty?

Opportunity for Reflection

During the experience, a personal reflective assignment should be included to list practices, attitudes or emotions, and experiences that were challenging or disruptive, even if not initially understood. If the experience includes group debriefs, the student should journal regarding those debriefs as well. Later, this journal will provide fertile ground for deciphering ethnocentric responses from biblical principles and addressing issues of interpersonal team dynamics. The assignment should culminate in addressing which personal values and ministerial issues were not familiar to the student and which values will need to be changed or which issues still need to be addressed. In general, reflective assignments such as this cannot be evaluated based on length or content, but will need to be analyzed qualitatively.

Opportunity to Teach

The experience should include opportunities to teach or preach across cultures using learner-centered practices of intercultural communication. Such situations should be observed and coached before presentation if possible. Here a student can be challenged to create messages that are biblically accurate, yet culturally engaging.

Evaluation

The purpose of detailed planning and evaluations should be explained up front; these experiences are not sightseeing adventures, but opportunities to observe, reflect, and identify areas students need to develop so that they may serve the body of Christ with their whole being.

A brief, culture-appropriate evaluation by the individuals who have interacted with the student in the field should be done just after the experience. Field-based observations may need to be tailored to each culture and may or may not be in written form.

The student should initially create the tailored evaluations during his or her planning stages prior to the field experience. Such thought-provoking planning will encourage students to anticipate the challenges they will encounter. In such evaluations, students should include both open-ended and specific questions, covering skills and abilities as well as cultural and emotional issues, in order to ensure the answers will reflect what the students are striving to assess. Institutional and field education goals should also be used for assessment. An evaluation template that contains the goal and purpose of each assessment question would be invaluable as the student begins to design the evaluations. The student-designed assessment will need to be reviewed and approved by the field supervisor.

A final personal assessment by the students should be assigned, which should include their evaluation of the culture in comparison to their own and a synthesis of cultural misattributions they felt others imposed on them and what they imposed on others. A review of their initial expectations and goals for the trip and a recognition of how or why those goals were or were not met should be addressed so that the students can craft a well-defended revision of—or affirmation of—their personal ministry vision statements.

Prayer of Transformation

Lord God, thank you. Thank you not only for the lives you have given each of us to glorify you, but also for the lives you have given others that we get to experience. We are grateful for your creativity in designing culture, people, and laughter. Thank you for the way you have made us. Thank you that one day every nation will bow and every tongue will confess, "You are Lord." Until then, please give us the desire and the wisdom to go beyond where we feel "safe" and to go where you want us to go. Help us not to pretend to be one, unified body, but teach us how to have the same attitudes toward each other as Christ has, so that with one mind and one voice we may glorify you and you alone. Amen.

Reflection Questions

1. What assumptions have you personally made regarding people of other cultures? How are these assumptions related to your family of origin? How have those assumptions about other cultures been challenged?

2. What cross-cultural or intercultural mentoring relationships have you been involved in? What misunderstandings had to be resolved?

3. How does your academic institution seek to recruit students from various cultures?

4. How does your academic institution address the needs of its culturally diverse student population?

5. What courses does your academic institution offer that prepare students to minister both cross-culturally and interculturally? What percentage of your student body enroll in those course?

6. Review the five imperatives for educating future ministers. Which of these will be most difficult for you to address with your students? Which of these do you already address in educating students for cross-cultural and intercultural ministry?

Further Reading

Elmer, Duane. *Cross-Cultural Connections: Stepping Out and Fitting In Around the World.* Downers Grove, IL: InterVarsity Press, 2002.

Lane, Patty. *A Beginner's Guide to Crossing Cultures: Making Friends in a Multicultural World.* Downers Grove, IL: InterVarsity Press, 2002.

Lanier, Sarah. *Foreign to Familiar: A Guide to Understanding Hot- and Cold-Climate Cultures.* Hagerstown, MD: McDougal Publishing, 2004.

Pocock, Michael, Gailyn Van Rheenen, and Douglas McConnell. *The Changing Face of World Missions: Engaging Contemporary Issues and Trends.* Grand Rapids: Baker, 2002.

PART 2

Players in Field Education

Students
Mentors

Chapter 5

Proactive Student Involvement

TAKING CHARGE OF LEARNING

WALTER KIME

Therefore, preparing your minds for action, and being sober-minded, set your hope fully on the grace that will be brought to you at the revelation of Jesus Christ. (1 Peter 1:13)

My mother came into my room, shook my shoulder, and called me out of sleep.

"Do I have to get up now?" I asked.

"Yes. It's the first day of school. You are a first-grader now."

The first day! This is the day I had been looking forward to all my life. There was no public kindergarten in our town, so this was my first step into the exciting world of academia. The day was wonderful. There was Miss Squire, a young, new teacher who was the best I had ever had. I had new friends, new books, and new activities to master. School was the greatest.

"Walter, it's time to get up," Mom whispered as the sun inched up on the second day.

"Why do I have to get up?"

"You have to go to school."

"Again? You mean I have to do it every day?"

So goes the family myth. After years of homework, tests, and degrees, there is one thing I now know about education—you have to do it every day. Every day God bathes us in a wealth of learning situations. We either set out each day to intentionally find these learning opportunities, or we remain content to stumble across just a few.

Learning How to Learn

Seminary education is about research and reports, tests and grades, and graduations. But it is also about stretching one's mind and abilities, deepening every relationship and growing spiritually strong. It is about learning to live faith-filled lives and becoming people of uncompromising integrity. The problem is that for much of students' educational life, they have learned to be passive. The teacher or professor knew exactly what the students needed to learn and graded the students on how well they acquired this information. As Malcolm Knowles wrote back in the seventies, "It is a tragic fact that most of us only know how to be taught; we haven't learned how to learn."[1] Having a healthy internship means being able to make the transition from being a "student" who is taught to being a "learner" who is proactive in his or her learning experience.

Jesus did not teach his disciples with didactic teaching alone. He preached to them and taught them key lessons. But he also taught them with parables—interesting little mystery stories that did not make much sense unless the listener became actively engaged in putting the images together. The Lord sent the disciples out—two by two—to do the work of ministry. When they returned Jesus asked questions, leading them to reflect on their experiences. Thus they were equipped for service. That was their "field education"—Galilean style.

Education at the seminary level comes down to being a matter of good stewardship. Alistair Petrie points out, "Stewardship, then, is a divine principle emphasizing our accepting responsibility for the possessions entrusted to us by somebody else, more than our giving away our possessions. This is our personal and corporate call to be stewards of the Kingdom of God."[2] The Lord gives students the opportunity to be equipped for their call through the seminary experience. At the end of the day, each one of them will accept or reject personal and corporate responsibility for the quality, the depth, and the living out of the education they receive.

So how can students "harvest" all that God has for them in this unique educational experience? Each student is to be proactive—actively engaged in all that he or she does. And what does that mean? For me it comes down to three basic factors: being action orientated, being relationally centered, and having good "horse sense."

---

1. Malcolm Knowles, *Self-Directed Learning: A Guide for Learners and Teachers* (New York: Association Press, 1975), 14.

2. Alistair Petrie, *Releasing Heaven on Earth: God's Principles for Restoring the Land* (Grand Rapids: Chosen, 2000), 22.

Being Action Orientated

Being action orientated means more than just being involved in doing ministry. It means being actively involved in one's learning in the classroom, in the field, and in one's life. In his first letter, the apostle Peter writes, "Prepare your minds for action" (1 Peter 1:13 NIV). For me, Peter's words describe what seminary should be all about. It is about preparing one's mind through high academic pursuits but also preparing one's mind so that he or she may be equipped for the good work God has called the student to do (2 Tim. 3:17). This is what theological field education is about—education leading to direct and effective action.

Touching Minds, Hearts, and Wills

For field education to be effective, it must touch one's mind, heart, and will. I think this is what Peter had in mind when this fisherman called each one of us to become shepherds. "As a fellow elder, this is my appeal to you: Care for the flock of God entrusted to you. Watch over it willingly, not grudgingly—not for what you will get out of it, but because you are eager to serve God. Don't lord it over the people assigned to your care, but lead them by your good example" (1 Peter 5:1b–3 NLT).

Field education is one place in a student's educational career where he or she must be actively involved. In order to have a healthy internship, each student is to be a truly proactive learner. Peter tells us that we are to be "willing" participants in our work and studies (1 Peter 5:2b). We are to be "eager" to know God, ourselves, and others deeply (1 Peter 5:2c). And we are to be "examples" to others, leading from the front (1 Peter 5:3).

In Peter's day a shepherd led his flock from the front. A shepherd led the sheep beside still waters, with his rod and staff he protected them, and he fed them—even in the presence of their enemy. That is what it means to be proactive and lead from the front. Can we do less? Students must develop their *minds* to think like a shepherd as they develop their integrity as well as their intellect. Students are to strengthen their *hearts* to live like a shepherd, as they grow in their passion for Christ and people. And students are to discipline their *wills* so that they lead like shepherds through their actions and accountability.

One's education cannot be limited to what is in textbooks and classrooms. Students must take it out to the streets—real ministry to real people with real problems. That is where they are to hammer out their theology and sharpen their understanding of Scripture. Students are to test what they learn from books and classrooms in the marketplace to see what is effective, what fits their own situations and their personal styles of ministry. To do that, students need to take risks, step out in faith, and put it into action. That is being proactive and no one can do that for a student. Each student must make a conscious choice to challenge and stretch his or her limits— every time out.

Stages of a Disciple

We are talking about an attitude toward learning as well as the act of learning. The Bible uses a specific word for this kind of learning—*mathano*. We translate the noun form of this word, *mathētēs*, as "disciple" and usually apply it to new believers who need to grow in their understanding of the faith. This is true, but it applies to everyone growing in a new discipline of life.

Discipleship expert Christopher Adsit writes,

> J. H. Thayer makes it clear that a *mathetes* is a special kind of learner—one who learns "by use and practice." Ah-HA! So we're talking about a person who not only thinks, but who *does*. He puts shoe leather to his convictions. . . . This kind of learning is taken in, practiced, and incorporated into a transformed lifestyle.[3]

Adsit goes on to look at 1 John 2:12–14. The following is what I have gleaned over several years from the fifth chapter of Adsit's book.[4] The passage identifies four levels in the Christian's walk. In 1 John 2:12, John talks about dear children, *teknon*, which means "infants." John uses a different word for children in 2:13a, the Greek word *paidion*, which can refer to anyone from toddlers through teenagers. In both verses 13 and 14, he uses *neaniskos* (we get our word *novice* from the root word), which points to those in their twenties and early thirties. Finally, John speaks to those who are "fathers" (*pateres*)—indicating adults or mature believers. Each one of these levels has different needs and requires different learning strategies.

A twenty-year-old (novice) does not learn the same way as an infant. A toddler needs a different approach to learning than a mature adult. Adsit points out the distinctive needs for each stage, as well as the unique teaching role needed for each stage. I have summarized it in figure 5.1.

Figure 5.1. Stages of Need		
Stage	**Need**	**Role**
Infant	Nourishment and protection	"Mother"
Child	Equipping	"Teacher"
Novice	Strength and skills	"Coach"
Adult	Motivation over the long haul	"Peer"

---

3. Christopher Adsit, *Personal Disciple-Making: A Step-by-Step Guide for Leading a New Christian from New Birth to Maturity*, 2nd ed. (Orlando: Integrated Resources, 1996), 31–32.

4. Ibid., 60–76.

This is easy to see as we look at the natural growth in a person's life. It is helpful in identifying the growth needs of people in our congregation. It is even more effective if we look at specific areas of a Christian's life and growth. For example, a person may be an "adult" in their use of Scriptures and yet a "child" in their prayer life. So the effective pastor would be a "peer" who encourages this person in his or her continued growth in understanding the Word and at the same time functions as a teacher in helping to develop the person's prayer life.

What I find exciting about this is that it helps me to see how I can grow in my ministry. I may be an "adult" in my Christian walk, yet I may be an "infant" in the pulpit if I have never preached a sermon. I may come to seminary as a "novice" in how I exegete the Word, yet still be a child in ministering to people who have just lost a loved one. Realizing these things helps me know what I need to learn, how I need to learn it, and what kind of mentoring I need as I grow in a particular area of my ministry and my life.

Becoming a Self-Directed Learner

Knowles says, "Fortunately, once adults make the discovery that they can take responsibility for their own learning, as they do for other facets of their lives, they experience a sense of release and exhilaration."[5] Taking responsibility for one's learning is exhilarating, yet it carries with it a greater degree of involvement on the person's part as a learner. This is what Knowles calls "self-directed" learning.

Being a self-directed learner means that we accept the responsibility for creating and organizing our learning experience. Traditionally, in field education this has been done through the use of a learning contract or covenant. These written statements of the student's learning objectives generally follow Knowles's steps of self-directed learning, which I summarize by remembering the four *D*'s—*Diagnosis, Designing, Doing,* and *Debriefing.*[6]

Diagnosis

To be proactive as a self-directed learner, a person starts with his or her felt need. Adults should be able to see, feel, and acknowledge the need to learn something new or different. The first step is to diagnose exactly what the person needs to learn. The four stages of growth mentioned above help the individual begin this process of diagnosis.

Knowles gives another tool by identifying six types of behavioral outcomes within the learning process (see figure 5.2).[7] Thus the next question becomes, which of the following does the person need?

---

5. Malcolm Knowles, *Modern Practice of Adult Education: From Pedagogy to Andragogy* (River Grove, IL: Follett, 1980), 46.

6. Ibid., 59.

7. Ibid., 240.

[handwritten notes:]
- strengths
- stretches
- unique calling
- BP placement
- character dev.

Figure 5.2. Behavorial Outcomes	
Knowledge	new information
Understanding	new application
Skills	new ways of performing
Attitudes	new feelings gained through success
Values	new priorities of belief
Interests	new activities

Designing

Each of these outcomes carries with it a different set of learning approaches. As one determines the nature of his or her learning needs, that person is moved to the second *D—Designing*. Here the learner is to develop a learning activity based on his or her assessment. In the classroom, this could be as simple as saying, "Here is what the professor wants me to do, and as I do these things, this is what I want to be sure to learn." Usually it is most effective to put these learning goals in writing and build in specific ways to be accountable.

For a student's internship, the learning design may be more complex. For example, in the field assignment, a student develops a learning contract stating the who, what, when, where, and how of the field learning experience. It is here that the student spells out objectives and the ways of measuring progress, identifies necessary resources, and clearly states what he or she plans to learn and how he or she will be accountable.[8] This is simply a mature process for accepting ownership of his or her learning needs.

Doing

The *Design* leads us to the actual *Doing* of what the student planned. The Navy SEALs have a saying that describes this step: "Plan your dive and dive your plan." Having diagnosed one's learning need and designed a plan, the student now "dives the plan." Students carry out their contract, document their progress, reflect on their experiences, and share their findings. Normally people will need midcourse corrections as they move through their learning activities; but by staying focused on their plan and their objectives, people can avoid chasing after interesting side issues and press on to reach their goals. That is "diving the plan."

Debriefing

This brings us to *Debriefing*. This is where students hold themselves

---

8. See chapter 7, "Covenant and Goal Development: The Aim for Success," for more information on goal development.

accountable. Did they actually learn what they set out to learn? Where is the evidence? How are they being accountable? This can be a time for rediagnosing their learning needs, or it may be a time to celebrate achieving their goal. It most certainly is a time of reflection and of acknowledging what God has been doing through the students as they have been action orientated in their learning.[9]

Being Relationally Centered

People ask me what field education is about, and I never had a good, brief answer for them until I read Robert Banks's book *Reenvisioning Theological Education*. Now I say, "You know, it's just yada, yada, yada." *Yada* is the Hebrew verb that means "to know." But it does not mean just to know the facts. It means to know completely, intimately, and experientially.[10] Ultimately, field education and ministry is about knowing God, knowing one's self, and knowing others at an intimate level.

Once students take their learning and ministry into the street, they realize that a central part of ministry is not how competent they are in their pastoral skills but how effectively they relate to people. Their model is Jesus, who engaged people personally. He asked people questions, challenged their belief systems, and called them to make commitments. "Jesus drew people into his ministry and empowered them to work alongside him or separately on his behalf."[11] Being in ministry is about developing relationships. Ministers are called to a deeper partnership with God, a healthier understanding of themselves, and a richer relationship with other people.

One example of this relational truth can be seen in Genesis, when Abram and Sarai believe God has called them to have many descendants. Being childless, they try to help God, and so Sarai brings her servant to Abram. This solution was socially acceptable and culturally legal in their day. But it was not God's plan. They had the right idea but the wrong mother.

In the last sentence of Genesis 16, we are told that Abram is eighty-six years old when Hagar gives birth to Ishmael. In verse 1 of the next chapter, we are told that Abram is ninety-nine years old. That is thirteen years between the end of chapter 16 and the beginning of chapter 17—thirteen years of silence. That is a long time for someone who is on a journey walking with God to a place God has yet to reveal to him.

But look at what happens as a result of their struggle. God finally breaks the silence and tells Abram, "I am God Almighty." The word used there is *El-Shaddai* (Gen. 17:1). After thirteen years of silence, God reveals something brand-new to Abram—a new name for God. This is the first time in

9. See chapter 11, "Assessment and Evaluation in Field Education," for additional resources.

10. Geoffrey Bromiley, ed., *The New International Standard Bible Encyclopedia*, rev. ed. (Grand Rapids: Eerdmans, 1986), 3:48.

11. Robert Banks, *Reenvisioning Theological Education: Exploring a Missional Alternative to Current Models* (Grand Rapids: Eerdmans, 1999), 105.

Scripture that *El-Shaddai* is used. Out of his struggle to serve God, Abram gains a new and intimate insight into the real nature of our God—the all-sufficient One.

But that is not all. Abram became Abraham (Gen. 17:5). He gains a new understanding of himself and who he is in God's eyes. No longer is he the "exalted father." More specifically he will be the "father of many." Thus out of their struggle to be faithful, both Abraham and Sarai, now called Sarah (Gen. 17:15), grow in their understanding of who they are and what God wants them to do and be.

But there is still more. God reaffirms his covenant with them (Gen. 17:7). What has happened to Abraham and Sarah also affects others. God reminds them of their new understanding of who the people of God are. They and their descendants for generations to come will be in a new relationship with God. Out of their struggle to be faithful to God's call, God reveals a new relationship with them. Abraham and Sarah both have a deeper understanding of who they are in God's sight, and a nation of God's people is established. That is the power of relationships in ministry.

We are to rightly divide the Word, be solid in our systematic theology, and competent in our pastoral skills; but the bottom line is that our effectiveness in ministry depends on our relationship with God, ourselves, and others. We cannot afford to forget or neglect this truth.

Having "Horse Sense"

Finally, to be proactive in one's studies and ministry means to have good "horse sense." Jesus says, "Blessed are the meek" (Matt. 5:5). We often think of being meek and being weak as the same thing. But the word translated "meek" is the word *praus*. To the Greeks this described an animal, such as a horse, trained to obey its master.[12] I picture a large, muscular stallion, raised up on its back legs, kicking out with its front hoofs, muscles bulging and steam snorting out of its nostrils. For the stallion to be meek does not mean it is "broken." For the stallion to be meek means the horse brings all its strength and energy under control to accomplish the purpose of its master. That is just plain good "horse sense."

We are called to be meek. We are to be under the control of our Master to achieve the Lord's purposes, using God's methods. We are not called to be successful, but we are called to be obedient. We are called to please our "commanding officer" (2 Tim. 2:4 NIV). That cannot be done by seeking peoples' approval or even a professor's praise. It takes faith and dogged determination to serve God no matter what the circumstances.

We see this kind of obedience in Joseph in Egypt and Daniel in Babylonia, as well as in the life of the apostle Paul. Joseph chose to be a willing slave and trusted God in spite of dire circumstances and even prison. Daniel decided

---

12. William Barclay, *The Gospel of Matthew, Volume 1* (Philadelphia: Westminster, 1958), 91.

to be faithful and please God even in the face of extreme authority figures and life-threatening situations. Regardless of shipwrecks, prison, and pending death, Paul resolved to set the example for others to follow. This kind of "horse sense" means to "work with enthusiasm, as though you were working for the Lord rather than for people" (Eph. 6:7 NLT).

Taking the First Step

To have a healthy internship and ministry means one must be proactive in the classroom and in service. To accomplish this, students must choose to be action oriented and self-directed learners in their education. Students must choose to be relationally centered as they keep people the priority over things. And students are to have the "horse sense" of a meek stallion under the control of the Master. That is being proactive in one's studies, ministry, and life.

Joshua was about to cross the Jordan River into the Promised Land. It would not be easy. It was a challenge that would take everything that Joshua and the people of God had to give. It was precisely at that point that God told this new leader, "I will give you every place where you set your foot" (Josh. 1:3 NIV).

God was going with them and would give them the land that was promised to Moses and their ancestors. But Joshua had to lift up his foot and place it down on the land. What an incredible image this is of how God chooses to work with people. God empowers, but we must move our feet. We have to be willing to step out in faith and walk into the promise of God, to be proactive—God's style.

You and I are called to live our lives with that kind of action—through that kind of faith. That is what field education is all about. The "ball" is in your court. It really is up to you—every single day.

Prayer of Transformation

God Almighty, our "El-Shaddai," who is enough in every situation of our lives: As you worked with Abraham and Sarah and taught them your Word and your way, so teach us now. Lord, teach us how to be good shepherds in our minds, hearts, and wills, that we may serve with faithfulness and be obedient to the call you have placed on our lives. Jesus, help us to be truly meek and bring all of our talents, gifts, and strengths under your control. Let us not be prideful or self-centered in our work. Protect us from the Evil One and from ourselves. Holy Spirit, fill us with such holy boldness that we ask for your direction with each step we take and have the courage to walk through every opportunity you open to us. In the name of Christ, Amen.

Reflection Questions

1. Reflect on a time when you grew in your understanding of God or yourself or other people. What did you learn in that moment? What were the circumstances? What were the conditions? What was there in that moment that opened you to a new understanding?

2. Consider what was said about learning in the discussion of 1 John 2:12–14. Make a list of five ministry areas where you feel a need to grow. These may be areas of strengths or weaknesses. How would you rate your need as a learner in each area?

AREA OF GROWTH	Infant	Child	Novice	Adult
1.				
2.				
3.				
4.				
5.				

What does this say to you about how you could meet these learning goals?

3. Select one of the learning areas that you would like to become more mature in. What do you need to learn: knowledge, understanding, skills, attitudes, values, interests? Design a learning goal for that learning area, and share it with your mentor or a friend for their feedback.

4. In your case, what will be the hardest part of being:
   a. Action orientated?
   b. Relationally centered?
   c. Under the control of your Master?

Share one of these concerns with your mentor or a friend.

Further Reading

Banks, Robert. *Reenvisioning Theological Education: Exploring a Missional Alternative to Current Models*. Grand Rapids: Eerdmans, 1999.

Kinast, Robert. *Making Faith-Sense: Theological Reflection in Everyday Life*. Collegeville, MN: Liturgical Press, 1999.

Knowles, Malcolm. *The Modern Practice of Adult Education: From Pedagogy to Andragogy*. River Grove, IL: Follett, 1980.

Macchia, Stephen. *Becoming a Healthy Team: Five Traits of Vital Leadership*. Grand Rapids: Baker, 2005.

Wardle, Terry. *Helping Others on the Journey: A Guide for Those Who Seek to Mentor Others to Maturity in Christ*. Kent, England: Sovereign World, 2004.

Chapter 6

Mentoring

THE OPPORTUNITY
TO LEAVE A LEGACY

DARYL SMITH

Summing it all up, friends, I'd say you'll do best by filling your minds and meditating on things true, noble, reputable, authentic, compelling, gracious—the best, not the worst; the beautiful, not the ugly; things to praise, not things to curse. Put into practice what you learned from me, what you heard and saw and realized. Do that, and God, who makes everything work together, will work you into his most excellent harmonies. (Phil. 4:8–9 MSG)

Let us start with a disclaimer! If you are like me, you open your mailbox every day or so, and a stack of ads drop onto the floor at your feet, calling you to buy, rent, attend, or read. It may be a seminar, a book, a CD, or a just-invented-best-ever Internet site. And amazingly, the subject often relates somehow to mentoring, coaching, or leadership (ah yes, they are all inter-related). It seems that a "DVD-of-the-Day Production Company" is stuck on autopilot, cranking out more and more of the same stuff, just with a new look. Let me assure you that this chapter is not one of those "have-the-answer-for-every-situation" resources. Nor is it a definitive work in the study of mentoring.

Instead, the point of this chapter is to share a piece of my life and ministry, along with helpful resources, in the hope of capturing a vision for how one's ministry life can become a dynamic force in the life of another person. I believe that mentors can *leave a powerful legacy*—in the lives of their students, the people they pastor, their co-workers, their family members, and those they hang out with at the coffee shop.

The Vital Role as a Mentor in Theological Education

Gone are the days when most students pack off to campus, settle in for a three- or four-year stint, get their heads filled with facts, relaunch into ministry, then unload all they have learned on an unsuspecting congregation. The educational and equipping scene is in dramatic shift. Students often start formal training after completion of a first career, so they come with life experience upon which to hang their studies. Many have families and jobs that must share time. Thus, ministry training becomes a moving pattern of dropping into a seminary's geophysical campus periodically to take a "live" class, spending time at work or with family, checking in on a computer in the late evening to attempt to finish a paper for an online class, then taking a Saturday to attend a seminar taught by the latest ministry guru. Seminary is now a 24/7 process.

Before getting into some detail about mentoring, let us first take a quick glance at how mentors relate to this changing model at seminaries or training centers and to the new face of students. My assumption is that a mentor will take regular, significant time to meet with his or her student—at least one hour per week, depending on the setting in which they are working.

On-Site Faculty

Researchers and conference speakers alike are now pointing to the fact that seminaries of the twenty-first century must rely on on-site faculty or mentors in the field if they are going to survive past this generation. Students no longer can or will isolate themselves to studies for several years and then begin translating those studies into ministry upon graduation. Seminaries are dependent upon "field faculty" to guide students in continuous integration of studies with practice—the best of theological reflection.

However, the thought of "nonacademics" (that means people without doctorate degrees) guiding graduate students in their learning still makes accrediting agencies very nervous. This idea is new enough that most accreditors cannot perceive anyone learning in a nonlecture setting, not sitting at the feet of a hallowed professor. They particularly do not like schools using the term "on-site faculty." So, field education professionals responsible for students' success in ministry must live somewhat subversively around their institutions because they take mentors or on-site faculty extremely seriously. Mentors are our future. Mentors are the future of the ministry. Mentors are vital in the kingdom of God.

Spiritual/Christian Formation Guide

I have never known a pastor who lost a ministry because he or she could not perform a wedding or an infant dedication appropriately. I have known many people who have left ministries because their personal and spiritual lives fell apart. No matter how skilled people are for ministry, if they are not continually being formed into the image of Jesus, they will fail.

As mentors, the spiritual or Christian formation of their students becomes the primary goal. Both terms have historical significance. Some will prefer the classic term *spiritual formation*. Others will add *Christian* to make sure that the formation is intentionally Christian. They can easily be interchanged. Whichever term one desires to use may not be as important as understanding its purpose. Obviously, mentors do not do the actual forming of another person. It is partnership with God's Holy Spirit working in the life of a receptive student. Mentors act as a "means of grace"—the tour guide who keeps pointing to where God is at work and where God still needs to work.[1]

The best spiritual formation model I have seen comes from Robert Mulholland. He defines spiritual formation as "the process of being conformed to the image of Jesus for the sake of others."[2] When one breaks that statement down into its parts, we see the strategy for mentoring.

- *The process.* It is intentionally begun but will never end; it is ongoing and growing.
- *Of being conformed.* We are being reshaped, made into something new.
- *To the image of Jesus.* This is not just some ordinary shape we are being conformed to. This is the image of the Creator who planted the original image in us and breathed our lungs full of the breath of life.
- *For the sake of others.* It is not about us. Both one's mentoring and one's ministries are for those who encounter God's love and life through us.

With spiritual/Christian formation as the overarching umbrella under which all else sits, mentors are constantly aware that their mentoring is not some generic sort of life coaching. Mentors are about spiritual guidance and *the shaping of a ministry vocation.* In the last section of this chapter, we will focus intently on the specifics of mentoring for Christian formation.

Theological Reflection Facilitator
A discussion of classical theological reflection might not include the

---

1. Rob Bell, *Velvet Elvis: Repainting the Christian Faith* (Grand Rapids: Zondervan, 2005), 87–89.
2. M. Robert Mulholland Jr., *Invitation to a Journey: A Road Map for Spiritual Formation* (Downers Grove, IL: InterVarsity Press, 1993), 15.

integration of academic studies and ministry practice. However, mentors are most helpful when they open the theological reflection box a little more broadly to include a wide range of issues for integration. Let us review a few of those issues.

First, if one desires to study theological reflection at a deeper level, there are many fine books available. Suffice it to say, mentors want students to see all of life and ministry from a theological viewpoint. Mentors want students to see where God is at work in daily living. Mentors want students to apply theological and biblical understandings to every situation they encounter in ministry.

Second, students must learn to create healthy accountability networks for life and ministry. A mentor can both guide and model this practice. We would hope that students will intentionally surround themselves with a group of three or four *safe people* with whom they may share deeply—people who will support them with prayer, guidance, and follow-up.[3] The best-case scenario would be a group that does not contain persons who might oversee the student in future ministry or be involved in ordination evaluation at a later date.[4]

Third, one of the most difficult steps in moving from academic studies to a ministry setting may be the practical integration of the two. When a student attempts to apply "head knowledge" to a "street-level crisis," the result can be terrorizing for the student (and yes, maybe also for the mentor who is observing). Mentors can ease the terror with gentle guidance, often giving a student the opportunity to talk through the what-ifs before the crisis arises.

An additional concern can be the student's desire to abandon study, once formal education is completed. A mentor can help students visualize the importance of maintaining a pattern of lifelong learning that continually informs ministry. As students learn to work the rhythm of integrating studies with daily life and ministry, they gain "hooks" upon which to hang future studies and gain tools for applying those studies to ministry.

Ministry Role Model

Daily life packs the greatest power for mentoring another person in ministry. The student will observe the mentor in the many ministry facets he or she performs. Mentors have the opportunity to demonstrate real-life ministry in a real-life setting. If a mentor is into faking a perfectionist pastoral role, the student will quickly sniff this out and miss the insights he or she needs from the mentor.

Students need to see their mentor struggle to balance family, sermon preparation, interruptions, personal conflicts, or whatever else makes up his or her particular setting. But it must not be left just at the observation

---

3. See chapter 10, "Building Biblical Community in Theological Education" for a more detailed discussion of the role of community in spiritual and leadership development.

4. See chapter 3, "Field Education and Theological Reflection in an Evangelical Tradition," for a more detailed discussion on theological reflection.

stage. It will be important for the student to process the ups and downs of the ministry life with the mentor. A major portion of the weekly interview between the mentor and student should focus on the real issues of ministry and how to work through them in biblical, theological, and healthy ways. *Think risky transparency!*

When the student is facing or has faced a struggle, the mentor can capture that opportunity to *actively reflect* with the student (mess-ups make great teachable moments). Here are some guidelines to follow. First, the mentor should approach the student with a positive and helpful attitude. If the student really messed up, he or she probably already knows it and feels sick having to face their mentor. Next, the mentor should ask quality, open-ended questions of the student, not just for a regurgitation of the facts.

Third, the mentor ought to make sure that the discussion is always one-on-one. A mentor should not work like the principal who walks into the classroom and yells at the teacher in front of his or her class. Of course there may be the occasion where the mentor must bring another person into the discussion because others are involved in the difficulty. But the mentor needs to start with the one-on-one even when he or she feels like yelling at the student in the church lobby. And finally, the mentor ought to discuss the things that went well in the problem. Then move to, "What did not work?" and "What would you do differently the next time?" This gives the student space to think through solutions rather than the mentor providing the "right" answer. More and effective learning will result.

Ministry Skills Coach

When the truth sinks in that mentoring is first and foremost a spiritual journey with another, one's tendency may be to give less attention to ministry skills. Mentors may fall into the trap of thinking that skills are insignificant or that they will come automatically. Usually that is not true.

Mentors find themselves in a balancing act between deep spiritual guidance and skill training. Spiritual formation and ministry skills are two sides of the same coin. The outer skill will likely not survive without the deep inner spiritual strength to sustain it. Yet, a deep inner life without the basic ministry skills to transport that spirituality into effective ministry will, at the least, make the ministry dramatically less effective than it otherwise would be.

Setting Growth Goals

Students must set specific *growth goals* for the time they will be mentored. A mentor's guidance will be vital in setting those goals.[5] In my mentoring, I ask students to set goals in the following order—a minimum of three growth goals, a maximum of four.

---

5. For more information on goal development, see chapter 7, "Covenant and Goal Development: The Aim for Success."

Personal Growth Goal

A personal growth goal focuses on what in one's personal life or spiritual life needs special attention during this accountability time. One student may start a regular Bible study regimen. Another may choose to put himself or herself into an accountable relationship with a spiritual director.

Family Relationship Growth Goal

A family relationship growth goal focuses on what relationship in one's life needs attention during this time. If married, the primary relationship would be with a spouse or children. If single, work may need to be done in the area of broken relationships with parents or siblings.

One of my midlife students struggled with a painful divorce from many years past. In the divorce process, he had lost all relationship with his high school children, who were now adults, married with children (his grand-children). As he set his growth goals for mentoring with me, he committed himself to rebuilding the lost relationship with his grown kids. By semester's end, with many dollars spent on phone calls and airline tickets, God had begun to restore the brokenness and father and children were back in communication with one another.

Ministry Growth Goal

A ministry growth goal focuses on the area of one's ministry that needs the most effort or where he or she wants to try a new "thing" in a safe setting. Some students will set goals that are much too broad to accomplish in any reasonable time, or that lack specificity. All growth goals need a clear target and measurable steps to reach that target. The mentor will evaluate the goals for clarity and practicality.

Never Forsake Excellence

Excellence is not the same as perfectionism. I prefer to define *perfectionism* as an unwillingness to admit a mistake or error. Often perfectionism causes persons to freeze up in fear of failure. Leaders who expect perfection are unwilling to accept mistakes by anyone, including themselves—often becoming irrationally judgmental. They are also unwilling to evaluate since that would admit lack of perfection. On the other hand, *excellence* is doing one's best but realizing that we will never reach perfection. The goal of excellence is to continually improve quality with regular evaluation of past performance. Excellence builds on the failures or flaws of the past.

If students are to grow in ministry skills—while pursuing excellence—they must be given regular and rich opportunities to attempt various facets of ministry. This entails a mentor guiding the student with broad exposure to all areas of ministry inside and outside the parish walls.[6] A mentor will need to

---

6. For me *parish* is defined as anyone a group of Jesus-followers has regular contact with, both inside the walls of a church facility and outside the walls.

open the doors for the student to experiment in a safe setting, while reducing the student's fear of failure. Since the fear of failure seems inbred to most humans, a mentor makes it possible for students to learn and experience some of the consequences of failing while providing a "student safety net."

The following equation summarizes the process of building ministry skill excellence:

Prepare the student for a ministry event
  + place the student into the ministry situation
    + evaluate the event
      + ask for student's learnings
        + discuss a more excellent way
          + give additional student practice (if necessary for the situation)
            + reinsert student into a similar ministry situation
              = Ministry Skill Excellence

Remember, mentors are shaping a ministry vocation in persons called by God to particular ministry roles.

Church-Planting Mentor

Church planting may be the most difficult vocation in the world. And in this age of rapidly increasing church plants, mentoring has become an imperative. In plain and simple language, church planters will not succeed without a mentor or "parenting church" to guide them along the way. Burnout of the team leader, "unhealth" in the congregation, and collapse of the ministry are all effects of "going it alone."

Ralph Moore, who has planted and guided hundreds of church plants across the world, does not allow one to start without the support and ongoing care of a "parent congregation."[7] That ongoing care includes continuous guidance from the parent church staff team or senior pastor.

For his doctoral research, Keith Cowart, a church planter and mentor to other planters, traced the success and failure records of several church planters and found that only those church planters with a walk-beside mentor were able to succeed in the plant.[8] Success was *not* defined as congregational size but by the health of the congregation, the health of the pastor, and whether the church plants were reproducing themselves in other church plants.

The opportunity to mentor a church planter is an awesome responsibility and privilege—never to be taken lightly since it is vital kingdom work. If a mentor is mentoring a midlife seminary student, chances are good that the mentor is mentoring a church planter or re-planter.

---

7. Ralph Moore, *Starting a New Church* (Ventura, CA: Regal, 2002).

8. D. Keith Cowart, "The Role of Mentoring in the Preparation of Church Planters of Reproducing Churches" (D.Min. diss., Asbury Theological Seminary, 2002).

Choosing a Style

The role of mentor has been described with many different synonymous terms. I prefer *coach* (we will discuss the significance of other terms later). That probably alerts you to my basketball and track background. But if you are a sports participant like me, you have experienced a variety of coaches.

Early in my career, I coached a seventh-grade boys' basketball team. Our high school varsity coach dragged us underlings to a coaches' clinic. The keynote speakers personified two, hugely contrasting styles. One was a ranting and raving coach from Indiana. He swore, yelled, and told profane jokes. In fact, his behavior was so offensive that I missed any helpful information from his presentations.

The other was John Wooden from the famed UCLA wonder years, those years when the team won eighty-eight straight games and ten out of twelve NCAA men's national basketball championships. He was gentle and soft-spoken. He shared his concern for fundamentals—even to how players put their socks and shoes on—and molding players into victorious people. He refused to use the word *win*. Instead, he challenged players to live to their full potential (victoriously) academically, relationally, spiritually, and athletically.

When I arrived at the Asbury Seminary Florida campus, our student association president was a former UCLA player. I asked him if this man I had met so many years earlier was for real. "What was it like to play for John Wooden?" His response said it all. "We dragged ourselves into the locker room after losing the eighty-ninth game, not knowing what to expect from Coach Wooden. Some of us had never lost a game in our lives. When he walked in, Coach Wooden simply asked, 'Did you give it your best?' 'Yes,' we responded. 'Then you were victorious! Let's go start a new winning streak.' And he left the room."

I saw in those contrasting coaches, before knowing what I was learning, *the difference between a manager and a mentor.* I also learned a lot about coaching. But even before "coaching" became a sports term, and now a life-guide term, it had a more profound meaning. Hundreds of years ago, coaches were vehicles to carry people—"royalty" types of people. Only *precious cargo* was able to ride in a coach. That says it all. When people are coaching (mentoring), they are carrying (guiding) precious cargo (ministry persons) from where they are today to where God wants them to be at the end of our term with them. That is the awesome and dramatic mission to which mentors are called.

A Mentoring Foundation

I would bet that none (at least most) of the mentors reading this book are doing now what they thought they would be doing at age twenty-two. And those career changes come for various reasons. For some it is termination by an employer. For others it is a sense of ministry call to a new direction. Or it might be the inevitable change that comes as life circumstances change. It might be adding a new job for additional income. Whatever the reason, most ministers find themselves in career or ministry transitions several times in their lives. And with the transition in vocational direction comes lifelong reeducation learning.

As a music education college graduate, I remember standing on my family's back porch at the beginning of September (still with no job after a summer off), peering out the screen door into the yard. I was trying to explain to my dad why I did not want to become a schoolteacher. In his generation you took whatever job you could find. I wanted one with *meaning*. Thirteen years later, when applying for a church ministry position, the senior pastor looked at my resume and wondered out loud why I could not seem to keep a job.

In the first five years after college, I worked as a university chaplain; a church music and youth director; the creator of a drug drop-in center; a graphic designer; a college campus pastor; a college fund-raiser; a home builder; a painter; a seventh-grade math and English, long-term substitute teacher; a seventh-grade basketball coach; an associate pastor; and a college church relations director. Obviously, some of those positions were held simultaneously, but none of them lasted longer than a year and a half. And there are many reasons for the many changes. One of those reasons was marriage, year three after college, and the need for a larger income and the required settling down.

More important than my continual job changes, however, was the wise guidance of two people who challenged me to start focusing on a vocational target. One of the two, in an isolated conversation, opened my mind to a picture of God's possible future for me. The other was a lifelong mentor, who listened, questioned, and guided. They both challenged me to work in my gifted areas; that is where I would find meaning. They encouraged me not to give up when *the ultimate* job did not open or when a great position fell through. In other words, they helped me pull my ministry call under the larger umbrella of *equipping persons for ministry*. While the specific jobs might change or I might receive income from several sources, they were simultaneously targeting toward the same *ministry-vocational* point.

The picture finally came extremely clear one day when a colleague disparagingly called me a "part-time person." Yes, I was working three or four part-time jobs to keep food on our table, but I was no "part-time person." For the first time, the pieces fit under my ministry-vocation umbrella. As you might suspect, I responded angrily because he was so wrong. The pieces of my life were on-target. My mentors had done their job, and my colleague just did not get it.

Additional and countless other mentors, some of whom I have met only through reading their books, came and went, leaving the residue of their influence on my life. Some mentors of the early years dropped off my radar after their impact was implanted. Others took their place. As I get older, I am finding that my mentors are coming from the oldest, senior generation and from the young adults who challenge my socks off to try everything new. And I am sure that my experience is not unique. As Laurent Daloz put it, "Many of us carry memories of an influential teacher who may scarcely know we existed, yet who said something at just the right time in our lives to snap a whole world into focus."[9]

The Original Mentor

You may remember wading through Homer's *Odyssey* during a college literature class. In Greek mythology, the original Mentor (proper noun), a friend of Odysseus, was left to care for Odysseus's palace and son, Telemachus, while Odysseus fought the Trojan War. "Mentor's task was to provide an education of soul and spirit as well as mind, an education in wisdom and not merely in information."[10] Athena, the goddess of wisdom, came to visit Telemachus but found suitors were after his mother, Penelope. Athena, in danger from the suitors, took the disguise of Mentor to protect and hide herself. Some time later, after twenty years of his father's absence, Telemachus set out in search of Odysseus. Athena, again in the form of Mentor, went as his guide. Thus, Mentor appears in mythology as both male and female, a symbol of wisdom and understanding who helps the young Telemachus grow from youth to adulthood.

Throughout our literature, we have sought to introduce characters who could walk the path with weaker or less-experienced folk—to guide, protect, and give counsel. It seems that we carry a hollow spot that depends on a mentor for fulfillment. Even if we cannot cite a personal mentor, we know deep inside that we need one. Do you remember Gandalf in *Lord of the Rings*, the "Skin Horse" in *The Velveteen Rabbit*, or Mother Willow in *Pocahontas*? They each carry the role of mentor to the characters in their stories.

The Theorists

While our literature and instincts tell us that mentor relationships are vital for succeeding through life passages, several notable theorists have put a research foundation under our notions. Three of the most prominent, and whose research has continued to be recognized, are Daniel Levinson, Gail Sheehy, and Maggie Scarf.

Daniel Levinson

In his book on men's developmental life stages, Levinson points to the necessity for each man, particularly young adults, to acquire a mentor.[11] He

---

9. Laurent Daloz, *Effective Teaching and Mentoring: Realizing the Transformational Power of Adult Learning Experiences* (San Francisco: Jossey-Bass, 1986), 21.

10. Keith Anderson and Randy Reese, *Spiritual Mentoring: A Guide for Seeking and Giving Direction* (Downers Grove, IL: InterVarsity Press, 1999), 35.

11. Daniel Levinson, *The Seasons of a Man's Life* (New York: Ballantine, 1978).

says that men face a major life transition every ten years, plus or minus two. The mentor becomes the stabilizer through the transitions. However, it is not unusual for mentors to change over time, often with a crisis between the mentor and student—when mentor and student break off the relationship. The crisis may be difficult at the time, but in healthy situations the relationship will usually return to a friendship at a newly shared peer level. Often a new mentor will take the place of the previous one.

Gail Sheehy

Maybe the first person to actually use the term *mentor* in modern print, and the most prolific writer on life stages, is Gail Sheehy. Her book *Passages* (now available in an updated thirtieth anniversary edition) first appeared in 1976 and immediately went to the best-seller list as she offered a road map of adulthood—an insight into human life stages that most every person will live through.[12] She followed twenty years later with *New Passages*, updating her life-stage theory with a primary focus on midlife and beyond, as baby boomers headed into their fifties.[13] Sheehy defines mentors as people with more life experience and older in age than the student.

Maggie Scarf

Maggie Scarf started her research targeting depression in women. It soon grew into an examination of the multiple facets of women's lives.[14] Daniel Levinson had only researched men's life passages, but Maggie Scarf believed that there were significant differences in the life passages that women progressed through. One of the primary differences she found was in the need for mentoring among women. She discovered that women whose primary life focus was marriage and parenting did not necessarily desire a mentor; they received most of their guidance from their mothers and patterned their lives after them. Those women who sought a career and put off marriage and parenting (even temporarily) expressed the need for a mentor just as frequently as the males in Levinson's work. Gail Sheehy's *New Passages* expressed this same understanding, as more women moved into careers and mentoring among women became more prevalent.

The Biblical Mentors

It may come as no surprise that the concept of mentoring did not begin with mythology or twentieth-century researchers. Mentoring is a biblical model for leadership. For example in the Old Testament, Moses was on the verge of burnout from problem solving, single-handedly, for the entire

---

12. Gail Sheehy, *Passages: Predictable Crises of Adult Life* (New York: Ballantine, 2006).

13. Gail Sheehy, *New Passages: Mapping Your Life Across Time* (New York: Random House, 1995).

14. Maggie Scarf, *Unfinished Business: Pressure Points in the Lives of Women* (New York: Ballantine, 1980).

nation of Israel. Jethro, his father-in-law, stepped onto the scene and taught him the art of delegation (Exod. 18). In the remaining years, Moses poured his life into Joshua, who led the Israelites from the wilderness travels into the Promised Land (Deut. 31; 34:9). In another generation, Naomi accompanied and mentored Ruth in her transition from marriage to widowhood to remarriage—setting herself into the genealogy of Jesus (Ruth 1–4). And who can forget the wild and crazy prophet Elijah? He took Elisha into his ministry until Elisha had developed enough to take over for Elijah (2 Kings 1).

The New Testament likewise is filled with models of mentors. Before the opening chapters of Jesus' life, while he was still a fetus in the womb, his mother, Mary, sought guidance, comfort, and care from her older cousin Elizabeth (Luke 1). In the earliest days of the Christian church, following Jesus' ascension to heaven, a rabid persecutor of the Jesus-followers, Saul of Tarsus, was dramatically converted. However, most Christian believers could not trust their ears and eyes at the change. So, Barnabas (his name meaning "son of encouragement") moved alongside the convert, willing to risk his life to facilitate Saul's acceptance into the Christian church (Acts 9). Through Barnabas's tutelage and partnership, Saul—now Paul—became the great missionary to the known Western world and author of major portions of the New Testament. Paul went on to mentor others, including young Timothy, who became his outstanding protégé (1 and 2 Tim.). Defining his mentor model, Paul wrote to Timothy, "You then, my son, be strong in the grace that is in Christ Jesus. And the things you have heard me say in the presence of many witnesses entrust to reliable people who will also be qualified to teach others" (2 Tim. 2:1–2 TNIV).

Since the world of the Old and New Testaments was male oriented, we obviously receive the stories of more male mentors than female mentors. One notable exception was Priscilla, who, along with her husband, Aquilla, invited the evangelist Apollos "to their home and explained to him the way of God more adequately" (Acts 18:26 TNIV) because he needed mentoring into a fuller understanding of the gospel. With her name appearing before her husband's, it is apparent that Priscilla was the primary mentor of the male Apollos. This was certainly unusual for the culture.

The ultimate mentor obviously was Jesus himself. Though he had many hangers-on and crowds following him waiting for the next miracle, he chose to give his special attention to only twelve. These twelve were taught, given the *real story* behind the parables, empowered for ministry excursions, and allowed to traverse Jesus' inner thoughts. See John 13–14 for a special summary of Jesus' final words to his disciples about his role on earth, about whom they were in relation to him, and about the roles they were to fulfill on earth.

Spiritual Formation Mentoring

Mentoring Has Direction

Should we say *leadership* has direction? It is nearly impossible to separate leadership and mentoring, since a key to servant leadership is mentoring. In fact, leadership writers Paul Stanley and Bobby Clinton state that leaders who finish well are those who have built a lifetime of mentoring relationship networks.[15] And those relationships must work in four dimensions—what they call the constellation model: upward mentoring, downward mentoring, mentoring within an organization, and mentoring outside an organization.[16]

Vertical Mentoring Relationships

Upward Mentoring

All leaders need to encounter the experience and insights of those who have gone before them, those who are wise enough to reflect on what they have learned and are willing to guide another leader along the path. Upward mentoring is intentionally seeking out someone with more leadership experience who can provide that guidance.

Downward Mentoring

Downward mentoring should not be mistaken for bossing or dictating the action of another person. Instead, it is when a leader recognizes potential in another person, usually younger or less experienced, and commits to training, guiding, and helping the younger leader grow to his or her full potential.

Horizontal Mentoring Relationships

Peer Mentoring Within the Organization or Ministry

We each need persons who will walk alongside us in our ministry vocation. Peers within the organization may be staff members or other congregants who know each another on such a personal level that they can hold one another accountable and provide encouragement. If relationships in a ministry are healthy, this type of mentoring is done quite naturally.

Peer Mentoring Outside the Organization or Ministry

The persons who provide this kind of mentoring may be friends, family, or other acquaintances who can provide a more objective view, a wider perspective. The most helpful collection of peer mentors might be persons from the nearby area who are not connected to one's ministry but share a common vision of life and ministry (e.g., pastors from nearby churches).

Mentoring Up

A new twist on the old term has appeared primarily in the business and

---

15. Paul Stanley and J. Robert Clinton, "Constellation Model," http://www.bobby clinton.com/articles/downloads/ConstellationModel.pdf., 1–2. The Constellation Model is expanded in their book *Connecting: The Mentoring Relationships You Need to Succeed in Life* (Colorado Springs: NavPress, 1992).
16. Ibid.

educational worlds. *Mentoring-up* mentors are those who have expertise in a specific area, no matter what their age or status. Back in 1997, Intel (the computer chip maker) launched this new mentoring model when they matched "people not by job title or by years of service but by specific skills that are in demand."[17] People were networked across the company to one another, to help each other grow and succeed at their work. In other words, find out who is the best person at any one skill or who knows the most about getting around a system (or organization), and let everyone else learn from that person.

This *mentoring-up* model looks a whole lot like the biblical view of the body of Christ, which finds its richest fulfillment as persons minister together, using their spiritual gifts (see Eph. 4 as one example). Hopefully we are already committed to this in our congregations. Certainly we experience it in normal, everyday life. Whenever we engage with a new piece of electronic equipment, we find the closest fifteen-year-old to teach us how to use it. That is *mentoring up.*

Types of Mentors

Before the toll road near our house was finished, friends from New York came for a visit to Orlando. When they left I-95 in Daytona Beach, heading west on I-4, they called us on their cell phone. They had a map in hand, but it did not give clear detail of the back roads to our house. However, with cell phone in hand, I was able to guide them through each turn, and before long they arrived in our driveway.

They had several levels of travel help available to them. They could have checked the Internet before they left home, trusted their map to get them here, asked for directions along the way, or talked to me on the phone—as they did. Better yet, they could have had someone in the car with them who had made the trip before and knew the way. That is another essence of mentoring—guiding.

Including *guiding* and *coaching*, Bobby Clinton has named nine roles or personalities that point us to a broader picture of mentors and mentoring relationships.[18] These roles are lived out in all four dimensions of mentoring listed above. All mentors fit one or more of these roles as they operate in one or more of the dimensions. By pulling apart these various layers individually, we will better understand the complexity of mentoring and the various roles mentors may play in each setting.

Discipler

A discipler is a mentor, usually one who is more spiritually mature,

---

17. Fara Warner, "Inside Intel's Mentoring Movement," *Fast Company*, March 2002, 116.

18. Clinton, "Constellation Model"; Anderson and Reese, *Spiritual Mentoring*; J. Robert Clinton and Richard Clinton, *The Mentor Handbook: Detailed Guidelines and Helps for Christian Mentors and Mentorees* (Altadena, CA: Barnabas, 1991).

who spends time, usually one-on-one, with a less mature individual, in an attempt to build the basics of Christian living into that other person. The goal is to empower the less mature person to follow Jesus as a mature believer.

Spiritual Guide

A spiritual guide is a mentor who provides accountability for the practice of spiritual disciplines and spiritual growth. Usually this involves a more intense relationship than discipling. The mentor gives specific direction related to spiritual questions and life issues.

Coach

A coach is a mentor who offers skill development (how to conduct a funeral or make a hospital visit, for example) and encouragement to use those skills.

Counselor

A counselor is a mentor who offers advice as well as an objective perspective of the student's self-view, relationships, life circumstances, and vocation.

Teacher

A teacher is a mentor who imparts knowledge and understanding of a specific subject for a specific time and need in a student's life. A church-planting mentor would be a *teacher mentor.*

Sponsor

A sponsor is a mentor who helps open doors, using one's influence or resources to help promote a student in his or her ministry career and personal development. Sponsoring might mean helping a person make a job connection or gain entrance into seminary training.

Contemporary Model

A contemporary model is a mentor who "models values, methodologies, and other leadership characteristics in such a way as to inspire others to emulate them."[19] As described earlier, this may be the most important way a young student can learn the ups and downs of ministry life from a mentor. It also may be the most threatening to a mentor since it requires transparency of the mentor's life.

Historical Model

Historical models are the same as contemporary models except that they are no longer alive. Instead, coming from the past, their mentoring is done as a student reads or studies them, autobiographically or biographically.

---

19. Clinton, "Constellation Model."

Divine Contact

A divine contact is a mentor whose intervention coincides with a specific need in the student's life and is perceived as God's guidance, whether the mentor is aware of the situation or not or if the mentor/student relationship carries any further.

Essentials for Mentoring

Mentors must always remember that mentoring is spiritual mentoring. Mentors are mentoring with a Jesus-kingdom purpose. Again, as mentors, they are in the *business* (pardon the phrase) of helping students be formed more and more into the image of Jesus so that the students' internal lives match the ministry acts they may perform, and so that the students' external ministry acts are deeply rooted in their personal relationship with the Creator.

Mentoring experts Keith Anderson and Randy Reese challenge us with a set of essentials that fit all models, all circumstances, all students, and all mentors and are a *must* for Christian, spiritual mentors.[20] They encapsulate all that we have said so far.

Spiritual Mentoring Is Relational

The Trinity set the relationship model into place at the beginning of time, and Jesus brought it into humanity with his incarnation. God has always been relational, and we are created with that same desire, even when we do not know it. Whether formal or informal, structured or casual, the best mentoring is a person-to-person relationship. It is the sharing of lives and hearts.

Spiritual Mentoring Is Autobiographical

This is at least the third time this point has been raised. Spiritual mentoring is grounded in the ordinary stuff of life. We each carry thoughts, feelings, dreams, and a multitude of experiences that will stay buried unless someone helps us mine those treasures. A mentor will help the student examine the stuff of life from both the mentor's experience and the student's, looking for the touch of God's hand and guidance.

Spiritual Mentoring Is a Partnership with the Holy Spirit

The Holy Spirit is already at work in every human's life, drawing him or her to God. Mentors become partners in the process. A mentor assists the student in paying attention to what God is doing and what God still wants to do inside the student.

Spiritual Mentoring Is Purposive

One's spiritual pilgrimage is not an aimless meandering. Despite its turns and twists, it is directed toward a spiritual purpose. "Our spiritual

---

20. Anderson and Reese, *Spiritual Mentoring*, 33–60.

journeys are not given to us complete with road map, trip outline or itinerary, only an invitation to discover what God has in mind for our particular excursion through time and space. It is the task of the mentor to help us sink deep enough into our own lives to discover that purpose."[21]

Spiritual Mentoring Requires Listening

Obviously a person does not *cause* spiritual growth in another person. However, a mentor can enhance it and encourage it. Ministers who look back on many years of ministry and have mentored numbers of people tend to offer answers, even before the questions are asked. If a mentor is to truly come alongside a student, sensitive listening is essential. A mentor listens to God, a mentor listens to his or her student's life, and a mentor helps the student to do the same.

Spiritual Mentoring Requires Adaptability

No cookie cutters are allowed in the mentor kitchen. Since spiritual growth cannot be packaged into a neat formula, a mentor needs wise discernment to get beneath the surface with a student. As a more experienced person, a mentor can easily look critically on a student, not allowing for future growth. The real need is to find the *real need.* And discerning mentors will ask questions that individualize their work with each one. If a mentor gets into a rut so that he or she "mentorizes" each person in the same way, that mentor has stepped away from reliance on the Holy Spirit and is just doing his or her own thing.

Spiritual Mentoring Belongs to the Priesthood of All Believers

Depending on whom you read, authors disagree on whether everyone can be a mentor. I believe it depends. Certainly not everyone will be a member of the clergy or a professional mentor. But I cannot imagine that every Christian is not or should not be a mentor to someone else. It is part of a Jesus-follower's DNA. We as leaders must open the doors for all who follow us to find their mentoring place, whether formal and official or coming alongside another person in need. Mentoring is a high calling and every Christian is invited.

Jesus' Model of Mentoring

Finally, we must take a more in-depth look at the ultimate Mentor and how he did what he did. Everyone else's model comes from and is an adaptation of his model. This may be a review for you, but think seriously about how each method below might come alive in one's mentoring, in new and creative ways.

Jesus Used Object Lessons

This idea is so obvious it probably goes without saying. Unfortunately,

---

21. Ibid., 48.

we Westerners tend to use verbiage (and yes, even our PowerPoints are filled with words) instead of visuals. Jesus drew attention to visible demonstrations of the truth he wanted his followers to learn. He used those things along the way, those objects at hand, to illustrate the truths he was trying to communicate.

Think for a moment of how many objects Jesus used to define the kingdom of God. You can probably name many. Remember the mustard seed, the farmer going out to plant, the yeast, the hidden treasure, and the fishing net? He described the influence of a believer as working like salt or light. Jesus challenged people to stop worrying since God cares for the birds, the lilies, and the hairs on our heads. When teaching on priorities, he illustrated with a coin, saying, "Give to Caesar what is Caesar's, and to God what is God's" (Matt. 22:21 NIV).

It is important to note that his object lessons were effective because from the *common stuff* of life he raised a powerful spiritual meaning. Sitting at dinner with his disciples on the night of his betrayal, he reached across the table and picked up a chunk of bread and the wine cup they had been drinking from—the normal Passover instruments. But instantly the normalness was gone. With his breaking and blessing, the common symbols were transformed into an eternal and sacred message of his body and blood given in love. This was the one object lesson that he commanded us never to forget. The challenge for mentors is to find appropriate object lessons and ones that are applicable to their students without being too simplistic.

Jesus Used Parables

Each parable was a case study on life. We use case studies in field education as an opportunity to broaden a student's understanding of many ministry settings, without each student having to actually experience the event.[22] In the same way, Jesus set up dilemmas for people to wrestle with. He used parables to emphasize relevant precepts and desired behavior patterns. Unfortunately, both his disciples and the broader crowd of followers often missed the point of his parables. Thus, he took the Twelve aside for further explanation.

When he wanted to teach listening and obeying, he talked about houses constructed on sand and rocks. When his point was prayer, he described a neighbor persistently beating on his friend's door at night to get food. When he was illustrating the spirit of giving, he pointed to a poor woman who offered only two coins, declaring her as giving more than the wealthy.

With a little creativity, mentors can use parables, case studies, or scenarios with their students. A mentor might rewrite them from reading he or she has done or from the Scriptures or, if the mentor has a Garrison Keillor bent, he or she might start originally.

---

22. See chapter 9, "The Use of Case Studies in Field Education," for further information on case studies.

Jesus Asked Questions

Rarely did Jesus provide answers. He usually responded to a question with a more thoughtful question of his own. Asking, not telling, is the partner to listening.

Jesus Used Probing Questions

When he wanted his listeners to get below surface thinking, he burrowed in with questions. In Mark 3:1–6, Jesus encounters a man with a withered hand who wants healing, and it is the Sabbath. Of course, the Jewish teachers, always scheming for a way to catch Jesus breaking the rules, hoped he would break the Sabbath law. Jesus, knowing what they were up to, challenged back with the question, "Which is lawful on the Sabbath: to do good or to do evil, to save life or to kill?" (NIV). That probing question had them cornered and made the point without accusing or lecturing.

We have already discussed how a mentor can ask questions that get the student thinking about solutions to problems or more helpful scenarios. Carefully crafted questions will give guidance without condemnation.

Jesus Asked Personal Questions

You did not hang around Jesus very long without getting transparent. If you did not come clean, he would call you out. When Jesus asked his disciples to declare his identify (Mark 8:27–30), he wanted to challenge his followers to put into words their understanding of him. He wanted their opinions, not just the answers they had heard among the crowds. He wanted a base line of how far their growth had come.

Yes, appropriate questions are imperative for working with a student. However, may I offer a word of caution about personal questions? Mentors never should push into deeply personal issues unless the student gives them permission. A mentor also will need to be ready to deal with difficult situations that may be exposed if he or she is allowed to probe deeply. Knowing a referral counselor is always helpful instead of attempting to counsel all comers.

Jesus Asked Provocative Questions

Occasionally Jesus' questions put the questioners into a dilemma where no response was acceptable for them to give. In one instance the Jewish teachers tried to corner Jesus by challenging his authority to cast out demons. "Answer me, and I will tell you by what authority I am doing these things. John's baptism—was it from heaven, or of human origin? Tell me!" (Mark 11:29–30 TNIV). With this provocative response, Jesus left them standing in disarray. Neither answer would work since the surrounding crowd was divided between the opposing responses; they were unable to publicly answer either way.

In one of my small groups, we have coined the phrase "Jesus-speak" to describe the statements Jesus made that do not provide easy answers—or seem to contradict themselves. With a student, "Jesus-speak" questions such as, "What if we canceled Sunday morning worship or met in a restaurant?" or "What if we hired a new staff person for that job so your husband wouldn't have to volunteer so much?" can push the student to deeper thinking and outside his or her normal box of perception.

Jesus Taught by Example

On the most important kingdom issues, there was no question about what Jesus thought or believed because his actions were so consistent with his inner life. The inner and outer lives were a perfectly matched set. This may be the most difficult issue for mentors because they are often so good at playing the professional minister role.

Students will learn the most about a mentor's view of ministry, and ministry in general, as they watch how the mentor interacts with staff, congregational members, and family members. Students will know mentors are truly committed to integrity as they watch mentors living with integrity in their private worlds. One of the first pastors I worked for refused to buy peanuts at baseball games despite the rules to not bring outside food into the stadium. He would buy peanuts before going to the game and send his sons ahead into the stadium. They would catch the peanuts as he threw the bags over the wall. His sons and his staff learned much from that pastor, but integrity was not one of the values learned.

If a student sees a mentor neglecting those closest to the mentor in order to feed his or her workaholic addiction—a frequent pastoral form of idolatry—students will either reject the mentor or begin to follow his or her sick patterns. After nine years as an associate pastor with two different work-aholic senior pastors, the model was deeply ingrained in my psyche. I nearly lived at the church. I stayed on call for a street ministry 24/7. I was burning the proverbial candle at both ends and, as our seminary vice president Dr. Steve Harper describes, cutting the candle into little pieces and lighting all those ends. Even a month and a half in bed with mononucleosis (from sheer exhaustion) did not get my attention to stop the bonfire I was creating. Fortunately, I finally joined a staff team whose leader enforced days off for all staff members and taught us how to take effective vacations. I have worked to keep Sabbath time sacred ever since.

Pastoral sage Eugene Peterson declares that lack of *self-care* (he calls it not taking *Sabbath*) is the greatest sin among clergy.[23] He calls us to stop playing God, believing that our ministry depends solely on us and if we dare to take a break (or recreate), it will collapse around us. Instead, what too frequently happens is that *we collapse in* the ministry from either heart attacks or moral failures. Bill Hybels of Willow Creek Community Church quotes the leadership expert Dee Hock, "It is management of self that should occupy 50 percent of our time and the best of our ability.

---

23. Eugene Peterson, *Working the Angles: The Shape of Pastoral Integrity* (Grand Rapids: Eerdmans, 1987), 71.

And when we do that the ethical, moral and spiritual elements of management are inescapable."[24] That is a huge percentage of our time. I wonder what ministry and family transformation might happen if we took Hock seriously?

Now back to Jesus. It does not take in-depth Bible study to realize that Jesus made self-care a priority. That is why the Jewish rulers were so frustrated with him. He did not fit their model of Sabbath—keeping the rules list checked off. Instead, he stuck to the heart of Sabbath, proclaiming, "The Sabbath was made for people, not people for the Sabbath" (Mark 2:27 TNIV). In the middle of every crisis or major event of his ministry, Jesus hid away to pray, refocus, and rest—to practice *self-care*. He usually dragged his disciples with him as a part of their instruction, although they and the crowds tempted him to perpetual action, to meet every need, to take a king's crown. It is also fascinating to note that most of those *Sabbath nights* were spent on mountaintops, a place from which one can see the upcoming valley more clearly—to regain God's perspective for the future.

Leaving a Legacy

Years ago Martin Luther King Jr. proclaimed the call to serve. This is the role of mentoring:

> Jesus gave us a new norm of greatness. If you want to be important—wonderful. If you want to be recognized—wonderful. If you want to be great—wonderful. But recognize that he who is greatest among you shall be your servant. That's a new definition of greatness. And this morning, the thing that I like about it: by giving that definition of greatness, it means that everybody can be great, because everybody can serve. You don't have to have a college degree to serve. You don't have to make your subject and your verb agree to serve. You don't have to know about Plato and Aristotle to serve. You don't have to know Einstein's theory of relativity to serve. You don't have to know the second theory of thermodynamics in physics to serve. You only need a heart full of grace, a soul generated by love. And you can be that servant.[25]

That would be my goal and the legacy I hope to leave as an imprint on lives who choose to let me mentor them. It is a high and spiritual calling.

---

24. Bill Hybels, *Courageous Leadership* (Grand Rapids: Zondervan, 2002), 183.
25. Martin Luther King Jr., "The Drum Major Instinct," at http://www.stanford.edu/group/King/publications/sermons/680204.000_Drum_Major_Instinct.html.

Prayer of Transformation

Gracious God, How awesome to remember that you were at work with us before time. You molded us and birthed us with your breath, into your image. Then you came to us as the model, yes the eternal Mentor to teach the way back home to you—and how to live victoriously on the way. We thank you! Now I ask that you'll empower me by your Holy Spirit for that same mission of mentoring. Always keep me being your servant, doing your will, in your way. And, God, may I live joy-filled in the high honor of planting your (and my) stamp on the life of another. Amen.

Reflection Questions

1. What is the biggest hurdle that you would have to jump to feel like you were leaving a true legacy in the life of another person?

2. If you had been Jesus trying to teach the kingdom of God to his ragtag band, what would have been most frustrating to you?

3. Which of Bobby Clinton's roles or personalities of mentoring most connect to who you are?

4. What is the one most applicable idea from this chapter that you will apply to your ministry in the next twelve months?

Further Reading

Anderson, Keith, and Randy Reese. *Spiritual Mentoring: A Guide for Seeking and Giving Direction.* Downers Grove, IL: InterVarsity Press, 1999.

Biehl, Bobb. *Mentoring: Confidence in Finding a Mentor and Becoming One.* Nashville: Broadman & Holman, 1996.

Daloz, Laurent. *Effective Teaching and Mentoring: Realizing the Transformational Power of Adult Learning Experiences.* San Francisco: Jossey-Bass, 1986.

Stanley, Paul, and J. Robert Clinton. *Connecting: The Mentoring Relationships You Need to Succeed in Life.* Colorado Springs: NavPress, 1992.

Zachary, Lois. *The Mentor's Guide: Facilitating Effective Learning Relationships.* San Francisco: Jossey-Bass, 2000.

PART 3

Tools for Field Education

Covenant and Goal Development
Mentor Supervisory Meeting
Case Studies
Biblical Community
Assessment and Evaluation

Chapter 7

Covenant and Goal Development

THE AIM FOR SUCCESS

KATHERINE KYTE

In your heart you plan your life.
But the LORD decides where your steps will take you.
(Prov. 16:9 NIrV)

Through internships, students can have unparalleled opportunities to work alongside veteran ministry leaders. Much like apprenticeships of old, students not only can learn practical skills of ministry from their mentors but also can gain invaluable insight and wisdom from them. Ministry students, by virtue of their formal "in-training" status, have access to pastors and other ministry leaders during their internship that average laypeople often do not have.

Aware of this privilege, students should want to do all they can to make the most of their experience. A significant way they can help themselves do this is through the exercise of setting goals and objectives. Breaking down the vision God has given them into progressive, attainable steps will serve them well, not only in their internship, but also in all aspects of their lives as they pursue God's unfolding call for them. A critical aspect of any internship is for the student to thoughtfully and prayerfully identify and develop personal goals for his or her time in training.

The exercise of setting goals might seem like a "no-brainer" to those who naturally like to think and plan ahead, but an understanding of the helpfulness of goal setting as a tool to help a person grow does not come naturally to everybody, perhaps not even to many. It is likely that only a few of us have had the blessing of having family or teachers guide us into any kind of meaningful goal setting at any point in our upbringing or education. Blessed are those children whose parents or teachers saw the benefits of periodically setting goals and objectives and took the time to pass these skills on to them! A common saying goes, "You cannot impart what you do not possess." If parents or teachers have not seen the need to acquire or to intentionally pass on goal setting as a life skill, then these perspectives skills—and their benefits—will not be engendered in us.

Most of us have had our goals delivered to us by someone else. Children are told what parents expect them to accomplish. Students are given syllabi and schedules for classes they must take. Seminarians may be expected by their school or denominations to acquire certain competencies. Our hope in goal setting for field internships is for students to either strengthen the goal-setting skills they may already have or to acquire those skills for the first time. Ideally, the desire is that through the goal-setting process students will come closer to a full development of the important life skill of regular, prayerful goal setting. It is good for students to understand that goal setting is an important way in which they can love the Lord, not just with their heart but also with their mind and strength (Matt. 22:37; Mark 12:30).

Initial Inertia

As mentioned above, not all students will arrive ready for their internships with established goal-setting skills. As would be expected, those who have been taught to plan ahead in life are at an advantage. Those who have not may find themselves resistant or intimidated as they anticipate the process. Whatever can be done to help demystify or make the process as constructive, simple, and positive as possible for these students is most helpful. Hopefully the process outlined in this chapter will contribute to that.

Over the years I have observed that personality type tends to play an observable part in students' natural ability and motivation in setting goals as they develop their learning covenants. More structured, organized, and methodical personalities seem to naturally take to goal setting, and these students often produce the most precise, well-worded and thought-out learning covenants. While these covenants are of a quality that could impress the patriarchs, the challenge with these students is to help them learn to be more flexible with their goals and in their assessment of their success or failure in their subsequent ministry. Setting goals, which can be a blessing, can come to feel like a curse for those who in their precision might tend to be overly sensitive or hard on themselves. Good mentors can be helpful to these students by teaching them more about grace—and about seeing goals as tools the students *use* rather than taskmasters that use *them*. In addition, good training in goal development can help students and others learn a healthy balance in creating more flexible and realistic goals and measures.

And then there are the more freewheeling, creative personalities. These students have progressed through life quite well through the power of their intuition, charm, and ability to improvise. These people are often some of the most engaging, ministry-motivated students, but they tend to express a kind of "allergic reaction" to goal setting, balking at the prospect of sitting down and thinking through what their needs and desires are. A common question is, "If the Spirit of God is responsible for the fruit, and I am following the Spirit's leading, then why should I have to set goals and objectives?"

Understandable as this sentiment may be, these students can still benefit by learning that goals and objectives can be their friends rather than annoyances that cramp their style—or cramp the Holy Spirit in his work. Many times at the end of a term, I have heard these same students report such things as, "At first I really didn't like having to write out my goals, but now I can see how much more God did in and through me after having been forced to think about it." Although the exercise of goal setting at first felt burdensome, the students discovered that the setting of goals—and reaching them—actually could become a means that the Holy Spirit used to bring more glory and praise to God!

Process of Goal Setting

Field education internships at our seminary require that learning covenants be submitted at the beginning of each twelve-week field unit. We explain that this learning covenant serves as a kind of charter for the student for that period of time. In collaboration with his or her mentor, the student is asked to set measurable objectives at the beginning of the term and then reevaluate his or her progress at the end of the term. We ask students to keep their objectives term-specific so that they can actually see and measure their progress over that time. Then for subsequent units, the students can adjust their goals and objectives based on what they have learned from their experience in the previous semester. Through this exercise—the updating and modifying of goals for each term—students can learn to keep abreast of their goals and objectives within an overall plan for their personal, spiritual, and ministry growth. This will help keep them from feeling overwhelmed by the size of overall goals and also will encourage them by enabling them to see incremental progress.

As mentioned above, different students are motivated differently. For those students who are more ambitious in their goal setting, I often say that if they have the goal of "evangelizing all of New England" during their first unit, it is likely that they will want to modify it the next time around! On the other hand, if a student in his or her overall desire to get to know the congregation in the church better sets a goal of "speaking to one parishioner" this term, then I would probably encourage the student to set a higher faith goal. In training students to set goals, I seek to strike a balance between encouraging students to trust God for bigger things and setting realistic, reachable goals that will serve to encourage students as they meet them.

Students need not be penalized for falling short of their goals. Falling short of reaching goals—and in the process learning to appropriately modify them—can be a vitally important part of the learning process. It also can help give insight into areas of strength and weakness, and how they bear on a student's sense of calling to ministry. Of course students can be encouraged to set higher goals that they want to trust God for by faith, but it is important to be sensitive to human nature and seek to avoid setting oneself up for discouragement.

Sections of the Learning Covenant

A cover sheet may be clipped to the front of the learning covenant, providing information that is important to the school or supervisor. On the cover sheet the student should list his or her name, relevant course information, and contact information. The student also should list the name of the internship site and mentor or supervisor and that person's contact information. Finally, there ought to be a place where both student and mentor can sign the document, signifying their ratification or approval. Figure 7.1 contains sample student instructions for composing the learning covenant.

The Job Description

The job description is the first of three sections of the learning covenant. It is intended to be a simple, straightforward outline of the role and responsibilities in a student's internship for that semester. It is common for students to simply cut and paste a copy of the job description that they have received from their internship into this section. It outlines for them the expectations of their work and the breakdown of their responsibilities and time usage.

In order to help students think through why they are doing what they are doing, students are next asked to respond to a couple of specific questions. First, they are asked to explain how they see their work as fitting into the big picture of the mission of the local and global church. They are invited to think beyond the mere accomplishing of tasks in their ministry and to reflect on the biblically revealed plan of God for the kingdom of God. It is exciting for students—and for everyone—to reflect on how our small, localized efforts actually play a part in contributing to the greatest enterprise of all time: the building and furthering of the kingdom of God!

Supervision and Resources

The second section enables students to think about what I consider to be a critical part, if not the centerpiece, of their field experience: the mentoring relationship. In this section, students are asked to outline how they desire their mentoring meetings to be handled as well as what they desire in their actual

Figure 7.1. Composing the Learning Covenant

Please submit in typing the information requested below. Please repeat each question or subject matter in the heading for each item. Single-spacing within a paragraph and double-spacing between paragraphs is preferred. A total of two or three pages will be sufficient.

Give careful thought to your learning needs as you prepare your responses. Keep your comments brief and concise, but do not give superficial responses. This is your learning covenant in which you are intentionally stating objectives for yourself as you engage in this ministry. Your signature is your commitment to work on these objectives, and the signatures of your mentor and the Director of Mentored Ministry attest to their readiness to assist you in meeting these goals.

A. Job Description
   1. Describe your *specific duties for this unit* as agreed to by you and your mentor.

   2. Briefly comment on how *your duties correlate with your learning needs* in preparing you further for Christian ministry (further elaboration to be done under Learning Objectives).

   3. State how your involvement during this unit will *help the church or organization fulfill its mission in the world.*

   4. Report any *financial arrangements* made.

B. Supervision and Resources
   1. Comment on what you desire in your relationship with your mentor (mentoring qualities, availability, spiritual counsel, etc.).

   2. List several topics for discussion (tentative dates may also be included) beyond your immediate ministry tasks/concerns which you plan to proactively discuss with your mentor over the course of the twelve-week unit. State how you would like to see the mentoring meetings handled or structured.

   3. Describe any resources (people, books, materials, etc.) you intend to utilize in meeting your objectives for this unit.

C. Learning Objectives (Unit-specific)
   Comment on your learning objectives for the three areas listed below. Remember that your written evaluation later will ask you

to assess your progress in meeting these objectives, and that your objectives are to be related to your learning and developmental needs. Although there may be some overlap among the three areas, be distinct and specific in your responses.

1. Ministry Knowledge (Knowing)
   Elaborate on the areas of knowledge you intend to gain from working in this unit. This has to do with matters of content about given subjects that relate to ministry. Choose 2–3 measurable objectives for this unit.

2. Ministry Skills (Doing)
   Comment on the ministry skills you want to develop in this ministry and what you will do to achieve this. Be specific, not general. Look at areas of professional development for yourself. Choose 2–3 measurable objectives for this unit.

3. Ministry Character (Being)
   State the personal characteristics and attitudes you desire to develop. Be specific. Do not focus on tasks or functions, but on personal qualities and attributes. Choose 2–3 measurable objectives for this unit.*

_____

* "Composing the Learning Covenant." © 2007 Gordon-Conwell Theological Seminary. Used by permission.

working relationship with their mentor. This is a wonderful opportunity for them to discuss with their mentors the dynamics of their relationship with a view toward the elucidating of expectations of both parties—and hopefully dispelling any unrealistic ones. This will build understanding with their mentors from the very outset of the relationship and help both the students and mentors form the best relationship and ministry collaboration possible.

In this section students can discuss such issues as their preferred leadership style (both giving and receiving), how they respond to criticism and challenge, and their desires for the handling of the spiritual aspect of their mentoring relationship. Some students reveal that they are looking for more of a spiritual friend, coach, or guide in their mentoring relationship. Other students are hoping for more of a systematic trainer, director, or supervisor for their internship experience. Some students want a mentor or supervisor who will teach them the ropes by working alongside them as they go, closely monitoring them, while other students want to be given a large degree of independence in their work, wanting the mentor to simply be available for advice as needed. Some relish close attention, while others feel stifled by it.[1]

Mentors, too, have their own style of leadership and their own assumptions about what students may or may not need in their supervision. Here is where students and mentors have the opportunity to discuss the dynamics of their relationship, their needs, styles, and preferences. Many unnecessary conflicts and problems can be avoided by taking the opportunity and time to discuss these issues and to get to know one another better through this process.

Next, students are asked to determine specific topics for discussion with their mentor or supervisor—one topic per week. Students and mentors will naturally talk together about current ministry concerns, but I also want students to make the best of their time with their specific mentor by intentionally "picking the mentor's brain" about a broader range of ministry issues. Each mentor has special and unique experiences and perspectives that no one else has had. The internship is a golden opportunity for a student to learn more about these experiences and the lessons that God has taught his or her mentor. Good mentors will be proactive in getting to know their students, their backgrounds, needs, vision, desires, and call, and students should be expected to be proactive as well. I ask students to select at least three topics, apart from current ministry concerns, that they wish to intentionally discuss with their mentors and to weave these into their mentoring discussion plan.

At the same time I also wish to promote balance and realism in the planning of mentoring sessions, as well as other learning objectives. Although students are asked to list dates and topics for mentoring meetings, it is not necessary that they have a different topic listed for every week. First, I know that discussions often can stretch over several weeks or can be revisited as new ministry situations arise. I also understand that urgent ministry concerns will eclipse other needs in any given week and it is good and appropriate for mentor and student to respond to these concerns together in depth. These times can be some of the greatest opportunities for learning. While I look for students to list at least three new topics of intentional discussion with their mentors in their learning covenant for a given semester, I also allow plenty of latitude in regard to length and variety of discussion. The main point is that a student exercises a healthy degree of proactivity in his or her mentoring experience, along with responding to current ministry concerns.

Learning Objectives

In the third section, "Learning Objectives," students are guided to move from the general to the specific as they outline their personal goals for the term. It is important that these objectives be term-specific and measurable. The categories of learning objectives are divided into three areas of focus,

---

1. See chapter 6, "Mentoring: The Opportunity to Leave a Legacy," for examples of these roles.

employing terminology commonly used in field education: goals for ministry knowledge, ministry skills, and ministry character—knowing, doing, and being. Here students are asked to set three specific, measurable goals for each area so that by the end of the term they will be able to have some kind of helpful measure of their progress (see figure 7.2).

I offer the formula, "By the end of this twelve-week period, I plan to accomplish _____ by doing _____." Students write their objective in the first blank and the measurable means to reach it in the second. For example, a student might write, "By the end of this twelve-week period, I plan to learn the skill of teaching adults by leading a ten-week adult Sunday school class on the Gospel of John." This basic formula can be elaborated on by having the student ask himself or herself even more detailed questions, such as, "What will it look like when I achieve this goal?" "What changes will I need to make?" "What resources do I need to utilize to reach this goal?" or "To whom will I be accountable to reach this goal?" Examples of learning objectives and more detailed questions may be found in figure 7.2.

I have found it to be relatively easy for students to state, measure, and reach their goals for *knowing* and *doing*; however, goals for *being* by nature tend to be more difficult to measure and take longer to attain. The saying "It takes a summer to grow a squash but years to grow an oak" is true when it comes to character development. It is expected that students would present at least some of the same character goals each time they write a covenant, so they need not consider this unusual or negative. They can be encouraged that even when they reset goals for knowing and doing in subsequent units, it is all right for them to continue to keep focusing on the same character goals, though perhaps coming at them from different angles.

This section is a critical one. As I often tell my students, "Aim at nothing and you're sure to hit it." By setting goals and reaching them—or even by only partially reaching them or not reaching them at all—they can learn valuable lessons about themselves and their limitations and especially precious truths about God and his ability and provision.

Balance in Goal Setting

Proverbs 16:9 states that "the mind of man plans his way, but the Lord directs his steps" (NASB). Sometimes students fear that goal setting might get in the way of or even express a lack of reliance on the work of the Holy Spirit. It is important to communicate a balanced perspective that while still insisting on the importance of goal setting, the overarching truth is that God is sovereign in our lives and ministries. There are many scriptural examples of God's people seeking God and making thoughtful, prayerful plans based on their sense of his direction and will (e.g., Moses, Deborah, Nehemiah, Paul) as well as admonitions to plan ahead and be wise (Proverbs, the parable of the ant, the teaching of Paul). At the same time, godly people also need to be ready to be flexible in their plans as the Holy Spirit may at any time redirect them in ways they cannot anticipate.

Figure 7.2. Writing a Learning Objective

There are three areas for which learning objectives are to be written: knowledge, skills, and character (knowing, doing, and being). The following is a *suggested exercise or method* for those who would like more direction and assistance in helping them discern and develop these goals, specific to each unit/term.

To begin, take three pieces of paper (blank) and at the top place one area on each paper. These will serve as your worksheets to prepare you to write objectives for your learning covenant.

For each area, consider one, at the most two concerns for each area:

1. A change that needs to take place
2. Some development that needs growth
3. A conflict/question/problem to resolve/answer/solve
4. A standard to be reached
5. An integration of theory and practice
6. A social or relational skill that needs refinement

First, state the concern as succinctly as possible. For example, try beginning, "By the end of the term I need to. . . ." (such as, discover my spiritual gifts; or, build leadership confidence; or, relate my theology of evangelism to child evangelism). Make sure that your objective is reachable. An objective is something that you can accomplish during the time of your mentoring relationship. Therefore, avoid life-goals.

Now, once you have gained an idea of concerns for each area, it is time for you to begin to formulate your objectives. Write two to four objectives for each of the three areas.

When you write your objectives, use the following example by asking the questions listed below:

1. "By the end of this twelve-week period, I want to be a more godly father by . . ."
2. What will it look like when you achieve this goal? E.g., "By leading my family in home worship twice a week."
3. How does your academic work relate to your goal? E.g., "By reading *The Reformed Pastor* and writing a summary on the pastor and his family."
4. How does this relate to your relationship with your mentor? E.g., "By spending a mentoring session discussing the life of the pastor and family, and learning from my mentor how he/she deals with his/her family."

5. What can reasonably be achieved in this time frame? E.g., "By interviewing fathers in the congregation and determining the climate of the church."
6. What changes will you need to make? E.g., "By being home for dinner each weekday evening and assisting in the cleanup afterward."
7. Where will you need to go? E.g., "By going to the library and developing a bibliography on effective fatherhood."
8. Who/what can be a resource for this goal? E.g., "By writing a reflection paper on the biblical aspects of parenting." E.g., "By discussing parenting with my spouse and then writing an integration paper on our discussion. This would include thoughts on how I might become a better father."

* A learning objective is not complete without the following:
* A time frame (the duration of the placement)
* A purpose (addressing a concern or need)
* A standard (measure)
* Accountability (supervisor/mentor)

Remember: One of the purposes of mentored ministry is to stretch you. The challenge is to go beyond what you are comfortable with and work on areas that require work and growth for future ministry.
Suggested length of Learning Covenant, 2–4 pages.*

---

* "Writing a Learning Objective." © 2007 Gordon-Conwell Theological Seminary. Used by permission.

To Have Competencies or Not to Have Competencies?

While most degree programs and courses have clearly spelled-out goals and aims for themselves—with corresponding knowledge and skills for students to acquire—a common discussion among field educators is whether they also ought to have a specific list of ministry skills or competencies that they require students to achieve in order to graduate. For denominationally based seminaries, this is not really debatable. Most denominations require that students seeking ordination with them have certain competencies in place, and thus they have little choice in the matter.

For interdenominational institutions such as ours, however, we realize that competencies are a real option, if for no other reasons than the trust that denominations put in us to educate their people and the tacit expectation of a certain level of ministry competency on the part of our graduates. Many interdenominational schools or seminaries do require competencies, and even one of our branch campuses has developed a modified version of competency requirements in which students can select from a list of "rotations" of ministry focus. (These include church planting, missions, preaching, teaching, healing ministry, counseling, administration, worship, discipleship, and culture.) So although we at our campus have opted *not* to have set competencies for our students, we seek to balance this by going to great pains in orienting our students and in preparing them to set clear, measurable goals for themselves in each learning covenant. We also rely heavily on the wisdom and expertise of denominational representatives and field education mentors to guide students in their goal setting.

Evaluation of Goals

While this topic will be covered in detail by a colleague in a later chapter, I wish to emphasize the importance of evaluation in goal setting. A well-thought-through learning covenant at the beginning and a corresponding evaluation at the end form sturdy "bookends" for students' field experiences. Evaluation helps complete the loop of learning. Like all field education programs, we receive end-of-term or end-of-unit progress reports and evaluations. It is here that students can report their progress on meeting their goals, and, even more importantly, through the process they get to spend meaningful time with their mentor in reflection not only on their specific goals but also on their goal-setting skills in general. Evaluation becomes a helpful and healthy reflection tool in itself.

It is a glorious thing when students see how they have been able to accomplish growth goals with the help of God! It is also a wonderful thing when they learn that it is all right to make adjustments to their goals in light of the realities of life and ministry, their responsibilities, and their limitations. Although I ask mentors to give a suggested grade for a student's unit (though by no means do all field education programs do this), I also stress that a grade not be based correspondingly on whether the student has absolutely met his or her personal goals completely or not. God's deeper goals may very well have been met for that student as he or she has learned important experiential lessons about ministry, self, God, and God's call through the process.

Prayer of Transformation

Dear Lord, thank you that you are at work within us both to will and to do that which pleases you (Phil. 2:13). Please help us to set goals worthy of Christ and of his call in my life. In this way help each of us to love you with all of our heart, soul, mind, and strength. Amen.

Reflection Questions

1. What are the positive benefits of goal setting?

2. How can goals and objectives be adjusted for different personality types?

3. Look at Matthew 22:37 and Mark 12:30. How do you love the Lord with all of your mind?

4. What are the three sections of a learning covenant or contract? Would you consider these sufficient or would you add or subtract any elements?

5. Look at Isaiah 55:8–9. How can you view your own responsible planning within the context of God's sovereignty?

Further Reading

Pyle, William T., and Mary Alice Seals, eds. *Experiencing Ministry Supervision: A Field-Based Approach.* Nashville: Broadman & Holman, 1995.

Zachary, Lois. *The Mentor's Guide: Facilitating Effective Learning Relationships.* San Francisco: Jossey-Bass, 2000.

Chapter 8

The Mentor Supervisory Meeting

THE HEART OF FIELD EDUCATION

HARLEY ATKINSON

*And what you have heard from me in the presence of many
witnesses entrust to faithful men who will be able to teach
others also. (2 Tim. 2:2)*

A weekly meeting or conference between the mentor and student might
very well be the difference between a good and a great field education
experience. Field education involves a relationship between a student and
a mentor whereby they agree to work together for the purpose of helping
the student in personal growth and professional development. Such a relationship demands mutual reflection, evaluation, stimulation, encouragement, correction, guidance, and prayer, all of which can be greatly amplified
during a weekly encounter.[1]

---

1. Many of the ideas and the outline for this chapter are drawn from an unpublished internship manual prepared by Canadian Bible College/Canadian Theological Seminary under
the direction of Marilyn Veley.

While a portion of the time a mentor and student spend together can be unstructured, most of the sessions should include some sort of agenda. In other words, the mentor and the student share the responsibility of bringing specific items to the meeting. Since the conference is designed for the benefit of the student, he or she should be ready each week to share an account of the previous week's activities and related issues. Likewise, the mentor should come prepared to discuss or analyze with the student facets of learning experiences he or she may have encountered in the past week and various topics related to ministry. Carefully intertwined throughout the selection of topics should be a strategy for evaluation.

A Word on Mentoring

While this chapter is concerned primarily with the regular meeting that should take place with the mentor and student, a few words are in order regarding mentoring.[2] Successful people, Ted Engstrom reminds us, never reach their goals without the enabling of a contingent of counselors who constitute a network of relationships.[3] One type of relationship that emerges in any discussion on leadership development today is the mentoring relationship. Mentoring is described by Engstrom as "the process of developing a man or woman to his or her maximum potential in Jesus Christ in every vocation."[4] The term *mentor* originates in Homer's *Odyssey* and in contemporary language depicts a wise and helpful friend, teacher, or leader "who uses his or her experience to show others how best to walk life's path, to accomplish goals and meet life's challenges."[5]

For centuries, a form of mentoring has been employed in the apprentice system in which young tradesmen would learn their trade under an experienced craftsman. In like manner, mentoring is germane to the field education process as the mentor passes on his or her knowledge, skill, and experience to the younger and less-experienced student. Mentoring a young man or woman who is heading toward ministry is a high calling, thus there are several qualities an effective mentor should possess. Surely, this is not an exhaustive list, but effectiveness in mentoring will be determined to a large degree on the ability to exhibit these qualifications:

1. Good supervising mentors possess significant expertise and ministry skills. It would be difficult to learn about ministry from someone who lacks expertise.

---

2. A more detailed discussion on the role and qualities of a mentor is found in chapter 6, "Mentoring: The Opportunity to Leave a Legacy," and chapter 18, "Equipping Mentors to Leave a Legacy."

3. Ted Engstrom, *The Fine Art of Mentoring* (Brentwood, TN: Wolgemuth & Hyatt, 1989), 3.

4. Ibid., 4.

5. Kenneth Gangel, *Team Leadership in Christian Ministry: Using Multiple Gifts to Build a Unified Vision* (Chicago: Moody, 1997), 257.

2. Good mentors are excited about sharing their expertise and skills with men and women who are heading into a similar field of ministry.

3. Good mentors are trusted and respected by their peers.

4. Good mentors are passionate about ministry and are committed to it.

5. Good mentors have a sense of vision about their ministry.

6. Good mentors are able to give good advice and sound counsel related to the student's ministry career.

7. Good mentors challenge their students to achieve greater performance.

8. Good mentors protect their students from harmful interference and criticism of others.[6]

Again, the process of mentoring is the process of developing an individual toward his or her maximum potential in Jesus Christ. The question for the mentor is, *How can I be most effective in a mentoring relationship with my student?* In addition to exhibiting the qualifications mentioned above, here are ten suggestions that will help make for a better mentoring relationship, and subsequently more productive meetings.[7]

Be Objective
While relationship is important in mentoring, the dynamic can be hurt if the mentor is too involved subjectively. The mentor should demonstrate the ability to see strengths and weaknesses clearly and to be candid with the student and be able to say, "This is what I see in your life."

Be Honest
The student's role is to absorb and learn as much as possible by observing and hearing from the mentor. Consequently, the task of the mentor is, with candidness and honesty, to help the student by telling that student things about himself or herself and his or her ministry that the student will need to hear. Mentoring is "a little like being a loving uncle or aunt, someone who will take you aside on occasion and tell you things you need to hear but frankly don't necessarily want to hear."[8]

---

6. Craig Donovan and Jim Garnett, *Internships for Dummies* (New York: Hungry Minds, 2001), 219.

7. Engstrom, *Fine Art of Mentoring*, 103–8.

8. Bobb Biehl, *Mentoring: Confidence in Finding a Mentor and Becoming One* (Nashville: Broadman & Holman, 1996), 100.

Be a Model

To be a role model in the context of field education means to demonstrate a commitment to ministry with a whole life posture or mind-set. Furthermore, it means the mentor can ask, "What did you learn by watching me as well as by listening to me?"[9]

Be Committed

To be successful as a mentor, one must be committed to giving away his or her life for the benefit of the student. The supervising mentor might ask himself or herself several questions: *Am I committed to the development of the student? Do I evidence a capacity for serving others? Do I have a dynamic balance between my needs and the needs of others? Or does everything revolve around my needs and me?*[10]

Be Open and Transparent

Good mentors are authentic. The student must see humanity—genuineness, transparency, and openness—evidenced in the life of the mentor.

Be a Teacher

While we should not equate mentoring with teaching, mentoring certainly includes teaching. Thus in a mentoring situation, teaching is much more than imparting knowledge. It may include passing on knowledge to a student, but more so it means helping that person raise his or her level of skill and lifestyle behaviors. For example, a student may have been taught the principles of effective sermon delivery and may even have delivered a sermon in class. Now, in the field education context, the student needs mentorship to help him implement the principles of effective preaching in a real situation.

Believe in the Student

There is a certain amount of risk involved in investing time, energy, resources, and emotions in mentoring a student. There is no guarantee that a student is going to turn out to be a worthy candidate for ministry, but one can increase the probability of success in a student's future by believing in his or her potential. Bobby Clinton describes this dimension of good mentoring in this manner:

> Mentors are people who can readily see potential in a person. They can tolerate mistakes, brashness, abrasiveness, etc., in order to see potential developed. They are flexible and patient, recognizing that it takes time and experience for a person to

---

9. Ibid.

10. Howard Hendricks and William Hendricks, *As Iron Sharpens Iron: Building Character in a Mentoring Relationship* (Chicago: Moody, 1995), 71.

develop. They have vision and ability to see down the road and suggest next steps that a protégé needs for development. And they usually have a gift-mix that includes one or more of the encouragement spiritual gifts: mercy, giving, exhortation, faith, word of wisdom.[11]

Envision the Student's Future

The mentor can help the student answer the question *How can I make a significant impact for God in my future and in my ministry?* Engstrom tells us how one can do that:

> Look into the eyes of your mentoree and see what he feels in his heart but has never thought yet in his head. He might feel like he has tremendous potential but will not allow himself to think that yet. He places limits on himself that the mentor has to eliminate. Help your protégé to see what you feel is his potential, even though he might not yet see it. Put that into words, don't just think it.[12]

Be Successful in the Eyes of the Student

It is important that the student feels that the mentor is successful at what he or she does—that he or she is a good youth pastor or dynamic preacher or outstanding minister to children. A student should feel that his or her mentor is someone the student would like to emulate in some ways.

Be Teachable

While this may seem an odd condition for effective mentoring, it is nonetheless a helpful quality. While it is indeed the responsibility of the student to learn, a teachable spirit on behalf of the mentor is helpful in at least two ways. First, if the mentor remains teachable, he or she models an attribute the mentor wishes the student to have. Second, the mentor may in fact learn from the student. A student well into his or her college or seminary preparation for ministry could very well have learned fresh insights about ministry that a supervising mentor may not be aware of. It would be detrimental to a mentoring relationship, as well as one's own ministry, to reject the student's insights based on the fact that he or she is simply a student, while the mentor is a "seasoned" pastor or minister.

The Supervisory Meeting and Facets of Mentorship

The field education experience will vary from student to student; but in any situation, there will be several facets of mentorship that emerge in

---

11. J. Robert Clinton, *The Making of a Leader* (Colorado Springs: NavPress, 1988), 131.

12. Engstrom, *Fine Art of Mentoring*, 107.

the regular supervisory meeting. The primary objective of the supervisory meeting is to offer the mentor an opportunity to assist the student in analyzing his or her ministry skills. However, the meeting also affords the mentor and student the occasion to address issues related to personal development, vocational calling, and theology.

Ministry Skills

Since one of the major objectives of field education is that the student experience ministry firsthand, it should be clearly understood that the mentor will spend considerable time assisting the student in analyzing his or her ministry skills. The supervisory meeting is the occasion when the mentor and student talk about the sermon, the youth talk, the children's sermon, the Sunday school lesson, and so forth. Were the announcements communicated clearly? Did the youth talk meet the needs of adolescents? How could the discipline problem be handled better? Was the student dressed appropriately for hospital visitation?

Personal Development

The weekly conference is an ideal context to talk about the student's personal growth or development. The mentor might address issues related to personality and temperament (e.g., anger control, patience, assertiveness), lifestyle habits (e.g., time management), or spiritual disciplines (e.g., prayer, Bible reading, fasting, worship). If the academic institution requires the student to complete an assignment related to personal development, this would be an opportune time to integrate it into the field education experience.

Call to Ministry

Another objective of field education is that the student will acquire a sense of confirmation toward his or her calling to a particular ministry or vocation.[13] The mentor can help the student answer questions such as:

- Is this type of ministry for me?
- Am I really called to serve God as pastor (or youth pastor, missionary, children's pastor, Christian education pastor, etc.)?
- How can I know the will of God for my life?

Theological Reflections

As the student interacts more and more with people in ministry contexts, he or she should increasingly see the relevance of biblical doctrines such as sin, grace, faith, and love. In addition, the mentor should be prepared to challenge the student to think theologically about various

---

13. See chapter 1, "Field Education and Vocational Discernment," for additional information.

aspects of ministry and relate theology to experience.[14] The mentor can assist the student in thinking theologically about ministry with questions such as:

- How is the Holy Spirit involved in the teaching/learning or preaching experience?
- Why is it important that children, youth, or adults have a proper concept of who God is?
- How do I confront sin in the life of an individual?
- What does it mean to be created in God's image? How is *imago Dei* related to self-worth?
- How do you distinguish between adolescent foolishness and sin?
- Why is it especially important to have a proper view of Scripture in a postmodern world?
- How do I help individuals work through failures in the Christian life? How does grace fit in?
- How do my theological presuppositions affect my ministry practice?

Addressing Difficult Situations

No doubt the ministry student will experience one or more difficult circumstances in his or her field education experience. It could be a run-in with a parent of one of the teenagers in the youth group, a disagreement with another staff person, or a confrontation with an elder or board member. If the situation has not been addressed already, the scheduled conference might be an ideal time to revisit the circumstances. The mentor should consider the following steps in assisting the student in working through a difficult situation.[15]

Step One—Facts

The mentor should check for the facts and clarify the details of the difficult situation. The mentor needs to clearly understand the circumstances surrounding the situation.

Step Two—Feelings

The mentor ought to be aware of the feelings the student has toward the other individuals involved in the experience. The mentor also should be aware of the feelings he or she holds toward the student and the event in which the student is involved.

Step Three—Reflection

The mentor can ask the student to reflect on the situation. The mentor

---

14. See chapter 3, "Field Education and Theological Reflection in an Evangelical Tradition," for additional information.

15. Engstrom, *Fine Art of Mentoring*, 107.

should encourage the student to share any hunches about the other people involved and to explore alternative courses of action she might have taken.

Step Four—Heart of the Problem

The mentor needs to help the student focus on the heart of the problem. The mentor can discuss how the student might have averted the problem by responding in different ways.

Step Five—Application

Finally, the mentor assists the student in making generalizations in terms of similar situations that might come up in the future. Part of supervising or mentoring is helping the student learn from various and diverse experiences so that the student will choose more competent responses to comparable ministry situations in the future.

Evaluating the Progress of the Student

A crucial feature of any field experience and critical component of the supervisory role is the evaluation of the student.[16] Lynne Schafer Gross proposes that "a good supervisor will let the student know how she or he is perceived on such traits as accuracy, dependability, willingness, quality of work, initiative, maturity, communicating about job-related problems, promptness, following instructions, relationships with others, ability to learn, and professional potential."[17]

There are a number of reasons for evaluating students, the most obvious one being to obtain and provide scores for final grades. However, evaluation also serves additional purposes. First, evaluation serves as an indicator as to where the student might need assistance or special help. Second, evaluation at a predetermined point in the process aids the student in seeing how far he or she has progressed since the onset of the field education experience. Third, evaluation might serve as an indicator to determine whether the student is ready to move on to another level or different responsibility. Fourth, evaluation might help the mentor report to the academic institution how well the student is doing. Finally and as already mentioned, the academic institution may use the evaluative input of the mentor to determine a grade the student will receive for completing the field education assignment.

Evaluation of a student's experience can be of two kinds—summative or formative. *Summative* evaluation occurs at the end of the field education and summarizes what the student has learned or accomplished by the time he or she has completed the experience. The results of the evaluation will

---

16. See chapter 11, "Assessment and Evaluation in Field Education," for a more detailed discussion on this topic.

17. Lynn Schafer Gross, *The Internship Experience* (Prospect Heights, IL: Waveland, 1987), 27.

normally be shared with the academic institution and possibly used to assess the final grade. *Formative* evaluation, on the other hand, occurs during the field education. Its purpose is to give the student feedback about his or her progress and growth. Usually the results of formative evaluation are shared only between the student and the mentor and serve to aid the student in determining what he or she needs to work on during the remainder of the field education. The supervisory meeting offers an ideal context for this type of evaluation.

College and seminary students, like other adults, often have fragile egos, and the responsibility of the supervisor, as evaluator, is to provide critical feedback to the student without causing undo anxiety and defensiveness. Adult education expert Stephen Brookfield suggests that a helpful evaluation process should include nine characteristics, to which Tara Fenwick and Jim Parsons add a tenth.[18]

1. *Clarity.* The mentor must make evaluative judgments with as much clarity as possible. The student should know at the outset what the criteria for evaluating his or her efforts are, and the mentor should articulate comments in terms and language the student understands.

2. *Immediacy.* When assessing a particular performance or activity, the mentor should make evaluations as soon after the event as possible. As learners, students will be best able to process and incorporate suggestions into their skill while the activity is still fresh in their memories.

3. *Regularity.* The mentor should make regular comments on the progress of the student's efforts (this is a good argument for having weekly meetings). Rather than employing only midpoint and end-of-the-field-education evaluations, ongoing assessment delivers more immediate information and, because of frequency, becomes less threatening.

4. *Accessibility.* It is important that the mentor is available as much as possible to the student for discussion regarding evaluations. The student no doubt will want clarification and will want to be able to talk about concerns or address any aspects of the evaluation that concerns him or her.

5. *Individualized.* It is essential that the mentor give clearly personalized attention to the student's efforts. However, it must be done in such a manner that the student realizes his or her whole being or personality is not under attack.

6. *Affirming.* Before addressing any issues of concern, the wise mentor will acknowledge whatever the student has achieved to this point. Such an evaluative strategy demonstrates that the mentor recognizes that which the student is doing well, while at the same time drawing attention to what might need improvement.

---

18. Stephen Brookfield, *The Skilled Teacher* (San Francisco: Jossey-Bass, 1990), 139–41; Tara Fenwick and Jim Parsons, *The Art of Evaluation* (Toronto: Thompson, 2000), 24.

7. *Future-oriented.* If evaluations are indeed to be of any value to the student, the mentor must give clear and specific suggestions to the student as to what he or she might do to improve performance or skills in the future. This, of course, is the raison d'etre for evaluation procedures.

8. *Justifiable.* The mentor must carefully describe how attending to the critique is in the best interest of the student. Students will want to know why they are being evaluated and that the reasons rise out of a concern for their development.

9. *Educative.* Ultimately, the purpose of evaluation is to help the student develop—both personally and professionally. Students may feel warmed or shamed by evaluations, but the important question is, are they educative?

10. *Selective.* Too much critique can be overwhelming to a student. Thus, it is important to focus on a few areas the student can work on. After all, any individual cannot work on or improve everything at once.

Most educational institutions will provide a guide for midpoint or formative evaluation. Furthermore, chapter 11 of this text, "Assessment and Evaluation in Field Education," will provide additional evaluative tools and insights for the mentor.

Ministry-Related Topics

Figure 8.1 contains a number of ministry-related topics that the mentor might cover with the student during the regular supervisory conferences. The list is designed to provide suggestions for dialogue rather than curriculum that must be covered, and it assumes a local church setting. As the mentor chooses topics for discussion, he or she should take into consideration criteria such as the student's major, future ministry goals, and personal interests. The mentor might go over the topics with the student in the initial session and determine what will be addressed over the course of the field education. Each topic includes several points to cover or questions designed to facilitate discussion.

Essentials of an Effective Supervisory Meeting

The entire process thus far described becomes the subject matter for the regular supervisory meeting. For supervisory meetings to reach their maximum potential, it is necessary that the mentor pay close attention to several essentials in addition to the guidelines given to this point.

Purpose

Like all meetings, the weekly supervisory meeting should serve a clear purpose and stay on the prescribed course. No one—including students—likes to be surprised by an unexpected item or confrontation. The purpose of the weekly supervisory meeting, as described earlier, is to assist the student in personal and professional development. It further exists to provide opportunity for reflection, evaluation, stimulation, encouragement, correction, guidance, and prayer.

Figure 8.1. Ministry Topics for Supervisory Conferences

Baptism
- What is the meaning and significance of baptism?
- What is the appropriate mode of baptism?
- How do you prepare an individual for baptism?

Communion
- When should Communion be served?
- How often should Communion be observed?
- Who should partake in Communion?
- What are some appropriate Scripture passages to use in the Communion service?
- How do you accommodate the sick and shut-ins?

Funerals
- What are the minister's responsibilities on the initial visit to the home of the deceased?
- How does the minister help the family with funeral arrangements?
- What is the order of a funeral service?
- How does the minister conduct the graveside service?

Weddings
- What are the state/provincial laws regulating marriage?
- What are the responsibilities for premarital counseling? How often should a pastor meet with a couple? What should be covered in the counseling sessions?

Organization and Administration
- What are the various types of church government?
- How is this church governed?
- What are the roles and responsibilities of elders and deacons?
- How does a church do long-range planning? Short-range?
- How important is goal setting in church ministry?

Leadership
- What is leadership?
- What are the qualities of an effective leader?

Hospital Visitation
- What do you say to a patient and family members during a hospital visit?

- What should be the length of a hospital visit?
- How can you involve laypeople in hospital visitation?

Pastoral Counseling
- What is the role of the minister as counselor?
- What are some ethical guidelines for counseling?
- What place should counseling play in a minister's overall workload? How do you schedule for counseling?
- When should a minister refer?
- How do you counsel individuals of the opposite gender?

The Minister's Personal Life
- How does the family fit into the minister's list of priorities?
- Does the minister take a day off? How do you protect that day?
- What kind of relationships should the minister have with people in the church? Should the minister have close friends in the church?
- How should a devotional life fit into the minister's schedule?

Sermon Preparation
- How do you prepare a long-range sermon calendar?
- What books should be in a pastor's library, especially for sermon preparation?
- How do you find good illustrations?

Evangelism
- How do we equip and mobilize individuals for personal evangelism?
- What are some strategies for reaching the lost?
- How do we best reach the lost in contemporary society?

Youth Ministry
- How does youth ministry fit into the contemporary church?
- What are some current youth ministry models?
- What are some key components for effective youth ministry?

Children's Ministry
- How does children's ministry fit into the contemporary church?
- What programs should be a part of an effective children's ministry?
- How do you recruit for children's workers? What precautions should one take in recruiting workers?

Christian Education
- What is Christian education?

- How does Christian education fit into the contemporary church?
- How do you recruit teachers? Do you look only for those with the spiritual gift of teaching?
- What are the qualities of a good teacher?
- How do small groups fit into the overall Christian education program?

World Missions
- How does world missions fit into the local church program?
- How do you create an interest in world missions?

Denominational Relations
- What is the relationship of the local church to the denomination?
- What are the levels of denominational structure (e.g., district, national headquarters)?
- What are some distinctives of your denomination?

Agenda

While an agenda for a two-party encounter will not be quite as crucial as it might be for a larger group such as a committee or church board, a meeting outline that is sent to the student beforehand will ward off any unwanted surprises. If the agenda items are of significance and the meeting follows the agenda, it ensures a more meaningful experience for the student and mentor alike. As indicated earlier, the agenda should include items related to the following: professional development (ministry skills, personal growth, call to ministry, and theology), difficult circumstances that might have occurred during the week, evaluation of the student's progress, and, as time permits, reflective dialogue related to various and appropriate ministry topics.

Preparation

Both the mentor and the student should come to the meeting well prepared. Meeting with a clearly identified purpose and having a written agenda will go a long way toward being prepared. The agenda should be developed far enough in advance to give both the mentor and the student the opportunity to come to the meeting prepared. Any necessary supporting documents should accompany the agenda to the student.[19]

Student Involvement

Weekly supervisory meetings that are characterized by mutual respect

---

19. Michael Anthony, "Working with Boards and Committees," in *Management Essentials for Christian Ministries*, ed. Michael J. Anthony and James Estep Jr. (Nashville: Broadman & Holman, 2005), 372–73.

and honest discussion will be most effective. If students are in any manner intimidated or if they are restricted from asking tough questions themselves, then the whole purpose of the weekly meeting will be undermined. The mentor should encourage the student to participate in the discussion, ask relevant questions, and freely share ideas and opinions. If there is a disagreement between the mentor and the student, the mentor should model a manner or approach to the difference that is inoffensive or innocuous.[20]

Meeting Place

The physical surroundings of the meeting place will either contribute to or detract from the effectiveness of the encounter. A restaurant or coffee shop will usually provide a friendly or relaxed atmosphere for discussion, unless the agenda contains items that are sensitive or private in nature. In the case that personal or confidential information is being discussed, the student may feel ill at ease in a public setting. The mentor's office serves as another meeting option, though the student may feel intimidated in such a setting. A third possibility is a neutral conference room. Wherever the meeting takes place, it should be reasonably quiet, well lit, temperature controlled, and equipped with comfortable chairs.[21]

Effective Communication

The final component of a successful supervisory meeting is effective communication. From the perspective of the field education mentor, effective interpersonal communication is characterized by at least three skills: attending, asking good questions, and responding.[22]

Attending

Attending is the skill or ability to listen attentively. It is at least as important as the ability to talk, if not of more value. Principles of active listening are legion, but some key behaviors that will lead to more effective communication in the supervisory meeting are summarized as follows:

- Carefully read nonverbal as well as verbal messages.
- Reserve judgment on the student until the entire message is heard.
- Avoid environmental and mental distractions.
- Do not bias the message through personal prejudices or value judgments.
- Acknowledge the student through verbal and nonverbal responses.
- Listen carefully to the intent of the student.

---

20. Ibid., 372.
21. Ibid., 373.
22. Harley Atkinson, *The Power of Small Groups in Christian Education* (Nappanee, IN: Evangel, 2002), 277–88.

Asking Good Questions

One of the keys to stimulating effective dialogue is asking good questions. The ancient art of Socratic questioning will help the field education mentor kindle helpful discussion with the student. In Socratic questioning, the mentor probes the meaning, justification, logic, or strength of a claim, position, or line of reasoning the student may make.

There are several categories of questions for the supervisor to draw from:

- Questions of clarification (What do you mean when you say . . . ?)
- Questions that probe assumptions (It seems that you are assuming . . . Is that correct?)
- Questions that investigate reasons and evidence (How did you come to that conclusion? or How do you know that . . . ?)
- Questions related to viewpoints (Does anyone else see this differently?)
- Questions that explore implications (If we were to follow that procedure, what might happen in our youth ministry?)
- Questions in response to a question (Why is this question so critical to understanding the nature of God?)[23]

Responding

How the mentor responds to the student in discussion is the third component to effective communication in the supervisory meeting. The mentor plays a critical role in creating a positive communication climate by the way he or she responds verbally and nonverbally to the student.

First, it is important to allow for silence. While it is sometimes difficult to endure prolonged silence, there are usually good reasons for a delayed response. Perhaps the query poses a difficulty and a good response demands some reflective thinking. Or maybe the potential response is risky or sensitive and the student wants to be careful in wording the answer.

Second, avoiding responses that communicate a message of nonacceptance will help create a positive communication climate. Nonaccepting messages include, but are not limited to, ordering ("You have to . . ."), threatening ("You better . . ."), moralizing ("It is your responsibility to . . ."), blaming ("It is your fault that . . ."), shaming ("How foolish can you be to . . ."), analyzing ("You know, your problem is . . ."), and interrogating ("Why did you . . . ?").[24]

Third, the mentor must be aware of the nonverbal cues he or she is sending. The mentor can convey positiveness through nonverbal behavior such as facial and vocal expressions, posture, hand gestures, and eye contact.

---

23. Richard Paul, *Critical Thinking*, 2nd ed. (Santa Rosa, CA: Foundation for Critical Thinking, 1992), 367–68.
24. Andrew Wolvin and Carolyn Gwynn Coakly, *Listening*, 4th ed. (Dubuque, IA: Brown, 1992), 289.

Likewise, he or she can send silent, negative messages that may discourage the student from developing a positive response in the meeting.

Fourth, the mentor must ensure verbal and nonverbal messages are congruent with each other. Every interpersonal communication experience involves both verbal and nonverbal messages, and generally, the messages are harmonious. So if the mentor tells the student he or she appreciates the student's work, the mentor reinforces the message by smiling and giving eye contact. If, on the other hand, the mentor says, "That was a job well done," but does so with a sneer or a roll of the eyes, the meaning is confused by different messages sent simultaneously.[25]

Finally, the mentor should concentrate on making his or her messages complete and specific. Johnson and Johnson remind us that while this may be an obvious supposition, a speaker often "will not communicate the frame of reference he is taking, the assumptions he is making, the intentions he has in communication, or the leaps in thinking he is making. Thus while a person may hear the words she will not comprehend the meaning of the message."[26]

---

25. David Johnson and Frank Johnson, *Joining Together* (Englewood Cliffs, NJ: Prentice-Hall, 1975), 114.

26. Ibid.

Prayer of Transformation

Heavenly Father, what an awesome responsibility you have given us—to mentor students in the ways of ministry. We are humbled that you would entrust us with such a noble and significant task. May the Holy Spirit guide us in the words we choose, the comments we make, and the insights we share in our weekly meetings. May each meeting be a blessed and fruitful experience. We pray that we would be willing to listen as well as speak, that we would be learners as well as teachers. Most of all, we pray that you would be honored in whatever is said and done in each meeting. Amen.

Reflection Questions

1. Why might the weekly meeting or conference be the difference between a good internship and a great internship?

2. If a student is intimidated in any way by his or her mentor, the weekly meeting will achieve less-than-desired results. What can the mentor do to make the experience as nonthreatening and productive as possible?

3. A number of ideas were offered in the chapter as to what might be addressed in the weekly meeting. Can you think of any other topics or issues that you might deal with?

Further Reading

English, Leona. *Mentoring in Religious Education.* Birmingham, AL: Religious Education Press, 1981.

Nichols, Michael. *The Lost Art of Listening.* New York: Guilford Press, 1995.

Sanders, Martin. *The Power of Mentoring.* Camp Hill, PA: Christian Publications, 2004.

Chapter 9

The Use of Case Studies in Field Education

WILLIAM TORGESEN

For the LORD gives wisdom;
from his mouth come knowledge and understanding;
he stores up sound wisdom for the upright;
he is a shield to those who walk in integrity,
guarding the paths of justice
and watching over the way of his saints.
Then you will understand righteousness and justice
and equity, every good path. (Prov. 2:6–9)

A young pastor enters into ministry, and within the first year he faces a head-on collision with a longtime board member who makes it abundantly clear that this bright-eyed young pastor answers to him, and to him alone. Quickly the bright eyes become blurry as the young pastor finds himself in a state of panic. What should he do?

An associate pastor has been serving in the church for five years under the leadership of a seasoned senior pastor. But now that beloved senior pastor has moved on, and the new pastor does not like the way the associate is doing ministry. The associate pastor does not know what he is doing wrong, but he is deeply discouraged and depressed. He ponders the options and begins to question whether this is the time for him to leave.

A woman takes a staff position with a mission organization, only to discover that the director does not get along with women. She soon realizes that there has been a long history of women being mistreated by this individual and his associates. She wonders how she could have missed such an obvious fault and what she could have done differently to avoid this mistake. Most of all she wonders what can be done to address this abusive situation.

These stories represent real issues and raise real questions. The greater question flowing from each ministry snapshot is simply this: What would you do?

Making a Case for Case Studies

These scenarios and many others like them prove that ministry can be complex and confusing. Each story represents a different situation consisting of different details, dynamics, and dimensions. Each story is placed in a unique context, and therefore it represents a unique case. Each case consists of individuals and groups that have their own history, language, customs, norms, and behaviors. In every instance we find individuals with their own personality styles and traits that ultimately drive their individual responses and reactions. Some respond passively; others react aggressively. In each situation we find ourselves trying to discern what a person could have done differently in his or her unique circumstance or what the church should have done to prevent such a crisis in the first place. In each encounter we are left to discover what we would have done given the same set of circumstances. That discovery leads us to a determination, and that determination influences the decisions we will make in the future. That is the role of the case study.

A case study by definition is a written story of a real event in real time with real people facing a very real problem.[1] Its very design presses us into the story so that we become participants in the drama. As we gather the facts and details of the story, we begin to interact as if we were in the narrative itself. Soon we find ourselves diving headlong into the crisis. As we wade through the confusion, we begin to think more clearly in terms of our own convictions and core values. Through the process we learn to make critical observations that will inform our decisions and actions should we face a similar situation in the future. Case studies can help us to learn from the mistakes and misfortunes of others, so that we do not repeat the same mistakes and experience the same pain as those who have gone before us. It is often said that history repeats itself, but the advantage of using case studies is that it does not always have to!

Case studies themselves have a long history in education. In 1870 the Harvard Law School began to use case studies as a tool to help legal students

---

1. William T. Pyle and Mary Alice Seals, "Tools for Data Gathering," in *Experiencing Ministry Supervision: A Field-Based Approach*, ed. William T. Pyle and Mary Alice Seals (Nashville: Broadman & Holman, 1995), 101.

to better understand sound principles of law. Students were required to interact with actual legal cases and then to reflect upon the dynamics and details of each case itself. The goal of such instruction was for the student to understand how and why legal decisions were made. The Harvard Business School picked up on this idea and began to use case studies to train their students for business management. Students were required to analyze real events from the business world in order to develop their capacity to make sound business decisions in the corporate world.[2] In both cases, the goal of the educational process was to allow students to interact with an actual event related to their field of study in order to prepare them for the future. In the 1960s case studies found their way into the theological schools and institutions. A decade later the Association for Case Studies was founded, and the use of case studies became normative for theological training among field educators.

Today, case studies can be found that address a variety of topics within a variety of ministry contexts. There are case studies that focus on administrative issues, conflict management, ethical dilemmas, racial divides, staffing issues, community development, family struggles, Christian values, and the list goes on and on. Case studies have been written within the context of the church, parachurch, mission, and social organizations. They can cover issues ranging from fighting among the staff to the financial mismanagement by a board member in the church. Case studies also address the difficult dilemmas we face in our culture today such as sexual abuse, suicide, or reaching out to the person with AIDS. They can present the painful realities of ministry, such as pastoral failure, pastoral depression, or even pastoral abuse. In each and every case, the goal of the case study is to bring one face-to-face with the realities of life and ministry and allow the student to wrestle with the tensions encountered.

Moving from Theological Reflection to Ministry Application

The goal of theological education is not only to help students think critically and biblically but also to help them live lives that are theocentric and Christocentric.[3] As students engage in theological truth within the classroom, they often find themselves struggling with the ability to transfer that content from theory into practice. As students read through book after book relating to ministry, they wrestle with what to do in ministry once they have graduated. In many instances, students are given vast amounts of information in a short period of time, and they have little time to process that knowledge or to consider how to put such information into practice. Case studies can provide a way to help students wrestle through their theological

---

2. Raymond Bystrom, *Slices of Ministry: The Case Study Method of Teaching and Learning* (Fresno: Pacific Seminary, 2005), 1–2.

3. For further discussion, see chapter 3, "Field Education and Theological Reflection in an Evangelical Tradition."

questions (presuppositions and tensions), to formulate their ministry convictions, and to grow in their ministry skill development.

Much like the goal of theological education, the goal of a case study is to help the student not only to think but also to act. James and Evelyn Whitehead, in their book *Method in Ministry: Theological Reflection and Christian Ministry*, remind readers that the ultimate purpose for theological reflection is to bring people to the point of an active response.[4] In a very real sense, a case study begs for a decision to be made by the reader. As students work through a case study, it is imperative that they remember the process is not complete until they arrive at the place of application. William T. Pyle, in the book *Experiencing Ministry Supervision*, states that theological reflection must move from insight to action, and if possible to strategic implementation.[5]

Knowledge is simply not enough. What students need is sound, practical wisdom. Wisdom by definition is the appropriation of biblical truth into the whole of a person's being so that it permeates life, guides conduct, and forms character. In other words, wisdom shapes a person's life. In the same way, the wisdom gleaned from the use of a case study should shape the student's understanding of ministry, but it also should shape the decisions he or she will ultimately make in ministry. Mentors need to help students to dig deep into the story. As mentors do this, they will help the students to attain the wisdom needed to navigate the difficult demands of ministry. If mentors can accomplish this task, then case studies serve as a great tool in helping students to form and develop their own ministry convictions and competencies.

The Value of Case Studies

One of the benefits of case studies is that they can be used in a variety of contexts. They can be used in the classroom, in the church, or on the mission field. They can be used in a Sunday school class to teach about ethics or in a small group to teach about conflict and reconciliation. Case studies have been used for adult education, youth ministry, leadership development, counselor training, community development, and the list continues to grow. Case studies also have a wide audience. They can be used by professors, pastors, mentors, or board members as they work with students, interns, staff members, or members of the church. Another advantage of the case teaching method is that learning can take place on many levels. The student learns valuable lessons as he or she interacts with the case study, but the mentor learns through the process as well. It is not uncommon for the pastor or church leaders to find themselves reliving a difficult season

---

4. James Whitehead and Evelyn Eaton Whitehead, *Method in Ministry: Theological Reflection and Christian Ministry*, rev. ed. (Lanham, MD: Sheed & Ward, 1995), 86.

5. William T. Pyle, "Theological Reflection," in *Experiencing Ministry Supervision: A Field-Based Approach*, 123.

in ministry and, as a result, rethinking and retooling their own responses and perspectives. When processed in ministry groups, theological reflection takes place on a grander scale as the group learns to discern together.

While there is great flexibility in the use of case studies, several creative methods are provided for consideration as part of a case study portfolio. Each of these scenarios have been tried and tested in the classroom, in the church, and within the context of mentoring relationships. While the examples are not exhaustive in scope, they do provide fuel for thought and creativity.

The Use of Case Studies for Conflict Management

One of the most effective ways to use the case study method is in the area of conflict management. It has been my experience that many students feel inadequate when it comes to the reality of church conflict. Case studies can be used to help students gain a glimpse into the various conflict issues that exist in the context of ministry. One way to use the case study in the context of a classroom is to have the students form into ministry groups, read through the case study, and then reflect upon the various aspects of the case together as a group. In an internship context, the students could join in a leadership group consisting of future leaders or a peer group from the church and accomplish the same results. As students study the case, they are encouraged to look at the individuals involved, the history of the conflict, the culture of the church, and the facts involved in the case itself.

While every case study has a primary focus of discussion, it is not uncommon to find smaller tensions working beneath the surface. As students study the case, they can often find layers of information that feed into the dynamics of the conflict. Students are asked to identify any relational conflict, congregational conflict, organizational conflict, systemic conflict, and then any staff infection. Students and mentors could be provided a rubric to help them work through the case (see figure 9.1). Such a rubric can help the students to consider more than just the obvious, but it also provides a standard for grading any projects.

Students can then begin to interact with the case study in several ways. They can think in terms of what could have been done to prevent the conflict from occurring in the first place. Second, they can consider what could be done to limit the conflict from spiraling out of control. Finally, they can process what could be done to bring about reconciliation and healing.

Once students have thoroughly diagnosed the conflict, they would be required to select from several projects. One option would be to prepare a plan for reconciliation that would first neutralize the existing conflict. Second, they would develop clear steps toward reconciliation. Then they would develop a strategy for resolving conflict in the future. Such a project would include addressing the steps they would take to resolve relational conflict between individuals, how they would address any congregational issues such as triangulation, and then the steps leadership would need to

Figure 9.1. Conflict Matrix

CONFLICTS	1	2	3	4	5
Relational Conflict Is there clear conflict between relationships? Is there a power issue among members of the church?	Student is unable to identify the relational conflicts involved in the case study.	Student is able to identify the significant relationships involved in the conflict but is unable to identify the cause and nature of the conflict.	Student is able to identify the key relationships involved and the root of the conflict, but is unable to identify the steps in order to neutralize the conflict.	Student is able to identify key relationships involved and the nature of the conflict, and is able to identify the steps to neutralize the conflict, but is unable to provide a plan for reconciliation and healing.	Student is able to identify the key relationships involved and the nature of the conflict, clearly understands the steps needed for reconciliation, and provides a plan for restoration and healing.
Congregational Conflict How is the congregation involved in the conflict? Is there politics involved? Long-standing members fighting with new members?	Student demonstrates no ability to identify the congregational conflict involved in the case study.	Student is able to identify the conflict involved in the congregation, but is not able to identify the cause and nature of the conflict.	Student is able to identify the key issues involved at the congregational level and the root of the conflict, but is unable to identify the steps in order to neutralize the conflict.	Student is able to identify key issues involved and the nature of the conflict, and is able to identify the steps to neutralize the conflict, but is unable to provide a plan for reconciliation and healing for the congregation.	Student is able to identify the key issues involved at the congregational level and the nature of the conflict, clearly understands the steps needed for reconciliation, and provides a plan for restoration and healing.
Organizational Conflict Is there administrative confusion aiding in the conflict? Lack clarity in job descriptions, poor policy, etc.	Student demonstrates no ability to identify the organizational conflict involved in the case study.	Student is able to identify the organizational conflict.	Student is able to identify the key issues involved within the organization and the root of the conflict, but is unable to identify the steps in order to neutralize the conflict.	Student is able to identify key organizational issues involved and the nature of the conflict, and is able to identify the steps to neutralize the conflict, but is unable to provide a plan for reconciliation and healing for the congregation.	Student is able to identify the key organizational issues involved at the congregational level and the nature of the conflict, clearly understands the steps needed for reconciliation, and provides a plan for restoration and healing.

Figure 9.1. Conflict Matrix (continued)

CONFLICTS	1	2	3	4	5
Systemic and Cultural Issues Are there outside influences? Are there denominational ties influencing the conflict? Are there strong family systems in place or history affecting the conflict? Are there ethnic or racial issues involved?	Student demonstrates no ability to identify the systemic issues involved in the conflict involved in the case study.	Student is able to identify the systemic issues.	Student is able to identify the key systemic issues involved within the congregation and how they relate to the conflict, but is unable to identify the steps in order to address the systemic dynamics.	Student is able to identify key systemic issues involved and how they relate to the conflict, and can identify the steps to address the systemic or cultural problems, but is unable to provide a plan for reconciliation and healing for the congregation.	Student is able to identify the key systemic issues involved at the congregational level and is able to identify the steps in order to address systemic or cultural problems, and provides a plan for restoration and healing.
Staff Infection Are there staffing issues involved in the conflict? Conflict between staff and board members?	Student demonstrates no ability to identify the staffing issues related to the conflict.	Student is able to identify staffing issues, but is unable to identify how these staffing issues relate to the larger conflict.	Student is able to identify staffing issues, and how they relate to the larger conflict, but is unable to identify how to address the staff infections.	Student is able to identify staffing issues and how they relate to the larger conflict, and is able identify the steps needed to neutralize the staffing conflict, but is unable to provide a plan for reconciliation and staff healing.	Student is able to identify staffing issues and how they relate to the larger conflict, and is able to identify the steps needed to neutralize the conflict, and has a clear plan for reconciliation and staff healing.
Conflict Management Overall understanding, diagnosing, and resolving conflict relationally and organizationally.	Student demonstrates no ability to manage conflict within relationships or the church.	Student demonstrates minimal ability to understand and manage conflict within relationships and the church.	Student demonstrates adequate ability to understand and manage conflict within relationships and the church.	Student demonstrates above average ability to understand and manage conflict within relationships and the church.	Student demonstrates exceptional ability to understand and manage conflict within relationships and the church.

take to move the ministry toward reconciliation. This might include steps to bring the congregation to a place of corporate repentance or to work the body through a season of spiritual healing. A unique by-product of working in ministry teams is that there is greater interaction of ideas and presuppositions, and this fosters a leadership environment and helps the students to better understand board and staff dynamics.

A similar project might be for the group to prepare a strategy for equipping the leadership and the church in the nature of conflict, the biblical response to conflict, the dynamics of church discipline, and the importance of reconciliation. Another group might be asked to write a philosophy of conflict management that is bathed in Scripture and describes the church's position and practice concerning church discipline. The projects themselves can take the form of a major paper, with each student taking one of the projects listed above, or the groups can present their projects to the class for discussion and feedback.

In the group discussion, one student provides the background to the case, including the name of the church, location, size, and makeup of the congregation. A second student would provide the history of the conflict, including significant individuals involved in the conflict. Another student would provide details that helped to provide fuel for the fire, or enabled the conflict to continue. A fourth student would provide the strategy for intervention to isolate the conflict and neutralize its effect. A fifth student would offer a plan to begin dealing with the conflict itself, working through the relational conflict and then providing a pathway for reconciliation. A final student would provide an overall strategy for bringing the whole church to a place where reconciliation becomes normative and part of the culture of the congregation. The presentation would then conclude with open discussion within the classroom. In a church context the peer group might present their project before the full board for feedback and affirmation.

Similar methods can be used individually with a student and his or her mentor. It has been my experience that when a student works through case studies with his or her mentor, the mentor soon takes the case study to the leadership board and the leadership board works through the process as well. The case study now becomes an equipping tool for the student as well as the church.

The Use of Case Studies for Administration

Case studies also can serve to help students develop their administrative abilities. Conflict often is the direct result of confusion and poor communication. Many times people do not know what to do, where to go, or how to get there. Staffing relationships deteriorate due to confusion over roles and responsibilities or goals and objectives. As students work through a case study, it is often clear that much of the conflict lies in poor administration. Organizational structure might be lacking, clear lines of authority could be unclear or nonexistent, or policies and procedures are clearly absent. As a result, the church or organization exists in an environment where discord and division is likely to occur. The tension is often a direct result of poor administration and management. It is not uncommon for a person to appear as if he or she is undermining the ministry when in fact the person is simply misguided or misinformed. At other times there are those who clearly take advantage of the confusion and push agendas through the cracks of the administrative walls of the church. In both cases, what is needed most are clear lines of communication, accountability, and organizational structure.

As always, the goal in using the case study is to move the student from the point of decision to a point of concrete application. One project might be for the student or group to develop a premarital and postmarital curriculum as a response to a case study addressing marital issues, or possibly a policy concerning divorce and remarriage. Another project might be to review a case that addresses declining attendance or a church that is stagnant. Here the student might identify the root causes for the stagnation, but the student also might prepare a plan for retooling the church. The student would need to address critical growth issues, determine how he or she might implement change in the culture of the church, and then provide a strategy for reaching the community that includes a plan for assimilation of new members.

Students could study a particular case to determine what administrative weaknesses are apparent or what management forms are clearly absent. The students can then create the organizational chart, ministry descriptions, definitions of roles and responsibilities, job descriptions, and even policies if the case calls for them. If the case demonstrates that the associate pastor is unclear of his role and responsibilities, then the students can create a job description that might fit that particular case setting. While the case study might not provide all the details necessary for the students to complete the job description, the lack of information forces the students to think beyond the surface and to consider what additional information would be vital to complete the project. When used like this, the case study moves the students from being reactive to being proactive as they work through the project.

One project that works well in a church setting is to have the student study a case where clear administrative details are lacking or insufficient. As the student recognizes the administrative voids in the case study, he or she soon realizes the damage that such voids can create within an organization or a staff. The student is now in the place to move to the point of application. With the help of the mentor, the student can be asked to help develop several key administrative articles for the church itself. This could take the form of creating several job descriptions, or possibly helping to write a policy manual for child safety. This then becomes a win-win situation as the church provides the experience for the student and allows the student to help in developing key documents for the church. The student learns why such administrative tools are needed, what happens when they are lacking, and how to create them when they are needed.

A great resource for working through administrative conflict is the book by David Luecke and Samuel Southard titled *Pastoral Administration: Integrating Ministry and Management in the Church*. Several case studies are provided that deal directly with management issues in the local church.[6] Michael Anthony's book *The Effective Church Board: A Handbook for Mentoring and Training Servant Leaders* also contains several case studies addressing such topics as financial difficulties and boardroom division.[7] The case studies themselves are rather short, but they provide for great group discussion. As students interact with the case studies found within the book, they often launch into a much larger discussion of similar events they have witnessed in the past.

The Use of Case Studies for Leadership Development

Case studies can be used effectively in leadership development and staff relationships. As teams work together, they begin to experience the diversity of ideas as they interact with the case material. Doctrinal issues come to the forefront, cultural differences may surface, and various assumptions can be challenged and even changed. The group begins with the dynamics of the case study, but the members soon realize that there are group dynamics surfacing that cause them discomfort. Many times the group will try to ignore these dynamics, minimize them, or at times allow differences to disrupt the team. At this point the case study becomes a springboard for more reflection upon their reactions as individuals and the division created among the relationships within the group. This becomes a great teaching opportunity for such issues as triangulation, power posturing, and interpersonal communication. It also becomes a wonderful opportunity to interact with principles of emotional intelligence as students assess their strengths and weaknesses in the areas of self-awareness and social competency. Daniel Goleman's book *Working with Emotional Intelligence* can serve as a great resource for students and mentors as they learn and experience the various concepts of emotional intelligence within the group.[8]

One of the major criticisms of pastors and leaders in the last several decades is that they relate poorly to people and they tend to be blind to their own blind spots. Emotional intelligence addresses how well we know ourselves, how well we understand our social context, and how competent we are to grow and mature in both areas. Case studies can be used to help students identify where emotional intelligence was evident or lacking in the life of a pastor or a board member. In one case an associate pastor displays

---

6. David Luecke and Samuel Southard, *Pastoral Administration: Integrating Ministry and Management in the Church* (Waco, TX: Word, 1986).

7. Michael Anthony, *The Effective Church Board: A Handbook for Mentoring and Training Servant Leaders* (Grand Rapids: Baker, 1993), 288–95.

8. Daniel Goleman, *Working with Emotional Intelligence* (New York: Bantam, 1998), 26–27. Another great resource is Daniel Goleman, Richard Boyatzis, and Annie McKee, *Primal Leadership: Realizing the Power of Emotional Intelligence* (Boston: Harvard Business School Press, 2002).

incredible social awareness by understanding the culture of the congregation and their readiness to make significant changes in the ministry, but in another case the senior pastor displays little social awareness and runs over everyone. Not only is the senior pastor blind to the state of the congregation, but he is blind to his own weaknesses as well. When his decisions are challenged, the pastor explodes into anger and threatens to leave. When the students evaluate such dynamics through the lenses of emotional intelligence, growth begins to occur in their own lives as a direct result.

Case studies also can be used in the area of leadership formation. As students wrestle through the various aspects of a case study, they are in fact formulating their own philosophy of ministry. As students work through an event, they find areas of agreement or disagreement. They may not like a certain approach to a situation, they may disagree with a doctrinal position, or they may react harshly to a pastoral response. Mentors need to look for these moments in the heart of the student and use these "flash points" to encourage the student to write down his or her thoughts and passions. Case studies are a great way for students to identify their values, mission, and vision for ministry and ultimately to form their own philosophy of ministry. People often learn best by learning from those who have made tragic mistakes in life or in ministry. In so doing, students learn what to avoid as much as they learn what to advance.

Case studies can be used to foster character development and accountability within the life of the student. This holds equally true of mentors, who may find that they too need to grow in these vital areas of ministry leadership. It is easy to forget how quickly anyone can fall! Case studies can serve as a vivid reminder of one's fallen flesh and just how easily power and position can corrupt even the best. They serve as reminders that it is typically a series of events that lead to pastoral failure, and that in most cases there was no accountability structure in place to help protect the leader from falling. Students and mentors alike can learn deep lessons through the lives of those who have fallen.

It is not enough to identify why an individual stumbled and fell. Students must move to the next level and identify what must be done to ensure that they do not make the same mistakes. A life plan can be developed that focuses on spiritual growth, ministry skill development, family health, physical health, and character development that includes goals, objectives, and strategies for ensuring growth in each area over the course of their lives. In addition, an accountability plan would be included, identifying significant relationships that will help them to grow in maturity and purity. The use of such tools may seem exhaustive, but they are well worth the effort if they provide protection.

The Use of Case Studies for Multiculturalism

Today we live in a multicultural world.[9] Case studies can help to reflect

---

9. See chapter 4, "Field Education and Cultural Awareness," for a detailed discussion on this topic.

upon what that means for individuals, and then what that means in terms of both local and global ministry. Case studies can be used to challenge and shape convictions for ministry in a multicultural world. They can provide a way to create diversity among the students themselves as they are placed in a more intimate environment with people of differing ethnicity, race, or social status. This alone is worth its weight in gold. As students wrestle with the issues of diversity, they are brought face-to-face with the reality that humanity is made up of different people, with different color, and with different histories and traditions. Case studies can be used to help students wrestle through their own prejudices, as well as to think through the barriers the body of Christ often builds when it comes to ethnicity and race.

One area that is often missed in discussions of division in the body of Christ is that of social status. In speaking of diversity, there is often failure in bridging the gap of social and economic differences. Scripture has plenty to say concerning the poor and marginalized and those who have been neglected and mistreated, regardless of race or ethnicity. Each and every one of these issues can be difficult to address, but it is monumental to work through them and think through the implications for ministry in a multicultural society. These issues can be hotly debated and can be the cause of incredible division, but much of the tension can be redirected as students process these critical issues in advance. Case studies are available that help students to reflect upon the need for multicultural ministry and the difficulties such ministries face in our society today. As students reflect upon the complex issues of diversity and social discrimination, values and convictions are shaped. Students can take these newfound values and prepare their own position on multiculturalism.

Case studies can be found that address community development and urban renewal. These stories identify the struggles many churches and parachurch organizations face as they attempt to bridge the culture they encounter every day. As students process the dynamics of a case addressing community development, they might discover that there are clearly issues in the church to address but there are also governmental roadblocks and community biases that prevent them from moving forward. Here the student might work with the church to address similar dynamics in his or her own community. The student might write a proposal to the city that seeks to invite city leaders into dialogue with the church in an effort to help the community. A student might lead a detailed demographic study of the church's community and then prepare a presentation to share with a board on building bridges to that very community. Students might work in peer groups to develop a plan to build a diverse leadership and present this to the class. Again, such projects could be completed as a team or as individuals, in the classroom or in the church context.

Another way to build unity in the body is to use case studies to address gender issues in the body. There is a great divide when it comes to the role of women in leadership, and case studies can be used to bridge the gap when it comes to gender differences. While case studies can be used to create discussion on the topic of roles and responsibilities for women in the church, they are far more helpful in addressing issues of personhood and worth. Case studies create an environment for dialogue, and dialogue, prayerfully, leads to understanding. Even the most conservative churches understand and recognize that women are going to serve in the church in many capacities, and it would be good for all students to grow in their abilities to relate with one another as men and women. Case studies provide a great environment to work through our differences and to think through ways that everyone in the body can be affirmed.[10]

The key is to look for teachable moments when statements can be probed at a deeper level and assumptions can be challenged. Each case provides an opportunity to lead the group to a whole new level of growth as dysfunctional behavior is identified and reconciliation is actually modeled within the group. In order for this to take place, it is critical to create a safe environment, where people can share openly and honestly while protecting the dignity of others as human beings. This alone is a great lesson for ministry.

The Use of Case Studies for Spiritual Formation

One of the great benefits of case studies is that they cause students to drill deep into their own ministry convictions, but case studies also help students recognize their own need for character development. As students draw upon the details of a case study, they begin to discover things down deep within their own souls. When dealing with conflict, it is not uncommon to find a student getting extremely hostile as he or she processes the details of a case study. It is no surprise that some students will force their convictions upon others in a way that is less than mature. While students interact with one another, it is not hard to imagine one of them expressing himself or herself in an inappropriate manner. After all, if church conflict can bring out the worst in the best of us, then why should one be surprised if character flaws are revealed during an intense discussion over a deeply held personal conviction? If the mentor is taking careful notes, he or she may find that there are deeper issues in the life of the individual that need to be addressed. This is especially true when the case study is dealing with painful topics such as sexual abuse or suicide. These sensitive issues must be handled with great care and counsel, but it is important that students do not miss these opportunities for growth.

One of the greatest gifts mentors can give to students is to help them find healing in their lives. This will pay big dividends down the road for their marriage, family, and the church. Too often the stress and pressure of ministry bring a person's hidden flaws and deep wounds to the surface over time. Usually by then it is too late. The damage is done and credibility is lost. Many

---

10. See chapter 13, "Working with Women Students in Field Education," for additional resources.

leaders become entrenched in their ministry, and due to their character flaws, countless people are wounded deeply along the way, and the ministry suffers. Mentors can provide a great service to students and to the body of Christ by helping students identify and acknowledge such issues before they head out the door for ministry. Here the mentor can come alongside students to guide them in seeking the proper care and counseling. As part of the case study, the student could develop a plan for his or her personal spiritual healing. Within this environment, the student can address specific issues such as anger, depression, addictive behavior, or even such things as just being plain rude and disrespectful. The student can develop a concrete strategy that would include specific reading in terms of his or her unique concerns and any counseling that would help the student to work through his or her specific issues.

Many times case studies address sensitive issues such as divorce and remarriage, euthanasia, abortion, or same-sex marriages. Students may reflect upon the issues involved, but ultimately they have to form their own convictions on such delicate matters. Such convictions must be anchored in the depths of God's truth. Many times students respond to the sensitive issues in a case study based on their emotions, and they find that their emotions lead them astray and often to anger. This is a great time for the mentor to bring the student or the group back into the presence of God. These serve as incredible teaching moments in the life of a student. When students are in the midst of their own inner turmoil, mentors can stop the discussion, turn to the Lord in prayer, and seek his guidance. Mentors can serve to remind the students that their beliefs and their behavior are to be governed by God's Word and not by our emotions or opinions. This also serves as a good time to have students write out their positions on such issues and provide biblical support for their beliefs. This would certainly be helpful when it comes time for the student to candidate for a position in the church and can be included as part of their candidacy material.

While these examples may not fit every ministry setting, they do provide a stimulus for thinking through creative ways for using case studies in your own unique context. The key is to think through ways to move the student through the process of theological reflection to the point of ministry application. The role of the mentor is to provide tangible assignments and projects that help students take what they have learned through the case study and implement such principles into actual practice.

Finding the Perfect Case Study

One of the greatest resources for finding case studies is the Association for Case Teaching.[11] The association provides an archive of countless case

---

11. For more information contact the Association for Case Teaching at P.O. Box 29443, Abilene, TX 79699-9443. The Web site is www.caseteaching.org. Case studies also can be located directly through Yale University at www.Library.yale.edu/div/case_teaching/

studies found in their *Case Teaching Journals.* A small membership fee is required for access to the journals, but the investment is well worth the return. In addition, a storehouse of case studies can be found through the association by using the Case Study Clearinghouse, which links the student to the archives provided by Yale Divinity School. While a small fee is required for each case study, they can be copied for classroom or ministry use. A summary of each case is provided for preview before any purchase might be made. The Association for Case Teaching also offers case studies located at Harvard University.

Numerous books have been written on the topic of case studies in theological education and ministry preparation. Kenneth Swetland has authored two books that provide a rich resource for case studies in pastoral ministry. The first book, titled *The Hidden World of the Pastor: Case Studies on Personal Issues of Real Pastors*, addresses the many tensions pastors face in ministry, such as staff conflict, financial problems, and worship wars.[12] Swetland's second book, *Facing Messy Stuff in the Church: Case Studies for Pastors and Congregations*, addresses tough topics like depression, suicide, AIDS, grief, and sexual abuse.[13] A great resource that is often overlooked is *Cases in Denominational Administration: A Management Casebook for Decision-Making* by Harold Phillips and Robert Firth.[14] While its title reflects a judicatory nature, the book contains excellent case studies that address a variety of administrative topics in incredible detail.

Another great resource for finding a quality case study is life and ministry itself. We live in a world filled with tension, and most of us have attended a church with more than a few problems. This should provide an ample supply of data to be used for fostering theological reflection. Case studies can be found in newspapers, magazines, journals, or in the very church we attend.[15] Every day there is a new story, headline, or event. The study of life itself can teach many lessons about living and help us avoid the mistakes others have made along the way in life and ministry.

Helping students to write case studies can be a rewarding exercise in theological reflection. These case studies can be written as individual projects with the aid of a mentor or can be done as a group assignment as each

---

case_list.html. Information concerning copy usage and any fees are provided at each Web location.

12. Kenneth Swetland, *The Hidden World of the Pastor: Case Studies on Personal Issues of Real Pastors* (Grand Rapids: Baker, 1995). A small fee of 35 cents is required per copy for using each case study found within the book. Information is provided in the copyright section of the book, along with mailing instructions for those using his case studies.

13. Kenneth Swetland, *Facing Messy Stuff in the Church: Case Studies for Pastors and Congregations* (Grand Rapids: Kregel, 2005).

14. Harold Phillips and Robert Firth, *Cases in Denominational Administration: A Management Casebook for Decision-Making* (Berrien Springs, MI: Andrews University Press, 1978).

15. Keith Bridston, ed., *Casebook on Church and Society* (Nashville: Abingdon, 1974), 211.

member contributes to the whole. A great resource for writing a case study can be found in *Slices of Ministry: The Case Study Method of Teaching and Learning* by Ray Bystrom.[16] In this book, Bystrom provides clear instruction on the principles of writing a quality case study. In addition, the Association for Case Teaching provides seminars and workshops in the case teaching method throughout the year.

Conclusion

Above all, the key to using case studies is to be creative and intentional. The case itself simply serves as a tool to allow for theological reflection, to develop ministry convictions, and then to develop specific skills and competencies for ministry. The more intentionally mentors and students use the case study, the more intentional the training provided for the student. As students come face-to-face with the events of real ministry, they will be better prepared for the real events they will ultimately face once they enter into ministry. May the Lord help us to become lifelong learners, those who learn from the lessons of the past so that we are better prepared for the future.

---

16. Bystrom, *Slices of Ministry*, 23–26.

Prayer of Transformation

Father, we are thankful for the lessons that you provide through your Word and through the lessons of life. Help us to learn through the pages of Scripture and through the pages of the past so that we will grow in Christlike maturity. Guide us as we wrestle through the complexities of life and ministry, and provide for us the wisdom that we need to navigate the critical issues we face in the church and the world every day and in every place. Help us to always remain humble and teachable as we grow in our abilities to serve you, O Lord. Help us to take what we learn and use it to better inform our decisions so that every decision delights your heart and brings glory to your name. Amen.

Reflection Questions

1. What is the role of the case study, and how can it be used to foster theological reflection?

2. What current issues facing your ministry or society might a case study address?

3. If you were to write a case study pertaining to a difficulty in ministry, what comes to the forefront of your thinking?

4. What are some creative ways in which a case study might be used?

5. What are some dangers when using the case study method? What are some extremes to avoid?

6. What perimeters might a group want to have in place before launching into a group case discussion?

7. Was there anything specific that resonated with you as certain issues were raised, or topics discussed? Was there anything that rubbed you the wrong way, and why?

Further Reading

Bystrom, Raymond. *Slices of Ministry: The Case Study Method of Teaching and Learning.* Fresno: Pacific Seminary, 2005.

Evans, Robert A., Alice Fazer Evans, Louis Weeks, and Carolyn Weeks. *Casebook for Christian Living: Value Formation for Families and Congregations.* Atlanta: John Knox Press, 1977.

Mahon, Jeffrey H., Barbara B. Troxell, and Carol J. Allen. *Shared Wisdom: A Guide to Case Study Reflections in Ministry.* Nashville: Abingdon, 1993.

Swetland, Kenneth. *Facing Messy Stuff in the Church: Case Studies for Pastors and Congregations.* Grand Rapids: Kregel, 2005.

——. *The Hidden World of the Pastor: Case Studies on Personal Issues of Real Pastors.* Grand Rapids: Baker, 1995.

Chapter 10

Building Biblical Community in Theological Education

PAUL PETTIT

Rather, speaking the truth in love, we are to grow up in every way into him who is the head, into Christ, from whom the whole body, joined and held together by every joint with which it is equipped, when each part is working properly, makes the body grow so that it builds itself up in love. (Eph. 4:15–16)

People who lose large amounts of weight in short periods of time fascinate me. Admittedly, some of these weight-loss endeavors are surgically or chemically induced. Still, many shed unwanted pounds the old-fashioned way: by sheer determination, gumption, discipline, willpower, or whatever you choose to call it. I marvel when I see loose-hanging clothes where tight-fitting ones were once the norm.

There is a lady in our neighborhood who walks each evening. At first I scoffed at her perambulating potential. *How much weight can a person really lose simply by walking around the neighborhood?* And yet, as time wears on, and the seasons change, I have been seeing less and less of the walking lady. She still makes her nightly appearance, but her form has changed; her shape has shifted. I am beginning to believe the well-worn definition that discipline is *a long obedience in the same direction.*[1]

---

1. Eugene Peterson, *A Long Obedience in the Same Direction: Discipleship in an Instant Society*, 20th anniversary ed. (Downers Grove, IL: InterVarsity Press, 2000).

In the same way that a person can lose a large amount of weight over time, a person can similarly change lifelong bad habits like impatience, pride, or slothfulness. All of us who labor in the fields of spiritual transformation and field education long to witness authentic life change. Reports from afar fail to satisfy our hunger to see those we disciple progress in their path toward Christlikeness. We want to see results. We want to know our efforts are not in vain. We also find it helpful and encouraging to see, before our very eyes, gains being made by those we minister to. This chapter touches on all three of the main themes of our text: character development, emotional intelligence development, and spiritual healing from past hurts. The specific intent of this chapter is to show how building biblical community groups can help students identify and grow in their own areas of giftedness, in addition to helping fellow students do the same.[2]

Tools for Groundbreaking

In my work as a director of spiritual formation, I have been tasked with assisting the spiritual health and growth of seminary students. What a tough crowd! In Kansas I planted Christmas trees in the fall and strawberries in the summer, but I believe the soil among some who are headed toward vocational, full-time Christian service may be even tougher. The campus is a tremendous place to work. But there is a pride that can subtly creep in somewhere between the many required trips to the chapel to hear from "the latest" speaker and isolated hours spent in the library researching and writing one more paper on "church programs that work." It's true, spiritual frostbite can occur among students who are preparing for a career in ministry toward others.

Obviously there are many different forms and approaches to implementing efforts toward having students experience life lived out in authentic biblical community. Some have used immersion; that is, living at retreat or conference centers for extended periods of time. Others use weekend retreats or summer experiences where Christian practices such as solitude, prayer, spiritual direction, and time devoted to various Christian disciplines are implemented.

At times, these approaches are extremely fruitful. In the academic experience, however, where calendars are filled with additional courses, exams, papers, and assignments, I have found that the following three disciplines, practiced regularly over time, help break up this potentially hard ground and surface deep-rooted problems the ministerial student must root out. I

2. Although I am labeling these groups *biblical community groups*, they are also known as care groups, transformation groups, theological reflection groups, vocational discussion groups, and even spiritual formation groups. I have used the term *biblical* because no matter what they are labeled, I believe they should uphold biblical values such as transparency, authenticity, confidentiality, and courageous love. And I use the term *community* because I believe the members of the group should strive to become more than simple participants; they should become *spiritual friends*.

encourage schools to divide their students into small groups (6–8 students) that regularly meet over an extended period of time.

Sitting in a Circle Helps Build Biblical Community

It is shocking how surprised some students become when they are asked to weekly sit in a circle with the same group of students for a two-year period. Part of our particular program of study involves a spiritual formation program. In it we ask students to join a weekly small group. Is not that a simple and straightforward request? It sort of sounds like a kindergarten conversation, doesn't it?

> KINDERGARTEN TEACHER. "Joey, you will need to learn to straighten up your area when you are finished, you will have to share the toys with all the other boys and girls, and once a week we sit in a circle and talk."

> JOEY. "But I don't wanna sit in a circle and talk!"

I have found various reasons why students do not want to sit in a circle and talk. First, we are just too busy. Boy, are we busy. "I don't have time to interact with my spiritual formation group because I'm too busy." I used to pause and wait to hear the list of busyness that some students could come up with. But lately, I have begun interjecting, "So you're too busy to sit in a circle?" It is harsh, but it is true. Have students who are preparing to deliver sermons, comfort the grieving, and sit at hospital beds and board meetings become too busy to sit in a circle with their fellow classmates once a week over the lunch hour? How sad is that?

Second, and this reason often goes unspoken, some find sitting in a circle and sharing frightening. What will people think of me? What should I say? What if I share some personal stuff and start crying? Over the years I have found that both men and women are frightened by small-group discussions. Maybe it is stubborn male pride, but especially in North America many men pick up an aversion to asking for help. Many students understand their need for assistance in the difficult disciplines of theological study, language acquisition, or the acquisition of leadership skills. But many of these same students are not yet aware of their glaring need for work in the critical areas of emotional intelligence, self-awareness, relational wholeness, courageous love, or authentic vulnerability. It is true; it can be really scary sitting in a circle of trust and sharing authentically. It can be equally difficult admitting we are flawed and that we need help and direction.

Another reason we shrink back from sitting in a circle owes to our fear of admitting past hurts. If we can just sit with our current friends, those we have already made headway with, we often assume we will remain in a safe place. However, Jesus often calls us out to the deeper water of relational development. There are those we need to meet who can learn from us, and there are those we need to learn from. Exchanging our life stories and struggles with fellow students opens us up to new insights and ideas on what God is doing in our life and where he may be leading us.

Authentic biblical community is not something we can manufacture or conjure up. In his classic work, *Life Together*, the German martyr Dietrich Bonhoeffer wrote, "Christian brotherhood is not an ideal which we must realize; it is rather a reality created by God in Christ in which we may participate. The more clearly we learn to recognize that the ground and strength and promise of all our fellowship is in Jesus Christ alone, the more serenely shall we think of our fellowship and pray and hope for it."[3]

Sharing Authentically Helps Build Biblical Community

It is difficult enough asking really busy people to sit in a circle once a week. And it would be quite awkward if we only sat in the circle staring at one another. (Too much silence and contemplation would be unfathomable at this early stage and in this particular age of ministry development.) So we ask students to verbally share with their fellow circle-mates what they are learning about themselves, God, and their vocational future. This too is difficult—difficult and scary. How much should I share? Is this a safe place, a confidential place? Oh no, I shared too much!

But authentically sharing (telling our own truth) is also incredibly healthy. Confession of struggle is good for the soul. Nothing cinches a circle like all the members realizing the failings they confess are not novel. Each of us involved in following Jesus is an imperfect disciple. The sooner we embark upon vulnerable, authentic communication, the better. This is true especially among those who are moving into ministry leadership positions, where telling the truth is paramount for effectiveness.

I smile every time I hear the old saying that ministry would be wonderful if it weren't for the people! We laugh, and it is the laughter of recognition, because inherently and intuitively we know ministry really is about the people. The apostle Paul said when we are filled with the Holy Spirit our authentic sharing will lead to our "speaking the truth in love, [and in so doing] we are to grow up in every way into him who is the head, into Christ" (Eph. 4:15).

One of the beautiful by-products of learning and sharing in a small group is the awakening that comes when we suddenly realize that others experience life differently than we do. It is so stretching and affirming to learn from other cultures, races, and ethnicities. In their groundbreaking work, *A Many Colored Kingdom: Multicultural Dynamics for Spiritual Formation*, the authors tackle the subject of learning together from and with those in other cultures and surmise, "Multicultural education is concerned with the sensitivity, skills, and spirituality necessary to teach

---

3. Dietrich Bonhoeffer, *Life Together*, trans. John W. Doberstein (New York: Harper & Row, 1954), 3.

all students more completely. It involves an awareness of their value as a human being that comes from understanding that God created each one in his image."[4]

Evaluating the Feedback of Others Helps Build Biblical Community

Sitting in a circle is tough. Authentically sharing is equally difficult. But try evaluating the comments and suggestions others in the circle make about you. If true spiritual formation means character change, and I believe it does, imagine how uncomfortable it can become when someone in my circle of trust points out, "Paul, you use humor as a defense mechanism," and everyone in the group nods in agreement.

I have never forgotten the day my own spiritual formation group told me I harbor a bad habit of dismissing legitimate concerns people have about me with lame attempts at making them laugh. Even though it stung a bit, it was too true to be ignored. I still remember my loud protestations. "That's not true. I don't do that," I countered. "You guys are starting to remind me of the preacher who walked into a bar with a parrot on his shoulder."

This three-part strategy (sitting, sharing, evaluating) works over time to help us become more and more the persons God created us to be. The more we sit with others who care about us, share what we experience and learn, and evaluate what these same brothers and sisters say about us, the more we move away from the dangerously destructive isolated individualism and vocational pride that set us apart from both the grace we crave and the very ones we are trying to minister to.

I have been humbled to witness, before my very eyes, students growing and changing to become more patient, kind, and loving. I have seen students work through conflict to become more healthy, vulnerable, and authentic. I have seen students come to the realization that they are more gifted to serve as a counselor than a preacher.

The circle of trust I am describing is no magic ministry bullet that sets sanctification in motion. But God, it seems, often uses our small-group friends saying what they see and putting voice to what they are observing to help us become what we long to become—healthy followers of the Savior living in authentic biblical community.

Obviously times arise in a small-group setting when the members need to have a difficult conversation. Even these encounters should begin and end with heartfelt encouragement. The apostle Paul modeled this when he described his ministry efforts in Thessalonica: "For you know how, like a father with his children, we exhorted each one of you and encouraged you and charged you to walk in a manner worthy of God, who calls you into his own kingdom and glory" (1 Thess. 2:11–12).

---

4. Elizabeth Conde-Frazier, S. Steve Kang, and Gary A. Parrett, *A Many Colored Kingdom: Multicultural Dynamics for Spiritual Formation* (Grand Rapids: Baker, 2004), 106.

Four Benefits of Biblical Community Groups

The following are only four of the numerous benefits to dividing students into small groups that allow for theological and personal reflection.

Friendship

The first benefit is that students are able to build strong friendships with students they may otherwise not have chosen. I am always amazed at the stories that emerge from within the small groups. A student will relay how someone in the group has an eerily similar background to his or her own. Another will reflect how he has become close friends with a group member through shared suffering. And another will share that she never thought she would become friends with a particular group member because of an inaccurate first impression, but over time she has learned to love and trust that particular member.

It is important to place students from different backgrounds and walks of life with each other. We all gravitate toward homogenous friendships. I gravitate toward students from the America's Midwest. I like to talk sports with guys. I normally choose to associate with those who are of my same age and financial bracket. But my friendships with those who are different from me always end up being rich experiences.

It is important to make friends with those who are different than me so that I can gain a broader perspective on who I am and who I am becoming. I need the insights and wisdom that come from those of other countries and cultures. And I need the advice of those who are both younger and older than I am.

Leadership

A second benefit of biblical community groups is the opportunity for students to experience peer-led leadership of the groups. Many have held leadership positions over those who are younger. It is fairly easy to lead a group comprised of those who may be ten or twenty years younger than the leader. However, leading one's peers requires a new set of leadership skills. Issues such as trust and respect play a larger role when the leader is around the same age or even younger than the group participants.

I have found no greater leadership challenge than giving someone a group filled with his or her peers and asking that particular person to lead them through a specific task over a given period of time. There are no shortcuts involved in peer-based leadership. Over time the group will reflect the qualities and characteristics of the leader.

Conflict

A third benefit of building biblical community groups is the opportunity it provides students to learn to work through relational conflict. When I first began leading small groups and coaching small-group leaders, I feared the onset of conflict. "*Uh oh, I heard Bill Johnson's group has encountered some conflict."* It is not that I enjoy or welcome group conflict now, but I no longer fear it as I once did. I have learned that conflict is a normal, natural part of a small-group process. And it is how students respond to and overcome quarrels and conflicts that show how mature or immature they really are.

The small groups are only a reflection of what the vocational Christian ministry student will encounter in the field. Learning to work through conflict in a healthy small-group environment is wonderful preparation for what will happen in churches, mission contexts, and parachurch settings.

Conflict can arise for many reasons. One student may not like the manner in which the leader facilitates the group. Another may not like a particular member of the group. Some students may complain that the groups are forced since they are compulsory. Of course, all of these same arguments could be made from the same students once they are assigned to a particular church or parish community. Rarely do we get to select our own parishioners! The bottom line: conflict is inevitable; how one handles conflict is optional.

Reflection

The fourth reason biblical community groups are such powerful tools for field education is the amount of time students are able to spend in theological and personal reflection. In a large lecture setting, students are rarely able to enter into personal dialogue with either the professor or fellow students. In a small-group setting, however, students are encouraged to reflect upon what they are learning and discovering about themselves and God as they settle upon their calling or vocation.

Specific exercises such as students being asked to share their life story can help fellow students understand the family environment or platform from which the student has arrived. And asking students to share their life dream or life vision can greatly assist a close circle of friends when it comes time to provide feedback or advice on a particular student's internship or vocational plans.

Biblical Community Groups: A Microcosm of the Marketplace

There are at least three reasons why adopting the biblical community group model for carrying out personal and theological reflection is one of the best methods available.

Teams

The first reason is that many church, parish, and nonprofit organizations now work in teams. Not only have for-profit marketplace businesses adopted a team-based model for doing business, but the idea has spread into the nonprofit world as well. Most are well versed in the world of committees in the work world. Ministry settings are similar. I once asked a student if he would like to lead a spiritual formation group. His reply was, "Oh, I don't need to be in one of those, I'm going into academic ministry!" I chuckled when I thought of how many committee, departmental, administrative, and student/alumni group meetings that same student may one day be called upon to meet with or even lead.

Another time I challenged a particular student with the idea of leading a small group, and he responded, "I don't think I need to do that. I'm planning on planting a new church." Any of you who have had anything to do with a church or parish start-up know just how many small groups are involved. In fact, at the nascent stages of a new work, all the groups are small groups!

People Skills

Second, nonprofit and ministry-based organizations are heavily dependent upon attracting leaders with people skills. I already have pointed out the obvious, that ministry is mostly about people. We all need those who can carry out particular and specific ministry skills. But mostly we long for those who have experience leading and working closely with people.

People skills like vision casting, conflict management, encouragement, counseling, and community building will score students in good stead when it comes time to deliver resumes and undertake interviews. Most of the church hiring committees I talk with want to know if the person they are interviewing has the specific gifts for the task, but they almost always end up asking as well, "Yeah, but have they ever really led anyone?" I had a professor who was fond of reminding so-called leaders that they should turn around and look over their shoulder from time to time to check to see if anyone is actually following. If no one was following, he would caution, then they were not actually leading. They were only out for a walk! Being involved in a biblical community group, and especially leading one, is one of the best ways to develop and enhance people skills.

Emotional Intelligence

The third reason these groups are so critical owes to the increasing importance of emotional, social, and relational intelligence in the ministry setting. More and more ministry practitioners are realizing that skill and task intelligence is only one part of what it takes to become an effective minister. More recent research carried out in the fields of emotional and social intelligence show that task skills are still vitally important, but no more or less important than the so-called *soft skills* of emotional and relational development.

In fact, in today's fast-paced environment of enhanced technological developments, some are saying that those with strong emotional and social intelligence skills are even *more desirable* as ministry employees. An example of this type of research is the much-discussed Sommerville study, a forty-year longitudinal investigation of 450 boys who grew up in Sommerville, Massachusetts. Two-thirds of the boys were from welfare families, and one-third held intelligence quotients below 90. However, IQ had little relation to how well they did at work or in the rest of their lives. What made the biggest difference was childhood abilities such as being able to handle frustration, control emotions, and get along with other people.[5]

All of these reasons and many more are why it is so important for field education students to spend time in small discussion groups critically reflecting upon what they are learning. Some critical ministry skills can be learned *only* in close interaction with other students. For example, if I am going to teach a group of young children to swim, it may be important for these students to read a book on swimming, and even for them to write a paper on swimming. But at some point I must get them into the water and let them have a go at it, if I am truly going to be successful as a swim instructor. And so it is with ministry development.

We must produce students who are competent in theology, biblical languages, biblical study, and all the rest. But should we not also produce students who are experts at knowing themselves and how they interact with others? Should we not be about the business of producing students who are incredibly self-aware, adaptable, trustworthy, optimistic, empathetic, and oriented toward serving God and others?

Lifelong Learning

Students embarking upon a lifetime of vocational Christian service should spend considerable time sitting, reflecting, and sharing with fellow students in a small group that is working on practicing living out the principles of authentic biblical community. However, this practice holds for those who teach and train as well. The benefits of authentic communication and learning in community are immeasurable and lead to balanced, healthy living. Some of the benefits include the hallmarks of emotional intelligence:

- *Emotional self-awareness*–recognizing our emotions and their effects.
- *Accurate self-assessment*–knowing our strengths and limits.
- *Self-confidence*–having a strong sense of our self-worth and capabilities.
- *Self-control*–managing disruptive emotions and keeping impulses under control.
- *Empathy*–understanding others and taking active interest in their concerns.
- *Teamwork*–creating a shared vision and synergy while working with others toward shared goals.
- *Social awareness*–having a "social radar," empathizing at the group level, recognizing and meeting others' needs.
- *Leadership*–inspiring and guiding individuals and groups of people toward common goals.

---

5. John Snarey and George Vaillant, "How Lower- and Working-Class Youth Become Middle-Class Adults: The Association Between Ego Defense Mechanisms and Upward Social Mobility," *Child Development* 56, no. 4 (1985): 889–910.

The future of ministry development calls for us to produce students who possess incredible organizational awareness, inspirational leadership, and teamwork and collaboration skill sets; and gifted future church and parish workers who can build authentic relationships while creating a shared, God-given vision and Holy Spirit synergy among a group of parishioners. May God help us to encourage the development of such students!

Prayer of Transformation

Father God, maker of heaven and earth, strengthen students everywhere who are planning and preparing to serve you and your kingdom. Help them grow and develop into all that you desire them to be and become. Bless those who are assisting and leading in the training, teaching, and supervising of these called ones. Into your watchful, loving care, we commit our grateful service. Help us to more and more live in authentic, biblical community for your glory and the spreading of your gospel. Amen.

Reflection Questions

1. Do you agree that learning about vocational Christian ministry in isolation is difficult? Why or why not?

2. What are the advantages of learning along with others and trying to implement values that are (a) authentic, (b) biblical, and (c) community oriented?

3. Why is it often difficult to open up and discuss in a small-group setting what we are really feeling or what we believe our emotions are really telling us?

4. Why is it important for a student who is going into vocational ministry to learn in a biblical community—one that practices values such as authenticity, vulnerability, openness, and compassion?

5. If someone in a small group has difficulty expressing or even recognizing his or her own feelings, how could the group assist that person in his or her struggle?

6. How can work in a small group help us better understand and implement the value of recognizing the various gifts and giftedness in the body of Christ?

Further Reading

Bonhoeffer, Dietrich. *Life Together.* Translated by John W. Doberstein. Harper & Row: New York, 1954.

Conde-Frazier, Elizabeth, S. Steve Kang, and Gary A. Parrett, *A Many Colored Kingdom: Multicultural Dynamics for Spiritual Formation.* Grand Rapids: Baker 2004.

Donahue, Bill, and Greg Bowman. *Coaching Life-Changing Small Group Leaders.* Grand Rapids: Zondervan, 2006.

Rosenburg, Marshall. *Nonviolent Communication: A Language of Life.* San Francisco: Puddledancer, 2003.

Chapter 11

Assessment and Evaluation in Field Education

Thomas Fuller

Do your best to present yourself to God as one approved, a worker who has no need to be ashamed, rightly handling the word of truth. (2 Tim. 2:15)

A key component to any educational process is the *assessment* of student learning and development.[1] Practically every academic course uses examinations and other (usually written) assignments to measure student progress toward stated learning objectives. For many students, these constitute the dreaded days of reckoning when they must demonstrate their mastery (or lack thereof) of the subject. There is an element of judgment involved; there are, likewise, elements of instruction and encouragement. For instance, in a history course, a learning objective may be that students, when given a particular historical event, will be able to write a thorough and cogent essay discussing the sociopolitical factors that led to said event. The essay, then, serves as a means of assessing what a student has learned about the facts of history and how he or she is able to synthesize that information into a

---

1. In the context of education, assessment refers to the broader work of determining the success of an initiative, for example, a degree program or student learning across the school, relative to stated objectives.

coherent explanation of history. While the emphasis in these assessments is too often given to the calculation of grades, the real question is, "What did the student learn?" or "How is he or she different (in terms of knowledge, skills, personal development) as a result of taking this course?" Based on what the assessment reveals, students and teachers are better able to plan for future learning and growth.

The assessment of student learning and development, rightly conceived and practiced, holds benefits for students and educators alike. By various means, assessment pulls back the curtain on the educational process to reveal how well things are progressing toward the desired end. With such knowledge, those involved in the process may gain encouragement or challenge, they may make adjustments to teaching and learning methodologies, or they may perceive strengths and weaknesses. The ultimate goal of assessment is to facilitate and direct future learning in the most needful and appropriate directions.

In theological field education, the primary means of assessing student learning and development is evaluation.[2] Students engage in supervised ministry experiences, not just for ministry experience alone, but for the opportunity to receive helpful feedback and direction for the sake of their ministry leadership development. This is the essence of evaluation: It is making judgments about students and their practice of Christian ministry for the purpose of giving constructive feedback and direction.

Assessment and evaluation are more than matters of academic concern and significance. In the preparation of vocational Christian ministers, they serve important formative purposes. Spiritual formation in general, and formation for ministry leadership in particular, requires an ongoing discipline of evaluation for the sake of self-awareness. The feedback one receives from mentors, professors, peers, laypersons, and others provides a mirror of sorts, in which a student can more clearly see himself or herself. This knowledge of oneself—one's strengths and weaknesses, gifts and passions, and much more—is a vital tool God uses to shape persons for his purposes. This is true not only for the minister-in-training, but also throughout one's ministerial lifetime. Growing "in the grace and knowledge of our Lord and Savior Jesus Christ" (2 Peter 3:18) and, thereby, growing in one's faithfulness and skill as a minister of Christ's gospel requires a discipline of evaluation.

In the practice of ministry, evaluation is not totally optional. It is taking place all the time in some form. Those who participate in, receive, or observe one's ministry are constantly making judgments about the minister and his or her ministry. The church parking lot and Sunday dinner table are some of the favorite venues for these evaluations. This is human nature, and it usually takes place informally and without due regard for the minister's or

---

2. In the context of education, *evaluation* refers to a process of determining the value of one's knowledge and understanding, character, and skills, relative to stated objectives.

ministry's improvement. The type of evaluation that lends itself to ministry leadership development, however, is different in several respects. It is conducted intentionally, with the minister as a willing and conscious participant; it is conducted with reference to particular criteria or goals; it is not concerned with perfection so much as with faithfulness and progress; and it has as its ultimate objectives the growth of the minister, the quality of the ministry, and the glory of God. By honoring these distinctive features, the practice of evaluation in theological field education can be a rich experience of learning and growth for all involved.

The purpose of this chapter is to highlight these core values as they are applied in the practice of evaluation in theological field education. In the opening section, the values will be distilled into several guiding principles that form the basic foundation for evaluation. On that foundation one can then build a healthy and beneficial process of evaluation. The latter sections of the chapter will address process—the who, what, when, and how of evaluating students preparing for vocational Christian ministry. It should be noted at the outset, however, that process is a highly contextual matter. What works for field educators in one place may not fit the needs and goals of those in another place.

Guiding Principles

If one goes to the pages of Scripture or to the history of the church looking for evaluation, at least as the formalized practice we know today, it will be nearly impossible to find. In other words, there is no well-established model for evaluating Christian ministers that has been handed down to us through the generations. Even so, one can easily look back over time and observe that judgments were made on the knowledge, character, and skills of God's servants of the past and that these were somehow communicated to them. God was certainly clear in denouncing false prophets and unfaithful priests, as well as commending the fidelity of the obedient and faithful ones. In truth, though, evaluation as a regular practice within the formal training of men and women for Christian service is a development of the last fifty years. Much has been learned in those years, and the quest for improvement continues still.

Like so many (all?) things in Christian ministry, ministry leadership development is more art than science. More specifically stated, developing leaders for Christ's church is a work of the Holy Spirit—a work in which the community of faith has the privilege and responsibility to participate. The ways and means of this work are not easily cataloged or distilled into prescribed formulae. We can learn from the past, observing in the Scriptures and church history how God has chosen to work in the lives of his servants to prepare them for their roles. Such a study reveals an endless variety of paths to faithful and effective service. In that variety, however, certain patterns emerge, allowing us to discern some of the constants in God's work of formation.

What follows are four guiding principles for evaluation in theological field education that reflect the values embodied in the Christian tradition and are consistent with practices in the discipline of ministry preparation.

Principle 1: Evaluation Is an Exercise in Healthy Christian Community

One of the richest passages on Christian community is Ephesians 4. Paul begins the passage with the admonition to "walk in a manner worthy of the calling to which you have been called" (v. 1). He elaborates on the ideal of walking in a worthy manner by commending humility, gentleness, patience, love, and harmony (vv. 2–3). These are signs of a healthy body, where the various members rightly recognize their unity in Christ and appreciate the diversity that comprises that unity (vv. 4–7). The "called"–which includes all believers and not just those called to special service within the church–must relate to one another with due regard for the marvelous way in which God has formed and continues to form his church. One facet of that marvelous work is accomplished through the service of those whom God has called and graced to serve as "the apostles, the prophets, the evangelists, the pastors and teachers, to equip the saints for the work of ministry, for building up the body of Christ" (vv. 11–12). These members function to feed, care for, and nurture the body of Christ so that it grows and matures appropriately (vv. 13–15). It is quite evident, though, that the enterprise of spiritual growth requires a whole-body commitment to certain habits and disciplines that create a fertile environment for the work of God's Spirit.

Healthy Christian communities speak "the truth in love" (Eph. 4:15). More than honesty, this is truth telling superintended by a selfless regard for others and a passion for the glory of God. Where these values prevail, truth will always serve the purpose of building up, repairing, reconciling, healing, and strengthening. That does not mean that what is spoken will always be easy to say or complimentary in nature. Some of the most loving words may be confrontational and critical. Even in those instances, however, healthy communities measure their words with humble and prayerful care, trusting that God will use them to accomplish his purposes.

Healthy Christian communities "encourage one another" (1 Thess. 5:11). One of God's great gifts to the individual believer is other believers. We are intended to live with and toward one another as instruments of God's grace. The Christian life is not a solitary journey, a private matter of "religion" between me and God. Rather, God binds believers together in Christ Jesus that we may encourage and build up one another in the faith. This should not be an occasional discipline of Christian community, reserved only for those times when one is down-and-out, but a consistent mark of believers' life together.

Healthy Christian communities "fan into flame" God's gifts (2 Tim. 1:6) so that they grow stronger. This was Paul's admonition to Timothy regarding God's call on his life and the spiritual gifts with which he was endowed. It was not an endeavor Timothy could undertake alone. Fellow believers play a vital role in cultivating an environment where God's call can be more clearly discerned and the gifts of the Spirit can be developed and employed effectively.

Evaluation of those who provide spiritual leadership is a practice consistent with these marks of a healthy Christian community. It should not be extremely awkward, therefore, to introduce the formal practice of evaluation into the life of a Christian ministry organization. The structure of it may be foreign to many, but the spirit and intent of evaluation should find a natural fit. In the best of circumstances, evaluation should be an expression of the faith community's mission to "build up the body" through practices that emphasize unity in Christ, truth, love, and the gifts and vocations of all God's people.

Principle 2: Evaluation Is Conducted for the Benefit of the Student

As a parent, I am constantly challenged to maintain a nurturing posture toward my children. Their growth and maturity is a matter of utmost importance, and how I relate to them plays a significant role in their development. My faithfulness to praise them for their achievements, to encourage them in their struggles, to instruct them in their learning, and to correct them in their mistakes, not to mention *how* I go about doing these things, has long-term implications for what kind of people they will grow up to be. But in the rush of everyday life, it is too easy to lose sight of this. The pressure to "take care of business" often reduces our relationship to tasks to be completed, schedules to keep, rules to keep, and so on. I need regular reminders that how I relate to my children in the mundane events of each day makes a big difference.

Theological field education is not parenting, to be sure, but it does share some common values, in the generic sense, with the parenting enterprise. In theological field education generally, and in the matter of evaluation specifically, educators and mentors have a nurturing agenda with students. Teaching is not just about the transfer of knowledge and skills, but in the best sense it is nurturing students in their overall learning and development, both personally and professionally. Theological field educators and mentors, like parents, are tasked, therefore, with praising, encouraging, instructing, correcting, and many other things. The healthy practice of evaluation will embody these values, with a view to what is best for the student and his or her formation for ministry leadership.

In the midst of academic protocols and assessment processes, it is easy to lose sight of working for the benefit of students. Evaluation can be reduced to a mechanical process—a slate of meetings to attend, a set of forms to complete, deadlines to meet—and the student's best interest can get lost in the mix. It is good to remember that educators and mentors are not evaluating a job, a position, or even a student only, but a person. People are complex creatures, and each one is unique. Each student's needs are different. Evaluation must ultimately benefit the student, which means that while necessarily standardized as a process, one size (way) does not fit (benefit) all. Personal (pastoral?) care must be taken to conduct evaluation as an exercise in spiritual discernment, so that it not only satisfies the academic requirements of a ministry leadership program but also edifies the student.

Principle 3: Evaluation Must Be Critical, Constructive, and Caring

There are potentially unhealthy extremes in the practice of evaluation. One extreme is disproportionately critical. This is usually practiced by those who are perfectionists in their perspective and whose personality type is disposed to "seeing the glass half empty." Quite often these critics mean well and have the best of intentions for the one being evaluated, believing that "telling them like it is" holds the most promise for promoting learning and growth. The other extreme, however, is weak on being critical, hesitant to offer an objective, sometimes unflattering, assessment of the student. The chief value for many evaluators in this camp is to nurture the student through affirmation of gifts and strengths and to encourage him or her at every turn. Positive reinforcement is the name of the game.

In the evaluation of students preparing for vocational Christian ministry, criticism and care need not be mutually exclusive values. In fact, for evaluation to yield maximum benefit to students, there must be a commitment to and a balance of criticism and care. The element that serves to bridge the gap between these potential extremes is the constructive factor—the value that keeps evaluation from veering off into the ditches of criticism or care on either side of the road and keeps the process moving forward toward the student's best interest and needs. Students do not need an exclusive diet of flattery, nor do they need to be told only what they are doing wrong or deficiently. They need critically helpful feedback from people who care about them and know what they are doing.

A word of caution is in order, however. Balancing criticism and care (or encouragement) is not as simple as making sure to offer the same number of critical comments as complimentary comments. Evaluation, in the best sense, is a relational exercise that defies mathematical precision. As with any relationship, it is vital to discern the needs of the student, the time and place for certain conversations, and a number of other factors in the course of offering feedback that will serve the ultimate end of the student's learning and growth.

Honesty is an essential component to any healthy relationship, and certainly the same is true for evaluation. Mentors want students to know the truth. But how mentors go about helping students to discover that truth, in concert with the work of God's Spirit in students' lives, is an endeavor to be undertaken with great care.

Principle 4: Evaluation Is an Essential Discipline for Lifelong Learning

The experience of evaluation, both for evaluators and for those being evaluated, feels very much like an academic exercise. In the context of theological field education, of course, evaluation is conducted as part of an academic course. This is not a bad thing; it is just an education thing. Consequently, however, people too often conceive of evaluation as one of the hoops to be jumped through to satisfy the requirements of an academic degree program or as an occasional process to endure as part of a personnel review. Thinking in these ways, people risk missing the point that evaluation is an essential discipline for lifelong learning and growth.

I regularly remind my students that upon graduation there will still be more they do not know about ministry than what they do know. My purpose in offering this reminder is not to discourage them but to impress upon them the importance of continuing to learn throughout their years in ministry. Formal training for ministry leadership, particularly theological degree programs, can only hope to lay a solid foundation for the faithful and competent practice of ministry. It is a vitally important step to take in responding to the call of God to serve the church in a vocational capacity. But Christian ministers must build upon the foundation of their formal training through learning and growth initiatives that will be largely self-directed. With the possible exception of ministers whose denominations mandate continuing education, most ministers must take ownership of their ongoing learning and development. It is essential not only for complementing the learning and growth of seminary days, but also for helping the minister maintain effectiveness in a world of constant change.

A variety of resources is available to the minister to aid in continuing education. There are additional degree programs, workshops, conferences, and the like. None of these, however, can take the place of personal discipline in the ministry setting itself. The minister's devotional practices, physical fitness, emotional fitness, and intellectual stimulation are well-recognized keys to staying sharp and vital as a spiritual leader. The practice of evaluation also has a place in this regimen. It serves as a means of accountability and assessment for progress made in any number of areas—spiritual, professional, relational, physical, or otherwise. Many ministers fall prey to the problem of good intentions never fulfilled. They can readily speak of the importance of lifelong learning and growth and what they need to do to foster continual improvement, but they stop short of developing a viable plan for the same. Consequently, the tyranny of the urgent and old-fashioned procrastination or laziness serve to keep needed growth in the realm of the intended but unrealized.

Learning goals are not just for academic coursework. They are useful tools for the serious pursuit of personal and professional growth. What students learn about the development and use of learning goals during seasons of formal training, including the practice of evaluation, can and should aid them in their lifelong learning endeavors. The feedback one receives from regular evaluation points to growth areas in the minister's life and work; it informs the development of learning and growth goals; it provides a measure of progress made toward those goals; and it sends a signal to those with whom and to whom one ministers that he or she takes seriously the pursuit of excellence for the sake of the ministry's effectiveness and the glory of God.

Who Conducts the Evaluations?

Programs of theological field education will vary from school to school with regard to the persons they involve in the supervisory process. The question of who conducts evaluations of the ministry student will likewise vary. At a minimum, every program designates someone to serve as a field supervisor or ministry mentor. This individual typically works most closely with the student in his or her ministry internship—helping the student develop appropriate learning goals, meeting with the student on a regular basis for reflection on the ministry experience, and observing the student as he or she exercises ministry leadership in context. The mentor thus is best situated to evaluate the student. In fact, the selection or enlistment of a ministry mentor should, among other things, be based on that individual's capacity for and willingness to evaluate the student in a way that is consistent with the guiding principles outlined previously.

Some programs enlist laypersons from within the congregation or ministry setting to participate in the field education process. These persons often function as a feedback group for the student, offering their perspectives on the student's ministry performance. The layperson's perspective is unique and valuable, complementing what he or she receives from others who are more professionally or vocationally oriented to ministry. The layperson can offer especially valuable insights on such matters as how the student relates to volunteers, how approachable he or she appears to those seeking counsel or wishing to address a problem, and the student's communication skills, just to mention a few.

The involvement of laypersons in the evaluation process should be moderated carefully by the mentor to ensure that their feedback is consistent with the overall objectives of the field education experience. In particular, the evaluation should not be used as an opportunity to grind an axe or advance an agenda. The learning goals for the internship should function as the primary framework within which laypersons' feedback is given. Opportunities for comment on other issues should be afforded, though carefully monitored to avoid overwhelming the student with an overload of feedback. If an evaluation form or instrument is being utilized, it is recommended that it be customized for use by laypersons. This would include rewording questions or items that are theologically esoteric and emphasizing those matters for evaluation to which laypersons can offer particularly useful feedback.

Peers in ministry also may participate in the evaluation process. These may include persons with whom the student serves in the ministry setting (other than the designated mentor and laypersons), as well as fellow ministry students who are engaged in ministry internships themselves. However, the evaluative capacities of these two groups differ significantly. The former group has the advantage of observing the student as he or she serves in the ministry setting, while the latter group is removed from the ministry setting and relates to the student in an academic environment. Each group has something valuable to offer to the student in the way of evaluation. Peers in the ministry setting can offer the unique perspective of teammates. Their evaluation is especially useful in evaluating a student's ability to work cooperatively with others and contribute to the larger work of the staff. It is said that if you want to obtain the most accurate reference on a minister, speak to the support staff (secretaries, custodians, and others) about them. They are often in the best positions from which to evaluate matters such as the servant spirit of the student, how he or she deals with stress, and attitudinal issues.

The student's school peers relate to him or her outside the ministry setting, and, in some cases, hear their classmate's comments and reflections on the ministry experience. While this limits their ability to evaluate him or her on ministry performance, it introduces other important dimensions to the evaluation process. Fellow students may evaluate their classmate's capacity for theological reflection and integration of theory and practice, they may provide an objective opinion on difficult ministry situations and their classmate's handling of those situations (via ministry verbatims or cases provided by the student), and they may provide valuable insight on the student's integration of personal identity and ministry identity. In the case of both groups, the evaluation methodology should be customized to facilitate the distinctive feedback each group can provide. Verbal evaluations and affirmations, captured through note-taking, are often most useful when soliciting feedback from these peer groups.

Almost all programs of theological field education require students to evaluate themselves. This is a vitally important exercise for the student for a number of reasons. First, it gives the student a voice in the evaluative process—one that is not only responding to what others have said about him or her, but offering an initial assessment of their own standing and performance in ministry. Second, it serves to develop the student's intrapersonal capacity. Self-awareness is an important issue for personal and spiritual health, and it has no small bearing on how one relates to others (the interpersonal). Third, comparing one's self-evaluation with the evaluations offered by others can help to clarify and (hopefully) to reconcile the often disparate matters of what I think about myself, what I believe others think about me, and what others actually think about me.

Self-evaluations are most useful in relation to the learning goals set forth at the beginning of the field education experience. Students should give an account of their efforts toward reaching the goal, being honest about their successes and failures, their frustrations and challenges, and the things they learned along the way. If the learning goals included evaluative criteria (and the best learning covenants do), then the student should address these. The focus in this evaluation should be given to progress, not just to achievement. Many (most?) matters of ministry leadership development defy an achievement or checklist approach. The more important questions are: "What did you learn?" "Where is God at work in your life?" and "Where do you go from here?"

Beyond evaluating themselves relative to learning goals, students also should take these opportunities to address the larger questions of formation for Christian ministry. Responding to the question "What did you learn about yourself in this ministry experience?" can provide a valuable opportunity for growth in self-awareness. More specifically, students should be challenged to continue the work of discerning their call, identifying their gifts, identifying areas or issues for special attention, and developing growth plans for the future.

What Should They Evaluate?

It is easier to speak in broad generalities about evaluating persons preparing for ministry leadership than to be specific about what to evaluate about them. But an effective process of evaluation requires some degree of specificity, for the benefit of both those conducting the evaluations and those being evaluated. In the effort to get specific about what to evaluate, theological field educators have developed numerous lists of competencies, skills, capacities, attitudes, understandings, knowledge, dispositions, behaviors, and so on. Likewise, certain denominations and judicatories have developed similar lists, grids, or profiles to use in the credentialing or ordination processes for their ministry candidates. These lists identify many of the same things, and they differ in many ways as well, usually reflecting the particular emphases of the tradition and culture in which they are developed. Truth be told, there is no definitive list of criteria for ministry fitness outside the whole counsel of the Scriptures. But looking to the Scriptures, and considering the list-making work of others over the years, it is useful to develop one's own list for the sake of evaluation.

Taken as a whole, any such list should constitute a profile of ministry fitness or ministry competency. As stated previously in this chapter, mastery of every area of ministry life and practice is a worthy ideal but ultimately impossible to attain, even over a lifetime in ministry. There will always be room for improvement in any number of skills; there will always be a need for giving attention to matters of character; and there will always be new horizons for learning and growth. Thus, any list of issues and competencies should be used not in a legalistic fashion but as a developmental tool for aiding continual improvement.

Figure 11.1 provides a list of issues to consider as one determines what to evaluate in the lives and ministries of those preparing for vocational Christian service.[3] Though it consists of seventy-two items, it is not an exhaustive list; one can always think of new matters that should be added.

---

3. The development of this list was aided greatly by the work of George Hillman, Doran McCarty, and Mary Alice Seals in the following books: Mary Alice Seals, "Evaluation in the Supervisory Experience," in *Experiencing Ministry Supervision: A Field-Based Approach*, ed. William T. Pyle and Mary Alice Seals (Nashville: Broadman & Holman, 1995), 133–37; George M. Hillman Jr., *Ministry Greenhouse: Cultivating Environments for Practical Learning* (Herndon, VA: Alban, 2008); and Doran McCarty, *Supervising Ministry Students* (Atlanta: Home Mission Board of the Southern Baptist Convention, 1986), 87–94.

Figure 11.1. Ministry Skills Evaluation

LEADERSHIP

Administrative practices	Knowledge of basic administrative processes involved in ministry leadership
Budgeting for ministry	Knowledge of processes for budget planning, approval, and monitoring
Business meeting moderation	Knowledge of business meeting agendas and parliamentary procedure
Communication skills (oral and written)	Ability to communicate clearly and effectively, both orally and in writing
Developing leaders/Mentoring	Ability to identify persons gifted for various leadership roles and to help them cultivate their gifts
Interpreting the ministry context	Understanding of contextual factors that affect the shape of ministry in a given setting
Leading change	Understanding of the principles and dynamics involved in proposing and effecting change in an organizational setting
Leading a Christian education ministry	Knowledge of basic principles and methods for Christian education; ability to organize a ministry that promotes spiritual growth among all God's people
Leading the church in missions	Understanding of the church's role in Christian missions; knowledge of resources for missions education and opportunities for missions support and involvement; ability to organize a ministry that promotes missions
Leading stewardship emphases	Understanding of the role of stewardship in the Christian life; ability to organize and lead a stewardship emphasis
Managing conflict	Understanding of the principles and dynamics involved in conflict; knowledge of resources and methods for helping resolve conflict; disposition to serve as a peacemaker and mediator
Organizational skills	Ability to organize and prioritize multiple tasks and responsibilities for the effective functioning of the ministry
Planning and goal setting	Ability to set appropriate goals and make detailed plans for achieving those goals, allotting sufficient time for the work
Recruiting, training, and motivating volunteers	Ability to recruit, train, and motivate volunteers for the effective functioning of the ministry
Relating to the community as a spiritual leader	Understanding of ministry identity and role as a spiritual leader in the community

Figure 11.1. Ministry Skills Evaluation (*continued*)

LEADERSHIP (*continued*)

Supervision of personnel	Knowledge of personnel policies and processes involved in hiring/staffing positions; ability to provide healthy and effective supervision to persons serving in the ministry organization
Understanding of denominational polity and resources	Understanding of denominational polity, structure, resources, and processes and how these relate to the functioning of the ministry organization
Understanding of financial reports and procedures	Knowledge of basic financial principles and procedures required for the sound fiscal operation of a ministry organization; ability to read a financial report
Vision-casting	Ability to articulate and promote a vision consistent with the mission of the ministry organization
Working with committees and other leadership groups	Knowledge of the leadership structure of the ministry organization and how the various components function together; understanding of the minister's role in relation to these groups

PASTORAL CARE

Care for the poor	Demonstrate an active concern for meeting the needs of the poor as an expression of Christian witness
Counseling	Understanding of the basic principles of Christian counseling; ability to provide sound biblical counsel to those seeking it
Crisis care	Ability to provide appropriate pastoral care to those experiencing various crises (illness, tragedy, divorce, family problems, loss of employment, etc.)
Encouragement	Demonstrate a hopeful perspective and offer encouragement through tangible acts of ministry
Equipping others for caregiving	Ability to recruit, train, and motivate others to serve as caregivers in the ministry organization and beyond
Hospital visitation	Ability to function appropriately as a pastoral presence to those who are hospitalized, to their families, and to medical staff
Marriage ministry	Knowledge of biblical teachings on marriage and the family, of issues to address in preparing for marriage, of church wedding policies, and of resources for premarital counseling, marriage counseling, and marriage enrichment; ability to provide premarital counseling, to officiate a wedding ceremony, and to provide counsel to married couples seeking help

Figure 11.1. Ministry Skills Evaluation (*continued*)

PASTORAL CARE (*continued*)

Ministry to the bereaved	Understanding of the stages of grief and of the needs of the dying and bereaved; knowledge of funeral practices and policies and of grief support resources available to those who suffer the loss of a loved one; ability to provide pastoral care to the dying and bereaved and to conduct a funeral service
Pastoral visitation/Soul care	Understanding of the role of the minister as a spiritual guide or director; demonstrate capacity to relate to other believers as a spiritual friend

PERSONAL AND SPIRITUAL ISSUES

Appearance	Demonstrate appropriate care for self and respect for others in one's outward appearance
Attitude	Demonstrate humility, high regard for others, slow to speak, not temperamental or rude, peaceable, passionate, and eager to serve
Biblical authority	Demonstrate a high view of biblical authority and willingness to submit to that authority in one's life and ministry
Calling and giftedness	Demonstrate increasing clarity about the nature and implications of God's call to vocational Christian ministry and one's particular giftedness for ministry leadership
Dealing with stress	Ability to work under stress and to find appropriate means for managing or relieving stress
Love for God and for others	Demonstrate a deep hunger for God and a passion for his glory, as well as an active love and concern for others
Discipline	Demonstrate capacity to exercise discipline in one's personal life and habits, as well as in one's professional life
Growth in faith	Demonstrate willingness and capacity for trusting God in all matters of concern, and push regularly on the boundaries of that trust
High ethical standards	Demonstrate high ethical standards in one's life and work, deriving from an acute sense of God's holiness and grace
Initiative and work ethic	Demonstrate willingness to take initiative with ministry tasks and responsibilities without requiring constant supervision; proper balance of work and leisure
Integration of theory and ministry practice	Ability to relate the wisdom of biblical and theological studies to the practice of ministry

Figure 11.1. Ministry Skills Evaluation (*continued*)

PERSONAL AND SPIRITUAL ISSUES (*continued*)

Money management	Demonstrate prudence and maturity in the management of personal finances—faithful stewardship, responsible in use of credit, prompt to settle debts, etc.
Practicing spiritual disciplines	Demonstrate faithful practice of spiritual disciplines, including but not limited to prayer, Scripture reading, meditation, silence and solitude, and fasting
Responsible and trustworthy	Demonstrate integrity in speech and actions; dependable when charged with tasks and responsibilities
Self-awareness	Demonstrate an increasing understanding of one's emotions and behaviors, where they derive from, and how they relate to one's identity in Christ
Self-care	Demonstrate appropriate concern for one's own health (physical, mental, spiritual) through those habits that promote it
Self-control	Ability to manage emotions (especially anger) and to speak and act in a manner reflective of the lordship of Jesus Christ
Servant spirit	Demonstrate the disposition to set aside one's own ego and needs to serve the needs of others; not unduly focused on obtaining praise or recognition for self
Sexuality	Demonstrate comfort with one's own sexuality and addressing the topic with others; ability to relate appropriately to persons of a different sex or sexual orientation
Teachable spirit	Demonstrate a passion for learning and growth as a lifelong pursuit
Theological grounding for life and ministry	Understanding of the role of theological reflection in the practice of ministry; demonstrate ability and willingness to ground one's life and ministry in theological convictions
Time management	Demonstrate responsible and efficient management of time; knowledge of available resources for improving time management

PROCLAMATION

Administering the Lord's Supper/ Holy Communion	Knowledge of the biblical teachings on the Lord's Supper/ Holy Communion and the doctrine of it in one's tradition; ability to lead a service in which the Lord's Supper/Holy Communion is served
Equipping others through teaching	Knowledge of the Christian Scriptures and Christian doctrine; understanding of the principles and methods of teaching for transformation; ability to teach various ages clearly and effectively

Figure 11.1. Ministry Skills Evaluation (*continued*)

PROCLAMATION (*continued*)

Justice advocacy	Demonstrate an active concern for justice, and function as an advocate for those who are oppressed, as an expression of the gospel
Organizing and leading others in outreach	Ability to organize and lead a ministry through which the ministry organization can meet and reach out to others in the church and community
Performing Christian baptism	Knowledge of the biblical teachings on baptism and the doctrine of it in one's tradition; ability to perform a Christian baptism
Personal evangelism	Demonstrate an active concern for sharing the gospel of Jesus Christ with others
Preaching	Ability to exegete faithfully a text of Scripture and to preach the message of that text with passion and clarity
Training others for evangelism	Knowledge of resources and methods for training others to proclaim the gospel of Jesus Christ in their daily living; ability to train and motivate others to be personal evangelists
Worship planning and leadership	Knowledge of the biblical teachings on Christian worship and the doctrine of it in one's tradition; ability to plan and lead services of Christian worship

RELATIONAL SKILLS

Dealing with difficult persons and situations	Ability to manage emotions, be assertive, maintain a pastoral attitude, and work for resolution of disagreements that benefit the body of Christ and the mission of the church
Empathy	Demonstrate the capacity to come alongside others emotionally in a variety of life experiences, to provide a beneficial pastoral presence
Flexibility	Ability to work within established structures as well as within ill-defined structures; demonstrate positive attitude and resiliency in responding to changes and surprises
Listening	Ability to attend faithfully to the thoughts, feelings, words, and actions of others as they attempt to communicate
Sense of humor	Demonstrate capacity to laugh at oneself, to not take oneself too seriously, and to evidence the joy of the Lord in one's life and work

Figure 11.1. Ministry Skills Evaluation (*continued*)	
RELATIONAL SKILLS (*continued*)	
With peers in ministry (collegiality)	Ability to relate to ministry peers with respect, encouragement, patience, and in a spirit of teamwork
With one's family members	Ability to relate to one's family members selflessly, to balance ministry responsibilities with family commitments, and to nurture family members spiritually and emotionally as the first order of ministry
With persons in authority	Ability to submit to those in authority, to show proper respect, to refrain from undue criticism or gossip, and to support and encourage them in their leadership role
With persons of different ethnic origin	Ability to relate to others across cultural differences, to show respect and appreciation for customs and traditions, to communicate the gospel in contextually appropriate ways, and to stand firm against prejudice and discrimination
With persons with disabilities	Ability to relate to persons with physical, emotional, and mental disabilities with respect; to value them as members of the body of Christ; to make necessary accommodations for their full participation in the life of the ministry organization
With persons of different ages	Ability to relate appropriately to persons of all ages, to understand generational differences and developmental needs, to provide for the unique spiritual needs of persons in each stage of life
With persons of various socioeconomic status	Ability to relate to persons of various socioeconomic status without intimidation or paternalism, to value them equally as members of the body of Christ, to not show favoritism

Likewise, this list may be more specific than one prefers or include issues that some find unnecessary to include in an evaluation. The nature and scope of the evaluation will serve to determine what should be included and what should be left out.

The various items are organized into five categories: leadership, pastoral care, personal and spiritual issues, proclamation, and relational skills. There is overlap in some of these items, though the description for each one should help to distinguish its meaning in this context.

It is unreasonable to expect that students would be evaluated on all of these issues on every occasion that evaluation is conducted. All of the issues are important, but no one is capable of giving adequate attention to all of them at the same time. The most valuable use of the list in any given term of supervised ministry would likely be as a pool of issues from which students and others could draw to set learning goals. The learning covenant for a defined term of supervised ministry should include no more than three goals taken from each of the five categories listed above. This allows students and mentors to give greater attention to those areas or issues that need developing most urgently.

When Should Evaluation Take Place?

In some respects, evaluation is taking place all the time in theological field education. Judgments are being made constantly about the student and his or her competency as a ministry leader. The majority of these evaluations are informal assessments, usually intuitive in nature, and rarely shared in an explicit way. They do, however, play a role in the ministry leadership development process, as they influence the way that others relate to the student. Students should be made aware of this fact, accept it as an abiding reality of ministry leadership, and learn to live with it in a healthy way.

Evaluation in the more formal and explicit sense should take place at a variety of stages during a term of supervised ministry. The nature and purpose of each evaluation event is somewhat different. At the beginning of the ministry experience, a student should undertake an evaluation of ministry competency to identify areas for attention in the coming weeks of supervised ministry. Some may refer to this as taking inventory. It amounts to establishing a baseline against which progress can be assessed at a later time. Looking to a list of ministry competencies (such as figure 11.1) or to profiles of faithful and effective ministry can help a student consider his or her standing relative to these standards. The student also may seek input from others who know him or her well or who have had occasion to observe the student in a ministry capacity. The results of this evaluation will primarily inform the development of the learning covenant for the term. The student will take the lead at this stage of evaluation, though the input of others is certainly an option as well. Those students who have already completed one or more terms of supervised ministry should refer to their previous evaluations for some initial direction in the beginning stages of a new term.

Some form of evaluation also should be taking place across the weeks of a term of supervised ministry experience. Much of this will take place informally, through conversations with one's mentor and the comments and counsel of others with whom or to whom one ministers. This anecdotal feedback is valuable in its own right. A student should take care to capture these remarks and responses through journaling or by other means of transcription. There is nothing altogether inappropriate about students taking the initiative to develop their own instruments for soliciting and receiving feedback in particular ways, such as sermon response forms, program evaluation forms, focus groups, and so on. However, this always should be done in consultation with one's mentor. More formal means of evaluation may be conducted during a term of supervised ministry. Lay committees often are used to provide students with feedback to various dimensions of their service. A student's mentor or others may also undertake evaluation during the weeks of service. These evaluations should not be comprehensive in nature, in light of the fact that one or more summative evaluations will be conducted at the end of the term. Evaluation, while valuable, can be overdone! It works best for these in-term evaluations to be formative in nature and carefully targeted toward specific ministry objectives, in essence, the student's learning goals.

The evaluations conducted at the end of a term of supervised ministry hold the most promise for providing a student with well-informed and considered feedback. Presumably, sufficient time has elapsed for those conducting the evaluation to observe the student in a variety of ministry situations, to become well acquainted with him or her, and to discern how best to offer practical wisdom that will benefit the student. This should not be done in a hurried way. Those who will participate in the end-of-term evaluation should be enlisted early in the term, they should be informed of the evaluation criteria early in the term, and they should be making notes (at least mentally, if not literally) throughout the term to aid them in the evaluation they will ultimately offer. While it is important to allow the maximum time to elapse before engaging in a final evaluation, it should not be done so late as to preclude an opportunity for the evaluators to take their time completing their forms or composing their remarks. Furthermore, time should be allotted for sitting down with the student to share the results of the evaluations and discussing their implications.

The final evaluations will give focused attention to the student's learning goals and progress made toward each one. This is also the most appropriate occasion for stepping back to consider the larger questions of calling and giftedness, relational capacities, leadership skills, growth areas for future attention, and suggestions of ways to pursue growth going forward. The final evaluations should not be anticlimactic. Neither should a student be taken by complete surprise by what he or she hears or reads in the final evaluations. Ideally, the final evaluations will summarize what the student has been hearing (or, at least, perceiving), both formally and informally, across the weeks of the term. This evaluation not only will look back to what has been and offer responses and judgments, but also will look ahead to what can be and should be and offer direction and encouragement.

How Should Evaluation Be Conducted?

The answer to this question is provided, in the main, in the sections preceding. The function and spirit of evaluation are addressed in the introductory remarks and in the section on "Guiding Principles." Likewise, most of the technical issues are addressed in the "Who," "What," and "When" sections. The remaining matters that deserve mention here are process and tools.

Before a term of supervised ministry experience begins, both students and those who will evaluate them need to be properly informed about and prepared for what lies ahead. While it may seem obvious to some that any form of field education would include an evaluative component, this should not be assumed and left to chance. Field education program directors should provide students with a thorough introduction to their program, taking care to explain the evaluative components, processes, and criteria. Ministry mentors and others who will participate in student evaluations likewise should be made aware of their roles and responsibilities as it relates to evaluation. It is important for everyone involved in theological field education to understand that evaluation is a critical component of the learning process and to commit themselves to their unique part in evaluation.

One part of this preparation should be the provision of forms or instruments to be used in the course of evaluation. Students and those evaluating them should have the opportunity to preview these materials, to learn about how they will be employed, and to be informed of their disposition after the supervised ministry experience is completed. This last issue is especially needful as it relates to privacy matters and to the use of student evaluations in broader processes of student assessment, academic program assessment, ministerial placement, or ordination and credentialing.

There is a variety of tools used for evaluation in theological field education. Most of these tools take the form of written documents, though some may be verbal or experiential in nature. Given the particular emphases of a theological field education program, the leadership will typically develop the tools to be used, with a view to the learning objectives of that program. For the purposes of evaluation at the beginning of a term of supervised ministry (when the primary task is taking inventory or identifying issues for special focus), a student may use a form that prompts him or her to examine specific areas, such as personal character, spiritual formation, and ministry skills. A list of ministry competencies (such as the one above, under "What Should They Evaluate?") is often used as a resource in this process. This evaluation tool should help the student establish a temporal baseline of ministry leadership development, it should be a resource for reference in the development of learning goals for the term, and it should foreshadow the criteria for evaluation at the end of the term.

In the course of the field education experience, other tools and processes may be used for evaluation. A student may be required to write narrative reflections on his or her ministry experiences, which the mentor or others evaluate and to which they offer formative responses back to the student. This can be especially useful for evaluating a student's integration of theory and practice or a student's spiritual and emotional responses to various ministry situations. A similar evaluation can be obtained through the use of ministry incident reports. A student may write a brief account of one or more ministry experiences and highlight what he or she learned about himself or herself and/or about the practice of ministry from the experience. A mentor and others involved in supervision and evaluation can use these artifacts of the student's ministry experience to provide helpful feedback and direction. Most of all, the mentor should keep regular notes (or a supervisory log) of observations, concerns, questions, affirmations, and suggestions across the weeks of a supervised ministry term. These notes do not constitute evaluation in themselves, but they do provide valuable data for conducting evaluation at a later time.

At the end of a term of supervised ministry, the student deserves a summative evaluation. This occasion affords the best opportunity for evaluating the student on the broadest range of criteria. Mentors and others who have observed the student in ministry may use forms provided by the field education program to rate the student's progress toward the stated learning goals. This objective format of evaluation—using Likert scales and/or checklists—should be used only for those evaluative criteria that lend themselves to such ratings.

In most other instances, a narrative format of evaluation is preferable. It allows for commentary and elaboration that is much richer and useful for the student. Narrative evaluations may be used to address learning goal progress, as well as larger issues of ministry leadership development. Given the demand of writing such extensive evaluations, the mentor may be the only evaluator asked to provide such feedback.

The student also may engage in self-evaluation, using the same narrative format. Mentor and student should share their respective evaluations with one another, bringing closure to the term of supervised ministry on a note of candid and constructive dialogue about what has been learned, where further growth is needed, and how the student can go forward to future growth. Beyond the use of written instruments or narrative evaluations, the student may also meet with ministry peers and/or a lay supervisory committee to receive verbal feedback. The mentor should moderate this meeting to ensure that it follows a constructive agenda. The student should not feel "ganged up on" but should experience the best of what Christian community and collective wisdom can offer. In all of these instances of evaluation, whether using material forms or group process, it is most helpful for the evaluation criteria to remain the same.

Conclusion

There is no more challenging or rewarding experience in theological field education than evaluation. Beyond forms and checklists, it consists of sharing godly counsel with a brother or sister as he or she strives to become all that God intends and desires. The standards for evaluation should be high because what is at stake in theological field education is nothing less than the preparation of men and women for the spiritual leadership of God's people. We share in the "upward call of God in Christ Jesus" (Phil. 3:14), which, Paul reminds us, requires a mature obsession with pressing on to greater heights of knowledge, character, and skill. Evaluation of those whom

God has called to serve the church is a great privilege and responsibility that is to be approached in a spirit of humility and love. Carefully and prayerfully practiced, God will use it to build up the body of Christ for the glory of his name.

Prayer of Transformation

God of all truth and compassion, may you grant wisdom to discern what is true, what is honorable, what is just, what is pure, what is lovely, what is commendable, what is excellent, what is worthy of praise (Phil. 4:8), that we may be perfectly fit to follow you who is the Way, the Truth, and the Life and may be faithful to lead others in your service. Amen.

Reflection Questions

1. In your life experiences, how have others' evaluation of you (coupled with their feedback) helped to shape your character, skills, and wisdom?

2. Have you experienced or observed instances when evaluation was poorly conceived or practiced? When evaluation was well conceived and practiced? What were the marks and by-products of each?

3. Are you satisfied that your evaluation of students preparing for Christian ministry properly balances assessment of past performance and planning for future growth? If not, then how can you revise your process to strike that balance?

4. With so many issues of ministry competency to attend to, how can a program of evaluation mediate between unreasonable expectations and responsible guidance?

Further Reading

McCarty, Doran. *Supervising Ministry Students*. Atlanta: Home Mission Board of the Southern Baptist Convention, 1978.

Seals, Mary Alice. "Evaluation in the Supervisory Experience." In *Experiencing Ministry Supervision: A Field-Based Approach*, edited by William T. Pyle and Mary Alice Seals, 125–37. Nashville: Broadman & Holman, 1995.

PART 4

Special Populations and Situations in Field Education

International Students
Women Students
Married Students
Distance Education
Difficult Situations

Chapter 12

Working with International Students in Field Education

LUKE BOBO

And I saw no temple in the city, for its temple is the Lord God the Almighty and the Lamb. And the city has no need of sun or moon to shine on it, for the glory of God gives it light, and its lamp is the Lamb. By its light will the nations walk, and the kings of the earth will bring their glory into it, and its gates will never be shut by day—and there will be no night there. They will bring into it the glory and the honor of the nations. (Rev. 21:22–26)

Twenty-two and counting! The Covenant Theological Seminary community—its faculty, staff, and especially the local and distance theological field educators and mentors—has the incredible privilege of training and shepherding seminarians from twenty-two different countries.[1] However, our training and impact does not abruptly end when these brothers and sisters graduate. Unquestionably, their seminary training will impact their families, their ministries, their countries, and future generations. These

---

1. At Covenant Theological Seminary, those persons in the field "classroom" who instruct, nurture, encourage, and guide our students are referred to as field education supervisors. Field education supervisors can be pastors, deacons, supervisors, professors, etc. These nontraditional classrooms range from churches to camps to parachurch organizations to not-for-profit organizations.

students hail from several distant lands, including the Netherlands, Togo, Hungary, China, Japan, Argentina, Korea, Peru, Canada, Hong Kong, New Zealand, Brazil, Ghana, Nigeria, and England. Providentially and ironically, God is bringing the nations to us! I am certain that Covenant Theological Seminary—the seminary of the Presbyterian Church in America (PCA) denomination—is not unique in this regard. Other evangelical seminaries also see an increase of international students on their campuses.[2]

On the one hand, God has entrusted to us—the theological field education community and the American church—an exciting opportunity. With this opportunity in a watching and cynical world, churches and other field education sites are exposed to the rich diversity of the kingdom. Welcoming, hosting, instructing, and interacting with these international students is simply a foretaste of Revelation 7:9, where the apostle John tells us that saints from every tribe, nation, and tongue will worship the Lamb of God together in sweet unity.

On the other hand, this influx of internationals to American campuses should give us goose bumps as we reflect on the gravity of our responsibility. International students coming to America present some formidable challenges not only to classroom professors but also to field educators and mentors. Broadly speaking, these challenges may be classified as ecclesial, cultural, social, theological, and technological in nature. Socially speaking, international students have different social constructs or schema that define learning, professor-student relationships, pastor-parishioner relationships, and field educator-student dynamics. Technically speaking, these students often come from educational systems not equipped with modern technology American theological students often take for granted (laptops, LCD projectors, or student portals).[3]

The classroom landscape is quite different now. The classroom is no longer comprised of just white males but of men and women at different life stages and of various ethnicities and socioeconomic classes. Indeed, seminary classes are now populated with men and women from different countries around the globe. Welcome to the global theological community!

Should field educators and mentors seek to assimilate international students into the mainstream of our American evangelical culture, churches, and field education sites? Or should field educators and mentors rather endeavor to accommodate these international students entrusted to their care? Is it necessary to alter one's pedagogical approach to theological education in general and theological field education in particular? This chapter will attempt to answer some of these questions.

---

2. See chapter 4, "Field Education and Cultural Awareness," for additional information.

3. As the name *student portal* suggests, a student is assigned his or her own portal accessible only by a student's login and password. On the portal, a student can download assignments and lecture notes, check academic progress, and complete field education paperwork.

International Student Forum

I convened several forums and one-on-one interviews with international students at Covenant Theological Seminary to get their input on several questions. These students have either graduated from Covenant or are still matriculating and currently in the process of doing their field work in evangelical churches, parachurch organizations, or not-for-profit Christian organizations. In all instances but one, these field education sites were directed by American evangelical Christians. In other words, all international students interviewed were indeed minorities or foreigners at their field education sites.

Those who participated in either a focus group or one-on-one interviews were from the following countries: Peru, Brazil, South Africa, Japan, Nigeria, Hong Kong, Hungary, and Togo. Seven men and three women participated in these sessions. Listed below is a brief profile of each participant. Provided is the gender, country, degree(s) sought or earned, and the length of time in the United States.

- Male, Peru, pursuing a Master of Divinity, has spent 9 years in the United States

- Male, Brazil, pursuing a Master of Divinity, has spent 2.5 years in the United States

- Male, Hungary, pursuing a Master of Divinity, has spent 2 years in the United States

- Male, Togo, graduated with a Master of Arts in Theological Studies, has spent 5 years in the United States

- Male, Japan, pursuing a Master of Divinity and a Master of Theology, has spent 3 years in the United States

- Male, South Africa, pursuing a Master of Divinity, has spent 9 months in the United States

- Male, Nigeria, pursuing a Master of Divinity, has spent 30 years in the United States

- Female, Japan, graduated with a Master of Arts in Counseling, has 5 years in the United States

- Female, Hong Kong, pursuing a Master of Divinity, has spent 9.5 years in the United States

- Female, Hong Kong, graduated with a Master of Divinity, has spent

39 years in the United States. This student previously earned a Master of Arts in Counseling.

Overall, these students said that their field education experience met these objectives:

- Field education facilitated an intersection between the classroom and a real-time [ministry] context. The field education context enabled the student to apply what he or she has learned in the classroom.

- Field education experience affirmed and sharpened known spiritual gifts.

- Field education helped the student discover *new* spiritual gifts and/ or perhaps a *new* ministry direction.

- Field education allowed the student to learn from "seasoned" veterans in ministry (pastors, etc).

- Field education helped the student to learn utter dependency upon the Lord.

In sum, these students said that their field education experience was positive and/or is presently a positive experience. I strongly encourage field educators, mentors, and school administrators to have frequent and less formal meetings with their international students to keep their fingers on the pulse of their students' field education experience (the highs and lows). My interaction with these ten brothers and sisters corroborated many of my own ideas and theories about the field education experience of international students. Their comments will be interspersed throughout this chapter.

Foundational Matters

Image Bearers

International students are human beings made in God's image, as Genesis 1:26–28 so elegantly and beautifully affirms. They are *imago dei* just as American Christians are. How do we image God? Before answering this question, remember that this unique distinction of being made in God's image is reserved only for humankind. No bird, no octopus, no giraffe, and no house pet is said to be made in God's image. Mankind is set apart from God's creation as uniquely crowned with inestimable glory and honor (Ps. 8). Only humankind was created to be like God.

Now back to the question: What does it mean to image God? Very simply, to image God is to mirror God. We make God known on earth as we image or mirror him. So, when a field educator or mentor looks at an international student engaged in his or her field education assignment, that person should see in the international student a certain reflection of God, who is a rational, moral, loving, ruling, creating being. This reflection may be of God's moral integrity. This reflection may manifest itself in a person's creativity in the arts, literature, or music or creativity in doing a ministry task or accomplishing a task in a novel and fresh way. This reflection may demonstrate itself by the love an international student has for his or her spouse. International students may reflect the likeness of God in their rational thinking and ruling (or leading) capability.

Indeed, an international student is an image bearer—one who does not just *"bear* or *have* the image of God but *is* the image of God."[4] International students, like *all* Christians, have an image that is defaced or tarnished, yet they remain image bearers as Genesis 9:6 and James 3:9 remind us. All Christians everywhere are presently in the capable hands of God—"the image refinisher." Once God is finished, every believer (international, American, or otherwise) will be like him, namely, Jesus Christ, who is the image of the invisible God (1 John 3:2; Col. 1:15–20).

Like American Christians, international students reflect the glory of God and thus deserve to be treated with the utmost dignity and respect.

Brothers and Sisters

God has graciously entrusted professors, field educators, and mentors with the educating of these international students. But who exactly are these men and women? Are they seminarians? Absolutely! Are they international students? Absolutely! Yet, these students transcend their international label much like we transcend our "labels." They are more than their national or cultural identity. Who are they? It is profoundly simple: they are beloved brothers and sisters in Christ.

Positionally, as brothers and sisters in Christ, we all are on equal footing before our Holy God (Gal. 3:28). We *know* this truth, but does our *doing* match our knowing? In other words, do we treat international students as truly brothers and sisters in practice? Dear reader, God's organizational infrastructure is quite flat: we are all accountable to him and him alone. God is over us. We all stand before God in the same state, as one friend puts it, as "beautiful messes." Any notion of superiority is squashed once all Christians understand that we share this common state.

Sadly, American Christian field educators and the American church have an inflated ego with regard to our importance. Yet, field educators and mentors share an ecclesial and familial bond with their international brothers and sisters in Christ unmatched in any other earthly institution. In God's economy we are to render to each brother and sister preferential favor and service regardless of race or national origin. We share the same

---

4. Anthony Hoekema, *Created in God's Image* (Grand Rapids: Eerdmans, 1986), 66.

plight—smitten by the sin parasite. And we have the same need—God's amazing grace. We share the same hope. We share the same destiny. We worship the same Lord. We are members of the same body of Christ. We are related by the blood of Christ. We are all beloved children of God!

All God's Children Have Culture

Woven through Genesis 1:26–28 is the realization that all human persons are creators of culture. We are mandated by God to create culture—literature, art, music, food, dress, idioms, customs, mores, and language. Moreover, we have the freedom to create the necessary tools to further develop culture. As we embark on these cultural initiatives, we image or reflect God. Fundamental to our "filling and subduing the earth" is making the earth livable. As we employ our God-given ingenuity to create culture, we make the earth livable.

The "we" includes all nations (of which international students are representatives) on the face of the earth. All people groups enjoy their unique cultural beauties (or glories) and artifacts. And because of the fall of man, we all sadly partake in the idolatries or shameful dimensions of our cultures too. Not only is every human being an image bearer of God, but every human being has been deeply impacted by his or her culture both positively and negatively. In other words, "our very way of thinking [and being or doing] is culturally conditioned."[5] As Americans, we have been undeniably conditioned by our American culture—the good, the bad, and the ugly aspects. And this applies to international students too. They have been conditioned by the good, the bad, and the ugly aspects of their cultures too. Nevertheless, all God's children have culture!

Many internationals, like many American Christians, locate their identity and worth in their culture. Thus, to curse or slander another's culture is to deeply offend the person. Consider this comment from a Nigerian graduate student (not part of my focus groups): "I am my culture; it's what I do; it's who I am; it's what I was brought up as. I am Nigerian and that's all there is to it."[6] Clearly this student's identity and culture are inseparably joined.

International students derive their values, beliefs, and social customs from their culture. Reflect on comments from two seminarians who participated in my forum—one from Brazil and the other from Hungary. The Brazilian seminarian said, "I derive aspirations and values from my culture." This student would readily admit that some of the values and aspirations derived from his Brazilian culture are praiseworthy while others are not.

The Hungarian student said this about meal etiquette: "We eat with both hands on the table whether we use both of them or not. It would be

---

5. Philip Harris and Robert Moran, *Managing Cultural Differences*, 3rd ed. (Houston: Gulf, 1991), 204.

6. Barbara Sparks, "A Sociocultural Approach to Planning Programs for Immigrant Learners," *Adult Learning* 12, no. 4 (2001): 22–25.

very impolite or rude in Hungary/Europe to keep one hand in our lap. It is just the opposite here [in America]." Just as an American adult learner brings his or her culture, which is pregnant with presuppositions, values, beliefs, fears, and life experiences (positive and negative), to the field education enterprise, so the international adult learner brings his or her culture, which is also pregnant with presuppositions, values, beliefs, fears, and life experiences (positive and negative), to theological education in general and field education in particular.

And one's culture also can affect the learning process. As William Romanowski puts it, "A culture can shape what we come *to know* and value—how we *understand* God's world."[7] So, one's culture has theological training implications. American businesses are acutely aware of the challenge that culture has on training.

In short, international students bring a worldview colored by their culture to the doorsteps of our theological schools and to the field education context. This worldview colored by the international students' culture is their "script." This "script" guides their doing (or praxis). All international students, in other words, have a philosophy of life that guides their learning, doing, and knowing. Romanowski aptly summarizes this point, saying, "Culture can be likened to a script that guides and explains people's actions."[8] This should not surprise us. An international student and an American Christian field educator, professor, or mentor will see and interpret things quite differently. The job of field educators and mentors is to understand the "script" of the international students. Do not be deceived. This is a huge but necessary task. International students do not arrive with an American "script" in hand; rather they come with their unique "script" conditioned by their culture.

Cultural Beings in "Foreign Waters"

God issued an effectual call to the patriarch Abraham to leave his *familiar* surroundings for *unfamiliar* vistas. Initially, he dragged his feet. Why? Abraham was called to leave family, friends, classmates, and neighborhood buddies; he was called to leave familiar markets, cousins, doctors, and barbers; and he was called to leave the security of knowing and being known in the city of Ur to go to a place that would be unfamiliar and less secure.

Like Abraham, international students have left the familiar for the unfamiliar. They are strangers on furlough in a strange land. International students are vulnerable cultural beings in "foreign waters." The challenge to matriculate at American seminaries is quite daunting for international students. These students face formidable challenges that are all at one time a complex technological, philosophical, social, academic, and cultural web.

---

7. William Romanowski, *Eyes Wide Open* (Grand Rapids: Brazos, 2001), 43; emphasis added.

8. Ibid., 42.

For example, one dear brother I interviewed, a native of Togo, tells of a horrifying account while attending a seminary in the South prior to transferring to Covenant. He remembers vividly the professor instructing the class to visit the online class bulletin board to retrieve assignments and the course syllabus. The problem? He had no inkling what that meant because students in Togo are not afforded such luxuries.

International students often are confused about cultural practices and habits and are reluctant to voice their opinions. One female student from Hong Kong who worked in a church nursery explained that she noticed a parent being lenient toward a disruptive child or bully. She wanted to say something, but because she was the minority, she opted to remain silent. She went on to say that in her culture, this situation would have been rectified immediately. The male student from South Africa who participated in my focus group recounted a similar experience while working in a nursery. He too decided to "zip his lip."

I cotaught an apologetics and outreach course at Covenant Theological Seminary, and I often told white American students in particular to be intentional about entering a context in which they are the minority. This can be unsettling and fearful. Welcome to the existential moment of international students. International students experience these same fears with regularity and great intensity.

Not Empty-Handed

International students do not come to the theological field education venture empty-handed. What does an international student bring to the theological field education table? One tenet or assumption of andragogy is that every adult learner brings something to the education enterprise.[9] It has been mentioned that international students bring their culture-colored worldview to the field education classroom. Yet they bring abundantly more than this to their field education and seminary contexts. For instance, they bring many years of fruitful ministry experience. Several of our international students at Covenant have pastored, led or served in parachurch organizations, or served on the mission field. Some of our international students have amassed volumes of ministry lessons learned. It would be wise of educators and mentors to reference these lessons learned frequently.

Our international students bring the wisdom of their culture (Prov. 8). Revelation 21:22–26 speaks of the glories that each nation will bring into the kingdom. One such "glory" educators and mentors can enjoy now and benefit from is the wisdom of international students. Their culture's wisdom has made their societies successful and prosperous, much as our culture's wisdom has made America successful and prosperous. However, it is quite tempting to think the American way of doing ministry is *the*

---

9. *Pedagogy* is the art and science of how children learn; *andragogy* is the art and science of how adults learn. Of course, there is overlap between these two disciplines of study.

right and supreme way and look with contempt on other cultures and their contributions.

For instance, it is easy to jump to the conclusion that Americans are the trendsetters and the ones to be emulated in all things. However, a Nigerian seminarian who participated in my study said, "A good work ethic did not originate with America." He is quite right. No one country has a patent on a good ethic. Educators and mentors should look for and consult with international students on ministry ideas and methodology.

For many international students, attending seminary marks a journey to a second vocation. Many of them had previous professional life experiences as lawyers, doctors, engineers, college professors, and high school teachers. It would be prudent (and dare I say biblical) if educators and mentors listened attentively to these men and women, who are intelligent and seasoned. International students do not come to America as an empty barrel ready to be filled; rather, they come with knowledge, life experiences (professionally and ministerially), and skills that can be utilized to enrich the theological field education experience. Let me suggest that educators and mentors assume the role of student at times and sit at the feet of international students and learn from them.

Improving Cultural IQ and Self-Examination

Missionaries, prior to going abroad, take time to study the language and culture of their final destination. They are essentially trying to bolster their cultural IQ or become culturally literate. Educators and mentors are called to do nothing less. Educators and mentors must prepare themselves and their congregations and ministry teams before the arrival of their international student. This can spare an educator or mentor and his or her international brothers and sisters some embarrassing and awkward moments.

For example, in Hungary, it is customary to give two kisses when greeting someone. In America, to plant two kisses on a lady would not only be insulting but also could be misconstrued as flirting. The Hungarian student who participated in my study has been embarrassed on several occasions when trying to give a lady two kisses on the face.

Globalization has effectively made people of all cultures one's "next-door" neighbors. The Internet and MTV have made us all global neighbors who exchange many cultural artifacts—dress, music, and ideologies (e.g., postmodernism). However, our global neighbors do not necessarily share the traits of our American culture, which include a "sense of equality, very direct style, individuality, [a] focus on the task at hand, and [a] willingness to take risks."[10] Rather, their cultural traits are often quite different from ours. And once they hit our shores, they will not necessarily know or adopt

---

10. Brooks Peterson, *Cultural Intelligence: A Guide to Working with People from Other Cultures* (Yarmouth, ME: Intercultural, 2004), 60.

the "traits" of our American evangelical culture. Our international students possess traits that in many cases are the polar opposite to ours. And those traits have made their societies run smoothly and successfully.

Culture Scales

In his book *Cultural Intelligence: A Guide to Working with People from Other Cultures,* Brooks Peterson describes five culture scales to help show the differences between various cultures. Below is a very brief description of these five scales.[11]

Equality Versus Hierarchy

One measure of cultural differences is a person's or culture's preference toward equality or hierarchy (see figure 12.1). The Nigerian participant in my study is accustomed to a hierarchal structure. He informed me that there is what is known as a "seniority allowance" in Nigeria. In that culture, the younger person does not challenge the elder even if the elder is just one year older. So imagine the fear and trepidation that would seize a Nigerian student if a field educator or mentor tells the student to approach and lovingly confront the pastor at the church.

Figure 12.1. Equality Versus Hierarchy	
***Equality* means people prefer to:**	***Hierarchy* means people prefer to:**
• Be self-directed	• Take direction from those above
• Have flexibility in the roles they play on a team	• Have strong limitations about appropriate behavior for certain roles
• Have the freedom to challenge the opinion of those in power	• Respect and not challenge the opinions of those who are in power because of their status and their position
• Make exceptions, be flexible, and maybe bend the rules	• Enforce regulations and guidelines
• Treat men and women in basically the same way	• Expect men and women to behave differently and to be treated differently

Direct Versus Indirect

A second measure of cultural differences is marked by the choice between a direct style of relating with others and an indirect style of relating with others (see figure 12.2). Interestingly, the male student from Japan who

---

11. Ibid., 37–55.

participated in my focus group said that when his Japanese friends want to be confrontational or direct they speak in English; otherwise, they speak in Japanese!

Figure 12.2. Direct Versus Indirect	
A *Direct* style means people prefer to:	**An *Indirect* style means people prefer to:**
• Be more direct in speaking and be less concerned about how something is said	• Focus not just on what is said but on how it is said
• Openly confront issues or difficulties	• Discreetly avoid difficult or contentious issues
• Communicate concerns straightforwardly	• Express concerns tactfully
• Engage in conflict when necessary	• Avoid conflict if at all possible
• Express views or opinions in a frank manner	• Express views or opinions diplomatically
• Say things clearly, not leaving much open to interpretation	• Count on the listener to interpret meaning

Individual Versus Group

A third measure of cultural differences is seen in the choice between a person's or culture's individual focus versus a person's or culture's group focus (see figure 12.3). A colleague at Covenant recounts this eye-opening story as he was teaching in Ghana. He was finishing one topic and preparing to move on to the next topic. Before he was allowed to do so, the students wanted to make sure everyone was ready to move on. In other words, group members huddled to make sure their fellow students understood the topic well before allowing the instructor to continue.

Figure 12.3. Individual Versus Group	
An *Individual* style means people prefer to:	**A *Group* style means people prefer to:**
• Take individual initiative	• Act cooperatively and establish group goals
• Use personal guidelines in personal situations	• Standardize guidelines

Figure 12.3. Individual Versus Group (*continued*)	
• Focus on themselves	• Make loyalty to friends a high priority
• Judge people based on individual traits	• Determine their identity through group affiliation
• Put individuals before the team	• Make decisions as a group
• Be nonconformists when necessary	• Put the team or group before the individual
• Move in and out of groups as needed or desired	• Conform to social norms
	• Keep group membership for life

Task Versus Relationship

A fourth measure of cultural differences is seen in the difference between a task motivation and a relationship motivation (see figure 12.4). Both the Peruvian and the Brazilian students who participated in my study said relationships far outweigh starting on time. And to ask, "How are you doing?" without really wanting to know how a person is doing is considered shallow in the South American and Hungarian cultures. Field educators need to be aware of when the cultures of international students can clash. For instance, the Japanese female student said that her task-oriented style often conflicted with the laid-back relationship style of a fellow Mexican student.

Figure 12.4. Task Versus Relationship	
A *Task* style means people prefer to:	A *Relationship* style means people prefer to:
• Define people based on *what they do*	• Define people based on *who they are*
• Move straight to business—relationships come later	• Establish comfortable relationships and a sense of mutual trust before getting down to business
• Keep most relationships with co-workers [seminarians] impersonal	• Have personal relationships with co-workers [seminarians]

Figure 12.4. Task Versus Relationship (*continued*)	
• Sacrifice leisure time and time with family in favor of work	• Sacrifice work in favor of leisure time and time with family [and friends]
• Get to colleagues quickly but usually superficially	• Get to know colleagues slow and in depth
• Use largely impersonal selection criteria in hiring (such as resumes or test scores)	• Use largely personal selection criteria (such as family connections) when hiring
• Allow work to overlap with personal time	• Not allow work to impinge on personal life

Risk Versus Caution

The final measure of cultural differences is observed in a person's willingness to take risks versus a desire to be more cautious (see figure 12.5). One Japanese seminarian recounted a story about attending a church leaders' meeting. In Japan, decisions are seldom arrived at during a meeting. Rather, meeting participants are encouraged to ponder the business discussed at the meeting, and a decision may come weeks or months later. So you can imagine this student's surprise when the next day a meeting participant was already behaving in such a way that communicated a final decision had been made at the meeting. This student was astounded. This created a conflict and left him asking, "When was the decision made?"

Figure 12.5. Risk Versus Caution	
A *Risk* style means people prefer to:	**A *Caution* style means people prefer to:**
• Make decisions quickly with little information	• Collect considerable information before making a decision
• Focus on present and future	• Focus on the past
• Be less cautious—in a "ready, fire, aim" way	• Be more cautious—in a "ready, aim, aim, fire" way
• Change quickly without fear of risks	• Change slowly and avoid risks

Figure 12.5. Risk Versus Caution (*continued*)	
• Try new and innovative ways of doing things	• Want more roles, regulations, guidelines, and directions
• Use new methods for solving problems	• Refer to past precedents of what works and what doesn't
• Have fewer rules, regulations, guidelines, and directions	• Stick to proven methods for solving problems
• Be comfortable changing plans at the last minute	• Not change plans at the last minute

Contrast of American Culture with the World

Figure 12.6[12] illustrates where America ranks in relationship to the five dimensions of culture discussed above. These traits have made this country immensely successful and prosperous. However, generally speaking, the traits or tendencies for the "rest of the world" line up with figure 12.7. Some would argue that the world is becoming more Westernized and that the circle in figure 12.7[13] is slowly migrating to the left. This may be true; however, international students nonetheless come to the United States with values and traits quite different from those of Americans.

A few comments need to be said about figures 12.6 and 12.7. First, the horizontal axis is not meant to imply that one can find or attempt to find a precise number for a particular culture because cultural traits are fluid, complex, and nuanced. (This probably explains why Peterson chose to use an oval and not a straight vertical line to illustrate the ranking of America and the rest of the world's cultures. This suggests that understanding a culture is not a precise science.) Of course, the danger of assigning a precise number to a culture is the false belief that we *know* it. This numeric scale is simply an easy way to illustrate similarities and differences along a continuum.

Second, beware of using these diagrams to oversimplify or overgeneralize a culture. Again, there are gray areas to be sure, and culture is a dynamic, complex, and nuanced organism. No two Americans think and act exactly alike; so too no two Nigerians think or behave exactly alike.

Finally, these scales provide us with a starting point to begin to understand how our culture may be different from and similar to that of international students. Peterson is helpful here, stating that "understanding culture

---

12. Reproduced by permission from ibid., 61.
13. Ibid.

is and should be, a messy and complicated business (and an enjoyable one) the deeper you get."[14]

Figure 12.6. American Rankings on Cultural Scales

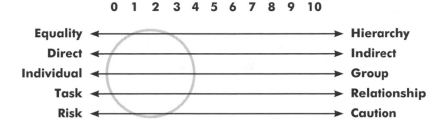

Figure 12.7. World Rankings on Cultural Scales

Figure 12.8[15] is yet another simple illustration of how the United States' culture compares to other cultures. What does figure 12.8 tell us? Generally speaking Canada is similar to the United States in cultural traits and practices while the Middle East is quite different. Admittedly, these figures are on one hand an oversimplification; yet, on the other hand, they do reveal some helpful data.

What are the implications for field educators and mentors who possess and work from one set of traits and serve alongside our international students who possess and work from another set of traits? The first implication is that field educators and mentors should not be naïve. Misunderstandings and conflicts are inevitable. Not only are we sinners but we also have different perspectives and different ways of doing things. Second, field educators and mentors need to jettison the idea that we simply need to be ourselves around international students, because being ourselves can be offensive to our international brothers and sisters. Third, field educators and mentors must prepare themselves and those who come

---

14. Ibid, 34.
15. Reproduced by permission from ibid, 69.

in contact with these students as well. Fourth, field educators and mentors must learn to tolerate ambiguity.[16] Field educators and mentors must be able to accept a degree of frustration and to be willing to wade into "nonprecise gray areas." Finally, field educators and mentors must be ready to intervene when an American Christian and international student clash or when two international students clash.

Figure 12.8. Scale of Cultural Differences

10 The Middle East, Asia, India, Africa

Eastern Europe

Western Europe and South America

5

England, Australia, and New Zealand

Canada

0 United States

Self-Examination

Field educators, mentors, and the entire theological education community must examine their own set of cultural beliefs, values, norms, customs, and behaviors when planning and designing field education programs. Additionally, they also must seek to understand the cultures of foreign students. One Japanese woman student said this: "Americans do not typically look beyond their own culture. Consider the local news. It simply covers local news and rarely covers international news." Theological field educators and mentors must reverse this reality and seek to understand their cultural biases and the cultural habits of international students.

As members of the dominant field education culture (field educators,

---

16. Harris and Moran, *Managing Cultural Differences*, 287.

mentors, and staff) seek to understand their own set of cultural beliefs, values, norms, and behaviors, they will begin to see the distinctions among diverse people groups. Thus, it is imperative that field educators and mentors seek to understand these different cultures and the often hidden cultural sensitivities. And because we American Christians are often shortsighted, we must take a risk and allow our international students to help us to *clearly see* our beliefs, values, norms, and behaviors. For instance, a brother in Christ and friend from South Africa commented after spending only three days in the United States, "I have noticed two things about Americans: one, they have a lot of choices, and two, they are individualistic." Field educators and mentors—allow your international students to serve as your mirror.

Looking Forward: Accommodation or Assimilation?

I asked my cozy group of international students about accommodation, assumptions, and assimilation. Most of them said that it was simply assumed that they were to assimilate into the ebb and flow of their field education site culture (no questions asked). Is this the right approach?

Assimilation

What do we mean by assimilate? In most cases our definition agrees with *Webster's New Collegiate Dictionary* that defines *assimilate* as "to absorb into the cultural tradition of a population or group (as in the community *assimilated* many immigrants)." We often speak of assimilating new members into our church. By assimilating we mean that a new member is expected to adapt to the language and dress of this church's culture and to adhere to its written (and unwritten) rules and its protocol. In many cases this works well if the members are of the same race, culture, and class. In most cases our churches and our field education sites have adopted this assimilationist perspective. When nationality, race, culture, and class are different, challenges will undoubtedly surface. However, to avoid conflict one is simply encouraged to assimilate.

Barbara Sparks cogently writes that "this [assimilationist] perspective suggests that all immigrants, regardless of race, ethnicity, or class level should eventually assimilate into the dominant Eurocentric white culture."[17] This perspective and understanding is not only assumed for international citizens assimilating into our American culture but it often applies to our international students assimilating into our field education site cultures too. In fact, my discussion with these international students bears proof of this unspoken requirement. In all cases, they were expected to assimilate. For many of them, it was not spoken but merely communicated nonverbally.

As brothers and sisters who will eventually worship in their own tongues and worship styles, is this the kingdom way? Should we allow our international students to wear clothing unique to their cultural setting and not a suit and tie, which is the standard uniform in our American churches? What

---

17. Sparks, "Sociocultural Approach to Planning Programs," 46–52.

are we sacrificing when we ask an international student to simply assimilate? When we ask our students to assimilate, do they consider themselves true ministry partners? I would contend that as evangelical hosts and hostesses, we must accommodate ourselves to our brothers and sisters.

Accommodation

God is fashioning one new community, a community where each Christian is invited to serve God in his or her cultural forms. The council that convened at Jerusalem serves as a case study here. The Jews did not mandate that the Gentile believers jettison their Gentile-ness but rather their sinful indulgences. To ask brothers or sisters to assimilate is to ask them to jettison their cultural thinking and ways of doing for the American evangelical ways of thinking and doing. To assimilate is to put their cultural ways of thinking and doing ministry on the shelf for now.

Our field education sites (and yes our seminaries' theological curriculums) need to take on a global perspective. In particular, I would submit that theological field educators and mentors must assume a more global perspective in planning, adapting, and executing their field education programs for international students. I am suggesting nothing less than our willingness to accommodate ourselves to our international guests of honor. We must generate new approaches to field education that consider the culture and differences of our new guests. No longer can we assume that "one size fits all." Most of our field education programs still operate under the assumption that all our students are of the dominant Eurocentric culture. No longer can we operate this way. Not only is this insensitive to our foreign students but it is also damaging to the witness of the gospel.

Our field education programs must accommodate the many national citizens who are matriculating at our schools. For many seminaries this will be unquestionably an awkward, frightening, and perhaps expensive proposition. Nevertheless, the surge of foreign students presents us with an excellent opportunity for teaching American theology students and our field education partners a vital truth inherent about the gospel—the need to contextualize our American evangelical ministry culture (methods, language, and unwritten rules) to make it accessible and accommodating to our international students.

Certainly our international students must assimilate to some degree. For instance, international students should obey the traffic laws. However, *what if* the field educator or mentor "takes the challenge of planning [field education] programs responsibly and democratically, [which] means generating new approaches that consider culture and difference and understanding how learning is used in social interaction within a situational context?"[18] *What if* field educators and mentors contextualized theological field education for our foreign students? This means being flexible and adaptable and accommodating different approaches. Do not be misled. What I am

---

18. Ibid.

suggesting is no easy feat. Practically this may mean eating food and engaging in practices unique to the international student's culture. God has given seminaries and thus field educators and mentors an awesome privilege and challenge to shepherd and train these foreign students before they return home. By accommodating themselves, field educators and mentors will model Christlike service as Christ accommodated and served us.

Charge to Theological Field Educators and Mentors

American Christian churches, professors, field educators, and mentors are afforded an incredible privilege—to train our brothers and sisters from the nations. Take a moment and reflectively consider the gravity of this opportunity. In God's providence, we actually participate in the international student's gradual transformation from one level of glory to the next (2 Cor. 3:18). We partner with God in another brother's or sister's spiritual maturation and ministry refinement and development. This partnership will involve tenacity and great patience. Training our international students will require accommodating ourselves, serving them and not insisting on our way (sounds like *love* as prescribed in 1 Cor. 13). I would like to suggest several helpful hints for training international students. Some of these hints are taken directly from the international students I interviewed.

Be Active Models

Field educators and mentors should actively model for their staff respect and dignity for their international students. I am calling all field educators and mentors to actively model before their staff and other seminarians (international and American alike) what selfless service entails. Field educators and mentors must show others the way in serving our international students in word and deed.

Take a Genuine Interest in the Person

We show international students worth and respect when we take a real interest in them as human persons and not merely as students. I had the distinct pleasure of leading a covenant group for two years at Covenant Theological Seminary. A covenant group is a small discipleship group in which members pray for each other, encourage each other, and hold each other accountable. One student from Togo said he believes this is the key for field education personnel. That is, take an interest in the international student as a person. This student commented that this covenant group encouraged him greatly at Covenant Theological Seminary by taking an interest in the affairs of Togo and his family (this student was here on political asylum and feared for his mother and immediate family, who were in grave danger). We prayed for his family. When he shared the financial struggles of his sister to buy school supplies for her children, we collected a very modest offering from the group members and presented it to this student. He immediately sent the collection to his sister. Everyone wants to be known and cared for. As field educators and mentors, we should be acutely aware of this universal truth.

Create an Environment of Mutual Learning

Several international students I interviewed said the field education sites in which they served just assumed the American Christian way to do ministry was the right way. This is ethnocentrism and is certainly unbiblical. This was not often communicated in words but rather in actions. As American Christians, we are often blinded by our cultural biases and habits. Remember, "White privilege blinds one to many things that are thought, said, and done."[19] Similarly, our American version of Christianity can blind us.

International students come to us with life and ministry experience: they can teach us. Therefore, in humility we must take time to listen to their input, ideas, and perspectives. Remember that "culture is like a diamond—hold the jewel to light, turn it, and we get another perspective."[20] I invite field educators and mentors to actively solicit the perspective of their international students. By actively listening to an international's student perspective, we effectively not only communicate dignity and worth, but we also communicate that he or she is truly an equal partner in the gospel ministry.

Practice Hospitality

I encourage field educators, mentors, and host pastors alike to practice hospitality. Scripture is quite clear that we are called to show hospitality to brothers and sisters in Christ (Rom. 12:13; 3 John). Hospitality (the New Testament word literally means love of strangers) conveys simultaneously intimacy, acceptance, and safety. Hospitality affords us the opportunity to share our very lives with our international students. The apostle Paul is our example, for 1 Thessalonians 2:8–9 makes it clear that he unselfishly shared his life with the church at Thessalonica. As field educators and mentors, we must invite international students to our homes. I was saddened when I heard Dr. Christine Pohl say during Covenant Theological Seminary's Spring 2005 Schaeffer Lecture Series that over 90 percent of international students have never crossed the thresholds of an American home during their stay in the United States.[21] This high percentage represents a tremendous opportunity, an opportunity for us to substantially lower this percentage.

---

19. Jeanette Rodriguez and Sharon Callahan, "Creating a Space in Oneself for the Other" (paper presented at the 27th Biennial Consultation of the Association for Theological Field Education, Chicago, January 2003), 60.

20. Harris and Moran, *Managing Cultural Differences*, 167.

21. The Francis Schaeffer Lectures are held twice a year. The purpose of this lecture series is to bring in noted speakers to address issues that the church is or should be struggling with. For this particular lecture series, we considered the topic, "Making Room: The Mystery, Riches and Challenge of Christian Hospitality," and Dr. Christine Pohl was a keynote speaker. Dr. Pohl is a professor at Asbury Theological Seminary and the author of *Making Room: Recovering Hospitality as a Christian Tradition* (Grand Rapids: Eerdmans, 1999). You may find the lectures at Covenant Theological Seminary's Ministry Resources (www.covenant seminary.edu).

Act as Translators and Escorts

In the hilariously funny film *My Big Fat Greek Wedding*, we get a glimpse (albeit exaggerated) into the Greek culture. The film is essentially about two distinct cultures—one Greek, one American—and culminates with a beautiful wedding. At the wedding reception, an aunt of the bride (both of Greek descent) kneels between the parents of the groom, who are American, to explain a Greek custom. As the bride's parents approach the podium and immediately before they present their gift to the bride and groom, the aunt says to the groom's parents, "This is what we do." Greek parents give meaningful gifts to their children. In this case, the parents hand the bride and groom a deed to a new home (which is, incidentally, next door to theirs).

Our international students need "translators" who explain *what we Americans do*. Several international students mentioned the necessity to have an advocate or "tour guide" to "lead them by the hand." Effectively, field educators and mentors need to walk alongside the international students. Escort them on "field trips" around the community, around the church, and around your home, and show them every room. Escorting them around your home may seem odd to the reader. However, for the sake of propriety, ask a Brazilian student what is different about a bathroom in an American home versus a bathroom in a Brazilian home.

Indeed, serving as translators of American culture and evangelicalism is a tall order. This is where we might solicit the help of seminarians to help us. Many international students need practical assistance like securing a driver's license or applying for a social security number or finding lodging. However, the needs of international students cover a vast range from these practical needs to living in our homes. Serving international students is a great laboratory for demonstrating a new quality of love for our brothers and sisters in Christ as John 13:34–35 reminds us. In other words, our treatment and care of brothers and sisters from foreign lands is a cogent and declarative apologetic.

Conduct Exit Interviews

I encourage field educators and mentors to conduct "exit interviews" with their international students. Essentially, the purpose for such interviews is to assess the students' experience at the field education site. Candid and honest feedback should be encouraged. Such feedback from "outsiders" often helps us to see our blind spots. The data collected can prove invaluable in improving or tweaking conditions for the next international student. Some practices may need to be retired. Very basic questions may be asked. What did you enjoy about your field education experience? How can we improve? How can we better accommodate students like you? Field educators and mentors should make it a point to stay in frequent dialogue with the seminary's administration to share what is going well and what needs to improve. Indeed, a team approach is strongly urged.

Prayer of Transformation

Lord, thank you for bringing the nations to us, and thank you for the awesome privilege to train these students—our brothers and sisters in Christ—from around the globe. May we as field educators and mentors assume the role of a servant and steward this trust well and to your glory.

Reflection Questions

1. How well does the church know the culture (especially, the cultural sensitivities) of the international student serving in her midst?

2. What assumptions have you made regarding your international students?

3. How well have you equipped international students to navigate the foreign waters of the American Christian church?

4. What can we learn from our brothers and sisters who brave coming to America for theological training?

5. How well do you know your international students? Do you know their joys, fears, and struggles?

6. What are the implications of asking an international student to assimilate? Can we find a balance between accommodating ourselves and asking our students to assimilate?

Further Reading

Harris, Philip, and Robert Moran. *Managing Cultural Differences*. 3rd ed. Houston: Gulf, 1991.

Peterson, Brooks. *Cultural Intelligence: A Guide to Working with People from Other Cultures*. Yarmouth, ME: Intercultural, 2004.

Chapter 13

Working with Women Students in Field Education

JOYE BAKER

So God created man in his own image, in the image of God he created him; male and female he created them. And God blessed them. And God said to them, "Be fruitful and multiply and fill the earth and subdue it and have dominion over the fish of the sea and over the birds of the heavens and over every living thing that moves on the earth." (Gen. 1:27–28)

When I first assumed the role of overseeing the internship program for the women students at Dallas Theological Seminary, George Hillman (our field education coordinator) explained that my responsibilities would involve meeting three different times with each potential female student. The first meeting would be a registration interview to help the student identify her internship. The second would be an appointment with the student, her mentor, and me, preferably at the internship site. The final meeting would be an exit interview with the student to evaluate and reflect upon her internship experience.

I looked forward to this opportunity to help our women students take what they had learned in the classroom and integrate it into practical ministry experience. Erin Stambaugh, administrative assistant at our Center for Christian Leadership, would be setting up all my appointments. She explained that George usually planned for fifteen-minute appointments for his registration interviews. This gave me my first hint that some differences might exist in the way to conduct field education for male students and female students.

My Doctor of Ministry project involved an analysis of the leadership challenges facing women seminarians.[1] Part of that study looked at the different leadership styles of men and women. Though care needs to be taken to not make broad generalizations, there remains sufficient data that men and women tend to interact and respond to circumstances and people in different ways. This being the case, George had no problem meeting with male students for fifteen minutes and accomplishing the task of determining the student's internship focus. However, I saw the first interview as an important time to get to know the female student, connect with her on a relational level, and then move toward identifying her internship options. Erin learned quickly that I needed at least forty-five-minute appointments! So began my journey to discover how to best serve female students.

A Brief History of Seminarian Women

"The first woman graduated from a seminary in 1850, but until the 1970s women continued to study in seminaries only in very small numbers."[2] Since the 1970s seminaries across America have opened wide their doors to women.[3] According to the Association of Theological Schools, women comprised 10 percent of seminary enrollments in 1972. The percentage climbed to 21 percent in 1979, 30 percent in 1990, 34 percent in 1999, and has remained close to 35 percent through 2006.[4] In the early years, seminaries focused primarily on training men for the pastorate. The past thirty-five years have seen seminaries broaden their focus and so create many new opportunities for women in the area of vocational Christian ministry. In 1989, Leon Pascal, the executive director of the Association of Theological Schools, characterized seminaries as undergoing a paradigm shift from a "clerical paradigm" (preparation of clergy) to a "community of faith paradigm" (a multipurposed nurturing of knowledge and understanding of a faith community).[5] This shift has allowed more women to come to seminary and prepare for a broad range of ministry contexts and positions.

1. Joye Baker, "An Analysis of the Leadership Challenges Facing the Dallas Theological Seminary Women Alumnae" (D.Min. diss., Dallas Theological Seminary, 2005), 12.

2. Joy Charlton, "Women in Seminary: A Review of Current Social Science Research," *Review of Religious Review* 28, no. 4 (1987): 306.

3. Beth Spring and Kelsey Menehan, "Women in Seminary: Preparing for What?" *Christianity Today*, September 5, 1986, 19.

4. The Association of Theological Schools, *Fact Book on Theological Education, 1972–1999* (Vandalia, OH: The Association of Theological Schools, 2000); and idem, "Fact Books/Annual Data Tables, 1999–2007," www.ats.edu.

5. Timothy Morgan, "Re-Engineering the Seminary: Crisis of Credibility Forces Change," *Christianity Today*, October 24, 1994, 75.

Gender Differences

A great deal of debate exists concerning the topic of gender differences. Some scholars believe there are inherent differences in the way men and women respond to circumstances and relationships. Other scholars support the belief that any so-called differences are cultural phenomena. Michele Green, in her doctoral dissertation, makes these summary remarks:

> Sufficient research evidence supports the existence of differences between men and women in epistemology, in social and communication behaviors, and in leadership style. However, not all researchers and scholars agree on the presence of male and female differences. An ideological debate continues between those who presume male and female differences and those who assume similarities that may have its roots in the feminist movement. The majority of researchers, however, acknowledge male and female differences even though they may disagree over their origin (i.e., whether they are sex-linked traits or socially constructed).[6]

Broad generalities require great caution, for certainly all men are not the same and all women are not the same, but studies done by such researchers as Steven Rhoads, Anne Moir and David Jessel, Leonard Sax, and Robert Saucy and Judith TenElshof, as well as many others, support the supposition that a majority of men and a majority of women respond in predictable ways.[7] This being the case, it becomes important to take these differences into consideration when designing a field education program.

With the advancement of medical science and especially brain research, studies have found that a high percentage of men and women differ in the construction of their brains. Anne Moir and David Jessel gathered information from scientific studies done around the world related to the differences in the brains of males and females. In their book *Brain Sex*, they state, "The sexes are different because their brains are different. The brain, the chief administrative and emotional organ of life, is differently constructed in men and in women; it processes information in a different way, which results in different perceptions, priorities and behavior."[8]

---

6. Michele Green, "The Preparation of Women for Ministry: An Exploratory Study of the Traditional Curriculum in Evangelical Seminaries" (Ph.D. diss., Loyola University, 2002), 65.

7. Steven Rhoads, *Taking Sex Differences Seriously* (San Francisco: Encounter, 2004), 14; Anne Moir and David Jessel, *Brain Sex: The Real Difference Between Men and Women* (New York: Carol, 1991), 5; Robert L. Saucy and Judith K. TenElshof, *Women and Men in Ministry: A Complementary Perspective* (Chicago: Moody, 2001), 52; Leonard Sax, *Why Gender Matters: What Parents and Teachers Need to Know About the Emerging Science of Sex Differences* (New York: Broadway, 2005).

8. Moir and Jessel, *Brain Sex*, 5.

Gregg Johnson, associate professor of biology at Bethel College, St. Paul, also confirms the biological evidence for gender differences. He states,

> Are men and women different? The evidence presented here suggests that we have some fundamental physiological and neural differences that are present at birth and predispose us toward certain behaviors dependent on gender. Let us hope that, by recognizing the existence of gender differences, we can better understand each other and help to maximize each other's potentials.[9]

We can observe these differences in the way men and women communicate, learn, and process and respond to relationships and circumstances in life. Before we consider how to specifically design a field education program for women, we need to understand some of the basic ways men and women differ (see figure 13.1).

Figure 13.1. Gender Differences

Men	Women
Responsibilities (Task-oriented)	Relationships (People-oriented)
Independent	Interdependent
Compartmentalize	Integrate
Goal-Oriented	Process-Oriented

Men and Women Prioritize Life Differently

Men tend to be more task-oriented, emphasizing responsibilities, whereas women tend to be more people-oriented, emphasizing relationships. Although men and women value and excel in both categories, the majority of women prioritize relationships over tasks and the majority of men prioritize tasks over relationships. Sally Helgesen's observations and interviews of four corporate women (in response to a study of five corporate men) led to the identification of eight distinctions in the way men and women lead. Helgesen concludes that the "attitudes and qualities in the words of women . . . above all emphasize relationships with people."[10]

In addition, James Kouzes and Barry Posner extracted from their study of leadership that because women focus more on relationships, women tend to emphasize heart issues more than men. As Kouzes and Posner explain,

---

9. Gregg Johnson, "Biological Basis for Gender-Specific Behavior," in *Recovering Biblical Manhood and Womanhood*, ed. John Piper and Wayne A. Grudem (Wheaton, IL: Crossway, 1991), 293.

10. Sally Helgesen, *The Female Advantage: Women's Ways of Leadership*, 1st ed. (New York: Doubleday Currency, 1990), 28.

"Female managers reported engaging in the leadership practice of encouraging the heart significantly more often than did their male colleagues."[11] Clearly, most researchers support the conclusion that women tend to emphasize the "heart" versus the "head."[12]

Although women value both categories, the majority of women prioritize relationships over tasks. In her early years of study under Lawrence Kohlberg in the 1970s, Carol Gilligan first identified this distinction of women valuing relationships over tasks and recorded her findings in her book *In a Different Voice*.[13] It becomes clear from her extensive research that relationships play a key role in the lives of women.

Men and Women Relate to People Differently

Men tend to value independence and women interdependence. "Where men have been identified by researches as 'separate knowers'—individuals who can approach knowledge objectively and reduce it to understandable parts—women tend to be 'connected knowers'"[14] Carol Gilligan concluded in her studies that men feel secure alone at the top of a hierarchy, securely separate from the challenge of others. Women feel secure in the middle of a web of relationships; to be at the top of a hierarchy is seen as disconnected.[15] Robert Saucy and Judith TenElshof, faculty members at Talbot Seminary, conclude from their research that "women define themselves in terms of relational attachment, while men in terms of individual achievement."[16]

Mary Belenky, Blythe Clinchy, Nancy Goldberger, and Jill Tarule collaborated to do extensive interviews with women of different ages, ethnic backgrounds, and social status. They identified women's desire to connect with other people and stated, "We have argued in this book that educators can help women develop their own authentic voices if they emphasize connection over separation, understanding and acceptance over assessment, and collaboration over debate."[17] In order for a field education program to most effectively prepare women for ministry, it must have a strong collaborative component. The majority of women enjoy working alongside other people in the context of teams or partnering with other men and women.

---

11. James Kouzes and Barry Posner, *The Leadership Challenge*, 2nd ed. (San Francisco: Jossey-Bass, 1995), 346.

12. Helgesen, *Female Advantage*, 55.

13. Carol Gilligan, *In a Different Voice: Psychological Theory and Women's Development* (Cambridge, MA: Harvard University Press, 1982).

14. Carolyn Duff, *Learning from Other Women: How to Benefit from the Knowledge, Wisdom, and Experience of Female Mentors* (New York: American Management Association, 1999), 42.

15. Gilligan, *In a Different Voice*, 62.

16. Saucy and TenElshof, *Women and Men in Ministry*, 239.

17. Mary Belenky et al., *Women's Ways of Knowing: The Development of Self, Voice, and Mind*, 10th anniversary ed. (New York: Basic Books, 1986), 229.

Men and Women Process Life Differently

Men tend to focus on one thing at a time and organize their lives in "compartments." Women can more easily connect all aspects of life together, which explains why most women typically multitask better than men. In his book *Why Gender Matters*, Leonard Sax cites studies that "provide further support for the notion that male brains and female brains are organized differently, with functions more compartmentalized in male brains and more globally distributed in female brains."[18]

In their book *Men Are Like Waffles, Women Are Like Spaghetti*, Bill and Pam Farrel state that "men process life in boxes. . . . Social scientists call this 'compartmentalizing'—that is, putting life and responsibilities into different compartments. As a result, men are problem solvers by nature. They enter a box, size up the 'problem,' and formulate a solution."[19] On the other hand, for women "every thought and issue is connected to every other thought and issue in some way. Life is much more of a process for women than it is for men."[20]

Cindy Rosenthal focused her research on female political leaders serving in state legislatures and in the Congress of the United States. Her list of sex-gender differences confirms the variety of different ways men and women respond to life circumstances and relationships.[21] Recognizing the ability and desire women have to integrate issues and relationships should be taken into consideration when implementing a field education program.

Men and Women Communicate Differently

Conversation lies at the heart of ministry, for ministry involves dialogue among people. Most women typically need to talk more than men and process information, rather than just focus on solving problems. Deborah Tannen's classic book, *You Just Don't Understand: Women and Men in Conversation*, reveals that in conversation, men seek power, whereas women desire to establish relationships. She states, "For most women, the language of conversation is primarily a language of rapport: A way of establishing connections and negotiating relationships. . . . For most men, talk is primarily a means to preserve independence and negotiate and maintain status in a hierarchical social order."[22]

Luba Chliwniak's research also confirms the difference in male and female conversational styles. She found that for women conversations are used to elicit cooperation or create rapport, whereas men tend to use conversation

---

18. Sax, *Why Gender Matters*, 12.

19. Bill Farrel and Pam Farrel, *Men Are Like Waffles, Women Are Like Spaghetti* (Eugene, OR: Harvest House, 2001), 129.

20. Ibid., 125–26.

21. Cindy Simon Rosenthal, ed., *Women Transforming Congress* (Norman, OK: University of Oklahoma Press, 2002), 23.

22. Deborah Tannen, *You Just Don't Understand: Women and Men in Conversation* (New York: Morrow, 1990), 77.

to negotiate status and engage in verbal competition.[23] In addition, Belenky's study discovered that one of the greatest desires of women is to have a "voice."[24] Helgesen concurs, stating that "women's way of leading emphasizes the role of voice over that of vision."[25] Carol Becker summarizes by stating, "Men tend to approach a conversation as a contest. Women tend to approach it as a connection."[26] It becomes particularly important to acknowledge these differences in communication styles between men and women when considering mentoring relationships in field education.

Specific Ways to Meet the Field Education Needs of Female Students

Previously, this book presented the different components of developing and implementing an effective internship program. When taking into consideration all these aspects of field education, the unique needs of women must be incorporated into the design of an internship program in order for female students to gain the optimum benefit from their practical ministry experience. The previous discussion of gender differences should inform decisions regarding site selection, but even more importantly they inform the choice of a mentor. On a number of occasions, female students expressed to me their frustration, discouragement, and disillusionment over the challenges they faced in their internship experiences. Many of the issues stemmed from their relationship with their site mentor, especially if they worked under a male mentor. The women interns appreciated the knowledge and skills they learned in their ministry setting, but they encountered limitations in areas of communication and theological reflection.

Mary sat in my office with tears welling up in her eyes as she related the difficulty she had talking with her male mentor. She also felt cheated because he spent extensive amounts of time with the male interns while often avoiding her or not including her. She dreamed of becoming a youth pastor one day, but she could not find a woman in that position to be her mentor. She learned a great deal under her male mentor but longed for the relational component that she needed in her internship.

Ronald Hornecker, in his chapter in *Experiencing Ministry Supervision*, addresses the challenges women face with these insights:

> Women students frequently are at some disadvantage in finding an adequate setting or supervisor. Attitudes toward women in ministry and views concerning appropriate roles vary with the setting and the supervisor. Some women will be unable to find settings where they can gain the experience they need to prepare

---

23. Luba Chliwniak, "Leadership in Higher Education: Influences on Perceptions of Women and Men Leaders" (Ph.D. diss., University of Arizona, 1996), 49.

24. Belenky et al., *Women's Ways of Knowing*, 18.

25. Helgesen, *Female Advantage*, 223.

26. Carol Becker, *Leading Women: How Church Women Can Avoid Leadership Traps and Negotiate the Gender Maze* (Nashville: Abingdon, 1996), 53.

for the role to which they feel called. Finding a woman minister who can function as a role model also may be difficult.[27]

This does not discount all the many things women can and do learn from men. Men hold most leadership positions in churches, so women seminarians often have little choice but to train under them. More churches have begun to hire women for various positions on their pastoral staffs, but it remains a limited number. In order for women students to gain the field education experience that will most adequately prepare them for vocational ministry, some will need to have male site supervisors. In these situations, the challenges primarily come in the area of theological reflection and sharing of more personal issues that the women may face.

Hornecker acknowledges, "Some male supervisors may be uncomfortable or uncertain about how to relate to a female student in a supervisory relationship."[28] Often it is neither appropriate nor wise for a man to advise a woman student regarding personal issues. Either the door will be closed to talking at all, as in Mary's case, or the conversations may encourage intimate sharing that could lead to an inappropriate relationship.

Field education settings, as well as students and mentors, are all different. For some, gender distinctions are minor; in others they have greater implications. But in either case, based on the previous information in this chapter, some effort should to be given to providing the best environment for women so that they can most benefit from their field education experience. The following suggestions offer some specific ways for field educators, site mentors, and students to design and carry out an internship program that will best prepare female students for a life of productive and satisfying ministry.

Suggestions for Field Education Coordinators

The field education coordinator has the responsibility of assisting students to identify the most suitable internship site and mentor. In order to do so, it is important that the mentor gain some background information on the student and understand the student's vocational goals. The following suggestions will help women students gain the most benefit from their relationship with their field education coordinator.

Ideally, Hire a Woman to Oversee the Internship Program for Female Students

If a man holds the position of field education coordinator and 25 percent or more of the student body consists of women, then hiring a woman at least part-time to oversee the internship program for the women students would

---

27. Ronald Hornecker, "Choosing a Ministry Placement and Field Supervisor," in *Experiencing Ministry Supervision*, ed. William T. Pyle and Mary Alice Seals (Nashville: Broadman & Holman, 1995), 31; see also Ronald Hornecker, "Choosing a Ministry Placement and Field Supervisor," in *Experiencing Ministry Supervision: A Field-Based Approach*, ed. William T. Pyle and Mary Alice Seals (Nashville: Broadman & Holman, 1995).

28. Hornecker, "Choosing a Ministry Placement," 31.

be the ideal situation. A male coordinator can administrate the details of the internship, but a female student will be more likely to share personal issues related to her internship with a female coordinator. It is not that a man cannot have successful conversations to help place a female student, but initial interviews and exit interviews will be more profitable and meaningful for a female student if done with a woman.

Field education experiences should closely align with vocational goals and placement. For some women, deciding on an internship can become a very emotional time as they seek God's direction for their future. Marital status often impacts the way they feel about making decisions, especially for single women. This can lead to tearful conversations. A woman coordinator can offer a female student a comfortable, safe environment where the student can express whatever she may feel. This opportunity to share openly will rarely happen with a male coordinator. If a woman student does share on a more personal level with him, appropriate boundaries often are breeched. This will either leave the student and coordinator at the very least uncomfortable, or, even more troublesome, open up the opportunity for inappropriate responses. Having a female coordinator will avoid these awkward situations. If this is not possible, then male coordinators need to develop some type of referral system in cases where they identify a female student who needs additional counsel.

Emphasize the Valuable Contribution Women Make to a Church/Parachurch Leadership Team

Field education coordinators need to develop ways to help the leadership in churches and other Christian organizations recognize the important contribution that women can make to a ministry team. God designed the world to function best with men and women partnering together to bring glory to God. Unfortunately some men resist the idea of women holding leadership roles in ministry. These reasons include "tradition, their view of what the Scriptures teach regarding women's roles in the church, irrational fears, and the possibility of negative experiences from the past."[29] The field education coordinator needs to respect various theological positions on women in ministry and yet address the men's concerns and assure them that including women on a ministry team will strengthen their ministry.

For too long women have been excluded from leadership positions. But even in some churches that believe that only men should fill the offices of senior pastor and elder, there remain many associate positions that women can hold. By inviting women to train for some of these positions (such as directors/ministers/pastors of children, youth, women, families, singles, pastoral care, small-group ministry, etc.), churches will gain the advantage of having a female presence and perspective on their staff, which will strengthen their

---

29. Sue Edwards and Kelley Mathews, *New Doors to Ministry to Women: A Fresh Model for Transforming Your Church, Campus, or Mission Field* (Grand Rapids: Kregel, 2002), 189.

leadership teams. "Women place a great value on enabling others, seeing projects holistically, empowering others, and achieving through others."[30] Their natural inclination to value relationships can help men embrace team-work and discover the strength of interdependence.

Often the field education coordinator functions in a public relations role. He or she will need to meet and talk with church and other ministry leaders to help them understand the value and contribution of women. The coordinator should be prepared to answer questions and give biblical support for women serving in vocational ministry.

Encourage Churches and Parachurch Organizations to Provide Internship Opportunities for Women

It is not enough to encourage churches and Christian organizations to see the value of women on their leadership teams. They need information regarding the benefits of offering internship positions to women. Now that seminaries and other Christian educational institutions have recognized the importance of training women as well as men for vocational ministry, women students need places to gain the practical ministry experience that will best prepare them to serve in churches and parachurch organizations.

Field education coordinators will need to meet with pastors and other Christian leaders to dispel any concerns or reluctance they might have concerning women interns. It is important for men in leadership to realize the necessity of female students training under male pastors because so few women serve in pastoral positions. One key to men feeling more comfortable inviting female interns to work alongside them is identifying a spiritually mature woman to mentor the woman student for her theological reflection time. This will relieve the men of that responsibility and avoid what might be an uncomfortable situation. Norman Cohen and Michael Galbraith note, "Even a strictly conducted professional mentoring relationship can still create impressions of impropriety, generate gossip, and even stigmatize the participants when it develops between males and females."[31] Some men in ministry will not risk the possibility of these problems. They need alternatives offered to them so that women students have equal opportunity to gain the practical ministry experience they need.

If a Female Student Plans to Intern Under a Man, Suggest She Find a Female Mentor to Meet with for Her Theological Reflection Time

Theological reflection is a very important part of the field education process. If a female student serves under a male site mentor, she can gain a great deal of knowledge and skills from him. He and she can engage in

---

30. Marian Ruderman, "Leader Development Across Gender," in *The Center for Creative Leadership Handbook of Leadership Development*, ed. Cynthia McCauley and Ellen Van Velsor (San Francisco: Jossey-Bass, 2004), 282.

31. Norman Cohen and Michael Galbraith, "Mentoring in the Learning Society," in *Mentoring: New Strategies and Challenges*, ed. Norman Cohen and Michael Galbraith, New Directions for Adult and Continuing Education (San Francisco: Jossey-Bass, 1995), 12.

conversations related to all aspects of ministry, and she can benefit from his years of experience. But having a female mentor to meet and talk with will allow the female student to delve more deeply into personal, emotional, and spiritual issues that she may face during her internship.

Carolyn Duff, who has done extensive study in the area of female mentoring, concludes,

> Women need women as mentors because only women can truly empathize with the experience of being a woman. We need women mentors because with other women we can act and feel and give as our true selves. In return, we will grow in confidence, strength, and accomplishment. Women will guide us toward the wholeness that is our vision and future.[32]

Relationships play a key role in the life of most women, and having an older, more mature woman to talk with can help a younger or less experienced woman process life issues unique to women.

It is best if the female mentor is somehow associated with the ministry in which the student serves. The mentor might be another woman on the ministry team or an older, spiritually mature laywoman who serves in some capacity of leadership in the church. Such a mentor will be familiar with the ministry setting and have the opportunity to observe the student. Sometimes no suitable woman is available to fill the role of a mentor. In this case, one option might be for a female faculty member to offer to meet regularly with the student for the reflection time. I have done this on a few occasions with encouraging results.

Gretchen planned to pursue a pastoral care ministry with women. She attended a small church in a suburb near Dallas Seminary. The director of pastoral care in her church was an older man who had many years of experience in lay counseling. He had offered her an internship with him. Gretchen realized this was a great opportunity to learn from this wise man and gain excellent ministry experience caring for the women in her church. No women served on the church staff, and she could not find any woman who fit the criteria to mentor her. She asked if I might consider being her mentor for her theological reflection time. Each week she met with me to process all God was doing in and through her life in the midst of her internship. At times she rejoiced and we praised God together; at other times she experienced brokenness, and we wept and prayed together. Gretchen felt free to confide in me and share openly and vulnerably. This would not have occurred with her site mentor.

Each student and each situation is different, but woman-to-woman mentoring will best enable female students to plumb the deepest parts of their hearts. As they spend time with one who most closely understands

---

32. Duff, *Learning from Other Women*, 4.

their questions and struggles, their mentor can respond in ways that will provide comfort and the needed help.

Become Acquainted with the Relational Dynamics of Men and Women Working Together

The field education coordinator will be most effective with women students if he or she has a good understanding of the different ways men and women relate, process and prioritize life, and communicate. It is worth the time to read a few of the books cited in this chapter to gain greater insight into gender dynamics. Listening is very important. Giving the woman time to express herself enables her to verbally process her thoughts and feelings and gives the coordinator the needed information to guide the student in discovering the best ministry setting for her.

Janet came to my office totally uncertain of what direction she wanted to pursue regarding an internship. I began by letting her share a little about herself and what she had enjoyed about her seminary training. I just kept asking her questions and encouraging her to explore the different options related to her ministry focus. She was interested in ministry to women but uncertain whether she wanted to serve in a church, parachurch, or overseas. We did not come to any conclusions at our first meeting, but we identified two or three different possibilities. We prayed together, asking for God's guidance, and she agreed to talk to people in various ministries. The following week she reported back to me. Ultimately she realized that working with the director of the women's ministry in her own church would best prepare her for whatever ministry setting she might find herself in the future. She needed the time initially to talk through all her thoughts and feelings so that she could discern God's will more clearly.

Women students also need encouragement. Some have served very little in ministry and lack confidence; others have faced negative experiences and feel angry or disillusioned. They need the freedom to share their fears or questions. They need reassurance that God delights in their desire to train for ministry and that he will be with them through their field education experience. Field education coordinators need to be cheerleaders or what Joyce Landorf Heatherly calls "balcony people."[33]

Be Aware That Women Often Follow a Different Ministry Career Path from Men

Joy Charlton offers some insightful observations regarding women:

> The career choice process is a different and more difficult one for women than for men. . . . Women are also concerned about work and family issues in a way that men are not. The trajectory of a ministerial career is based on a male model—men are expected to settle into a career at the same time that women are expected

---

33. Joyce Landorf Heatherly, *Balcony People* (Austin, TX: Balcony, 1984).

to marry and have children. Timing and commitment issues are salient for women in a way they are not for men.[34]

Field education coordinators need to recognize these gender differences so that they can best advise their female students.

Marital status impacts a woman differently than a man. If a woman is single, she wonders if she will eventually marry, knowing that becoming a wife most likely will change the direction of her life. If a woman is married, she may be limited in her options regarding ministry, depending on the flexibility of her husband's occupation. She often wonders how motherhood will impact her desire to serve Christ.

These marital and family issues influence a woman student's attitude toward selecting an internship. Needing to make decisions about the future often surfaces a great deal of emotion for some women. The field education coordinator needs to prepare for these emotional responses and give the female student the opportunity to express her fears, doubts, and questions. Women often need to release their feelings first, and then they can more clearly think through decisions they need to make regarding future plans.

Suggestions for Site Mentors

Site mentors serve in a variety of ministry settings. Some hold positions as pastors or ministers in churches, others work in parachurch organizations or on the mission field, and some serve as counselors or teach in academic institutions. Whether men or women, site mentors have the responsibility to give direction and oversight to students seeking practical ministry experience. Site mentors hold a key place in preparing the next generation of Christian leaders. They will function as mentors to men and women who will grow and mature best in the context of a relationship with a person who models Christian character and passes on valuable and needed knowledge and skills.

This chapter focuses on the unique needs of women students. It is important to remember that all women students are not the same. They have different temperaments, life experiences, spiritual gifts, natural abilities, passions, and dreams. First and foremost, site mentors function as mentors for the women training under them. As mentors, they should go behind a woman to encourage her, in front of her to guide her, face-to-face to listen to her, and beside her as a companion.[35]

Generally speaking, the following suggestions should be considered in order for either a male or female site mentor to offer the most beneficial field education experience for a woman student.

---

34. Charlton, "Women in Seminary," 307–8.

35. Myra Bloom, "Multiple Roles of the Mentor: Supporting Women's Adult Development," in *Learning Environments for Women's Adult Development: Bridges Toward Change*, ed. Kathleen Taylor and Catherine Marienau, New Directions for Adult and Continuing Education (San Francisco: Jossey-Bass, 1995), 63–72.

Help the Woman Student Find a Female Mentor for Reflection Time if You Are a Male Mentor

Since men hold the majority of staff positions, especially in churches, women will often need to intern under a man. Some men prefer not to have a female intern. Often there exists a "good old boys network," and the presence of a woman disrupts the male-only environment.[36] Ruderman offers additional reasons some men are reluctant to mentor women: (1) Men tend to meet together informally through sports and other social outings where it might be awkward to include a woman. (2) Others may disapprove of the relationship. (3) It may be misconstrued as a sexual advance. (4) Men are unwilling to engage in relationships with women.[37]

Though these issues sometimes exist, they need not prevent women from training under men. The solution rests in designing a program that allows women to benefit from the knowledge and skills of men without crossing inappropriate relational boundaries. Men and women first should be brothers and sisters in Christ who join together in the family of God to help one another grow and mature. The best solution is to encourage the female student to ask a spiritually mature woman to meet with her for her theological reflection time.

As part of my Master of Arts in Christian Education studies, I completed my internship under Dr. Michael Lawson, chairman of the Christian Education Department at Dallas Seminary. I fulfilled many typical office responsibilities during my internship. In addition, since my ministry goals focused on ministry to women, Dr. Lawson provided oversight as I participated on a committee that developed a women's ministry concentration for our Master of Arts in Christian Education and Master of Theology degree programs. At the same time, I met weekly with a small group of other field education women students to do theological reflection.

In his role as my site mentor, Dr. Lawson functioned as a mentor to me in many ways by helping me learn all the aspects of working in a seminary setting. Ultimately he paved the way for me five years later to join the faculty of the Christian Education Department. Although there existed limitations in my relationship with Dr. Lawson related to sharing very personal issues, my needs to discuss more intimate areas of my life were met through the women in my theological reflection group.

Sometimes a female student cannot find a woman to serve as a mentor at her internship site. In this case, a female faculty member could offer to meet with the student regularly to reflect about her internship. As I mentioned earlier in this chapter, I have personally fulfilled that role for a number of female students. Woman-to-woman mentoring remains most appropriate, effective, and wise, especially when dealing with personal issues.

---

36. Craig Donovan and Jim Garnett, *Internships for Dummies* (New York: Hungry Minds, 2001), 226.

37. Ruderman, "Leader Development Across Gender," 294.

Provide Your Female Intern a Listening Ear

Whether you are a male or female site mentor, female interns need opportunities to talk about aspects of the ministry experience. "Being heard confirms that she has something valuable to say and that her voice deserves to be heard."[38] As mentioned earlier, women tend to be verbal processors, so giving them time to express themselves contributes to their learning. Bloom offers some helpful insights:

> If mentors are to care for students, they must accept the necessity of challenging learners to think more precisely, more broadly, and more profoundly. They often accomplish this by asking questions. . . . Mentors try to frame questions that enable learners to reveal their inner intelligence and clarity of thought. . . . The mentor builds on the foundation of what the learner already knows, thereby validating and confirming her capacity to know.[39]

Let your student know you are available to answer any questions or to help her with any problems she may face in her internship. Set aside time for her to share her thoughts and feelings related to her ministry experiences. Walter Jackson summarizes by saying,

> Personal relationships are a valuable resource for learning in ministry. . . . Conversation about the student's effectiveness in relationships, especially biblical and theological reflection about these relationships, will help the student learn and grow. In addition, the relationships developed with primary supervisors or theological educators are of immense importance.[40]

Giving time to listen validates a woman and the contribution she makes to the ministry and will increase her self-confidence and self-esteem.

Offer Your Female Intern Encouragement and Affirmation

In addition, women thrive in an environment of encouragement and affirmation. They often step into an unfamiliar environment as they begin their internship. Some lack confidence or certainty about their ministry gifting. Women can experience fear in the areas of failure, making mistakes, risk taking, not being liked, change, overcommitment, and success.[41] They need support and patience. They will more readily receive constructive criticism if

---

38. Bloom, "Multiple Roles of the Mentor," 66.

39. Ibid., 69.

40. Walter Jackson, "An Introduction to Theological Field Education," in *Experiencing Ministry Supervision: A Field-Based Approach*, 10.

41. Julie Baker, *A Pebble in the Pond: The Ripple Effect: Leadership Skills Every Woman Can Achieve* (Colorado Springs: Cook, 2001), 26–29.

it is offered in an atmosphere of praise and acknowledgement of things they have done well.

Alison, a third-year seminary student, was three months into her children's ministry internship when she made an appointment to talk with me. As her field education coordinator, I assumed the role of mediator between the site mentors and the female students. When Alison began her internship, she already had a number of years of experience in children's ministry. Her site mentor (a woman) never praised Alison for the many things she did well. No matter what Allison did, her mentor either suggested ways she could improve or criticized her. Allison became more and more discouraged and began to lose confidence in her abilities to work with children. It was not that she was not open to constructive criticism, but she also needed reminders of her strengths and specific ways she successfully ministered to the children.

Because women value relationships and often evaluate themselves based on those around them, the words they receive powerfully impact the way they think and feel about themselves. "Several psychologists argue that an inner sense of connection is the central organizing force in women's development. . . . This stands in contrast to the more male-oriented theories of development, which emphasize independence and autonomy at the expense of relationships."[42] A woman interprets words through a relational grid that can either negatively or positively impact her, depending on the message. "Mentors express care for students by engendering trust, issuing challenges, providing encouragement, and offering visions for the journey."[43] Women students will thrive in an environment of men and women who praise them and encourage them to become all God designed them to be.

Encourage Your Female Intern to Join a Small Group or Have a Close Friend

Women need other women with whom to share life experiences. Titus 2:3–5 stresses the importance of older women teaching truth and passing on life skills to younger women. As you work with a female intern, find out what type of relational support system she has in her life. Because women tend to filter life through a context of relationships, they need to build into their lives people (especially other women) with whom they can be honest and transparent.

Normally over the course of a lifetime, a person will have a number of different mentors. In *Connecting: The Mentoring Relationships You Need to Succeed in Life*, Paul Stanley and Robert Clinton present eight different categories of mentors and also include a chapter on peer co-mentoring.[44] Friends can act as mentors to one another as they support and encourage one another.

---

42. Ruderman, "Leader Development Across Gender," 276.

43. Laurent Daloz, *Mentor: Guiding the Journey of Adult Learners* (San Francisco: Jossey-Bass, 1999), 30.

44. Paul Stanley and J. Robert Clinton, *Connecting: The Mentoring Relationships You Need to Succeed in Life* (Colorado Springs: NavPress, 1992).

Help the student to see the value of building nurturing relationships into her life to enhance what is offered to her in her field education experience.

Take into Consideration the Uncertainty of a Woman's Future Goals

Because relationships tend to be a priority to women, decisions regarding marriage and family often have a significant influence on a woman's ability to consider future goals. Patricia Aburdene and John Naisbitt's research supports the fact that women face many challenges related to balancing work and ministry and their personal lives. "Women do not identify exclusively with their careers, as most men traditionally have."[45] In addition, Beth Spring and Kelsey Menehan discovered in their studies that placement becomes complicated by churches being reluctant to hire women, ministries not having the budgets to employ women, and negative perceptions from laypeople.[46] These factors deeply concern women and often will impact them during their internship as they think about future ministry options.

Single women often face an additional barrier to being hired, particularly in churches. Not being married is often seen as a liability rather than an asset. Albert Hsu makes this observation: "Qualified single adults are passed over because it is believed that their single state means that something must be wrong with them. Single adults are viewed as immature or naïve, unable to understand the issues of marriages and families."[47] Often, marital status determines whether or not a woman is considered for a leadership position. This often leaves them frustrated and discouraged when they experience one rejection after another.

These issues and others related to marital status and family responsibilities weigh heavily on most women. A site mentor's awareness of the way women view and prioritize life will allow the student to share her uncertainty and/or fears related to future ministry goals and challenge her to trust God to guide her toward God's will for her life.

Suggestions for Female Students

Field education exists for the purpose of offering students the opportunity to move from reading, listening, and studying about ministry to doing ministry. Students have the chance to observe men and women working in the various aspects of Christian service and to practice what they have learned in the classroom. A student's relationship with his or her site mentor often determines the success of the internship experience. Ministry is first and foremost about men and women teaming together to bring glory to God, serving the needs of people, and carrying out Christ's work on the earth.

---

45. Patricia Aburdene and John Naisbitt, *Megatrends for Women*, rev. and updated ed. (New York: Fawcett Columbine, 1993), 132.

46. Spring and Menehan, "Women in Seminary," 18–21.

47. Albert Hsu, *Singles at the Crossroads: A Fresh Perspective on Christian Singleness* (Downers Grove, IL: InterVarsity Press, 1997), 86.

Women have a significant place in God's economy, and, thankfully, they now have the opportunity to gain the biblical and theological training that can equip them to effectively impact the world for Christ. The following suggestions address the unique needs of female students and can help to enhance their internship experience.

Learn How to Communicate Effectively with Men

Whether the site mentor is a man or woman, a student will find herself working with men in most ministry settings. Men hold the vast majority of leadership positions, especially in churches. Though personalities will vary among men, most men tend to have certain styles of relating and communicating that differ from women. Understanding and appreciating these differences will help a woman succeed in ministry. Reading books such as those suggested at the end of this chapter will give helpful insights into effective ways for a woman to understand and communicate with men. Remember that most men are more task-oriented, so they will normally prioritize the implementation of ministry. Male conversations tend to focus on knowledge and skill issues and less on the relational component of ministry. Some men may not demonstrate sensitivity to the needs of the people around them. And often men have more difficulty articulating feelings and emotions.

A female intern must learn to not take things personally but to develop the confidence and courage to address appropriate issues with men related to ministry issues. She needs to seek wise counsel from other women to help her accept and respond to the challenges of working with men. God created men and women to partner together in ministry (Gen. 1:26–28). An internship experience should include opportunities for female students to engage with and work alongside men to help prepare her for a life of ministry.

Deborah Tannen addresses the issue of communication between men and women and how this impacts their relationships in the home, the church, and the workplace. Though she is careful to recognize some of the dangers in developing general categories for all men and women, she makes the following statement:

> Pretending that women and men are the same hurts women, because the ways they are treated are based on the norms for men. It also hurts men who, with good intentions, speak to women as they would to men, and are nonplussed when their words don't work as they expected, or even spark resentment and anger. . . . There *are* gender differences in ways of speaking, and we need to identify and understand them. Without such understanding, we are doomed to blame others or ourselves—or the relationship—for the otherwise mystifying and damaging effects of our contrasting conversational styles.[48]

48. Tannen, *You Just Don't Understand*, 16–17.

When women join men on leadership teams, they can come face-to-face with this communication problem. Often effective communication must be learned just like any other skill. Success can be achieved as men and women acknowledge their differences and learn to appreciate the unique way God has created male and female, thus allowing these differences to strengthen ministry rather than bring conflict and confusion.

If Your Site Mentor Is a Man, Seek Out a Female Mentor for Your Reflection Time

Daloz observes, "It is noteworthy that when I asked the mentors and students what their most important duty was to each other, the women overwhelmingly named honesty and openness as central. . . . The men placed less value on honesty, more on activities like providing guidance and fostering independence. . . . It is a fascinating distinction and seems to bear out the speculation about the female need for connection, the male's need for separation."[49] This difference does not mean a female intern cannot and should not interact and learn from her male site mentor. But in order for her to have the most comprehensive opportunity to reflect on all God is doing through her internship, she will want to have a woman mentor to meet with also.

A woman mentor will provide a female student with the opportunity to share personal, possibly intimate issues of her heart that would not be appropriate to share with a male mentor. With a woman, the student has the freedom to express emotions, share concerns she has observed in her ministry setting, and confess areas of her life that God may be revealing as inconsistent with the teachings in his Word. Deeper levels of honest sharing can best be accomplished woman to woman.

Schedule Regular Times of Theological Reflection with Your Mentor

Men and women who hold ministry positions tend to be very busy people. A student needs to be proactive in setting up times for theological reflection. Ideally, this should happen once a week for at least an hour. Since we have learned that a woman student will gain the most when given the opportunity to verbally process issues related to the relationships and circumstances in her internship, theological reflection becomes a key part of her field education experience.

Take advantage of the reflection time, not only to share observations and concerns, but also to ask questions and learn from the wise counsel of your mentor. If your mentor is a woman, be willing to share openly and honestly the issues of your heart. I advise my women students to make a list of things they want to discuss before meeting with their mentor. Take advantage of the opportunity to sit and talk with one who has years of ministry and life experience. Seek God's guidance and maximize your reflection time. Ultimately your proactive initiatives will enable you to gain the full benefit from your conversations with your mentor.

---

49. Daloz, *Mentor*, 216.

An internship allows you to take what you have learned and apply it in a ministry context. But when you leave the classroom and enter into the real world of ministry, you often come face-to-face with new and unexpected challenges and discover things about yourself that you may not have been aware of. Issues of fear, anger, doubt, impatience, and so on need to be recognized, articulated, and discussed. It takes time to build a relationship with your mentor that engenders a safe place to reveal confusing and disruptive feelings. Guard yourself from allowing the doing of ministry to rob you of the time to reflect on what God wants to do in your heart. Communicate to your mentor that you value a regular time of reflection to facilitate the personal and practical things you desire to accomplish in your internship experience.

Recognize the Value of Processing with a Small Group or Close Friend

Elizabeth Inrig states, "I believe it is impossible for any woman to grow to maturity apart from healthy female relationships in the body of Christ."[50] Women understand one another and can identify with one another's feelings and perspectives on life. Mentors rarely have time to discuss all the issues involved in a field education experience. Conversations with close friends also can offer opportunities to process internship concerns. Seminary or Bible college are ideal times to develop close friendships. Often these women will become lifelong friends and confidants, even if you end up serving in different ministry locations. Committed friends share the common struggles faced by women in ministry and can best support and encourage one another.

Dallas Seminary requires students to be part of a spiritual formation group for two years. Their group time ideally occurs before they enter their internships. The groups consist of all men, all women, or married couples. They meet weekly to enable one another to learn that life change happens best in the context of community. These groups become a support network as the students move into their internships and provide an additional set of people with whom to interact about various issues that arise in real-life ministry. If you do not personally have a close friend or group of friends, pray for God to lead you to those who can come alongside you (and you for them) as prayer partners and confidants. Friends can provide the additional support you will need to survive and overcome the challenges faced in serving in Christian ministry.

Understand That the Career Process for Women Often Follows a Different Path from That of Men

Women tend to have different seasons of life depending on their marital status and family needs. A woman might begin working in church as a single woman and then marry. If she and her husband decide to move because of his work, she will then need to find a new place of ministry. If children come along, she may choose to stay home with her children, give her time

---

50. Elizabeth Inrig, *Release Your Potential: Using Your Gifts in a Thriving Women's Ministry* (Chicago: Moody, 2001), 112.

in a lay capacity in her local church, and later return to vocational ministry when her children are older. A single woman might have elderly parents with health problems and decide to move closer to them to oversee their care. Men rarely find marriage, fatherhood, or family needs determining decisions related to vocational ministry. Their lives tend to stay more consistent unless something within their ministry experience causes them to make a change.

Limited staff positions for women in ministry also must be considered. A woman may need to start with a part-time position or take a different position than she might ideally desire. When I graduated from Dallas Seminary, I accepted a one-year position as the receptionist in the Christian Education Department there. That led to a part-time position mentoring and advising women students. In the meantime, I completed my Doctor of Ministry degree and began teaching some women's ministry courses. Five years passed before I became full-time staff and was offered an adjunct faculty position.

Often women have to demonstrate the contribution they can make to a leadership team. Historically men have assumed all of the paid positions of leadership in a church. Women have served in churches for centuries but without compensation. If women will be patient and show their support in partnering with their brothers in Christ, the men will normally appreciate the value of their presence and gifts and open more and more doors of opportunity for them. It may take time, but God will honor a woman's willingness to trust his timing and ways.

Conclusion

Field education represents a strategic part of a seminary student's preparation for ministry. Men and women alike need to integrate their biblical and theological training into practical ministry experience. God calls them to partner together in complementary ways to enhance and strengthen the body of Christ and impact the world. He made men and women to be uniquely different in the way they reflect his image. Female seminarians will profit most by participating in a field education program that values and accommodates these differences. By doing so, both men and women will benefit as they learn to appreciate and maximize their unique characteristics and discover ways they can best serve the body of Christ together.

Prayer of Transformation

Dear Father God, we thank you that each person is fearfully and wonderfully made. You have chosen to create some to be men and some to be women— each in your image, designed to rule and subdue the earth together. We pray that women will be valued for the unique and needed contribution they can make to the body of Christ and given open doors of opportunity to be used by you to bring your love and hope to a lost and searching world. In Jesus' name we pray, amen.

Reflection Questions

1. In your experience, have you observed differences in the way men and women relate, communicate, and prioritize and process life issues? Give a couple of examples.

2. Do you agree that men mentoring men and women mentoring women is usually the most effective and appropriate practice? Or do you think a female student can be mentored the same by a man or a woman? Why or why not?

3. Are you in agreement with the suggestions given to field education coordinators, site mentors, and female interns? Are there any you disagree with? If so, why?

4. What additional recommendations would you make to enhance a woman student's field education experience?

Further Reading

Farrel, Bill, and Pam Farrel. *Men Are Like Waffles, Women Are Like Spaghetti.* Eugene, OR: Harvest House, 2001.

Moir, Anne, and David Jessel. *Brain Sex: The Real Difference Between Men and Women.* New York: Carol, 1991.

Rhoads, Steven. *Taking Sex Differences Seriously.* San Francisco: Encounter, 2004.

Saucy, Robert L., and Judith K. TenElshof. *Women and Men in Ministry: A Complementary Perspective.* Chicago: Moody, 2001.

Sax, Leonard. *Why Gender Matters: What Parents and Teachers Need to Know About the Emerging Science of Sex Differences.* New York: Broadway, 2005.

Tannen, Deborah. *You Just Don't Understand: Women and Men in Conversation.* New York: Morrow, 1990.

Chapter 14

The Impact of Field Education on Marriage and Family

MARY SANDERS AND JEFF SANDERS

Little children, let us not love in word or talk but in deed and in truth. (1 John 3:18)

Field education affords a wonderful opportunity for a seminary student to begin to "test out" what ministry will be like. Field education provides students the occasion to put into practice their seminary learning and to use the gifts God has given them. It is also a time for students to try on the "ministry cloak" that will be theirs to wear upon graduation.

For the married student and for married couples with children, the field education experience takes on additional significance as the couple begins to learn more about the impact that ministry will have on their family. For many couples entering field education, ministry has been a theoretical idea. Field education offers a pragmatic encounter where students and their families can begin to look at the ways in which ministry will impact their relationships and to strategize about how they are going to enter this experience well.

With any vocation a couple pursues, there comes particular implications for family life. Christian vocational ministry holds underlying assumptions for a married person, which include a strong marriage and a supportive spouse and family. These common assumptions can create unique challenges for a couple entering ministry. The nature of ministry's demands coupled with the expectation of a strong, vibrant marriage can set up a double bind for couples. A strong marriage, like a strong ministry, requires time and energy, both finite commodities. Couples entering ministry must learn how to negotiate this tension. The field education experience is an excellent time for couples to begin the conversation about how they are going to hold this tension in practice and how they are going to handle the implications and expectations that come with serving in vocational ministry. It is our belief that it is possible to have both a thriving marriage and a thriving ministry, but it does not just happen.

We have two objectives in this chapter. The first is to explore issues that we have seen emerge for couples and families during the field education process. In addition to our work with seminary couples, we each have experienced field education as the student and the spouse. Our second is to provide practical tools to assist couples in their conversations as they begin to navigate vocational ministry together.

Expectations

For many couples the field education experience is their first opportunity to engage in hands-on ministry. Many arrive at seminary having sensed God's call or invitation to prepare for ministry but have not actually worked in a ministry setting. Students describe experiencing various thoughts and emotions as they approach this step. Excitement, fear, anticipation, and dread are common emotions for students and spouses at this point. They are asking many questions: Can I do this? Do I know enough? Will people like me? Will people respect my ministry? How will we fit one more thing into our busy lives? Will we have enough time as a family? What if my spouse hates it and I love it? What if we both hate it?

This is also the time when students and spouses begin to become aware of expectations. The person entering field education at a particular site will inevitably run into a cross section of potentially competing expectations. The student holds expectations for what the process may teach him or her about ministry, the student's fit for ministry, ministry's fit with family, and so on. The spouse holds expectations about what his or her part will be, and the ministry setting holds expectations for them both. Some of these are known to each of the parties, and others are assumed, and yet they all begin to unfold during the field education experience.

I (Mary) was fully supportive of Jeff pursuing his Master of Divinity degree and seeking ordination as a minister. I was eager for him to prepare to formally minister to others. I was excited when he got to the place in his program that he was ready for his field education experience. I also remember the first uncomfortable moment when one of my assumed expectations surfaced.

Jeff had interviewed for an associate pastor position. He had initially met with the senior pastor for lunch and upon returning shared that the pastor would like to meet me. My first thought was to wonder why, but I agreed to go to lunch with the pastor and Jeff the following week. Our meeting must have gone well because shortly afterward they offered Jeff the position. Jeff was to be formally introduced to the church a few weeks later.

One day when Jeff was at class, the pastor called. When I told him that Jeff was not home, the pastor asked if he could leave a message for Jeff. He said that the church board would like Jeff to prepare an introductory talk to share with the congregation on Sunday morning. I was busy writing the message when he added, "Oh and the church would also like you to share." Without thinking, I blurted out, "Well, I'd rather die than do that!" After an awkward silence, he assured me that it could be very brief but that they wanted the church to get to know me. The pastor and congregation were very kind the following Sunday. I survived and I have always been grateful that the pastor did not alert the search committee about potential problems with "the wife"!

Before we had even entered the church door, I learned an important thing about my assumptions regarding my role in Jeff's ministry. I had always viewed us as a team and expected to support his ministry endeavors with that mind-set. I expected to support Jeff and his work in the church by loving him, caring for our children, praying for him, tending to our home, and being a listener and encourager. My church activities would be chosen after careful prayer and attention had been given to our family needs first. As an introvert, my expectations never included standing up in front of five hundred people on a Sunday morning sharing my testimony! The event became the first of many opportunities for Jeff and me to look at how our assumptions and the ministry's expectations coalesce and strategize about what to do when they did not.

Expectations abound in ministry settings, and it is impossible to fulfill all of them. Field education is a great time to begin to look at how the unique gifts, strengths, and interests God has given the student individually and the student and spouse as a couple fit or do not fit with the expectations of the student's ministry setting. Our encouragement is for students to use the field education time to begin to sort through and practice what they will do when others' expectations and their expectations do not fit together. This can be incredibly challenging to do, particularly if it means sharing with a supervisor or a church member that the student will not be able to do some-thing that has been asked or assumed of him or her.

A pastor friend was called to a congregation of about five hundred people in a smaller city. He had been there only a week when one of the older women in the church scheduled an appointment to meet with him. After several minutes of introductions and exchanging pleasantries, the woman shared why she was there. She was the unofficial chair of the women's ministries program, and they had been praying and felt that God wanted the pastor's wife to lead the Bible study for the upcoming year. She proceeded to say that the pastor's wife has "always" done this and they wanted to "invite" his wife to do that as well.

Our friend swallowed hard as he tried to think quickly what to say. He thanked her for the invitation and promised to pass it on to his wife. He then added that his wife was in the process of thinking and praying about how God may want her to be involved and did not have clarity about that yet. She would add their invitation to the things she was praying about and let her know. The woman was a bit taken aback and not too happy several weeks later when her "invitation" was turned down.

It was challenging for the pastor and his wife to do that, especially since they were brand-new to the church and wanted to establish connections quickly. Yet, they held true to what they knew about themselves and their family. His wife truly had no interest in leading a women's Bible study. She did not have a gift for teaching or a desire to do so. They had young children and the weekly prep time alone felt overwhelming to her, much less teaching the study! Had she fulfilled that expectation, she would have missed the ministry opportunity that came several months later. The church began an outreach to pregnant single women, and she was the first to sign up. She had a huge heart for people, and she thrived as she poured herself into the women and children she served.

However a couple decides to work through these issues, it is evident that family is uniquely tied to ministry as a vocation and to the various expectations of others who participate in the ministry. It becomes imperative, then, for the couple to determine how they are going to deal with the challenge of expectations as they move forward. Any time spent working this out during the field education stage will aid in the health of the family, as well as provide a healthy foundation for future ministry.

Boundaries

Another area that can impede or aid in the health of couples and families beginning the field education process is that of boundaries. In family systems language, a couple is its own system that is imbedded within many other systems. Couples are part of their extended families, their communities, their church communities, their city, their state, and so on. A boundary is what defines one system as a separate unit from another.

Historically, when a man entered church ministry, it was often viewed by the church as getting the whole family. Dad was the pastor, mom was the pastor's wife, and the kids often were expected to contribute in some way as well. This setup, while advantageous to the church, often was challenging to the minister's family, with them paying a tremendous price physically, emotionally, financially, or some other way. Today with the plethora of ministries, more women in seminary, and many couples both in the paid workforce, ministry has become increasingly complex. While this has lent a greater freedom for spouses to participate as able, expectations continue to be a real pressure for ministering families to deal with. As individuals and couples begin to examine those expectations and determine how their family will be involved, the need for establishing healthy boundaries becomes vital.

Healthy boundaries around the family are essential for long-term ministry. Field education can be a good place to begin forming and setting those boundaries around the student and the family. Healthy boundaries establish the space between the ministry setting and the family. It can be challenging to establish these boundaries. It is understandable that a person hired to serve in a ministry setting wants to do a good job. Often this means making himself or herself available and accessible in numerous and excessive ways to the ministry setting the person is in. After all, it will only be until they get established, get their feet under them, and build relationships, and then they will "cut back."

What invariably happens is that the ministry setting becomes accustomed to whatever the level of giving the minister and family does. After some time, ministers and their families realize that they cannot continue to give at that level, and they try to "cut back." This then creates problems between the family and the ministry setting. It is important to keep in mind that you can always loosen a boundary, but it is much harder to tighten or change a boundary, particularly in a ministry setting.

While the area of boundaries may look a bit different depending on one's ministry setting, the need for them remains the same. The following examples are based on real people whose lives have been impacted in this area.

Jim was the pastor of a rural church in a town with a population of 1800. He and his wife, Carol, have three children. The town and church loved this family. They are down-to-earth folks who really care about people. Since their church was small, Jim, Carol, and their kids served many roles in the church. Jim was the senior pastor, youth pastor, and worship leader. Carol played the piano and co-led worship on Sundays with Jim. She also was responsible for special music whenever the need arose for community gatherings, weddings, funerals, and such. Their children were gifted musically and academically and had very tender hearts for the Lord and people. They opened their home for Bible studies, youth group, and community outreach events.

After twelve years, the intensity and the pressure began to wear on Jim and Carol and their kids. They were faced with either radically changing their level of involvement in the church or leaving because they just could not keep it up. They made many attempts over several years to cut back, including hiring a part-time youth pastor and adding a volunteer music director, but it was not enough. The church elder board began to comment about Jim not being at every meeting and over time began to question his commitment to the church. It became increasingly uncomfortable for Jim and Carol, and they ended up leaving. They moved to a larger community, where Jim became an associate with the hope that things would be better once he was not in charge.

Karen was a worship pastor in a suburban church. She had wanted to be a worship pastor for as long as she could remember. Karen was not married and did not have children, but she had a large extended family who lived nearby and with whom she was quite close. She received a seminary degree, completed her musical training, and landed her first pastoral position. She was incredibly creative and had tons of energy. She motivated people easily, and soon the worship teams and the choirs had grown to capacity, and everyone was commenting about how tremendous the worship had become.

Karen was continually thinking of new things to add to worship, which meant supervising more groups, more meetings, and more practices. She was at church early in the morning and stayed late on many evenings. She often held meetings in her home. She rarely had a vacation, seldom took her "day off," and spent most of her free time doing some church-related activity. Her parents noticed her absence from family gatherings that she normally would have attended. Karen assured them that she was still getting established at the church but it would get better. She continued this for seven years. Occasionally the pastor or a parishioner would comment that she should take some time off. But they never pushed it because she was so incredible at her job and the church loved her. This all came to a screeching halt one day after she had made a series of very poor choices, resulting in several people being hurt. The incident was such that reservations about her character surfaced and her entire ministry was called into question. The situation blew up. The church took sides, and many left. The whole incident resulted in her being let go. She is no longer in ministry and has gone through an incredibly painful time as she has tried to sort through it all.

There are many different kinds of boundaries. Boundaries will look different for every family, and there is no formula for how a family must tend to this area. Boundaries help systems to function in healthy ways. Without them, a ministering family runs the risk of being engulfed by the deluge of needs that are inherent in vocational ministry. If they are too severe, a family runs the risk of being seen as cold and indifferent.

How will students create the space between them and their ministry? How will students and their spouses create a healthy boundary around their family? How permeable or closed will those be for their families? How much will students share about ministry happenings with their spouses? How will students guard their children's space? Will expectations for their children and their behavior be different from any other child? Will students open their home for ministry events? How much will the ministry setting know about their families? Will students use their families in illustrations? If so, how often, and do they need their families' approval? How many functions will the students and their families attend? If an important family event and an important church event land on the same evening, which one wins out? How challenging is it for students to say no? How are students at handling conflict? These are all boundary-related questions.

Sometimes implementing a boundary can feel unkind or unspiritual. No one likes to hear "no." However, if long-term ministry is a student's goal and the student wants to invest his or her life in people for the sake of the gospel, then it is imperative to learn this skill. As students enter their field education experience, they will have many opportunities to practice. We would encourage students to take advantage of those opportunities and to be in conversation with their spouses as they figure out what healthy boundaries will look like for their family.

Roles

Every couple goes through a period early in marriage when roles are established in order to fulfill family functions and needs. This process can include intentional, talked-through decisions that a couple makes. Some couples use their dating relationship and premarital counseling as times to begin their conversations about roles and to make some initial decisions. Other couples choose their family and marital roles almost by "default." This is often manifested by the husband and wife continuing roles modeled by either their families of origin or other influential couples. However couples choose their roles, they arrive at seminary and to their field education experience having already chosen and practiced specific roles.

As a couple enters new scholastic pursuits, their lives can look very different than they did before this new change. Often the addition of school demands a geographical move, job change(s), and always the inclusion of class and study time into the couple's life together. While difficult, the couple then adds the new role of minister to their list as the student enters field education. The uniqueness and intensity of this role can be challenging for couples to adjust to.

Also, depending upon the couple's cultural and denominational backgrounds and biblical understandings, their accepted and customary roles of either men or women in ministry (and gender ideology more broadly) may be challenged or even evolving. Previously held assumptions and understandings can be strongly held and difficult to work through. If a couple is stuck in this type of conversation or at very different places, it is important that they have someone with whom they can talk through the issues. Most schools have professionals in place who can assist couples with these difficult situations.

Of all the adjustments and changes that I (Jeff) went through during our seminary experiences, I believe that our role changes while Mary was in her internship was one of the most challenging for me to deal with. Our marital roles as they pertained to our children and our home fell largely along traditional lines. I was the primary breadwinner, Mary a full-time homemaker and part-time student. Our roles remained largely the same during her program. She took classes one day a week and studied after the kids had gone to bed or on Saturdays when I was home. While she certainly felt the load, there were minimal changes required of me.

That all changed during the year that Mary had her field education experience. By then we had a kindergartner, a second grader, and a fifth grader. Mary worked long days, many evenings, and Saturdays, and our roles underwent a major change. Mary had my full support and blessing to pursue her dream of attending seminary. It was not until that year, however, that my support had to change from verbal encouragement to support that I displayed in my actions. Suddenly I needed to take on a major portion of all that was going on at home. While I thought I knew what to expect, I really did not know all that was involved. There were times the role changes felt very uncomfortable, and I felt completely overwhelmed. Yet, I knew that if Mary was truly to have the time and space she needed to complete her internship, then I needed to step up to the plate and show my support of her in this very tangible way.

There were some days that I did this better than others. Mary knew when she left the house and I said "Have a good day" whether or not I meant it. She told me once that I had two ways of saying "Have a good day," and while I used the same words, they held very different meanings. There were days when the kids were fighting, the house was a disaster, we needed groceries, I had work from my job to do, and the walls felt like they were caving in around me, and the day had just started. Yet, she had to be at her internship.

On those mornings "Have a good day" really was more like a pleading for her not to go. It was somewhat like our dog, Trevor, who sits and watches us intently getting ready to go off to work in the morning. He adds a few whimpers here and there, and then when we turn to say good-bye, he is still sitting there staring with big, sad eyes. No words are necessary, but he has gotten his message across, and we leave feeling guilty and bad that we have to leave him home alone all day.

The other "Have a good day" held with it the message that we are with you in this and everything is going to be fine here—you go and do what you need to do, and do not worry about us. I knew when I sent Mary off with that message that I was supporting her with my actions as well as my words and that I had taken on this new role.

As couples head into ministry, the area of roles will surface again. Just as roles fulfill functions and needs within a family, they also fulfill functions and needs within a ministry setting. It is often an unfamiliar process for students entering field education to begin negotiating the roles they will fill in their place of service. The internship is always a combination of the site and mentor attempting to match some ministry needs with a person who is hoping to fill those needs while learning more about ministry. It would be unrealistic to suggest that a student will write his or her own job description. Yet, it is important for the student to begin to express what roles in ministry he or she is challenged or invigorated by and if there is an area of the organization he or she would like to learn more about or seek involvement in.

This is an important time for the student to come to terms with the reality that he or she will have choices regarding the roles in ministry filled over his or her years of service. The process of determining what roles students feel God is calling them into, what roles they enjoy fulfilling or understand the necessity of fulfilling, and/or what roles they really are hoping/planning for someone else to take over is complex. It can be incredibly helpful for the student to begin including his or her spouse in the conversation. This is true both because the spouse knows the student and his or her giftedness better than anyone and because role choices will always affect the spouse and family.

Some helpful questions to begin to ask one another during field education are what roles does the student envision playing in his or her spouse's ministry? What will be required of each person in order to fulfill the field education requirement? What kinds of role adaptations may be needed? Can the student continue in all the roles he or she has been doing, or does the student need to give some up? If so, who will take them on? Which of the students' roles are nonnegotiable? How many roles is the student willing to take on in his or her ministry setting?

Time

Time is a commodity that students and their families may not take into account when considering their field education experience. It is evident in Scripture that God decided to create day, night, and time, as we know it. It seems important to acknowledge that God created time before he created people. He set up the structure of this world before he allowed us to inhabit it. God has given everyone twenty-four hours each day in which to live, love, sleep, and serve. Research continues to teach the important ramifications of solid sleep habits in our lives. Assuming solid sleep, everyone then must decide how to spend their waking hours. The constraints of time in those choices are real and tangible. Everyone lives out their ministry within their confined humanity, and that includes the confines of time.

Ministry is unlike many other paid positions in that it is very difficult to assess how much time a certain opportunity or task may require. Ministry is rarely a scheduled nine-to-five job. This is often a new dynamic for families of students, particularly if they have not been intimately involved in ministry work previous to the internship. People involved in ministry, like people involved in any occupation, have differing assumptions and expectations concerning time and "work." During the field education process, the student (and spouse) may be presented with many differing opinions. These will have a dramatic effect upon the field education and can greatly influence the couple's thinking concerning ministry in general.

One of our observations is that ministry families often are living in a world where to say yes to one opportunity demands saying (or living) no to another opportunity or thing. So, the question becomes what or whom is the student willing to say no to in terms of time? This question can dramatically change what students are willing to agree to in terms of new or expanded opportunities. It also seems appropriate to point out that the most difficult decisions are not those choices between a good and a bad option. The most difficult decisions related to time are determining the best option(s) from among several good choices.

We know of one wise pastor who feels very strongly about this issue of time and its impact on the health of a pastor and the pastor's family. He requires that any student intern he has keep a record of his or her time. To be included in the log are hours slept, God time, family time, personal time, class time, study time, and hours worked at church. It is not enough for the student to log the hours; he has the student bring the log to his or her mentoring time each week. He knows that a student's ability to manage time will have a great impact on his or her health, the health of the family, and the health of the ministry. He told us that often students grow impatient with the amount of time they spend talking about time. After all they are eager to "do ministry," and they protest that life will not always be as busy as it is during seminary. He assures them that it will be just as busy if not more so.

Their time logs then become part of the discussion as they discuss ministry opportunities. When the big projects come along or the Christmas or Easter seasons begin, he challenges them to look at their time and figure out where the hours will come from. He is giving them a tremendous gift in allowing them to wrestle with and learn this very important ministry skill.

Self and Family Care

In the gospel account of Mark, one of the teachers of the religious law asked Jesus, "Of all the commandments, which is the most important?" Jesus answered, "The most important commandment is this; 'Hear, O Israel! The Lord our God is the one and only Lord. And you must love the Lord your God with all your heart, all your soul, all your mind, and all your strength.' The second is equally important: 'Love your neighbor as yourself.' No other commandment is greater than these" (Mark 12:28–31 NLT). In bringing the teacher to the beginning of the Shema and then heightening the second commandment to equal importance, Jesus was overtly challenging the religious focus and practice of the religious leaders of that time. In an era when external devotion and sacrifice were primary, Jesus focused upon inner devotion to the true God and a way of living with one's self and others that naturally flowed from that devotion.

The church has long given verbal assent to this teaching, and we have heard many wonderful messages regarding loving God and loving our neighbor. What often gets tagged on, if at all, is the "as yourself" part. The text is clear: "Love your neighbor as yourself." Jesus' admonition to love others includes an expectation that we would love ourselves. It is OK to talk about it. However, it can be viewed as selfish in the church (and in seminary education) to really live out Jesus' teachings regarding self-love and care. We almost hear the word *self-love* in the same way as we hear *self-indulgent*. Are we not supposed to deny "self"? Yet the two are very different. What does loving self mean for a servant leader or field education student and his or her family? In addition to Jesus' verbal teachings, it is evident in a study of his life that he spent time alone in prayer, rested, and even withdrew from the crowds in the midst of supercharged ministry opportunities. What are we to make of that, and how do we apply his example for ministry in our own lives? While we do not want to directly contradict Jesus' life and teachings, self and family care clearly have not been a tremendous focus in the preparation of ministers over the centuries.

We believe that this conversation and the following issues are spiritual in nature and have direct importance to the field education process for the couple and family. The three issues we would like to focus on here are energy, finances, and stress. We see each of them as a part of overall self and family care and ultimately self-love. In ministry it is easy to make distinctions between worldly and spiritual, and often things related to one's humanity can get lumped into the worldly category and therefore treated with less importance than the spiritual things. We would like to encourage students to consider these things as spiritual in nature.

Energy

Energy is, in our experience, a part of human nature and reality that often is not considered or spoken of while a family is involved in field education. Like time, energy is a finite commodity. We do not have a limitless supply, and yet personal energy is a commodity that tremendously impacts work and relationships—especially family relationships. It is helpful for students to understand how they are wired. What things energize them? What things drain them? How do they get refueled? What kinds of ministry tasks energize them? What kinds of relationships? Who are the people that help them to recharge?

These kinds of questions become increasingly important as the demands of ministry, school, and family life collide. It is also important for students to understand what energizes them as a couple and a family. Refueling is an absolute necessity for individuals and couples involved in vocational ministry.

Finances

Finances are influenced by whether or not the internship is paid, how the time given to the internship detracts from other paid work (both by the student and his or her spouse), and how the energy necessary for the internship affects one's ability to pursue additional paid work. It is imperative to create space for conversation related to finances and, again, helpful to consider them spiritual conversations. The Bible is full of cautions regarding money. We have never heard of anyone entering ministry to become wealthy. Yet, we have watched many couples hesitate to bring up the subject of money with their church and consequently deal with incredible amounts of stress as they try to survive financially. It can feel very awkward to approach the subject of money in the field education process, almost as if it is unspiritual. However, this is a perfect time for a couple to recognize that paid ministry includes both pay and ministry. Both of these (remuneration and service) are important pieces of a unified whole. Both radically affect the entirety of family life for the long term, and field education provides a practical time frame to continue (or at least begin) these discussions.

Stress

We all understand that new opportunities, especially job changes, bring stress into the family system. We also understand that all of us react differently to stress (even good stress). Families can respond to new opportunities and the accompanying changes by either becoming more connected to one another or by being pulled farther apart. But there are many other ways to respond to stress. It is important to understand what the patterns as a couple and family tend to be during stressful times and to both monitor and manage the stress while participating in field education. Monitoring stress includes honest self-appraisal, recognition of patterns, and acknowledgment of what is really happening in each partner (and children if applicable). Managing stress is entirely different. This includes assuring that one's responses to stress are somewhat healthy and that the student is able to recognize what is causing the stress and make changes accordingly. The ways in which couples and families respond and react to stress during the field education experience can hold insights into how they will hold up under the stress of ministry.

Again, there can be a not-so-subtle perspective that would attempt to diminish these and other issues of self and family care into a category titled "worldly." These would be compared unfavorably to other matters of "eternal" or "spiritual" significance (often interpreted as anything having to do with ministry). We caution against creating a dichotomy of "spiritual" and "worldly" issues, finding that an approach that honors the breadth of one's life and the complexity of all of one's life choices is extremely helpful in ministry and ministry preparation.

Spiritual and Personal Formation

One common theme that has surfaced while sharing with students involved in field education is that of spiritual and personal formation. Field education is often the beginning of a career path in which talking about God is integral. Much of ministry time is spent sharing about God, encouraging others in the delight and importance of knowing God, and admonishment toward obedience of God. Men and women who have been involved in the gospel ministry express the tension between their need to be conversant about God and their own inner being and relationship with God. There is a difference between talking about God and talking with God. There is also a difference between encouraging the spiritual formation of others and pursuing one's own spiritual and personal formation.

When we talk of spiritual formation, we are including the facets and personal choices involved in our individual relationships with God. These can include, but are not limited to, the quality of our personal piety, recognition of and involvement in our own spiritual growth, and the practices we adhere to in order to develop our inner relationship with God. When we talk of personal formation, we are including our understanding of the effects of our personality, emotional intelligence, and relational capacity and skill. This, again, is not an exhaustive list but is intended to offer a place to start the conversation.

Field education offers consistent opportunity for students and their families to recognize and deal with these important issues in their lives and ministry. Yet, those more individually focused moments are not what we wish to focus on here. It is the interplay between two developing spouses and their family that we wish to discuss. As a couple enters the internship process, it is necessary to remember that each spouse is developing. They, like every couple, are simply developing differently. Different circumstances offer different choices and opportunities related to spiritual and personal formation. Whether the field education experience is positive or negative, the opportunities inherent in the experience for students may leave the supporting spouses feeling a bit left out. Over time that may cause spouses to question whether their level of "formation" or "spiritual growth" is adequate and whether they will be able to keep relating well with their spouses in this area.

In our experience, this area of conversation can be impacted by two very human temptations, competition and fear. While spiritual and personal formation are certainly not a competition between spouses, it is worth noting that we are all forming and this will be a time when each spouse forms differently. Because the student's formation may be happening during overt involvement in a ministry setting, that does not diminish the formation of his or her spouse. The spouse may be forming in a different type of work setting or while caring for the children at home.

Both men and women have shared with us regarding their difficulty in this area. On our best days, we listen well to our spouse's stories of formation and growth, encouraging them in their walk of development and faith. On other days, we may experience concern that we will be left behind or are not quite spiritual enough ourselves, and the fear these thoughts bring can hit us like a big wave. It is helpful to consider these experiences as part of the process. In field education, a couple is simply faced with an exaggerated process, if you will. Due to the spiritual and personal nature of ministry, the student, his or her spouse, and their family simply experience and hear much more about formation. It is an important part of the experience and language of internship. It is also an area where conversation and solid listening can set each member of the family free to embrace the ways God is working in and developing them.

One additional component to the issue of spiritual and personal formation is the development of the children whose parent(s) are involved in field education. It can be a temptation for parents who are busy entering a new endeavor to overlook the impact the season has upon their children. Some of the questions related to how field education affects one's children and their development involve the ages of their children. Children are dealing with different developmental issues at age three than they are at thirteen years of age. While the pursuit of education by one parent certainly involves sacrifices by everyone in the family, the question becomes "how much sacrifice?" There can be a very real expectation on the part of parents that their children will adjust and form well in every "good" situation that their parents feel is appropriate. And, of course, what is more "good" than ministry?

Here we would like to caution parents entering into field education experiences. A marriage and family therapist who was one of Mary's supervisors stated that "children are great at gathering information but terrible at interpreting it." It is important to check in with children to see how the changes, challenges, and joys of this new season are affecting them. Ultimately, their parents are the people who know them best, are most committed to their spiritual and personal formation, and are responsible to the Lord for encouraging solid, life-giving formation in the lives of their children. Children may not feel comfortable asking questions, advocating for their desires, and particularly expressing their frustration to their parents. We believe that the more the concerns and observations of children are heard during field education, the stronger and more meaningful ministry can be for the entire family in the future. Ministry is often a very public experience for the family of the minister, and while parts of that can be enjoyable, some can be awful. We believe it is important to engage in conversation that includes all the voices when trying to encourage the spiritual and personal formation of every family member.

Fit for Ministry

It also can be during the field education time when both the student and his or her spouse deal with fresh questions about their adequacy and fit for ministry. These fresh questions, when combined with old fears or even failures, can create a potentially acidic thought process. It is extremely helpful for the couple to process how old expectations (their own or others that have been shared) and experiences are affecting them during this new adventure. One idea we offer is for both partners to try to stop themselves and carefully consider what is happening when their thought process includes the words "I should" or "I should be." While a helpful motivational tool for some, the internal "should" phrases may be indicative of conflicting expectations, ideals, or experiences crashing together. It also may be helpful for one or both spouses to seek help in this process if they are feeling stuck.

For both the student and the spouse, one of the most emotionally charged areas inherent in the field education process is that of future ministry and its meaning in their lives. It can be very difficult (and even scary) to bring up for discussion the "now what?" type of questions. We would suggest that it is a critical time and a particular gift of field education to offer a reason for a couple to ask of each other, "Do we believe this is the best direction for us?" We also believe that it is important for both to come to some sort of agreement on the answer!

Field education is a time when the development of ministry strength areas, revelation of growth areas, and new learning regarding ministry, personal, and relational issues come together. These are then joined together with those realizations and new learning gathered by the supporting spouse and family. Ideally, they all give the couple (and family) new clues, ideas, and perhaps direction for future ministry. These also may be critical pieces in leading the student, spouse, and family to an awareness of further education, healing, or understanding that is needed as they continue in their pursuit of obedient and meaningful service. We encourage this type of real conversation among couples and families involved in field education. It is our experience that when willing to freely ask and discuss meaningful questions during this process, their marriages and ministry together invariably become stronger.

Conclusion

We began this chapter by suggesting that the field education experience is a unique opportunity for seminary students to put their seminary learning into practice, use the gifts God has given them, and begin to learn the impact that ministry will have on their families. We also stated that learning during the field education experience is not limited to the student. The student's spouse and children all are learning along with the student they love. Our stated objectives for the chapter were to explore issues that we have seen emerge for couples and families during the field education process and to provide practical tools to assist couples in their conversations as they begin to navigate vocational ministry together.

In an attempt to address our initial objective, we explored several issues that we believe emerge for couples and families during involvement in field education and continue in vocational ministry. These issues were expectations, boundaries, roles, time, self and family care, spiritual and personal formation, and the couple/family fit for ministry. Each of these issues can be an integral part of a couple's discovery related to ministry impact in their relationship and in the relationships they share with their children. While certainly not exhaustive, these issues provide a breadth of topics for discussion that can be a beneficial part of the learning that can occur during field education.

In order to provide practical tools to assist couples in this process, we have chosen to offer many questions throughout the chapter that could aid in the discussion. We have chosen to blend our observations, the experiences reported by others involved in field education, and questions that we believe could prompt real, meaningful dialogue for a couple. It is our hope that mentors will help both the student and his or her spouse to individually explore the material in this chapter and then join together as a couple in discussion. We believe that an exploration of these issues and related questions invites a couple into a process of learning that will greatly enhance their relationship and the field education opportunity and help to set up a healthy foundation for lifelong ministry.

Prayer of Transformation

Sweet Jesus, we ask your blessing on the couples who have answered yes to your invitation to prepare for ministry. Please give them wisdom, insight, and courage as they embark on this new adventure. We ask you to strengthen their relationships with you and with each other. Amen.

Reflection Questions

1. How does the seminary experience compare to what you thought it was going to be?

2. How do you envision yourself entering this internship process as a family? How involved does your spouse anticipate being?

3. Are both you and your spouse continuing to sense God's invitation and leading toward vocational ministry?

4. How are you going to incorporate the internship into your schedule? What things need to happen in order to add this to your life?

Further Reading

Markman, Howard, Scott Stanley, and Susan Blumberg. *Fighting for Your Marriage: Positive Steps for Preventing Divorce and Preserving a Lasting Love*. San Francisco: Jossey-Bass, 1994.

Parrott, Les, and Leslie Parrott. *Your Time-Starved Marriage: How to Stay Connected at the Speed of Life*. Grand Rapids: Zondervan, 2006.

Wangerin, Walter. *As for Me and My House: Crafting Your Marriage to Last*. Nashville: Thomas Nelson, 2001.

Chapter 15

Working with Technology and Distance Education

TARA HORNBACKER

Therefore, as you received Christ Jesus the Lord, so walk in him,
rooted and built up in him and established in the faith, just as you
were taught, abounding in thanksgiving. (Col. 2:6–7)

The implementation of technology and distance-learning practices are the most distinctive cultural and pedagogical shifts for theological education in the last twenty years. At our seminary, e-mail has replaced much of the communication that used to be handled by phone calls, formal letters, and face-to-face (F2F) interactions between students, faculty, and administration. We have traded in paper notes and memos in on-campus mailboxes for electronic missives in our e-mail in-boxes.

Field education is distance education by its very nature. Field educators have been engaged in a form of distance education since the beginning of their practice with the movable feast of ministry settings as classrooms. Since field educators are accustomed to distance learning, they can model the best practices for other academic disciplines in theological distance education. Cyberspace classrooms created with educational software platforms offer quality twenty-first-century educational experiences. This revolution, however, has not been without deep division among academics. Field education is poised to assist institutional adjustment in the shifting landscape of ministerial preparation through distance learning.

Field education has named the ministry setting as the primary textbook for reflective learning in theological education. Most field educators also assign traditional texts to accompany the student in his or her ministry settings, according to the student's own learning goals. Still, the ministry setting and its rich offerings of location, identity, and mission is the basis for the action/reflection model of learning in field education. The majority of these settings are beyond the doors of the seminary, which automatically make them *distance*-learning opportunities. Technology affords the opportunity for teachers and learners to increase their connection during those off-campus experiences, thus enhancing the interactions of students and faculty and deepening the educational experience as never before. This chapter is concerned with the new realities of distance education and the technological advances available to theological education today.

What Has Changed?

Many students, fresh from college, are accustomed to an online environment. Most second- or third-career students arrive at educational institutions with experience and facility with e-mail and the Internet. Educational technology has progressed from overhead transparencies through PowerPoint presentations to fully downloadable multimedia presentations. In my institution, every faculty member is responsible to teach at least one course either completely online or as a hybrid/blended course (a class consisting of both online and F2F components). In a recent faculty search, one of the noted skills was the "ability/willingness to teach in an online environment." The Internet is a way of life in our culture. When I asked an incoming class of seminarians how they were looking for a new church in the community, every one of them answered, "Internet search." Our students use our online services to register for classes, submit papers for (F2F and online) classes, receive the seminary newsletter, and communicate with one another and faculty. Text messaging and wireless access have resulted in new etiquette and expectations for classroom participation.

Manufacturers of educational software have created educational platforms, programs that schools can use to put their courses on the Internet. These platforms are increasingly user-friendly for both teachers and students. New andragogy has developed around distance education and teaching online that will require retraining for most of our faculty.

Challenges and Obstacles

Entry into the distance-learning environment for graduate theological education has its challenges as well as opportunities. Some faculty and students determine that online classes are not appropriate learning environments for some classes because the courses require a community that they feel cannot be created without face-to-face interaction. These faculty members will need to learn methods for creating communities in an online environment. Others have cautioned that students could hide their "real selves" from the instructors and classmates. However, safeguards can be put into place to ensure against pretenders and imposters. The hesitations abound for this newer form of educational format. Educational institutions and faculty must attend to these concerns together with students and their constituents.

Faculty, administration, and students should approach one another's questions concerning teaching and learning in an online environment with care, "bearing with one another" as the biblical text would admonish all involved. Just because one *can* do something does not necessarily mean one *should* do it. Taking time to adapt and adopt the appropriate technologies will make the transition to distance learning go more smoothly.

Hopes and Dreams

Field educators often have dreamed of better contact with their students, supervisors, peer committees, and teaching sites. Technology makes that dream a reality, whether it is the *old* technology of telephones and "snail mail" or the *newer* technology of e-mail, the Internet, and the various media they can access. The danger in writing about technology is that with new developments all the time and the rapidity of change in the distance education field, anything I say here may be dated by the time it is printed. Still, an introduction to the basics of distance learning and technology as we know it today may be helpful as we look ahead to field education for the twenty-first century.

Distance-Learning Platforms or Course Management Systems

In order to put a class online, software developers have created programs that allow educators to post syllabi, make assignments, facilitate small-group interaction, participate in "real-time" as well as asynchronous (students are online at different times) discussions, and to communicate to all, a part of, or one person in the class. The actual design of the page one sees when the class site is opened depends on the course management software program used. There are many programs now available, from Moodle, which is an open-source platform, to BlackBoard, WebCT, and other proprietary programs that allow the instructor to design and edit the course. Students participate in the learning process by posting to discussion boards, participating in conference groups, or communicating as individuals, or in chat rooms.[1] The course management system (CMS) provides a framework for the instructor to design and manage the course and the place for the students to access assignments, interact with others in the class, and submit their work. Depending on the complexity of the CMS, the instructor can post lectures,

---

1. It may be helpful for readers to download a distance-learning glossary from the Internet. Some words have come into common usage among distance educators but are yet to be adopted by wider audiences. Many terms are defined here, but a good glossary will facilitate the reader's understanding.

create and administer quizzes and exams, attach audio or video files, or post a link to any other site with a video a student might benefit from seeing. Basically, the instructor/administrator with editing rights to the course site can post any document that can be put in an electronic format on the learning site. Handouts become links to documents or other sites on the Internet.

Most students catch on to using the Web-based learning tools quite readily. Faculty, as the instructional designers, need to devote extra time to learning to use the CMS. Navigation of a CMS and most e-learning software is intuitive. For teachers and administrators, a well-informed IT (instructional technology) person is critical to the success of the distance-learning program. Students do need additional orientation time to become accustomed to using the courseware and to become acclimated to the new learning environment.

For field education, a CMS can increase the contact between the student in the field and the seminary. As a starting point, if all students enrolled in the field education program were given access to the course online, the handbook and other course materials could be posted for easy access. Theological reflection forums could be established with students assigned to small groups for interactions and case studies. This also facilitates the conversation between students out in the field.

Alternatives and Augmentations

If the faculty member would like to begin without investing quite so much time and effort in working with a CMS, then an electronic mailing list can be a useful tool for theological education. Educators may start a mailing list by using free services such as Google Groups or Yahoo! Groups. These provide the framework for electronic discussion groups using e-mail to communicate.

Another alternative that uses technology, but not the Internet, is the conference call. Depending on budgetary constraints, this is one method that can be used to process case studies when students are around the world. The conference call technology is not hard for students to use, as long as they have access to a phone. If the calls are all in North America, the phone rates can be quite reasonable.

Using videos or DVDs is an excellent use of technology for preparing supervisors, training teaching/peer committees or supervisors, or even introducing individual students to theological reflection. DVD or video production can be rather expensive, particularly if one wants to go beyond the "talking head." A good return on investment (ROI) is possible if the program is large, as there is an economy of scale. Another ROI factor is the travel expense for faculty to do on-site training. Instead of sending faculty to each site a number of times, students could lead their own training for their respective sites using DVDs or videos.

Teleconferencing is a format with which some schools are having great success. Students may be in several locations, with video capabilities to view and respond to a professor and class at another location. This option does tend to be rather expensive, but some campuses already have the equipment. Another option that might be considered is interactive work with webcams. These are small video cameras mounted on computers that can record and broadcast the computer user. Some CMS have the capacity to show webcam interactions. The drawback to this technology currently is the varying ability of students to receive webcam broadcasts. Unless students have high-speed Internet access, it takes too long to download and play the webcasts.

Podcasting is a newer technology. A podcast is an audio or video (digital medial) file that has been converted to an MP3 format, which can then be downloaded by the student and played using an MP3 player or a computer. This format for educational technology is gaining in popularity. Webcasting is also becoming more widely used. It is the Web version of a radio or television broadcast.

E-portfolios are new to higher education. These are electronically based portfolios that students can edit and append during their seminary careers. E-portfolios might contain important papers, faculty commendations or narrative evaluations, student journals, or other writings. For seminaries that require a capstone course with a portfolio, this is an excellent tool. Field education documentation that is done by electronic means could be easily included in such an environment.[2]

This is by no means an exhaustive listing of technology alternatives employed by distance learning. New means and methods are being introduced constantly. In choosing to use specific technologies to either enhance an F2F course or increase the connecting possibilities between teaching sites and students, achievement of educational purposes, goals, and objectives must be primary. It may be seductive for some to play with the latest electronic technology; however, technology is meant to serve the educational purposes rather than the other way around.

Teaching and Learning in Cyberspace

It is important to consider which aspects of field education can be brought to an online experience. How does the concrete nature of ministry setting and the students' reflections upon their ministry in that setting translate to online conversation? If one looks at the components of field education itself, what is transferable might become clearer. One of the most important components of every field education placement is the action/reflection model of learning. How might a field educator create a teaching/learning environment that is conducive not only to conversation but also to reflective practice?

---

2. To read more on e-portfolios, a Web search reveals a number of services. One free service that also includes work with assessment and rubrics is www.rcampus.com.

Structuring a course so that students' reflective practice might be cultivated and evidenced usually happens in group interaction in an F2F course,
or by case study processing.

These interactions happen best in a community of practice that has the
underpinnings of a listening and learning community. In a recent meeting
of the Association of Theological Field Educators (ATFE), participants in
a workshop concerning online learning in field education asked how one
builds community in the distance-learning environment. It is important to
remember that the definition of community here is a *learning community*.
The task of the field educator is to facilitate the learning of the ministering
person through the completion of the students' learning goals.

One of the distinctions field educators must consider in creating that
learning community is that they are not doing this in a spiritual vacuum.
The Holy Spirit is a recognized partner in the learning community. As such,
when developing the learning community for a theological education, prayer
with and for one another is an integral part of the class. Students who do
not know one another (or even some who do!) may not trust one another
immediately. The Holy Spirit working in the midst of the learning through
prayer gives the gift of community—it is always a gift, not something that is
constructed. However, know that some environs are more welcoming to the
Holy Spirit than others. Field educators recognize that their students come
to seminary to be shaped and formed as persons of prayer for the sake of
the ministries they have been called to before God. Therefore, teaching and
learning in cyberspace, as in an F2F situation, must be bathed in prayer on
the part of the student as well as the teacher.

In secular distance-learning courses, there are forums or areas where
students share what is going on in their personal lives or at work, travel
plans, and so on. In designing theological education courses, several
forums should be added to the actual course site. The site should include
a prayer forum (place for asking for prayer or sharing praises), a social
forum (place to chat and go "off topic" for fun), and several small groups
for assignments or other working groups in addition to the announcement
forum (place for general announcements for the course or the calendar
reminders).

Each of the forums within the course Web site has a function. Forums
invite the gift of community in a specific way. Students are required to post
to some forums. In the beginning of each course, students might be required
to introduce themselves by sharing their favorite music or pastime. Sharing
information about one's self is an icebreaker and helps to build a learning
community. Students will not be going out for coffee or sandwiches between
classes together in an online class. It is the responsibility of the faculty and
instructional design team to structure ways of building community through
online sharing.

One of the marked differences for teaching online is that the assignments need to be more specific than one might generally have in an F2F

class. Details that might be explained through question and answers in an F2F course have a way of disappearing in the online environment. Specificity and detail in assignments help the students to be successful and feel at ease with expectations.

A teaching style that is dependent upon appearance and visual cues will need to be modified in distance learning, unless there is extensive use of DVD and visual broadcast material. In an online environment, both teachers and students need to use words with precision and care. Without the tonality of audio to assist in interpretation, words can be misunderstood. Although it may seem rather infantile, the use of emoticons (;-} , for example) can clarify a statement, or set the tone for a comment.[3] These simple combinations of keystrokes representing emotions are helpful in discussions when one cannot hear a voice or see a face.

In a classroom setting, the instructor would not count the words or necessarily the number of times a student speaks in class. Generally instructors note the class participation, but it is not as specific as the online course work. For example, in a spiritual growth group that is online, each week the students have required reading and then are required to post an original 50- to 100-word response to the reading. They are also required to read everyone else's posting that week and respond to two of their colleagues' postings (25–50 words). Just reading and not responding (a behavior that is termed "lurking") is not acceptable participation. Our faculty members have commented that one can more successfully lurk in an F2F classroom than in an online environment. Participation in class discussion is more easily tracked electronically.

Students who prefer to ponder questions before answering them sometimes have difficulty in discussion-based courses. An online course gives time and grace to students who prefer inner processing to verbal processing. My experience has shown that there is a balancing of course discussion activity between the introverts and extroverts when they move to an online environment. An unexpected outcome of distance learning has been students' improvement in their writing skills and ability to think critically. When all discussion must be articulated through writing, the students become more adept in written discourse.

Teaching and learning in an online environment requires some changes in how students and teachers approach course work. Our seminary requires that the professors have their syllabi posted to the registrar's Web site and available to students six weeks prior to the first day of classes. This change has happened because online course sites for distance-learning classes are open six weeks prior to the first class meeting. Another driving reason behind this advance notice for students is the fact that our student population is no longer primarily residential. We, like many other seminaries, have

---

3. Further definitions and examples can be found at http://whatis.techtarget.com/definitionsSearch/0,290008,sid9,00.html.

residential students, commuter or local students (who drive up to 150 miles to attend classes), and Connections students.[4]

Students in the nonresidential Connections program usually have other employment along with their student status. They need to plan ahead for their reading and course work, so in order to help the students be as successful as possible, our faculty agreed to opening the course sites six weeks prior to the course start. It has worked so well with our Connections students that the entire student body now receives this same early start opportunity. Planning on the part of teachers has to move ahead proportionately in order to meet these deadlines.

Another change in teaching and learning is the rhythm of the week and the course work. In a traditional F2F class, the faculty has a block of three hours per week in the classroom with the students, or perhaps two classes of one and a half hours each. An instructor sees students in the classroom at specific times, in informal meetings around the campus, or during set office hours. Class preparation for those class meeting times are set by the professor, and this has been the rhythm of academic life for most who teach in higher education.

In an online environment, there are not usually set class meeting times. Students can post at any hour or sequence during the week. Professors need to log on to the course site and monitor the conversations and discussions at least once a day. Students also need to be just as responsive to one another and the course material. The course and assignments are all set up ahead of the course actually beginning. In the author's courses, there is a course itinerary, which lists on a weekly basis, the assignments due and activities expected (see figure 15.1). Adjustments and changes can be made during the life of the course, but, remember, students have planned their course work and additional life commitments around what was published. Last-minute modifications may meet with marked resistance.

Professors need to post office hours for online courses, just as one would for F2F classes. During those posted hours, a closed door with a sign reading "Privacy Requested: Online Office Hours" can afford the instructor some undisturbed hours with online students. The beauty of that is also that the instructor can have those "online office hours" from his or her home office or with a laptop from the local coffeehouse with free wireless access. There are some advantages to this for students and faculty!

Distance-learning technology enhances connections with students in the field. A weekly reflection journal on a critical event in their ministry setting that is shared in a small group can enrich the whole class. It also affords the calm assurance to students that they are not alone in this endeavor.

---

4. The distance-learning program for the M.Div. degree at the seminary in which the author teaches is called the Connections program. Our sister seminary, Earlham School of Religion, named their distance-learning program Access. Schools use various terms for their programs, when online classes can lead to a degree.

Figure 15.1. Example of Weekly Assignments			
Semester I Classes begin	Thr		8/30
1st Weekend Intensive	Fri		8/31
Bring to weekend intensive Bible, Ministry Formation Handbook, your calendar Content/Context review of Transforming Church Boards	Sat		9/1
	Sun	W E E K 1	9/2
	Mon		9/3
Read: Grounded in God	Tue		9/4
	Wed		9/5
	Thr		9/6
	Fri		9/7
	Sat		9/8
	Sun		9/9
	Mon		9/10
Weekly Log #1 Self Assesment Due Learning Serving Covenant due with Learning Goals	Tue	W E E K 2	9/11
	Wed		9/12
	Thr		9/13
	Fri		9/14
	Sat		9/15
	Sun		9/16
	Mon		9/17
Weekly Log #2 Permission for Verbal Communication form due Metaphor for Ministry due	Tue	W E E K 3	9/18
	Wed		9/19
	Thr		9/20
	Fri		9/21
	Sat		9/22

Some distance educators in higher education have found that teaching online takes more faculty time than teaching an F2F course. My seminary counts each F2F course as one unit of faculty time and each online course counts as 1.5 units of faculty time. Pacing is essential for students and faculty. Palloff and Pratt offer these suggestions for all distance educators and their students:

1. Set a specific time each day to read and respond to messages rather than doing it throughout the day.

2. Wait to respond to a message that upsets you and be careful of what you say and how you say it.

3. Establish clear priorities for dealing with messages and categorize messages by importance and need to respond.[5]

As an educator, one also must be aware that off-the-cuff remarks that one might make in a classroom become published statements in an online environment. One of our professors learned that lesson in a most difficult manner when one of his longer responses to a student found its way in published form around the church. This was an unintended use of a professor's work, but it is a reminder of how problems might arise. Students and professors will need to covenant with one another that what is said (written online) in this course, stays in this course. Confidentiality must be obtained and guarded for the protection of the students as well.

This is particularly true when case studies are being discussed in the online course work. While this forum is safer than just sending e-mail back and forth, since the course site does not allow persons access unless they are enrolled in the course, there are still concerns to be addressed specific to field education placements. In order for the students to feel the freedom to discuss the deeper issues they find in the setting, there must be assurance that the discussion forums and their contents are not shared beyond the members of the class.

The freedom to share from a ministry setting provides one of the unique characteristics of field education for both the teachers and learners. Students bring events and personal experiences from situations in their own settings to the table for theological reflection. This gives rich and real texture to the question: Where is God in all this?

Some field education programs do not have a classroom component to their placements. Adding an online environment offers the opportunity for each student to bring forth issues and to receive feedback from an entire group, rather than only the professor or the on-site supervisor. Students

---

5. Rena Palloff and Keith Pratt, *Building Learning Communities in Cyberspace: Effective Strategies for the Online Classroom* (San Francisco: Jossey-Bass, 1999), 51.

learn from their own learning goals, as well as from others' by the interaction afforded in the online course work.

Structuring a Course

Instructional design for a field education course will include the major elements one would encounter in a more traditional F2F seminar for theological reflection. If the seminary does not have an F2F course component for field education, adding an online area for assignments, reflections, and community for learning can enrich the experience for everyone. The faculty for field education can decide which elements of a reflective learning community are appropriate curricular pieces to include. When first moving to an online environment, it is helpful to meet with other teachers, curricular design specialists, and instructional technology experts to reimagine the course. Taking an F2F syllabus and posting it online "doth not a successful distance-learning experience make!"

Beginning with the course goals and objectives, the instructor examines the assignments and activities that will create the best atmosphere for learning. In the traditional classroom, lectures or didactic sessions, discussions, case study presentations, and sharing of the week's challenges and learnings take up the bulk of the class time. In the online environment, small-group assignments and presentations develop a sense of community. Shared leadership in facilitating the small groups develops a sense of ownership and effective leadership styles.

Whether the student is responding only to a faculty member or to a cohort of learners, the first step is for the student to describe his or her own setting and the learning goals for the field education experience. In an F2F class, students turn in their learning goals and share a short description of the setting in the first classes. In larger F2F environments, small groups can be used effectively so that each person has an opportunity to be heard.

In the previous courses, if there have been documents or forms the student, peer committee, or supervisor was to fill out, these same documents may be posted electronically. The user can then access the document, fill it out, and return it online. In some cases, a user might print out a form accessed electronically and then, after filling out the form, return it by regular mail. If a teacher has a document that needs to remain in the exact same format, the document may be saved to an Adobe document (pdf) format and then posted to the course site. Users could see, download, and print the document, but it could not be changed or manipulated electronically.

Case studies often are processed in field education classes, and they can be processed in an online environment as well. The person facilitating the discussion needs to post the open questions and guide the discussion carefully. Students need clear guidance as to their responses in processing a case study so that each area is fully examined before moving to the next. For example, after the case study is posted, students would be asked to take some time in prayer and then post any clarifying questions they might have.

The students would have two days to post any clarifying questions and the presenter to answer them. Then, the presenter would be asked to enter a "listening mode" and "lurk" while the others processed the case study. (The presenting student would be asked to respond at the close of the processing.) In the next two days students would be asked if there are areas in their own lives that this event is particularly touching. Following the harvest of personal experience, the facilitator would ask a section of questions gathering professional and educational wisdom, theological understanding, presenter's ministry, and then a final section of questions for evaluation, when the presenter would be invited to verbally participate in the discussion. Each section of questions could be asked over the course of twenty-four to forty-eight hours. This gives the students enough time to ponder each movement of the case study but still keep the discussion moving asynchonistically.

Course management systems (CMS) allow the instructor to set up forums that are private for these and other sensitive discussions. The teacher can set up several different types of groups for whatever educational purposes that are needed. Students may be enrolled in several different groups according to the need of the curricular elements. The faculty sets the settings for each course, and most course sites are not open to visitors, only to those enrolled. Within each class, the faculty can set up groups that are either available or hidden from the other groups in the class. CMS are flexible, and software designers are adding new elements rapidly.

Conclusion

If all this seems like a blur or exciting but still a blur, there are several books mentioned in the bibliography that can carry this topic much farther than this one chapter has been able to do. In addition, several educational institutions have excellent certification programs to learn to teach online. A blessing of taking this course work is that as a teacher, one is refreshed in the basics of assessment, grading rubrics, creating learning goals, and understanding learner-centered collaborative education. Outstanding resources on distance learning are available online.[6]

When our seminary first began to use technology in the classroom, each week was a new learning experience. Then, when the distance-learning program was instituted, our seminary took two years of planning, meeting, and training before the first courses were offered online. The seminary hired a person who had taken extensive training in distance learning and had the services of an institutional technology department to help us think through and plan the courses. A team was created to assist each professor with the course design and ideas for distance-learning andragogy/pedagogy.

We had brown-bag lunches during which we discussed books provided to

---

6. See http://www.irrodl.org. This Web site lists journals and organizations for distance-education research as well as conferences that one might attend to learn more.

us by the seminary.[7] During one of the brown-bag lunches, one of our faculty suggested we team-teach paired courses in this new system. For two years we followed that format and were gifted with new discoveries about each other's teaching styles and curricular offerings. It was a blessing for our faculty as a community. We eventually unpaired the courses so that students could have more flexibility in taking course work, but the experience was lasting as an introduction to teaching online. There is nothing like the buddy system when we are learning new tasks!

There were times during the expansion of the curriculum to the online environment when the learning curve seemed to increase exponentially. Looking back on those first few courses, we learned so much about each other as teaching faculty and about our own educational practices that our F2F courses improved. Teaching in the online environment required us to examine course structure, learning objectives, and outcomes more carefully.

May your explorations of field education, distance learning, and technology lead you to uncharted territories, to the glory of God and to our neighbor's good.

---

7. Our seminary provided time and space for us to learn about teaching online in a hospitable environment. The administration wisely provided training and texts for each faculty member to increase our sense of comfort with teaching in this new system.

Prayer of Transformation

Creator God, you who bring fresh understandings through the Holy Spirit, enliven our teaching and learning that we might follow Jesus Christ with passion and clarity. Embolden our hearts and minds so that all we do may be for your glory and our neighbor's good. We pray in the precious name of Jesus. Amen.

Reflection Questions

1. If your school does not have a classroom component to field education, how might adding an online class component facilitate learning?

2. If your school has an F2F class included in the field education program, what enhancement would an online component bring to the course requirements?

3. How might students' spiritual lives be deepened by guided Internet contact during the semester?

4. What changes would your institution need to make in order to have an online class in field education?

Further Reading

Duffy, Thomas, and Jamie Kirkley. *Learner-Centered Theory and Practice in Distance Education: Cases from Higher Education.* Mahwah, NJ: Lawrence Erlhaum Associates, 2004.

Hess, Mary. *Engaging Technology in Theological Education: All That We Can't Leave Behind.* Lanham, MD: Rowman & Littlefield, 2005.

Paloff, Rena, and Keith Pratt. *Building Learning Communities in Cyberspace: Effective Strategies for the Online Classroom.* San Francisco: Jossey-Bass, 1999.

——. *Lessons from the Cyberspace Classroom: The Realities of Online Teaching.* San Francisco: Jossey-Bass, 2001.

Chapter 16

Dealing with Difficult Situations in Field Education

Doran McCarty

*After this the Lord appointed seventy-two others and sent them
on ahead of him, two by two, into every town and place where he
himself was about to go. (Luke 10:1)*

When asked to name mentoring problems in field education and supervisory settings, participants in my mentoring workshops have responded with enough problems to fill a chalkboard. However, problems in mentoring also offer opportunities for growth and maturation. Does a mentor really want a student to have a completely problem-free internship? Does a mentor want the student to never have conflicts with the mentor or any of the church staff? Does a mentor want the student to never face criticism from the congregation? Does a mentor want the student to have an entirely hassle-free opportunity to learn about ministry?

Pardon me, but when is ministry truly hassle-free? Will students really learn about ministry in completely idyllic situations? Let us suppose that a student has a kind of irenic internship. What happens when he or she goes to a parish and has to face the realities of church leadership? Is it possible that the student needs to see firsthand how a minister or leader handles difficulties so the student will be able to apply those principles in his or her own ministry setting?

I remember two of my friends getting married. Lois was from a home where the parents never raised their voices or quarreled in front of the children. On the other hand, Jack's parents expressed their feelings aloud, including criticisms. So the first time in their marriage when Jack confronted Lois, she was sure the marriage was over. I have seen young ministers experiencing this in their first church as well, having never been close to conflict and criticisms in the church. The internship is where the student can experience these difficulties and be sheltered by his or her "student status" and a sensitive and effective mentor.

One of the best ways to avoid mentoring problems is to have a good training program for the mentors.[1] While a training program will not eliminate the problems, mentors who have been in my mentoring training courses have told me that they knew how to approach the problems now.

While some of the challenges a student may face come from participants in his or her ministry, others come from within the mentoring relationship itself. Mentors and students face traps that can hinder the effectiveness of the field education experience. The sincere mentor or the responsible student may be surprised by one or more of these traps. When that happens, it is easy to despair and believe that dealing with these traps is all that a person does. But that does not have to be the case. Since these traps are prominent in mentoring, this chapter addresses some of these potential problems and how to deal with them when they come.

Personal Traps Affecting Mentoring

Some of the mentoring traps come from what the individuals (mentor and student) bring into the mentoring relationship. Some of these traps are more on the student's end and some are on the mentor's end. A mentor and his or her student would be wise to be sensitive to these areas.[2]

Identity Issues

All persons face identity problems, but identity issues are especially difficult for younger students. These younger students are not only taking on a new role—moving from student to minister in their field education setting—but also are struggling with the move from adolescence to adulthood. These younger students may tend to think that at a magic age, they will have it all together (as they perceive their seminary professors and

---

1. See chapter 18, "Equipping Mentors to Leave a Legacy," for more specifics on mentor training. The training program should be a requirement for the certification of a mentor. Training is important because it brings the mentors on board as team members with the school. Training will help mentors realize what the school expects from them and the students. The mentors will understand the reasons behind certain requirements and will be given some of the tools needed for the mentoring process.

2. I want to thank John Hopkins for his insight into this area. Also, it should be noted that other areas of potential problems (such as mentoring across gender and mentoring across culture) are addressed in their own chapters in this book.

mentors do). However, they fail to realize everyone struggles to "put it together."

The younger students are not the only ones wrestling with identity issues, though. Many seminaries have second-career students who are older than the traditional seminary students. They move from a successful career to a neophyte student minister. They too may struggle with this new identity, both within the school and in the ministry location.

In the ambiguity of unsure identity, a strain on the student personally and the mentoring relationship in general can take place. Nevertheless, this wrestling with identity (along with testing one's calling) is one of the primary growth areas in a student's life.[3] The mentoring experience can become a safe environment to deal with issues of identity and testing one's calling. In dealing with students, mentors can provide a model by sharing their own continuing identity struggle. This self-revelation by the mentor takes insight, honesty, and courage on the part of the mentor.

Change, Loss, and Resistance

Students in general are in the midst of change in their lives while in school, but this is especially true during the time of their internship. During the internship, a student leaves the familiarity of the academic classroom and experiences life differently in churches and organizations that are unlike the student's academic institution. As a result, change is happening internally and externally in the student's life at the same time.

Some of these changes may involve loss and change, even if change is for the better. Whenever there is a loss or change in the life of the student, the mentor may expect anger in the life of the student. The anger may be internalized and denied or expressed and justified; but anger is one sign of loss and change. Anger can be seen in such signs as withdrawal, pouting, emotional explosions, or constant resistance. The mentor should be prepared to deal with the anger in order to proceed with the mentoring task.

Sometimes what results is resistance on the part of the student during these times of change. Mentors meeting resistance in their students fight an uphill battle. Mentors may feel as though they are pushing a car uphill by themselves, but resistance is no great mystery and can be unraveled. A mentor needs to tell the student that he or she perceives resistance and work with the student to check the source of that resistance. This is the honest way to handle resistance. A mentor cannot help by closing his or her eyes to resistance or becoming legalistic and making demands regardless of resistance. The most helpful thing is to flush out the resistance so that both the mentor and the student can see the resistance and deal with it. Where there is resistance by the student in a field education setting, resistance will likely be a problem in his or her ministry vocation after graduation.

---

3. See chapter 1, "Field Education and Vocational Discernment," for a more detailed discussion on calling discovery.

Individualism and Authority

While I applaud some individualism and independence, these characteristics also can hinder mentoring and ministry. The internship and corresponding mentoring should help a student recognize how the attributes of individualism and independence help and, conversely, when these attributes do not. A pastor of a church or a leader of an organization will succeed when he or she learns to develop teamwork. Field education is a good place to test out the student's ability to work as part of a team.

Individualism and authority usually come into conflict. Unfortunately, some ministry students believe they are accountable to no one but God. As a result, authority issues can surface as an important part of a mentoring relationship. From the mentor's end, he or she may be afraid to assert his or her rightful authority and not confront a student. Or a mentor may abuse his or her authority and be overly demanding. To prevent this situation, lines of authority should be drawn in the covenant between the seminary and the ministry setting at the start of the internship.

Students may struggle with the use of their own authority as well. For example, a group of seminary students went overseas as volunteers for the summer. In their service, many of these students took an authoritarian approach to their work. As a result, all but one couple was sent home. Not only were they unfamiliar with the culture and the work, the students endangered the relationships of the vocational missionaries with the government of the host country. What a teachable moment this was to learn about the proper use of authority.

Assigned Responsibility

Each field setting and person in the mentoring relationship must accept responsibility. Unfortunately, the student may want the mentor to assume what should be the student's responsibility, or the student may even want the mentor to "rescue" him or her. If so, there may be trouble if the mentor assumes more responsibility than called for in the covenant. A good covenant includes the limits of responsibility of each field setting and person.

The mentor needs to maintain accountability of the student and be supportive. A mentor should note clues that show that the student is having problems dealing with responsibility. Those who rely on religious clichés or phrases such as "the Lord's will," "praise God," and "the Devil made me do it" may be avoiding responsibility. While theology includes the will of God, praise, and demonic temptation, these also may be used as escape mechanisms. Students may even avoid taking responsibility for the good things because if they did, they would have to bear the responsibility for the problems as well.

A mentor will need to observe the student's ability to take initiative. If a mentor is very task-oriented, he or she may make a list of tasks the student should do. This might be helpful in the short run, but the student must learn to take initiative and bear the responsibility for the results.

While a healthy work ethic is vital, the mentor should be careful not to impose personal patterns of work on his or her individual student. For example, the student may work more intensively but for shorter periods of time than the mentor. A workaholic mentor should not impose his or her work neurosis upon the student.

One other issue related to student responsibility is that of passive-aggressive behavior. While quietly acquiescing to the mentor's wishes for a while, the passive-aggressive student may blow up or in some way try to sabotage the mentoring relationship. This type of person often has difficulty taking initiative in some situations. Mentors need to note when students acquiesce to their suggestions but do not carry the suggestions out or fail to act on them enthusiastically. Mentors need not examine the task perhaps as much as what is occurring in the mentoring relationship. After all, this passive-aggressive behavior no doubt will carry on when the student gets into a parish.

Family and Financial Problems

Family problems that surface may be serious and capable of destroying the student's effectiveness. Erosion of the home in American society influences the minister's home as well. The student's family problems can easily arise with the amount of time demanded at a field education setting. If the spouse is not in sympathy with his or her partner's ministry vocation or does not appreciate the ministry setting, problems are certain.[4] Mentors, too, can be affected by problems at home.

Finances also may create a strain on many students who may face great economic pressures compared to people in other professions. Younger students may still have college loans to pay off. Mature students may be financing their children's college educations. Mentors need to be sensitive to the fact that tension connected with inadequate finances may affect the functioning of students. I recall leading a mentoring seminar at a seminary where the director of the program said that he could not ask his students to do a rigorous mentoring program because the tuition and living expenses were so high that almost every student had to work long hours to meet expenses.

Mental and Emotional Health Issues

Perhaps the single most devastating thing that can happen in mentoring is to have a student who is mentally or emotionally unhealthy. Students are no less exempt from mental and emotional health problems than the general population. With the additional stress of ministering in a field education setting, it is possible for a student with fragile mental health to "crack up."

When faced with an unhealthy student, a mentor can end up spending

---

4. See chapter 14, "The Impact of Field Education on Marriage and Family," for a more detailed discussion on this topic.

an inordinate amount of time with that student. The mentor also should consider the legal ramifications of the situation. When a mentor sees signs of mental health problems, he or she should contact the seminary director of the field education program and seek help for the student. The mentor should not become vulnerable by keeping the problem to himself or herself. It is not the mentor's role to offer therapy to a student with mental health issues, because this affects his or her role as a mentor. These situations move beyond the scope of the normal mentoring relationship and should be dealt with by trained professionals.

Cross-Generational Mentoring

Cross-generational mentoring is a reality in today's society. There are many mentoring relationships where age differences between mentor and student can adversely affect their ability to work together. However, many mentoring relationships do well in spite of age disparity. Variance in age does not assure problems, but both mentors and students should be aware of potential problems and should identify early signs of problems in order to address them.

Younger mentors who work with older students should not discount the wealth of wisdom that these older students offer. Age often gives a person perspective as well as information. There is usually a great deal of teach-ability found in these older students. They often want more training in a new situation than the mentor offers. Sometimes these older students only need assurance that their previous experience is applicable to the present situation. At the same time, these older students need to be encouraged to continue to be open to new ventures.

Older mentors who work with younger students need to recognize that these students think differently and have different expectations. Many younger students do not come from Christian homes and had no early Christian nurture. Their concept of church is often different, and their chosen style of worship is new. They depend more on relationships than structure. The younger generations are less likely to have denominational or institutional loyalty. Their work ethic may differ from the traditional Protestant work ethic. All of these can become sources of conversation in the mentoring relationship.

Cross-Vocational Mentoring

There are many kinds of cross-vocational mentoring situations. There are senior pastors who mentor students serving as ministers of music, education, youth, or children. There are denominational workers who mentor Christian social ministry workers. There are professors who mentor student pastors and those in other church ministries. Many have proven to be successful cross-vocational mentors, and many have experienced difficulties.

Mentors who find themselves in these cross-vocational situations need to remember that they do not need to have all the answers. In fact, the "know-it-all" mentor can create a serious problem in a cross-vocational setting. For example, the student serving as a youth minister may find the cross-vocational mentor operating out of a stereotype of a youth program from the mentor's own youthful years without recognizing today's realities.

Mentors who find themselves in these situations need to remember that there are other resources to help. This is where the resources of the school can play a key role. But more important, remember that the technical skills of a particular ministry vocation are only one part of the field education experience. The starting place of all good mentoring is the understanding that it deals with personhood as well as tasks. While the mentor may admit at the beginning that he or she does not have the technical ability to deal much with some vocationally focused tasks, the mentor can deal with personhood issues.

Situational Traps Affecting Mentoring

Besides the personal traps just mentioned, there are also situational traps that affect mentoring. When these situations arise, they have to be addressed.

Unhealthy Systems

It is just a fact that some churches and organizations provide adequate structure for good mentoring and others do not. Sometimes a mentor may be able to change the system to provide the appropriate structure, but this type of change may take a long time. In these types of settings, it is important for the mentor to be honest with the student before the internship begins. It is better that the student enter the relationship aware that adjustments will have to be made to provide good mentoring. Having a very clear covenant will help to provide the kind of structure needed as well.

In some churches or organizations, the overall system is overly task-oriented. In these situations, it will be important for both the mentor and the student to insert personhood issues into the mentoring program and to be sensitive to personhood issues. In other systems, the overall scheme is so person-oriented that they overlook the basic tasks that need to be done. These systems are preoccupied with individual hurts, injustices, theories, and feelings. In these systems, students need covenants with quantifiable goals and review times so they are held accountable to the goals.

Unclear Roles

Sometimes in a field education setting, the roles may be unclear for either the student or the mentor. For example, consider a second-career student who decides to do the internship with his or her home church and pastor. This student had been a member of the church for a number of years prior to school. Before the student entered seminary, he or she had been elected to the church's budget committee. Now the student and the pastor are in a field education experience, with the pastor serving as the supervisor of the student. This blurring can create role problems, especially if the two later are at odds over a budget issue.

In another case, a student may have to answer to multiple voices in an internship setting. Many mentoring programs include the field education professional at the school, the on-site mentor, and a lay committee, as well as church committees in the area where the student works. Plus there are the actual ministry constituents. In this case, who is the student ultimately responsible to? In the past, management theory determined that only one person could be a supervisor of an employee and that supervisor, in turn, was accountable for the employee. In the past two decades, though, this autocratic view of leadership in management has changed with the development of participatory or democratic management. This management style includes people at all levels in evaluation and decision making. Even students participate in decisions. Therefore, shared mentoring in seminary programs is not unique.

The covenant is a tool for helping define the different mentoring roles. Student mentoring should be divided among the parties involved so that each knows the most productive way to help while staying within the limitations of their roles. This is consistent with my definition of mentoring as a "support system."

Mentoring is not a "lone-ranger" undertaking but the development of a mentoring support system. I had an older, experienced pastor who attended my training workshop who said, "Doran, send me a boy, and I'll take care of him." I knew that I was in trouble. He supervised only one year.

Shared mentoring has built-in problems, though. For one thing, it opens the gate to game playing. Students may play the game "mentoring split," pitting one mentor against another. Or persons involved in the mentoring task may fail to recognize or adhere to the divisions in the mentoring role. Their actions may undercut the role of the direct, local mentor.

The covenant should make clear the roles of all involved parties and organizations. When a person or group begins to violate the covenant, one or more of the other people involved needs to call for a clarification. As circumstances arise, some areas may not be as clear, creating the need to renegotiate the covenant. If a student plays "mentoring split," the other parties involved should be alerted as well.

Mentoring Friends

Related to the topic of unclear roles is the topic of mentoring friends. While one might not seek to supervise a friend, there have been mentors who found themselves having to do so.[5] In these awkward situations, there may be role, authority, and emotional confusion. The alert mentor will talk with the friend and define their respective roles and when the roles apply. There need to be clear signals about when the two are in the roles of mentor and

---

5. I wish to thank Bob Mills for his work in this area.

student and when they can relax in the role of friends. Probably no person more than the mentor realizes that the mentoring authority is not because of his or her inherent superiority but rather it is a responsibility that comes with the position. It is wise for the mentor to indicate that to the friend.

Friends often feel a sense of betrayal when a mentor-friend agrees with another person rather than with the student in a situation or assessment. When the mentor discusses the mentoring role with the friend at the beginning of the new mentoring relationship, the mentor should clarify the possibility of this happening and assure the friend that this does not mean he or she is being rejected.

The covenant can help avoid problems when a person has to supervise a friend. Mentoring can be contained within the framework of the covenant, while "normal" relationships remain outside the scope of the covenant. I had a friend with whom I used to double-date who entered the Doctor of Ministry program that I supervised. I told him that when we went to lunch we were David and Doran; but when we had mentoring meetings, I was mentor and he was student. Such an understanding also should be communicated to any other students since they will know of the friendship and worry that they will be left out.

It would be a mistake to ignore possible concerns that might arise from a friend mentoring a friend. Of particular concern is how the relationship will change. From the beginning both parties need to discuss the implications for this new dimension in their relationship. Some might assume that nothing will change and that the relationship will move along as it always has. This assumption is dangerous in mentoring. There may be a temptation not to clarify personal and systemic expectations, but this is necessary for good mentoring. The best time for this discussion is before either party agrees to accept this new relationship.

From the beginning it must be clear what the new roles will be in mentoring. How will the roles change? What is expected by the mentor and the system? A friend can supervise a friend and have a stronger relationship. It can bring them to a new level of appreciation for one another. However, many relationships are without structure and intentionality, and good mentoring demands both of these. Since one or both may not want structure and intentionality, they must decide whether they can tolerate these within their friendship.

Mentoring at a Distance

Mentoring at a distance is a reality in religious circles.[6] For example, many seminary students serve student pastorates and their actual mentor may be some distance away from the student. It is not only a religious phenomenon, however. It is not uncommon today for a business enterprise to practice

---

6. See chapter 15, "Working with Technology and Distance Education," for the latest research on this topic.

mentoring at a distance. One of my daughters lived in Kansas City and her mentor was in New York City. Her husband supervised people in New York City, Miami, Puerto Rico, and the Dominican Republic from Kansas City.

My philosophy of mentoring focuses on taking care of personhood and task needs. Nowhere is the need for this focus clearer than when mentoring at a distance. The personhood challenge is to be sure the student does not transform loneliness into alienation. Mentoring the task needs probably means helping a student serving at a place where no one has ever succeeded at the task before. In fact, the student may be working in a difficult situation for the very reason that it is not easy, for had it been easy, someone else would have succeeded before.

Geographical distance between the mentor and student can interfere with the mentoring task. In these situations, mentors may be tempted to play the game "wooden leg" and say, "If I were only closer, I could do a good job of mentoring." But good mentoring (i.e., support) may be especially needed where geographical distances are great.

No one denies that geographical distances are a challenge to mentoring, but good planning can ensure good mentoring. The mail, e-mail, and the telephone can be used. Mentoring sessions may be planned to coincide with denominational meetings attended by both mentor and student. Mentors can plan to make longer visits with students. There is no substitute for full cooperation between mentor and student.

The covenant is very important when mentoring at a distance. A clear and complete covenant gives the student a "mentor" at hand inasmuch as he or she can regularly review the covenant. This is a situation where a covenant may need to outline monthly goals and activities. The mentor may have to lead in renegotiating the covenant every few months under these circumstances.

There are several potential problems with mentoring at a distance. One is frustration. The student faces crises without immediate access to the mentor. The student gets little feedback or feedback that is too late for help or affirmation. Mentors also can face frustration. If the mentor is a high control person, he or she faces anxiety and sometimes anger. The mentor cannot understand some of the actions the student initiates because he or she cannot keep in touch adequately to meet the mentor's control needs. If the mentor is a self-starter, he or she may not understand the dependency or approval needs of the student.

Mentors need to make opportunities for observation. During medical internships, the mentoring physician can observe the intern perform medical tasks such as surgery. The student also has the opportunity to observe the mentoring physician "make rounds" in the hospital. The student observes the questions the mentoring physician asks the patients and can dialogue with the mentoring physician later. The medical profession would not supervise students at a distance. However, many religious situations must depend on mentoring at a distance.

Where there is distant mentoring, mentoring conferences on the field are limited. The student and the mentor may plan to have conferences at denominational or professional meetings they both attend. Phone calls may be used to supplement mentoring conferences. These limited mentoring conferences must be well planned so the time is not eroded by extraneous conversation.

Mentoring at a distance lends itself to the mentor imposing an agenda. The mentor needs to work with the student to set the agenda. Often the distant mentor will not have firsthand knowledge of the local situation.

Distant mentoring works against developing mutual communication. The mentor has to depend heavily on correspondence, phone conversations, and e-mail and newsletters. The student can resent the impersonal communication and feel that the monthly reports submitted to the mentor are only "bureaucratic" necessities.

Evaluation is often difficult even in the best mentoring situations; distance adds to those evaluation problems. When the mentor is at a distance, it is difficult to get data and test it out in order to make a good formal evaluation. Good evaluation is more than numbers on a page; it is testing out hunches about personhood issues. Because of little contact, the student may not take the mentor's evaluation seriously.

The mentoring visits should not be "drop by" visits but well-planned visits. Since the visits may be few, they may need to be lengthier. The mentor and student should give each other full attention. Prepare an agenda. Give the student materials. Visit with the family. Tour the church building and at least part of the church field. Wrap up the meeting with a thankful word to the student and to God.

Free Church Tradition and Student Pastorates

In many denominations bishops or superintendents have the responsibility of appointing ministers to settings, but the free church tradition has largely left the calling of ministers to the local churches. Often ordination or education is not required. This means that many seminaries of these denominations or traditions have students who are already serving in student pastorates. Most of these are single-staff churches (only a student pastor) and have no one on the staff to supervise them. The field education professional has to be alert to this situation and work out a satisfactory mentoring situation. He or she may have to call on another pastor in the vicinity or a denominational official. This also means that the mentor is not usually on-site. While good mentoring can occur under these conditions, special care has to be taken. Certainly this situation can become a problem. This is a systemic problem many field education professionals face and and to which they have to adjust their system to cope.

Role Changes

Sometimes in mentoring situations the roles change for either the student or the mentor. A student may find himself or herself starting out in one role but transitioning into another role during the internship. For example, consider a student who goes to a church with the full responsibility for the youth in the church. During the year, the church finds that they have the financial resources to employ a full-time youth minister instead of a part-time student intern. As a result, the student is faced with a role change. The student can transition from being in charge of the youth ministry to assisting the new youth minister. Or maybe the church offers the student a different role (such as working with senior citizens), and he or she has to decide whether to make this shift or not.

Hopefully in situations like this, the student can see the importance of the role change and make the change graciously. Also, it helps when the student can be part of the planning that leads to the role change. In most of these cases, the change requires a renegotiation of the field education covenant.

But role changes also occur with mentors. Sometimes, there is a need to change mentors during a student's term of service. I have experienced mentoring changes for a variety of reasons. Pastors change parishes, become ill, die, or get fired. Whenever mentoring change happens, it is a stressful situation for the student. I consider it important to communicate to the student that he or she will not lose credit for the course and that I will provide a mentor even if I have to do it myself. Obviously, I do not expect this to happen very often.

When a mentor change takes place, there needs to be renegotiation of the covenant and new assignments. A student may have feelings of betrayal by the changes. The change may result in a student being put into an area of responsibilities where he or she has no experience and little expertise. A wise seminary field education director will consider the situation and help the student adjust happily. This is also a time when there is a possibility of game playing.

When a student or a mentor wants to bail out of the mentoring setup, I appeal to the covenant that they have negotiated and of which I was a part. Maybe they cannot tolerate one another or have a different philosophy of ministry, but that is what the student will face in his or her ministry career. This again can become a wonderful learning opportunity if handled properly.

Forced Termination

Quality mentoring involves an intentional focus on the growth of persons and the effective accomplishment of tasks. Sometimes, though, after repeated attempts at course corrections and perhaps even a probationary period, further action is required. Termination of the intern may be necessary as a last resort. "This won't happen to me" might be the last words spoken by the mentor who is not prepared to address the matter of termination. A mentor needs to approach termination with a plan.[7]

---

7. I thank Bob Mills for his work on forced termination.

One of the keys is for the church or organization to have a personnel policy and procedure manual that spells out the reasons and process for termination for all of its employees, not just student interns. This policy and procedure manual should address legal issues as well. But having the manual in place is not enough. The next step is to actually follow those procedures when needed.

Having a good evaluation procedure in place is vital in this process. In having these evaluations, it is important that these written records be honest and accurate. Too many times evaluations are seen as just routine with no negative remarks. This casual use of evaluations will hinder any termination procedure that is needed. Honest evaluation that details difficulties is necessary for termination.

There also needs to be a system of notification when performance or attitude is below expectations and the covenant has not been fulfilled adequately. If the performance or attitude is below expectations, the mentor needs to establish a period of probation so that further action will be no surprise to the student. During this probationary period, the mentor should make himself or herself available for any correction the student needs to make.

In addition to the church or organization, the seminary also should have a system in place to deal with termination. This should include both preparing for problems before they occur and steps to be taken when they do occur.

Termination is seldom easy or comfortable for anyone. Nevertheless, termination is a reality in mentoring and should not be taken lightly. If all options have been exhausted, termination may be necessary. When this happens, termination should be approached with planned deliberation. And remember that in any multiple-staff situation, other staff persons need to be consoled and assured that the termination of one person poses no threat to them.

Communication Problems

My daughter came home from second grade one day crying and angry. When my wife asked her what was wrong, my daughter told her mother that her teacher had called her best friend a "horse" just because her friend had a cold. After understanding the situation, my wife patiently explained the difference between being a "horse" and being "hoarse."

Communication is a difficult enterprise. Mentors and students can expect communication problems. Communication is mysterious enough when both parties try to make communication work. Greater communication troubles arise in mentoring when there is inadequate structure, resistance, or unclear goals. Both mentor and student operate in each situation with their own ideas, facts, experiences, feelings, and dreams. Difficulties in communication are compounded even more when mentoring is cross-cultural.[8]

---

8. Because of the unique challenges in working with cross-cultural students, there is an entire chapter in this book dealing with the subject.

Communication is the vehicle for mentoring. When the vehicle is faulty, adequate mentoring cannot occur. Mentoring may even be harmful rather than helpful without adequate communication.

Listening Is Key

Poor listening is a major problem in communication. Public schools spend millions of dollars teaching remedial as well as regular courses in reading, yet we spend more hours a day listening than reading. Who has ever taken a course on listening?

Good listening improves communication. One should actively listen rather than just sit in the geographical locale of the speaker. One can determine whether he or she is actively listening by asking, "Am I spending as much energy and concentrating as much when I listen as when I speak?" The mentor or student who does not listen with concentration can expect to be heard with the same indifference. One of the best ways a mentor can teach communication is by first modeling good listening skills. A mentor who listens actively communicates a caring attiude, showing that he or she thinks the student is important.

Mentors and students can structure communication for clarification purposes. The mentor may need to ask the student, "What did you understand me to say?" The student may answer, "I understood you to say . . ." Feedback provides opportunity to see if what was said was appropriately communicated. A student should not say to the mentor, "What you said was," but instead, "This is what I heard you say."

Listening is more than hearing words. Good listening also is perceiving the feeling behind those words. Words alone do not always bear the message. There are feelings behind the words that may be a cry for help. Good listening is accomplished with both the ears of the mind and the ears of the heart.

Importance of Context

Another thing to consider in communication is context. Everyone communicates within a context. The context includes things such as family background, cultural background, goals, education, and existing pressures. For example, a mentor within five years of retirement works from a different context than the twenty-five-year-old person in his or her first ministry position who dreams about future job possibilities. The person from one culture comes from a different context than a person from another culture. Words may not mean the same from person to person. Each person reacts differently to ideas.

Regional idioms also may cause misunderstanding. Wendell Belew, former missionary of the North American Mission Board of the Southern Baptist Convention, told a story about sending a seminary student from Mississippi to preach in the hills of Kentucky. He instructed the student to stop at a certain place, pick up an elderly woman and take her to church.

Later that week, when Belew called the woman and asked the woman how she liked the young man, he was surprised to find out that she had been offended. The young man had offered to "carry her" to church. The Mississippi idiom of "carrying" people resulted in a gross communication problem.

The context of authority can either create or alleviate communication problems. Observing an associate pastor lead a seminar, I noticed no one responded when he asked for feedback. After an hour, the pastor affirmed what he had heard from the associate, and from that point on there was stimulating dialogue. Titles, over-under relationships, personal charisma, and forced relationships can create communication problems. Mentors can examine their communication with students by monitoring whether they are communicating as a parent, a peer, a professor, or in some other role. They may even become conscious of when they change communication styles.

The setting influences communication. If the mentoring session occurs in the mentor's office, the mentor's role and authority is heightened because the student is on the mentor's turf. The desk behind which the mentor sits communicates that something is between them. Free-flowing communication usually occurs more in a neutral place or at least one not closely identified with the mentor. The mentor and the student should sit facing one another with no barriers between them. A man who is a sought-after expert in his field told of a job interview during which the dean sat behind his desk the whole time. The man perceived the dean as arrogant and impersonal. Consequently, he turned down the job offer.

Body Language

Body language refers to bodily reactions or mannerisms. Everyone interprets body language, whether conscious of it or not. I have heard people say, "I knew he wasn't telling me the truth because he couldn't look me in the eye." People communicate by what they do with their bodies as well as by their words. They communicate with the way they look at one another, whether they cross their arms or legs, whether they lean toward or away from the other person, and by where they sit in relation to the other person. Usually people are unconscious of their body language. In a nonthreatening mentoring relationship, mentors can interrupt conversations to discuss the meaning of any observed body language seen in the student.

Following a mentoring training conference, I apologized for a colleague whose inappropriate remarks demonstrated that he did not understand what was being said. The leader said to me, "Yes, I noticed you cleared your throat every time he started to speak." The leader had picked up my unconscious body language. I could have offered some excuse about sinus drainage, but the truth was the leader had picked up my response when this particular person spoke.

Formal Versus Informal Communication

We experience formal and informal communication in everyday life.

For example, behind-the-scenes diplomatic negotiations often further international understandings more than the formal statements made by diplomats. Formal statements may be made to save face and maintain traditional positions; but behind the scenes, diplomats may deal with issues in a realistic way.

Mentors and students will find these same conditions in formal and informal communication. Informal communication may help solve problems in ways that formal mentoring sessions cannot. Informal luncheon discussions may solve more problems than formal mentoring sessions. It is not the meal that makes a session informal but the consciousness that the participants are no longer in a formal setting.

Healthy Confrontation

Much of what has been discussed so far in this chapter can be seen as sources of confrontation in the mentoring relationship. Confrontation and challenge is normal in a mentoring relationship, but confrontation may be uncomfortable for the student or the mentor or both. Confrontation can put a relationship to the test. However, meaningful confrontation from a friend may enhance the relationship when it is seen as coming from someone who has demonstrated a caring attitude. Confronting is caring, and it may be even more productive in a mentor relationship.

There is a myth, based on no fact I know, that there is no confrontation where Christians operate. Ancient history and contemporary examples dispute that myth. I usually find that where there is no confrontation, there are mindless people. Instead of avoiding confrontation and conflict, we do better when we learn how to handle them in a Christian manner. There is confrontation and conflict in all human relationships. It should not surprise us, then, that these appear in mentoring relationships.[9]

Let me distinguish between confrontation and conflict. People often use these terms interchangeably but, if at all possible, we should distinguish between them. Confrontation is simply facing, challenging, and encountering. In contrast, conflict is antagonistic, incompatible, contradictory, and irreconcilable. When confrontation reaches the level of conflict, bad things can happen. Military cemeteries, divorce, and bankruptcy courts attest to this. People can lose their jobs and status. People do not always make up and live happily ever after. People may lose future opportunities.

Authors and speakers have made the term *conflict management* popular, but I believe this is an inappropriate term. One may be able to manage confrontation to some extent, but not conflict. If one could manage conflict, one could manage avoiding it. I prefer to speak of "handling" conflict rather than "managing" it.

As a mentor models healthy confrontation, the student also learns how

---

9. This material on confrontation and conflict is an expansion of the ideas in Doran McCarty, *Working with People* (Nashville: Broadman & Holman, 1986), 107–23.

to confront others in a healthy manner. The student who does not learn how to confront situations or people now will have problems in ministry in the future. Many ministers (and even mentors) have this very problem because they themselves never learned healthy confrontation skills. The student needs to learn not only to confront but also how to confront in a way that is productive. Mentoring can be a valuable teaching tool in learning this art.

Reasons to Confront

It is important to confront healthy people who can change. Neurotics need care from therapists rather than confrontation from a mentor. A mentor will gain nothing by confronting a sick person. Of course, a mentor does not have an option when an unhealthy person creates conflict.

Mentors also need to confront people who can make a difference. Each quiver has only so many arrows, so mentors need to make them count. Good mentors challenge those students in whom they see value.

There are times when the results of confrontation are not worth the effort. You will remember the old saying that a dog can whip a skunk, but it is not worth the effort. This can include some emotionally unhealthy people who actually have a need for constant confrontation to feed their ego. There are legitimate reasons and times for confrontation. In each case, it is important to remember that confrontation is not punishment but an opportunity to learn.

Care

One of the reasons to confront at times is to express care to another person. This is not as contradictory as it sounds. David Augsburger, in his book *Caring Enough to Confront: How to Understand and Express Your Deepest Feelings Toward Others*, created the term "carefronting."[10] Unless we care, we will not confront. We may care for the well-being of the other person, our own welfare, the status quo, an organization, a possession, an idea, or a dream. But we will not confront unless we care.

Clarify

Another reason to confront at times is to seek clarification. When we need to clarify, we may have to confront. For example, another person may have answers that we need but do not have. That person must tell us the information we are seeking or we will not know. If that person does not volunteer the information we need, we will have to ask (which is a form of confronting). Such confrontation also breeds creativity through the meeting of differing ideas in the clarification process.

Change

A third reason to confront at times is to bring about change. Good can

---

10. David Augsburger, *Caring Enough to Confront: How to Understand and Express Your Deepest Feelings Toward Others*, rev. ed. (Glendale, CA: Regal, 1980).

actually come from confrontation. People and organizations can change for the better. Whether we want to change or guard the status quo against change, we will have to confront. At some point everything changes, and without confrontation the particular changes may not be desirable.

Grow

Finally, people need to grow. Some people need to be confronted in order to stimulate growth. If the mentor does not confront, the student may continue in his or her unproductive patterns. The same principle applies to organizations.

Why Do We Avoid Confrontation?

Proverbs 27:5 says, "Better is open rebuke than hidden love." In light of the truth of that passage, why do we avoid confrontation? I can observe several reasons for this.

"It Is Not Nice (or It Is Not Christian) to Confront"

We carry emotional baggage from childhood marked with "it's not nice" tags. Mothers tell sons not to fight because "it's not nice." They separate quarreling siblings, usually sending them to different rooms so they cannot even communicate. Cultural baggage adds to the avoidance. Some cultures avoid confrontation (or the Euro-American form of confrontation), and other cultures make confrontation typical. I notice that my Italian friends have little difficulty with confrontation. They confront intensely and love no less.

Christians with sentimental notions about religion say, "Christians don't do things like that!" This attitude risks equating meekness, kindness, and gentleness with acquiescence. Jesus, as shown in the New Testament, did not avoid confrontation with either friends or foes. We may not confront in order to keep peace and harmony. But avoidance of confrontation does not create (or conserve) peace and harmony; rather it equates peace and harmony with passiveness.

Fear

Another reason we avoid confrontation is that we fear getting hurt or hurting someone else. People can get hurt, especially when confrontation turns to conflict, and avoidance spares their fragile egos. However, healthy people are not so fragile and can stand healthy confrontation. Instead of falling to pieces, healthy people often gain strength from confrontation that is done in a proper way.

Passivity

The last reason we avoid confrontation is that some people would rather switch than fight. They think that appeasement will make problems go away. Even though the passive person knows that something needs to be said about a particular situation, he or she will remain quiet and just hope that the situation will work itself out. Or, at the very least, that the problem will remain unseen. One interpreter calls them "abdicrats" since they would rather abdicate their "throne" than contend.[11]

Marks of Good Confrontation

With such sensitivity about confrontation, how can we make confrontation take place in a way that is healthy and beneficial? Much lies with the person doing the confronting. There are several qualities of a person who does well at confrontation.[12]

Caring

Nothing takes the place of caring. Whenever we care, we have won a large part of any battle. If we do not care, we will not confront.

Insightful

The apostle Paul spoke of discernment in Philippians 1:9: "And it is my prayer that your love may abound more and more, with knowledge and all discernment." People who do well at confrontation possess such discernment. An insightful person can conceptualize a situation rather than become angry.

Courageous

Insight is not enough. An effective confronter has courage to initiate action and withstand the wills of others. People are tempted to surround themselves only with people who agree with them. That is comforting but ultimately counterproductive. It only insulates the person for a short time and may allow the pressure the person faces to increase over time.

Patient

Finally there is patience. Patience is not passiveness but keeping attention on an issue without aggressiveness. A person who confronts and then retreats will not be effective. The competent confronter keeps pressure on others until they are open to negotiation. Change comes from thawing a situation, changing it, and refreezing it so that it stays in place. If one does not have the patience for the changed situation to freeze, it will drop back to its original level.

When Confrontation Becomes Conflict

Healthy people often can solve problems without conflict. Proper

---

11. William Schutz, *FIRO: A Three-Dimensional Theory of Interpersonal Behavior*, 3rd ed. (Muir Beach, CA: Will Schutz Associates, 1998).

12. See chapter 6, "Mentoring: The Opportunity to Leave a Legacy," for a more detailed discussion on these qualities.

confrontation, of course, may help avoid conflict altogether. Conflict costs. The cost may be time, energy, self-esteem, money, or relationships. The costs are real. Marriages break up and churches split. As one analyzes conflict, he or she should determine whether the conflict is worth the costs.

However, even in best-case scenarios, situations sometimes move from confrontation to conflict. While conflict cannot always be avoided, there are some things that can be done to help the situation.

Anticipate Conflict Before It Happens

Remember that people are at a disadvantage when conflict surprises them. When one anticipates conflict, one can prepare for it. Anticipation helps avoid flashes of anger followed by damaging verbal abuse. Good anticipation allows a person to plan strategy rather than claim a position without careful thought.

Identify the Source of the Conflict

Conflict may be either personal or systemic. If personal, the conflict may be a struggle within a person or between persons. Systemic conflict, on the other hand, involves organizations, institutions, or relationships. The nature of conflict is not always clear, and the apparent issue may only be a smoke screen for deeper issues. Sources of conflict may be reality, fantasy, fears, or dreams. Conflict may come from history or the present. The problem may be logistical, informational, status, or a clash of values. All of these need to be considered. We teach people to read books, but effective leaders need to know how to read situations as well. This is critical in handling conflict.

It is also important to know the depth of the conflict. The more people care about an issue, the deeper the conflict may be. People may vote politely on a resolution about Iraq but fight vehemently over dividing a Sunday school class. An issue that deals with the whole of life generates more feelings than conflict over a single issue. When an issue is a surface one, it may not create a threat if people treat one another with dignity. A complex issue that threatens principles or a way of life can become turbulent.

There are personal aspects of conflict as well. The person who controls the systems is important since he or she can either calm or excite conflict. In a large bureaucracy, the system tends to control the system itself. People make investments in the system and want to protect themselves and their emotional—and maybe financial—investments. This creates conflict when they believe someone threatens their investments.

Know the Dynamics of Conflict

There are dynamics in conflicts. Each conflict differs, and individual factors contribute to the differences. These factors can include personalities, timing (is there a pressing need for a resolution?), time limits (is this an ongoing systemic conflict or a short-term conflict?), nature of the decision, the position of the people involved (level of leadership between parties), and the relationships involved.

When dealing with a conflict, it is important to determine the phase of the conflict. Authors have described the phases of conflicts as:

- anticipation
- conscious but unexpressed differences
- discussion
- open dispute
- open conflict

It is a serious problem if a person is unaware of the specific phase of the current conflict. One cannot turn back the clock to an earlier phase. Trying to deal with conflict without understanding what phase it is in can be disastrous. Furthermore, when a person closes his or her eyes to the progress of conflict into a new phase, that person leaves himself or herself at a disadvantage.

When conflict is long-term, it grinds people down. If they know that the conflict is situational rather than chronic, they may be able to sustain their equilibrium. People have to deal with long-term conflict differently than short-term conflict.

Develop Good Attitudes

People need to develop good attitudes toward conflict as a way to prepare themselves. Emotional conditioning before conflict happens is key. A person needs to be both tough and tender during conflict. A person who becomes surly, belligerent, passive, or acquiescent toward conflict has not prepared adequately for conflict.

Positive results come when a person believes there is the possibility of a mutual solution. Western society is very competitive, but that competitiveness may get in the way during an attempt to handle conflict. People are made in God's image, so even those who engage in conflict with a person deserve the person's respect. Each person has the same right as the other to state his or her opinions.

Consider Alternatives

What are the alternatives? Make a list. How will I try to settle the conflict? Win-win? Win-lose? Lose-lose? What approach will I take? Passive? Aggressive? Passive-aggressive? Assertive? Do I have to have a life-and-death struggle now, or can I live to fight another day, perhaps with advantages I do not have now?

Make Decisions

Effective leaders will have to make decisions during conflict. Timely decisions help settle conflicts in early stages. The leader has to make decisions rather than forfeit decision making. No decision is perfect, but decisions can be effective.

Since decisions are not perfect, it is unwise to absolutize decisions. In 1936, American financier Bernard Baruch said that if you could guarantee that he would be right 51 percent of the time, he would make a million dollars a day on the stock market. The temptation to make absolute decisions puts things in black-white, right-wrong, or perfect-useless categories when every decision is a mixed bag.

Once the decision is made, the leader needs to implement the decision. No decision is more effective than its implementation. Conflict remains until there is good implementation. Decision without implementation opens the door for more conflict.

Care for People's Needs

People in conflict need care. They have crises that need attention. The wise person takes care of others' hurts regardless of where they are in the conflict. All people deserve respect. When one is disrespectful, he or she can even alienate supporters.

Prayer of Transformation

Lord, may we be strengthened with all power, according to your glorious might, for all endurance and patience with joy (Col. 1:11). May we have the patience with others and caring for others that you have shown us. In Christ's name, amen.

Reflection Questions

1. Why are personhood issues so important in mentoring relationships? How can you make sure that personhood issues are being addressed?

2. Why is the covenant such an important instrument in field education? Are there some things missing in your current covenant that need to be there to avoid the problems addressed in this chapter?

3. Based on what you have read in this chapter, are there some things that need to be addressed more in either the mentoring training or the student orientation for field education at your school?

4. Are you the type of person who avoids confrontation, or do you overuse confrontation and conflict in your relationships? What is the role of healthy confrontation in field education?

Further Reading

Coll, Regina. *Supervision of Ministry Students*. Collegeville, MN: Liturgical Press, 1992.

Hunter, George I. *Supervision and Education-Formation for Ministry*. Cambridge, MA: Episcopal Divinity School, 1982.

Jones, C. David. *The Pastoral Mentor*. Richmond: Skipworth, 1980.

McCarty, Doran. *Supervising Ministry Students*. Atlanta: Home Mission Board of the Southern Baptist Convention, 1992.

———. *Supervision: Developing and Directing People on Mission*. Nashville: Seminary Extension, 1994.

Nelson, William. *Ministry Formation for Effective Leadership*. Nashville: Abingdon, 1988.

Pyle, William T., and Mary Alice Seals, eds. *Experiencing Ministry Supervision: A Field-Based Approach*. Nashville: Broadman & Holman, 1995.

PART 5

For Field Education Professionals

Talent Inventories
Mentor Training

Chapter 17

Comparing Natural Talent Inventories for Use in Field Education

PHILLIP SELL

As each has received a gift, use it to serve one another, as good stewards of God's varied grace. (1 Peter 4:10)

Theological field education is a venue where students can explore their calling to vocational ministry and the focus that their vocational ministry might take in the future. In my nine years of exploring "calling" with students at Trinity Evangelical Divinity School (TEDS), it has become clear that there are three kinds of students (relative to their calling) who enroll in our graduate programs of study. Some students enroll with no clear sense of calling to vocational ministry; they are pursuing studies for enrichment to their spiritual life and are exploring the possibility of being called to vocational ministry or perhaps another vocation. Other students enroll with a clear sense that God is calling them to vocational ministry, but they are not sure what the focus of that ministry will be (missionary, pastor, youth pastor, etc.). Still other students enroll knowing that they are called to vocational ministry, and they have a clear sense of focus on a particular kind of ministry.

Each of these kinds of students can be aided in clarifying their calling or in focusing their calling by having a clearer picture of their God-given talents. In the Office of Supervised Ministries at TEDS, we have found that the use of natural talent inventories can greatly accelerate a student's progress toward talent identification and talent development.

But why natural talent inventories rather than spiritual gift inventories, especially at a school devoted to ministerial professional development? Before we can answer that question, it would be good to explore what the term *natural talent* means. A good definition of a natural talent is provided by the Gallup Organization: "Talents are naturally recurring patterns of thought, feeling, or behavior that can be productively applied."[1] When talents are honed by experience and knowledge, they can become a "strength," which the Gallup Organization defines as "the ability to deliver consistent, near-perfect performance in a given activity."[2]

From a Christian perspective, natural talents are given by God, as Creator, to all humans by virtue of being made in the image of God. Ideally these natural talents, like all resources in life, are to be used to honor God and to serve other humans. "Natural" talent is not meant to convey something less valuable than "spiritual" gifts, which are given to all believers at some point subsequent to conversion to Christ as Savior. Both the natural talents endowed at human birth by God as Creator and the spiritual gifts endowed subsequent to spiritual rebirth by God as Savior are a significant stewardship to our Lord.[3] Therefore, the first reason to use natural talent inventories is that they give additional insight into the God-given talent base entrusted to a person by God, their Creator.

A second reason to use natural talent inventories is that they are more rigorously designed and validated than the spiritual gift inventories currently being used in evangelical Christian circles. Because the natural talent inventories explored in this chapter have uses within business, academic, and ministry settings, greater funding was available to refine and validate these instruments with a rigor absent in spiritual gift inventories that have a limited church and ministry market. In both of the natural talent inventories examined in this chapter, we can be reasonably sure that the questions, in fact, assess the talent that they are exploring across both gender and cultural boundaries.[4]

---

1. Albert L. Winseman, Donald Clifton, and Curt Liesveld, *Living Your Strengths: Discover Your God-Given Talents and Inspire Your Community* (New York: Gallup, 2003–2004), 4.

2. Ibid., 5.

3. In comparing hundreds of student profiles that utilize both natural talent inventories and spiritual gift inventories, there is a high degree of correlation between the results from the various instruments. The strongest threads of gift and talent are usually indicated in multiple assessment instruments, whether assessing for natural talents or spiritual gifts. It should not surprise us that there is correlation between the work of God as Creator and Savior.

4. This is not to deny the usefulness of spiritual gift inventories but simply to note the discrepancy in validation between them and the natural talent inventories assessed in this chapter.

Development and Administration of Two
Natural Talent Inventories

Both of the assessment instruments discussed below are devoted to ascertaining an individual's natural talents as described above. Each instrument's origin is delineated, and the key ideas that are foundational to each instrument are described. A brief description of each of the instruments is provided, including the delivery and scoring system for each instrument. Certification requirements and training expenses for entry-level qualification and certification is also provided, to give the reader an idea of the probable costs associated with the use of each instrument.[5]

Clifton StrengthsFinder

The Clifton StrengthsFinder was developed by Donald O. Clifton and is published by the Gallup Organization.[6] Clifton for many years was a professor at the University of Nebraska and later formed a company called Selection Research Incorporated, which assisted specific industries to identify the talents necessary for potential recruits to be top performers in their industry. This brought Clifton into contact with the "best of the best" in various industries, helping him identify the characteristics that would be desirable for future employees in that particular industry. One of his foundational concepts is that "to produce excellence you must study excellence."[7] This led Clifton to pioneer and champion "positive psychology," which focuses on people's strengths rather than on pathologies and on how to help people flourish rather than simply function.

Clifton later became the chairman of the Gallup Organization, the global management, consulting, training, and polling company. This provided even greater resources for research into human talent that could be productively applied. After over thirty years of research in business and education settings concerning human talent, he attempted to map human talent comprehensively with what would eventually become the Clifton StrengthsFinder (hereafter CSF). Extensive research and validity testing, including the data of over two million people, has yielded an instrument that identifies thirty-four talent themes to be applied in the work domain (see figure 17.1) and that has validity across cultures, genders, and languages.[8]

---

5. The author holds basic certification in both instruments. Costs provided were accurate at the time of publication, and while these costs are likely to go up over time, the information is still helpful to give the reader an understanding of the relative cost of each inventory.

6. Information about the Gallup Organization and Gallup University can be found at www.gallup.com.

7. Marcus Buckingham and Donald Clifton, *Now, Discover Your Strengths* (New York: Free Press, 2001), xiii.

8. Much of this summary on Clifton and the development of the StrengthsFinder comes from the Gallup Organization, *Strengths Performance Coach for Faith* ([Princeton, NJ: Gallup, 2005], 1–18), a publication provided with the paid seminar.

Figure 17.1. Clifton StrengthsFinder Talent Themes Descriptors

Achiever
People who are especially talented in the Achiever theme have a great deal of stamina and work hard. They take great satisfaction from being busy and productive.

Activator
People who are especially talented in the Activator theme can make things happen by turning thoughts into action. They are often impatient.

Adaptability
People who are especially talented in the Adaptability theme prefer to "go with the flow." They tend to be "now" people who take things as they come and discover the future one day at a time.

Analytical
People who are especially talented in the Analytical theme search for reasons and causes. They have the ability to think about all the factors that might affect a situation.

Arranger
People who are especially talented in the Arranger theme can organize, but they also have a flexibility that complements this ability. They like to figure out how all of the pieces and resources can be arranged for maximum productivity.

Belief
People who are especially talented in the Belief theme have certain core values that are unchanging. Out of these values emerges a defined purpose for their life.

Command
People who are especially talented in the Command theme have presence. They can take control of a situation and make decisions.

Communication
People who are especially talented in the Communication theme generally find it easy to put their thoughts into words. They are good conversationalists and presenters.

Competition

People who are especially talented in the Competition theme measure their progress against the performance of others. They strive to win first place and revel in contests.

Connectedness

People who are especially talented in the Connectedness theme have faith in the links between all things. They believe there are few coincidences and that almost every event has a reason.

Consistency

People who are especially talented in the Consistency theme are keenly aware of the need to treat people the same. They try to treat everyone in the world with consistency by setting up clear rules and adhering to them.

Context

People who are especially talented in the Context theme enjoy thinking about the past. They understand the present by researching its history.

Deliberative

People who are especially talented in the Deliberative theme are best described by the serious care they take in making decisions or choices. They anticipate the obstacles.

Developer

People who are especially talented in the Developer theme recognize and cultivate the potential in others. They spot the signs of each small improvement and derive satisfaction from these improvements.

Discipline

People who are especially talented in the Discipline theme enjoy routine and structure. Their world is best described by the order they create.

Empathy

People who are especially talented in the Empathy theme can sense the feelings of other people by imagining themselves in others' lives or others' situations.

Focus

People who are especially talented in the Focus theme can take a direction, follow through, and make the corrections necessary to stay on track. They prioritize, then act.

Futuristic

People who are especially talented in the Futuristic theme are inspired by the future and what could be. They inspire others with their visions of the future.

Harmony

People who are especially talented in the Harmony theme look for consensus. They don't enjoy conflict; rather they seek areas of agreement.

Ideation

People who are especially talented in the Ideation theme are fascinated by ideas. They are able to find connections between seemingly disparate phenomena.

Includer

People who are especially talented in the Includer theme are accepting of others. They show awareness of those who feel left out and make an effort to include them.

Individualization

People who are especially talented in the Individualization theme are intrigued with the unique qualities of each person. They have a gift for figuring out how people who are different can work together productively.

Input

People who are especially talented in the Input theme have a craving to know more. Often they like to collect and archive all kinds of information.

Intellection

People who are especially talented in the Intellection theme are characterized by their intellectual activity. They are introspective and appreciate intellectual discussions.

Learner

People who are especially talented in the Learner theme have a great desire to learn and want to continuously improve. In particular, the process of learning, rather than the outcome, excites them.

Maximizer

People who are especially talented in the Maximizer theme focus on strengths as a way to stimulate personal and group excellence. They seek to transform something strong into something superb.

Positivity
People who are especially talented in the Positivity theme have an enthusiasm that is contagious. They are upbeat and can get others excited about what they are going to do.

Relator
People who are especially talented in the Relator theme enjoy close relationships with others. They find deep satisfaction in working hard with friends to achieve a goal.

Responsibility
People who are especially talented in the Responsibility theme take psychological ownership of what they say they will do. They are committed to stable values such as honesty and loyalty.

Restorative
People who are especially talented in the Restorative theme are adept at dealing with problems. They are good at figuring out what is wrong and resolving it.

Self-Assurance
People who are especially talented in the Self-Assurance theme feel confident in their ability to manage their own lives. They possess an inner compass that gives them confidence that their decisions are right.

Significance
People who are especially talented in the Significance theme want to be very important in the eyes of others. They are independent and want to be recognized.

Strategic
People who are especially talented in the Strategic theme create alternate ways to proceed. Faced with any given scenario, they can quickly spot the relevant patterns and issues.

Woo
People who are especially talented in the Woo theme love the challenge of meeting new people and winning them over. They derive satisfaction from breaking the ice and making a connection with other people.*

---

* Clifton StrengthsFinder Talent Themes Descriptors. Used by permission of the Gallup Organization.

The CSF champions positive psychology with its focus on enhancing normal human functioning rather than focusing on dysfunction. It also believes that talents are formed early in a person's life and solidified by the early teen years. This explanation of talent formation relies heavily on research concerning brain development. The brain channels synapse patterns in such a way that some synapse patterns become routinely practiced and some barely develop, thus each person has distinctive patterns that become the foundations for some natural talents being formed and others being undeveloped.[9] This process is completed by the early teen years, and thus Gallup does not suggest administering the CSF before the mid to late teen years.

The Gallup Organization describes the CSF as follows:

> The Clifton StrengthsFinder is a Web-based talent assessment instrument from the perspective of Positive Psychology. Through a secure connection, the Clifton StrengthsFinder presents 180 items to the user. Each item lists a pair of potential self-descriptors, such as "I read instructions carefully" and "I like to jump right into things." The descriptors are placed as if anchoring polar ends of a continuum. From each pair, the participant is then asked to choose the descriptor that best describes him or her, and also the extent to which it does so. The participant is given 20 seconds to respond to a given item before the system moves on to the next item.[10]

When this process is completed, the person taking the CSF is given a readout listing his or her top five talent themes, with the most strongly indicated talent first and the next four in descending order. Each talent theme is given a brief description of how that talent theme is expressed.

This might seem like sparse information if one does not understand how codes are accessed to unlock the CSF. The Web site and the code to open the CSF can be accessed only by purchasing a Gallup Organization book that further explains all of the signature themes and gives ideas on how to develop those talent themes into strengths through the infusion of skill and knowledge (factually or though experiential awareness). Each of these books cost about $25 and lists on the dust jacket or on the inside cover a Web site to access and a onetime-use code to unlock the CSF. (Used books will most likely contain a code that has already been used and thus is invalid.)

One of the books that provide access to the CSF is *Now, Discover Your Strengths*, which focuses on the business applications of the CSF with descriptors of the talent themes but also has chapters on how to manage people according to their talent themes and how to develop a

---

9. Buckingham and Clifton, *Now, Discover Your Strengths*, 48–56.
10. The Gallup Organization, *Strengths Performance Coach for Faith*, 8.

strengths-based organization.[11] *StrengthsQuest* focuses on high school and college students by helping them to use and develop their talent themes for directing their educational experiences and to a lesser degree for focusing their vocational choice.[12] *Teach with Your Strengths* applies the CSF to the classroom setting for teachers.[13] *Living Your Strengths* is an application of the CSF to the church and its ministry and is a product of the Faith division of Gallup, which has been in existence for about six years. It focuses on talent themes and their place in church ministries and how to create a strengths-based congregation.[14] In 2007 the Gallup Organization unveiled StrengthsFinder 2.0, which uses the same thirty-four signature talents and descriptors as the previous version and thus does not in any way alter conclusions formed based on the original version of the CSF.[15]

Because the CSF does not require certified facilitators to access the instrument, it is plausible to think that the Gallup Organization might not do further training. They do, in fact, offer training in the CSF, not for gatekeepers to limit access to the instrument, but rather for coaches of individuals who have taken the CSF. The first level of coaches training through the Faith division of Gallup University currently costs $2,500, which includes some online training modules as well as two days of classroom training. At the end of this training, the CSF coach has access to the top five signature themes of the person he or she is coaching and some strategies to help move that person from talents to strengths. After completing ten favorable reviews by those being coached, the CSF coach will be certified as a coach by the Gallup Organization. The Faith division plans to provide two more levels of coaches training, each at a similar cost. Gallup is rethinking what will be included in each training level, but the upper levels will probably include access to the entire theme sequence (all thirty-four talent themes in ranked order) of the person that is being coached, some individual Gallup coaches training for working with teams, and perhaps training in using CSF in marriage and premarital counseling settings. Contact Gallup University's Faith division to see how these upper levels of training are conceptualized in the future.

IDAK Career Match

The IDAK Career Match was developed by John Bradley, the president

---

11. Buckingham and Clifton, *Now, Discover Your Strengths*.

12. Donald Clifton and Edward Anderson, *StrengthsQuest: Discover and Develop Your Strengths in Academics, Career, and Beyond* (Washington, DC: Gallup, 2002).

13. Roseanne Liesveld, Jo Ann Miller, and Jennifer Robinson, *Teach with Your Strengths* (New York: Gallup, 2005).

14. Winseman, Clifton, and Liesveld, *Living Your Strengths*.

15. Tom Rath, *StrengthsFinder 2.0* (New York: Gallup, 2007). This book is in many ways a simplified restatement of the material covered in their other books, especially Buckingham and Clifton's *Now, Discover Your Strengths*.

of the IDAK Group Incorporated, which distributes the IDAK Career Match and the Talent Discovery Guide[16] Bradley's journey into identifying natural talents started while working at employment agencies in Nevada and Texas in the 1960s.[17] In 1973 he became a researcher at the University of California at Davis, exploring student aptitudes. During that time period, he published an employment discovery manual based on natural talents. Bradley later enrolled at Western Theological Seminary in Portland, Oregon, and began to wrestle with leadership development and career assessment within a specifically Christian context. Refinement of natural talent identification pressed forward for the next four years, and in 1983 Bradley had refined his Talent Discovery Guide and the fifty-four natural talents that are at the foundation of all IDAK publications.

A half-million-dollar grant allowed Bradley, together with the Rosemead Graduate School's psychometrics faculty, to validate the instrument that became the IDAK Career Match. Part of that validation included examining sixty-thousand career options with the natural talents identified in the Career Match. Bradley was confident that the Career Match represented talents that applied across the board to all career options. The IDAK Group has become specialists in midcareer transitions and vocational planning based on natural talents. They work with for-profit companies, educational institutions, churches, and mission organizations. Bradley's book *Discovering Your Natural Talents* explains in simple terms much of his thinking about natural talents.[18]

The theoretical underpinnings of the IDAK Career Match are really quite simple. All people have God-given natural talents that are endowed at birth, and it is when these are utilized that a person derives the most satisfaction, enjoyment, and effectiveness in vocation and ministry. Conversely, working in skill areas that are not supported by natural talents leads to limited effectiveness and an inordinate drain of our personal energy. Therefore, the key is to discover one's talents through the productive experiences that have been most enjoyable. Despite the simplicity of this model, it can be difficult to discern these talents without an inventory because interests, values, personal and family vocational expectations, and educational investments can all prevent a clear picture of what a person's natural talents really are.

The IDAK Career Match is a professional-grade vocational guidance instrument that costs $125 to purchase and have scored (although educational institutions buying in bulk may be able to purchase them for around $85). It combines natural talent identification with specific suggestions about vocational settings and specific duties in those settings. Extensive guidance is given about how to find the right vocational setting and how to get in contact with key persons in

---

16. Information about the IDAK Group can be found at www.idakgroup.com.

17. John Bradley, discussion with the author, February 2007.

18. John Bradley and Jay Carty, *Discovering Your Natural Talents* (Colorado Springs: NavPress, 1994).

that vocational setting. The IDAK Career Match exercise booklet starts with a process for selecting work clusters that are interesting to the client. The client examines hundreds of work settings that are then reduced down to his or her top fifteen work settings. The next phase of the process is to answer 168 questions that are weighted as to the relative enjoyableness of different activities that relate to the fifty-four natural talents that the IDAK Group assesses (see figure 17.2). The person then identifies his or her most enjoyable experiences in life to further focus on his or her natural talents. The last section of the IDAK Career Match helps the person through a testing process to identify his or her top five work values out of twenty-two possible value options.

Figure 17.2. IDAK Talent Descriptors

1. Concerning Communication

A. Using Words

Writing Words

Writing clearly understood reports, letters, e-mails, essays, stories, scripts, advertisements, contracts, curriculum, magazine articles, or the like.

Conversing

Talking one-on-one, sharing ideas and feelings, discussing current events, exchanging views, explaining things with a high degree of mutual understanding.

Giving Speeches

Using a lecture style of persuasive communication as in a graduation ceremony, political address, business luncheon speech, keynote speech, or sermon.

Teaching by Lecture

Using a lecture style to instruct others regarding a subject, topic, or idea in a classroom, club, association, church, or other group meeting with limited spontaneous audience interaction.

Broadcasting/Telephone

Communicating clearly through telephone or electronic media such as video, radio, CD, or audiocassette recording.

B. Being Artistic

Designing

Expressing my thoughts or feelings through sketches, illustrations, graphic arts, theater set designs, murals, or other design projects.

Painting

Expressing my thoughts and feelings through oils, pastels, watercolors, and chalk.

Using Colors and Patterns
Expressing my thoughts or feelings through colors or patterns such as in interior décor, clothing, makeup, jewelry, house paint, photography, and the like.

Using Shapes and Forms
Expressing my thoughts or feelings through shaping forms as in sculpturing and photography or designing layouts as in architectural designing, landscaping, furniture arranging, and the like.

Using Handcrafts
Projecting my thoughts or feelings through handcrafted items made of wood, leather, cloth, metal, plastic, or the like.

C. Performing

Composing/Arranging Music
Expressing my thoughts or feelings by writing, composing, or arranging works of music.

Acting/Imitating Mannerisms
Imitating mannerisms of others through role-playing, acting, telling jokes, doing character impersonations or mime in either informal conversation or theatrical settings.

Group Moderating
Guiding a group discussion, hosting a panel presentation, or coordinating discussion between several people or groups.

Singing or Instrumental Performing
Singing or playing an instrument in front of others as part of an orchestra, choir, ensemble, duet, or band, or as a soloist.

Giving Presentations with Audience Interaction
Giving presentations in front of others with spontaneous audience interaction such as seminars, workshops, announcements, selected readings, product service demonstrations, and management briefings.

2. Concerning Relationships

A. Multi-relational
Bonding quickly to form new friendships (within minutes or hours).

B. Familiar Group Relational
Preferring to be with people I already know. Also willing to meet new people or work on a task by myself.

C. Singular Relational
Preferring to be by myself, reading, studying, or working on a project. Also willing to be with selected people I know well.

3. Concerning Functional Capacities

A. Organizing Time and Personal Space

Ordering My Time and Priorities

Consistently organizing my daily schedule to get the most important things done: appointments, deadlines, errands, projects, or the like. Getting a lot done in a day.

Ordering My Space

Keeping my surroundings well organized and my household items in their place without much effort. Routinely putting things back where they belong.

B. Being Creative

Creating

Coming up with new ways to do things, improving routine tasks or traditions with new viewpoints, questioning outdated regulations or procedures.

Imagining

Spending time imagining new stories, theories, or science fiction ideas, philosophical concepts, or the like (also referred to as daydreaming).

Inventing

Inventing new technical gadgets, electronic devices, machines, chemical formulas, plant hybrids, and the like.

C. Supervising Others

Developing/Initiating New Ventures

Recruiting others to a new vision and supervising their start-up efforts as in starting new projects, programs, organizations, clubs, companies, and the like; also dramatically improving a program, company, etc.

Long-Range Logistical Planning

Mapping out the long-range details to meet my employer's, club's, family's, or board's goals: finances, equipment, personnel schedules, or travel itinerary.

Managing Established Groups, Organizations

Supervising others in an "established" department, club, group, or organization over an extended period.

D. Using Body, Hands, Fingers

Being Physically Coordinated or Physically Active

Using my body, arms, and legs together as in athletics, physical labor, construction work, gardening, or the like.

Using My Hands and Arms

Preferring activities such as repairing or maintaining (car, furniture, clothes, equipment), building or assembling (cabinets, machines), using hand or power tools.

Operating/Driving

Operating or driving moving vehicles such as a car, truck, farm/construction equipment, boat, aircraft, or stationary equipment, machines, or the like.

Using My Hands and Fingers

Preferring precision detail projects such as building small-scale model kits, soldering, casting jewelry, calligraphy, or drafting.

E. Helping Others

Tutoring (Nurturing)

Helping another to cope with disabilities or learning problems as in specialized training, coaching, tutoring, therapy, or rehabilitation over an extended period of time.

Being of Service (Nurturing)

Assisting others by being available when they need my help with their projects and programs to the neglect of my projects.

Counseling (Nurturing)

Patiently helping people over a period of time to resolve personal or emotional problems: dating, marriage, self-image conflicts, spiritual concerns, abnormal behavior.

Reassuring and Supporting Others (Nurturing)

Identifying with another's hurts and frustrations, giving encouragement, comfort, and support without necessarily trying to solve their problems.

F. Using Intuition

Evaluating People's Character

Accurately assessing another's integrity or sincerity including motives, underlying thoughts, or attitudes during initial encounters.

Making Future Projections

Accurately predicting the general public's responses to future events as in: politics, clothing fads, business trends, or other future concerns.

G. Being Persuasive

Negotiating

Successfully settling disputes between two or more people, acting as a go-between, arbitrating, negotiating contracts, being a peacemaker, or the like.

Selling

Successfully convincing others to buy and pay for a product or service, recruiting volunteers, fund-raising, closing the sale.

Promoting

Motivating others to consider something that I am excited about:

new book, new restaurant, great sale item, new viewpoint, and the like.

H. Observing Details

Observing Physical Environment Details

Seeing small details others often miss indoors or out-of-doors: street signs, small plants, unusual rock formations, animal tracks, rust, scratches, cracks, and the like.

Observing Printed Details

Seeing details others often miss in newspapers, manuscripts, books, blueprints, and maps, including misspellings, "typos," or grammatical errors.

Observing in Three Dimensions

Visualizing a three-dimensional object from a two-dimensional drawing such as a building from a blueprint, a cabinet from a sketch, a dress from a pattern.

I. Using Numbers

Calculating Numbers

Working quickly and accurately with numbers and figures; adding, subtracting, multiplying, and dividing without much effort.

Recording or Auditing

Routinely counting and recording how many items are on a shelf, in a box, in a room, in a warehouse (taking inventory).

J. Problem-Solving Procedures

Mechanical/Technical Troubleshooting

Tinkering with mechanical, electrical, or technical items (attempting to repair) as in clocks, engines, electrical circuits, door locks—not necessarily being skilled with tools.

Solving Problems

Thinking deeply about people relations, problems, logical reasoning concerns that come up at work, home, club meetings, activities, or the like (not necessarily mechanical or electrical problems).

K. Researching for Information

Researching/Investigating

Collecting a lot of information from different sources about a subject for present use, a new purchase, or future reference (may include field research).

Remembering

Recalling names, numbers, or other details quickly and accurately without much effort.

Classifying

Routinely arranging and maintaining information, reports,

photographs, and recipes for easy and quick reference (file systems, catalog systems).

L. Reasoning and Contemplating

Analyzing to Understand

Wanting to learn most anything, curious, studying a subject, object, or opinion to determine its good/bad points and how it compares with other items.

Appraising/Estimating

Bargain hunting; accurately estimating the monetary value of a car, house, antique, collectable, or business opportunity and its economic potential.

Synthesizing

Putting together different parts to make a whole as in a project or report; selecting ideas, concepts, or objects in order to fit them together in a useful way.

M. Making Decisions

Quick Reflex Action

Spontaneously and skillfully responding to another person's accident or emergency situation such as a child choking, kitchen fire, stalled car, or person drowning.

Taking Risks

Committing my time and my finances, without undue stress, when there is an equal chance of success or failure.*

---

* Any reproduction or use of talent names, categories, or definitions by any means is prohibited without permission from the IDAK Group. Used by permission.

When the IDAK Career Match has been scored, a report is sent out that has the following components:

1. An *Aptitude Summary Report* lists the client's top ten preferred organizational settings for work. It also lists the top fifteen work positions/duties that could be woven into the client's preferred organizational settings. The next section takes each of the fifty-four natural talents and ranks each for its intensity in the client's life in terms of both feelings and actual experiences. The last section of this first report is a ranking of the client's work priorities/values. The top five are considered significant to work satisfaction.

2. The *Career Match Report* takes the client's top ten preferred type of organizational settings and lists up to five specific job titles within each organizational setting that is tied to the client's unique blend of natural talents.

3. The *Employer Search Guide* lists each kind of job according to its CONI (Christian Organizational Numerical Index) system reference number for ministry and nonprofit organizations and its SIC (Standard Industrial Classification) number for business and industry settings. From these codes the client is given guidance as to who to contact in those organizations and industries to explore possible jobs. Web sites are provided for job searches in ministry organizations, the government and military, and business settings.

The findings are a cornucopia of vocational information. Step-by-step processes for switching vocational settings are supplied, and usually a private consultation (or including the client's spouse) is provided with the IDAK counselor/consultant.

The IDAK Group also has a Talent Discovery Guide, which is a three-page, trifold instrument printed on card stock that can be purchased through an IDAK counselor/consultant for about $6.50, with discounts for bulk orders. It asks participants to identify their top ten most enjoyable activities from work and other settings. They then evaluate which of the fifty-four natural talents were engaged in each of their favorite activities. In theory the natural talents that get the most bubbles filled in from the ten most enjoyable activities are probably their dominant natural talents. The Talent Discovery Guide does expose the client to the fifty-four natural talents, but it lacks the rigor and the vocational guidance of the Career Match. Obviously if the person picked ten different enjoyable activities, the results would be at least slightly different. The Talent Discovery Guide might be useful for church ministry placement when coupled with other instruments and when cost prohibits the use of the Career Match, but it should not be considered a substitute for the Career Match when serious vocational guidance is needed.

The IDAK Group recently unveiled an online version of the IDAK Talent Discovery Guide. The online versions costs $27 and has increased validation rigor over the hard-copy Talent Discovery Guide. Like the hard-copy Talent Discovery Guide, the online version starts with identifying the person's ten most enjoyable activities, but it also adds two validation improvements that make the online version better than the hard-copy Talent Discovery Guide. The first improvement involves increased specificity concerning how often a particular talent is used relative to one of the ten most enjoyable activities: the client must choose from three options (often, occasionally, or rarely) instead of two (yes or no), thus weighting answers more precisely.

The second improvement is that each natural talent has validation questions that help the client to discern if the natural talent with high scores is validated by questions that probe the presence of that natural talent in the person's life. This kind of validation helps to offset the client's bias. Be aware that the validation questions are an optional part of the online Talent Discovery Guide, but I would recommend it to anyone taking the online version. Both of these improvements make the online version of the Talent

Discovery Guide an affordable option (in comparison to the IDAK Career Match) and a more rigorous version of the Talent Discovery Guide than the hard-copy version.

The online Talent Discovery Guide can be accessed directly at the IDAK Web site (www.idakgroup.com/TDG), without the involvement of an IDAK-trained counselor/consultant. However, to be able to order, administer, and consult using the other IDAK Group materials (the Career Match and the hard-copy *Talent Discovery* Guide), the counselor/consultant must be certified by taking the Level I and II training, which costs $395 and takes a few days to complete. The training provides the foundational principles of the IDAK Career Match and proven counseling and coaching techniques for helping clients in career choices and transitions. The IDAK Level III training teaches an intensive autobiographical interview process to better identify and clarify the natural talents of the client and costs $950. IDAK Level IV Training costs $2000 and consists of refining skills related to the job search process and more in-depth coaching.

Shared Foundational Concepts

The theoretical bases of these two natural talent inventories share some commonly held concepts about natural talents that are important to take into account in teaching about talents, especially when assisting students with their sense of calling to vocational ministry. By *commonly held*, I mean that although their exact language and emphases might be slightly different, the training concerning natural talents shares some foundational ideas about natural talents and their place in vocational guidance.

Natural Talents Are Innate and Confirmed Early in Life

These natural talents appear very early in life and are not alterable after the late teen years. As Christians, we would affirm that they are God-given tendencies and abilities. The Bible emphasizes that God has not made humans with a cookie cutter but that we are all distinctly gifted (1 Peter 4:10), and this concept extends beyond our spiritual gifts to the talents given us by the one Creator.

Vocational Satisfaction Is Based in Large Part on Engaging Natural Talents

The Gallup Organization emphasizes developing a strengths-based organization, and the IDAK Group invokes what they call a "60/40 rule," that vocationally we should spend *a minimum of* 60 percent of our vocational time in activities that draw upon our natural talents and *a maximum of* 40 percent of our vocational time on activities in which we have developed work skills that are not grounded in our natural talents. If it becomes 50/50 or worse, there is a very good chance of burnout and vocational dissatisfaction.[19]

---

19. Bradley and Carty, *Discovering Your Natural Talents*, 37.

We cannot gain satisfaction within a vocation simply by working hard at it. It must tap into the way that God has wired us as a person in our natural talents. A corollary to this idea is the Gallup Organization's emphasis that "weakness fixing" or trying to become "well rounded" is not a good vocational strategy (in terms of vocation talent, not moral weakness or character faults).[20] Again the biblical emphasis on gifting and the image of the body of Christ with different functions integrate nicely with these ideas (1 Cor. 12:14–31). This would also call into question the idea of the omnicompetent pastor who does all ministries well by virtue of being ordained.

Clues Can Be Found That Might Indicate the Presence of a Talent

The IDAK Group has clearly built their natural talent inventory around the concepts of *enjoyable*, *effective*, and *energizing* as being key indicators of the presence of a natural talent in an activity. The Gallup Organization gives some additional criteria for a natural talent being present, such as *yearning*, that is, you have a natural draw to the activity; *rapid learning*, that is, you pick up an activity very quickly; and *flow*, that is, you pick up the steps to certain activities automatically.[21]

There also can be subtle or not-so-subtle pressures to make vocational choices that are not based in one's talents and gifting. Parental or societal pressures may nudge (or in some cases shove) a person toward a vocation that is not suited to the person's talents. Often people make vocational choices based solely on the perceived earning power of that vocation. In Christian circles, values often cloud vocational choices grounded in talents and gifts. Because a person values a particular kind of ministry or admires people who do a particular kind of ministry well does not mean that an individual has the gifting necessary to do a similar kind of ministry. Sometimes even mentors or teachers, in their zeal for their own vocational calling, can be too quick to urge a person to follow in their footsteps without adequately assessing the gifts and talents of the individual to help them find their own vocational place in the world. All of these are obstacles to finding a vocational fit based in gifts and talents.

Talents Can Be Developed but Not Generated

While a person cannot bring a talent into existence by hard work, he or she can develop a talent. A talent for communication can be honed by courses in public speaking, homiletics, and gaining experience on a debate team. The Gallup Organization is particularly strong on this point, noting that a talent does not become a strength without the addition of knowledge (both factual and experiential) and skill. Please note that the Gallup Organization uses the word *skill* differently than the IDAK Group. The Gallup Organization defines *skill* as an important component to add to a

---

20. The Gallup Organization, *Strengths Performance Coach for Faith*, 7.
21. Ibid., 13.

talent to help it become a strength. The IDAK Group considers a *skill* to be an activity or proficiency that is necessary to fulfill one's job description but is not undergirded by a talent.[22]

The "You Can Be Anything You Want to Be" Mantra Is Wrongheaded

Anyone with minimal exposure to the American public school system has heard the mantra that a person can be anything he or she wants to be with enough hard work and discipline. Positively, educators are urging students not to set artificial limits on their aspirations, but this is also a deceptive message. To be excellent in a vocation is not just about hard work, education, and dedication; it also must tap into a person's gifts and talents in a significant way. Thus, in order to serve ministries well, vocational guidance must look at gifts and talents as well as aspirations.

An Evaluation of Natural Talent Inventories

How does one compare and contrast two diverse natural talent instruments and be fair to each? One way that I found insightful was to categorize their natural talents according to Howard Gardner's highly acclaimed theory of multiple intelligences as articulated in his book, *Frames of Mind.*[23] Gardner posits that each human has multiple innate intelligences that enrich life.

Linguistic intelligence is a natural intelligence for the use of language, displaying a "great sensitivity to the use of words . . . sensitivity to the order among words . . . and sensitivity to the role of language in explanation."[24] This is obviously crucial for poets, writers, teachers, and public speakers. *Musical intelligence* is the natural intelligence to compose and often create sound and patterns of sounds that are pleasing to the ear. People with this intelligence often have "tones in their heads."[25] Musical intelligence is crucial for both composing and performing music. *Spatial intelligence* is described by Gardner as "the capacities to perceive the visual world accurately, to perform transformations and modifications upon one's initial perceptions, and to be able to recreate aspects of one's visual experience, even in the absence of relevant physical stimuli."[26] It is crucial in many sciences, architecture, and of course the visual and spatial arts. *Bodily-kinesthetic intelligence* focuses on "bodily movements and the capacity to handle objects skillfully."[27] This is most obvious in dancers, athletes, acting, and many forms of manual labor and machine operation. *Logical-mathematical intelligence* most fundamentally "refers to the actions one can make on an object, the relations

---

22. Ibid., 8–9.
23. Howard Gardner, *Frames of Mind: The Theory of Multiple Intelligences*, 2nd ed. (New York: Basic Books, 2004).
24. Ibid., 77–78.
25. Ibid., 101.
26. Ibid., 173.
27. Ibid., 206.

that obtain among those actions, the statements (or propositions) that one can make about actual or potential actions, and the relationships among those statements.[28] This intelligence is foundational for scientific and logical thought. *Intrapersonal-interpersonal intelligence* is a natural intelligence that allows a person to be particularly aware of his or her own inner state of being and to be sensitive to the inner state of being of other persons.[29] This is a critical intelligence for many philosophers and religious leaders and more obviously for those in counseling and care vocations.

The range of intelligences identified by Gardner are an excellent grid to evaluate the range of natural talents assessed by the two natural talent inventories (see figure 17.3). The assumption is that each kind of intelligence will have corresponding natural talents. The key is coverage of all of Gardner's categories of intelligence by a particular natural talent instrument, not necessarily the number of items that each natural talent inventory might have in a particular area of intelligence. (You'll notice that the IDAK Career Match has twenty more natural talents than does the Clifton StrengthsFinder.) Gardner would stress that any particular activity might be using more than one category of intelligence to function correctly. This makes the categorization of some of the talent terms from the two natural talent instruments a bit difficult, but overall the conclusions drawn from comparing the instruments to Gardner's intelligence categories are so pronounced that they will not be affected by changing the placement of a few natural talents into different categories. With this additional framework in place, evaluation of the strengths and inadequacies of the two natural talent instruments for giving vocational counsel to theological field education students would be the logical next step.

Evaluation of the Clifton StrengthsFinder
Admirable Qualities

There are many admirable qualities of the CSF. The online format for taking the CSF is a clear plus for those who are accustomed to using the Internet and are comfortable with online tests. The books from which a client receives the codes to take the CSF are very helpful in explaining the thirty-four talent themes, so that understanding the significance and meaning of an individual's top five signature talents from the CSF is readily available without additional assistance. This arrangement is user-friendly and convenient. In addition, the combination of book and inventory for approximately $25 is very reasonable.

Another admirable quality of the CSF is its complex and textured identification of natural talent themes related to leadership and organizational development. In figure 17.3, which compares the two natural talent inventories through the lens of Howard Gardner's theory of multiple intelligences,

28. Ibid., 129.
29. Ibid., 239.

it becomes clear that the CSF has most of its natural talents located in the logical-mathematical intelligence and intrapersonal-interpersonal intelligence categories. These categories have great significance for leadership and organizational development, making the CSF very well suited for giving insight to those who will be in leadership positions and responsible for developing organizations.[30] This would certainly describe most pastoral ministry vocations; thus the CSF can be very helpful in identifying talents for the leadership and the organizational development aspects of the pastor-in-training's ministry and field education experiences.

Deficiencies

However, for all of its admirable qualities, there are a number of deficiencies in the CSF that limit its usefulness in theological field education and pastoral preparation. The first deficiency is that only the top five signature talents are given to the client once he or she has completed the CSF. The Gallup Organization data banks have all thirty-four talent themes sequenced from most indicated to least indicated for all persons who have taken the CSF. The Gallup Organization itself admits that a person's top ten to twelve talent themes are probably used with some regularity, but nonetheless it will give only the top five.[31] Receiving my "Theme Sequence" for all thirty-four talent themes helped me not to feel like some key aspects of my talents were missing, because those "missing" components were in my top dozen but not my top five talents in my talent sequence.[32] I would like to see Gallup's initial report generated from the CSF include the top ten to twelve talents.

The Gallup Organization is clear that the reason it does not give the entire theme sequence to the client is that many will go immediately to the bottom of the sequence to see what talent weaknesses they should fix. This "weakness fixing" approach violates all the CSF stands for but can be irresistible to those who have this propensity. The Gallup Organization also might argue that giving more than five talent themes might dilute a person's focus in developing their top talents into strengths.

Another deficiency of the CSF is that a few of its talent themes and their descriptions sound less-than-desirable for devoted Christians than the Gallup Organization anticipated. The development of the CSF within business venues might be the source of some of the descriptor difficulties. For example, people who exhibit the "competition" talent theme are described as, "measuring their progress against the performance of others." Seminarians

---

30. The emphasis on leadership talents and organizational development talents certainly would be consistent with the fact that the initial research for the CSF by Clifton was focused on various sectors of the business community.

31. This assertion was made by Curt Liesveld of the Gallup Organization in my "Strength Performance Coach for Faith" training at the Gallup University, July 2006.

32. My "Theme Sequence" was given by virtue of going through the first level of CSF coaches training. For an additional cost a client can get his or her "Theme Sequence."

Figure 17.3. Talent Assessment Instruments Categorized by Howard Gardner's Theory of Multiple Intelligences

GARNER'S CATEGORIES OF INTELLIGENCE	IDAK CAREER MATCH (54 Talents)		CLIFTON STRENGTHS-FINDER (34 Talents)	
Linguistic Intelligence	Writing words Conversing Public Speaking Broadcasting	Teaching Giving presentations Group moderating	Communication	
Musical Intelligence	Composing/arranging music	Singing/instrument		
Spatial Intelligence	Observing detail-environment Spatial perception 3D Designing Painting Using color and patterns	Using handicrafts Using shapes and forms Ordering space Observing printed details		
Bodily-Kinesthetic Intelligence	Acting/imitation mannerisms Physical coordination Hand/arm coordination	Hand/finger coordination Operating/driving Quick reflex action		
Logical-Mathematical Ingelligence	Creating Imagining Inventing Calculating numbers Recording/auditing Technical troubleshooting Researching/investigating Problem solving Remembering	Classifying Analyzing Appraising/estimating Developing/initiating Planning Setting time and priorities Making future projections Risk taker Synthesizing	Achiever Activator Adaptability Analytical Arranger Command Competition Connectedness Consistency Context	Deliberative Discipline Focus Input Intellection Learner Strategic Belief Futuristic Ideation
Intrapersonal-Interpersonal Intelligence	Managing Negotiating Selling Promoting Multi-relational Familiar group	Singular relational Tutoring Being of service Counseling Reassuring and supporting Character discernment	Developer Empathy Harmony Includer Woo Individualization Maximizer	Positivity Relator Restorative Self-assurance Responsibility Significance

Gardner's catgories of intelligence used by permission; Howard Gardner, *Frames of Mind: The Theory of Multiple Intelligences,* 2nd ed. (New York: Basic Books, 2004). IDAK Career Match talent names used by permission; any reproduction or use of talent names, categories, or definitions by any means in prohibited without permission from the IDAK Group. Clifton StrengthsFinder talent names used by permission of the Gallup Organization.

often will note that Scripture enjoins believers not to compare themselves with others (John 21:21–22; 2 Cor. 10:12–13; Gal. 6:4). Thus, that which is conveyed as a positive talent theme by the CSF may be seen as a moral failing by those engaged in theological field education.

Similarly, the description of the "self-assurance" talent theme with its emphasis on self-confidence may strike many seminarians as incompatible with God-confidence. In the same way the "significance" talent described as "wanting to be very important in the eyes of others" might seem overly self-centered for Christian sensibilities. These talents may need to be reframed by the theological field educator to help seminarians embrace the positive aspects envisioned by the CSF.

A third deficiency of the CSF revolves around its coaches training. The first level of the coaches training in the Faith division of the Gallup Organization is about five times as expensive as the initial training for the IDAK Group's Level I and Level II training. This expensive trend is projected to continue for the CSF in its anticipated Level II and Level III training. Despite its high cost, the CSF coaches training has less value-added components for the coach than most assessment instruments training. Most other instruments use their training to certify the trainee to have a gatekeeping role for a client's access to the instrument as well as give additional insight for coaching the client. Instead, the CSF is available to anyone who purchases the Gallup books, and the initial coaches training provides little information that cannot be accessed by a careful reading and application of the books from which the client got the access code. I have heard repeated complaints from people who, after having met with a certified CSF coach, have found it not to be as "value-added" as they had hoped. One value-added component that could be added to the initial CSF coaches training would be the ability to access the entire theme sequence for their client at a minimal cost.

The most serious deficiency of the CSF is the limited scope of natural talents that it assesses. The comparison chart based on Howard Gardner's theory of multiple intelligences clearly shows that the CSF does not focus on some major forms of intelligence but is rather narrowly focused on logical-mathematical and intrapersonal-interpersonal forms of intelligence with only the very broad "communication" talent theme covering all linguistic intelligence. This is not simply a result of it having twenty fewer talents than the IDAK Career Match. Rather, whole categories of natural talent are woefully underrepresented or ignored altogether.

It seems that the studies of the "best of the best" were primarily focused on business, academic, and other professional settings. In a research "Frequently Asked Questions" section published by the Gallup Organization, they write:

> Since 1998, The Clifton StrengthsFinder has been used by Gallup's initial diagnostic tool in development programs with various academic institutions, faith-based organizations, major businesses, and other organizations. The Clifton StrengthsFinder has been used to facilitate the development of individuals across hundreds of roles including: manager, customer service representative, salesperson, administrative assistant, nurse, lawyer, pastor, leader, student, teacher, and school administrator.[33]

One suspects that not many artists, dancers, construction workers, musicians, plumbers, or interior designers were included in the research. These gaps in kinds of intelligences represented in the talent themes is particularly

---

33. The Gallup Organization, *Strengths Performance Coach for Faith*, 18.

damaging for church-related assessment. Church ministry communication is highly varied, including oral, written, visual, musical, and other forms, and will only continue to be more varied in the increasingly multimedia future. The restricted range of communication talents in the CSF limits its value for church settings and its utility for institutions preparing people vocationally for parish ministry. In addition, the lack of inclusion of kinesthetic intelligences in the CSF limits its utility in identifying natural talents that could be applied in more concrete service projects in the church and in the community.

Evaluation of the IDAK Career Match and Talent Discovery Guide
Admirable Qualities

There are many admirable qualities that the IDAK Career Match possesses. Most significantly the IDAK Group's range of natural talents does not miss any major domains of intelligence as delineated by Howard Gardner. This would indicate a more comprehensive coverage of the range of possible natural talents than the CSF. Significantly, the Christian context of much of the development of the IDAK Career Match has precluded the use of terms that are "loaded" for Christian audiences.

Other admirable qualities include the comprehensive nature of the IDAK Career Match process. It is one of the few instruments that not only identifies natural talents but also gives very clear career guidance as to environments and duties where those talents could be practiced. It also provides processes as to how to make career switches if that is necessary. Also its training for its counselor/consultants provides high value-added skills for the IDAK Career Match consultant. Without training the instrument cannot be purchased or scored, and there are many additional skills provided in IDAK Level I and Level II training for a fraction of the cost of the CSF training.

Deficiencies

Despite these admirable qualities, there are some drawbacks to using the IDAK Career Match. The first is cost—both in time and money. While the IDAK Career Match provides plenty of value for the money, it does have a considerable up-front cost for the financially strapped theological student. It also takes more than six to eight hours to complete the IDAK Career Match, which is available only in hard copy. This means that considerable time must be given to filling out the instrument, after which it must be sent to Oregon to be scored with the results mailed back to an IDAK-trained consultant. The IDAK Career Match is to be followed by an intensive interview with an IDAK-trained consultant/counselor. Again, this process can be too time consuming and costly for the academic institution to absorb.

The online version of the Talent Discovery Guide could be the best IDAK Group product for general use in theological field education. It uses the full, fifty-four-talent list of the IDAK Group and has the convenience of an online product that can be accessed without an IDAK counselor/consultant. It has increased validity compared to the hard-copy Talent Discovery Guide and is priced comparably to the CSF. The chief drawback is that unlike the CSF, it does not have a book to provide deeper insights into the person's top talents and how to develop them. While there is some help for development on the IDAK Web site, this development process traditionally has been provided by IDAK consultants/counselors and may still need their input for the online Talent Discovery Guide to have full impact.

Conclusion

Theological field educators constantly wrestle with helping students to understand and focus their pastoral vocational calling. Natural talent inventories can be significant tools to assist students with this focusing process. Both the CSF and the IDAK Group instruments can provide natural talent input that can be valuable to the student. The CSF may have some advantages in helping students refine their understanding of their leadership and organizational development natural talents, but the IDAK Group gives the more comprehensive map of natural talents. The online version of the Talent Discovery Guide may be the best overall, affordable priced natural talent assessment for a broader range of natural talents, especially when combined with insights from an IDAK-trained consultant/counselor.

Prayer of Transformation

Father, you are the source of all that we are. As Creator you have endowed us with talents, and as Savior you have granted us spiritual gifts. We are, as the psalmist would say, "fearfully and wonderfully made." Allow this wonderful truth to guide our view of ourselves and to guide our assessment of others who have their own unique endowment from you. Guard us from envy of the gifts of others and from questioning your wisdom in your gifting of us. Grant us the faith to press on to use our endowments fully and the discipline to hone gifts until they are fully developed. May our gifts serve others lovingly and bring honor to your name. Amen.

Reflection Questions

1. Reflecting on your ministry context and emphases, which one of the natural talent inventories might best serve your ministry?

2. Do you balk at or embrace the idea of including "natural talents" in the assessment of students for ministry preparation? What theological reasons do you have for your stance on "natural talents"?

3. Can you think of natural talents that are not covered by the two assessment instruments referred to in this chapter?

Further Reading

Bradley, John, and Jay Carty. *Discovering Your Natural Talents*. Colorado Springs: NavPress, 1994.

Buckingham, Marcus, and Donald Clifton. *Now, Discover Your Strengths*. New York: Free Press, 2001.

Clifton, Donald, and Edward Anderson. *StrengthsQuest: Discover and Develop Your Strengths in Academics, Career, and Beyond*. Washington, DC: Gallup, 2002.

Gardner, Howard. *Frames of Mind: The Theory of Multiple Intelligences*. 2nd ed. New York: Basic Books, 2004.

Liesveld, Roseanne, Jo Ann Miller, and Jennifer Robinson. *Teach with Your Strengths*. New York: Gallup, 2005.

Rath, Tom. *StrengthsFinder 2.0*. New York: Gallup, 2007.

Winseman, Albert L., Donald Clifton, and Curt Liesveld. *Living Your Strengths: Discover Your God-Given Talents and Inspire Your Community*. New York: Gallup, 2003–2004.

Chapter 18

Equipping Mentors to Leave a Legacy

DARYL SMITH

But that doesn't mean you should all look and speak and act the same. Out of the generosity of Christ, each of us is given his own gift. The text for this is,

He climbed the high mountain,
He captured the enemy and seized the booty,
He handed it all out in gifts to the people.

It is true, is it not, that the One who climbed up also climbed down, down to the valley of earth? And the One who climbed down is the One who climbed back up, up to highest heaven. He handed out gifts above and below, filled heaven with his gifts, filled earth with his gifts. He handed out gifts of apostle, prophet, evangelist, and pastor-teacher to train Christians in skilled servant work, working within Christ's body, the church, until we're all moving rhythmically and easily with each other, efficient and graceful in response to God's Son, fully mature adults, fully developed within and without, fully alive like Christ.
(Eph. 4:7–13 MSG)

The mentoring of student-pastors may be the greatest single factor in determining their future ministry success. However, to assume that a pastor or leader will provide effective mentoring without mentor training is like sending a tenth-grade biology student into a surgical suite and expecting a successful heart transplant to result.

This chapter is for those of us (professional field educators, pastors, team or ministry leaders, etc.) who face the awesome task of equipping mentors for their vital role.[1] As one who has walked both sides of the mentor/field educator street, this is my story. Hopefully, my perspective will provide a mirror off which you can reflect your work. If you read the earlier chapter to mentors, you will find some overlap of key concepts but with different emphases. I am assuming that you are working in an academic institution or local church setting. If that is not true, you will need to translate for your context.

As mentor equippers, we are not beginning some new trend. There are mentor models in the Old and New Testament Scriptures, in epic stories, and in contemporary fiction. Several developmental theorists—including Daniel Levinson, Maggie Scarf, and Gail Sheehy—have researched human development for many years. They have concluded that all persons need mentors to find full human development. However, I believe mentoring has moved to center stage in the last twenty years or so, primarily due to the growing study of leadership and with it the growing understanding of the vital role mentors play.

A Bit of My Story

For a number of years I was an associate pastor given the responsibility to provide ministry opportunities for seminary students who took supervised ministry classes. No one talked to me about mentoring or trained me for the job, so I took full advantage of the students who came my way. I appointed them to my vacant Christian education positions, turned them loose on the children or teens for a semester, and forgot about them. I filled out a couple of evaluation forms at the end and sent them on their way while I awaited a new bunch of recruits for the next semester. I thought I had done my job, and I was pleased to have the *willing* volunteers. It never dawned on me that there was more to supervised ministry than managing a system or that I should be doing something to help shape the seminary students' vocational call.

The first few sections of this chapter will look at the importance of mentors and our roles in their successful mentoring. Near the end I will describe our seminary's actual mentor training model as a sample for your reflection.

Mentors Are Necessary for Theological Education

You have probably seen the research or heard the conference speakers pointing to the fact that seminaries of the twenty-first century must rely

---

1. The use of *you* throughout this chapter is intended for field educational professionals and those responsible for training internship mentors.

on on-site faculty or mentors in the field if they are going to survive past this generation. As you know, seminary education is in cataclysmic change. Students no longer can or will isolate themselves to studies for several years and then begin translating those studies into ministry upon graduation. Often students come to us from a first career, wanting to take a few classes and quickly move on into ministry, all the while balancing their business, family, and church ministry. Seminaries are dependent upon "field faculty" to guide students in continuous integration of their studies with practice—to make intentional, theological reflection as natural as breathing. In addition, with many denominations charging forward with church planting, research shows that church planters nearly always fail if there is not someone to walk beside them through the first few years of the new plant. Thus, our future as ministry-equipping centers and the future ministry of our students depends on the mentors we train.

Mentors Must Be Trained

If you drop into any leadership conference, you will almost immediately find a heated corner discussion as to whether leaders are made or born. The best answer is yes. The same is true for mentors. Some persons seem to exude a natural instinct for mentoring. Others need special help to get the picture. All mentors need additional training, even if it is only to help them understand the model that you are working with in your institution. Any time that field education materials are updated, it is important to recall mentors for upgrading.

You, as an equipper of mentors, must decide which model works best for you. You may choose a one-day event or a weekend retreat. As a curriculum designer by training, I try to create events that cover the learning-styles spectrum. With time and location limitations, I tend to lean toward lecture and discussion, but I always incorporate other activities that engage the other learning styles.

Our actual equipping of mentors must provide the basic tools of mentoring while building a relationship between the mentor and the institution. The equipping sessions and materials should help mentors move from a supervision perspective to a pouring-their-lives-into-another-person perspective. And that is usually a dramatic shift.

Start from a Spiritual Formation Perspective

Do not skip spiritual formation just because the mentors coming to you are ministry leaders. Before we think about the nuts and bolts of meeting academic requirements or teaching ministry skills, we must think about partnering with God in the shaping of people into the likeness of Jesus—both the students and the mentors who work with them. Pastors (and mentors) fail in ministry because their spiritual and personal lives fall apart—rarely do they fail because their skills are inadequate.

In chapter 6 of this book, I discussed Christian or spiritual formation at length. I quoted Robert Mulholland's definition of spiritual formation as "the process of being conformed to the image of Jesus for the sake of others."[2] Mulholland's view is that we are in a lifelong process of transformation. That transformation is to take the shape of Jesus. And it is not about us. It is for the sake of other persons. If we do not start training mentors with Christian formation as the foundation, the remainder of what we teach them will be meaningless for ministry. And our mentors must experience the same ongoing transformation in their lives that we are expecting them to guide in the lives of our students.

Focus on Mission, Not Supervision

All mentors must supervise students, but if supervision is the mentors' sole perspective, they will never understand the mission to which they are called. You may need to confront this topic head-on. If you have mentors who have come through the "old school" model as I did, they may have difficulty understanding that life is about mission. Even persons who pastor regularly often get caught in the "job" mentality. They complete a certain number of hours per week or a certain set of tasks, and the work is done. In fact, some of my students have encountered mentors who were counting the days to retirement. They had long since burned out and were disgruntled and bitter, and the student had to take charge of the ministry and guide the mentor. Needless to say, we do not use those mentors a second time.

On the other hand, I have found that most ministry leaders or pastors have a deep longing to make a difference in the ministry of some young leader's life. They dream of leaving a positive and powerful legacy. As ministry leaders begin to understand that our goal is to turn them loose to pour their lives into a ministry student for the kingdom of God, they catch a new flame in their hearts. For some, the flame has burned for years. For others, the flame has died. For most all mentors, the mentoring process reignites the mentor's passion for ministry. In fact, mentors often come to me overwhelmed with gratitude for allowing an idealistic student to spend a semester with them. As pastors, they had lost the vision they started ministry with. Through mentoring they are re-visioned for their own ministries and have helped launch another person into ministry at the same time.

Build Expectations Between Your Institution and the Mentor

If you are working as a professional field educator in an academic institution, you are responsible for meeting accrediting requirements for specific classes. If you are in another ministry setting, you must meet your ministry's expectations. Whatever the case, it is important to be clear about what you expect of the mentor, the student, and yourself. Once a crisis has arisen, it is too late to set an expectation in place. It is better to be straight and clear from the beginning.

---

2. M. Robert Mulholland Jr., *Invitation to a Journey: A Road Map for Spiritual Formation* (Downers Grove, IL: InterVarsity Press, 1993), 2.

Raise the Bar

Do not accept mediocrity. That is the disease of our culture. Instead, expect the best. Expect *excellence* from your mentors and yourself. If you set a low level of accountability, they will meet it.[3] If you set a high bar, they will strive for it and amaze themselves at how well they do.

It is important when you set the bar for accountability that you be specific about what excellence looks like. For example, mentors should meet with students at least one hour per week. They must not fail at that, or they must make it up, not just skip it. If mentors must attend training sessions to be a mentor in your program, then they must attend the training before they mentor your student. I have discovered that when I set a training time, there are usually several who tell me they cannot come. When I offer a makeup date or the option of watching a four-hour video, they somehow can find the time to attend the original training session.

Sometimes ministry leaders are so busy they will not take your equipping seriously unless you communicate to them the necessity of doing it. Others are arrogant (did I actually use that word? I believe it is true) enough to believe that they do not need training to mentor. They assume that mentoring is like falling off a log—no equipping required. Those are the mentors I take off my list.

On our Asbury Seminary Web page, we list these basic requirements as a starting point:

1. A theological/ministry degree
2. Five years of ministry experience following the completion of that degree
3. Participation in a mentor training session (offered twice each year)
4. Completion of the mentor profile, submitted to the Mentored Ministry office
5. Completion of the Mentor-Student Contract
6. Commitment to help students determine their Growth Goals
7. Completion of the Mentor Evaluation at the end of the semester

We are somewhat flexible on the first two items if persons have an equivalency in education and experience. Otherwise we hold a pretty hard line. It helps that the students are required to complete the mentored ministry class for graduation so they can apply pressure to mentors who are delinquent with forms or other items. (Let me add that most mentors come through with flying colors, delighted at the ministry opportunity they have had.

---

3. In chapter 6, I explained the difference between perfectionism and excellence. Perfectionism becomes intolerance and is immobilizing. Excellence is striving for the best while acknowledging that we never can be perfect. Thus, we evaluate where we did not do well and build on that understanding to do our "better-best" in the future.

Often mentors are frustrated when another student is not immediately available for them.)

Use a Mentor Profile

Your institution may have a set of forms for background checks on everyone on staff. Hopefully, you have a sexual harassment policy in place. If your mentors are coming from a denomination where regular accountability is practiced, you may not need to perform a new background check. If the mentors do not come from a reputable institution or ministry, a background check could be very important.

In addition, you need a way to find out who your mentors are, their ministry thinking and their leadership philosophy. Do they share the same values that you want your students to gain? Are they on the same theological page? Mentors must own what you are doing, not just fill a space so students can complete a class.

We have created a simple two-page form that asks the basics of name, address, academic credentials, ministry record, and so on. It then goes on to get at what we believe is most important. We ask mentors to respond to questions about their leadership style and how they use teams and small groups in their ministry. We ask them to reflect on their motivation for ministry and what they believe they bring to the table for mentoring. And, finally, we ask them to define their current ministry for us. It is those reflection questions, along with any other information sources, that we use in accepting or declining a mentor for one of our students.

Check for Ministry Skills and a Teachable Spirit

If you do not know the potential mentor and a mentor profile does not give you all you need, try to find out how well the mentor performs basic ministry skills. You may need to ask the potential student if he or she knows the person well. You may need to contact denominational leaders who oversee the mentor.

We can live with a person whose ministry skills are not the best, but a teachable spirit is imperative. Mentors must see themselves as people on-the-grow. They are not just advice sources or bosses of the students. They are partners in an adventure together, even though they have greater experience than their student.

Enforce Confidentiality and Safety for the Student

Each mentor training session comes to silenced attention when I tell the mentors that they will be fired if they ever break a confidence with a student or if they sexually harass a student. If a mentor breaks confidence with a student—unless the student is dangerous to himself or herself or to someone else—the student is pulled from that relationship and we never use that mentor again. You probably have had friends (or yourself) whose ministry lost credibility because someone broke a confidence shared in a time of deep need. Thus, mentors, as a rule, should have future authority over a student (e.g., in a denominational setting) if what a student shares in a field education experience might come back to haunt them.

In the same way, if a student is ever mistreated or is sexually harassed by a mentor, the student is immediately pulled from the ministry setting and the mentor relationship. (The same, of course, holds true if a student betrays a relationship.)

This is the one time during a training session that mentors know I am very serious. I do not apologize for appearing firm—because I am. What I also notice is the pained look and nodding of heads from many mentors who have lived with the grief of a betrayed confidence or destroyed relationship.

Encourage Healthy Relationships Between Mentors and Students

Beyond all that we discussed above, encourage mentors to take time to build healthy relationships with their students. Mentoring can be so much more than the one-hour-per-week interview. That time will have a set agenda. If a mentor meets the student for nonscheduled time—say, at the nearest coffee shop—the student will soon discover what really makes the mentor successful and the mentor probably will be more transparent than in the formal setting.[4]

Equipping Models

With the shifting of seminary education from the residential campus to include 24/7 online classes, the equipping of both students and mentors must be nimble enough to meet the needs of each individual in each specific setting. This rapidly changing seminary scene can create anxiety. Yet, it also provides amazing possibilities for those who are willing to creatively flow with it. While it is impossible to guarantee the quality of training when equipping mentors one never sees, there are tools to increase the level of training success.

Think Face-to-Face First

I am changing my mind. Years before anyone was thinking of online education at our seminary, I was agitating for us to get started with it. At the time, I was taking a class that explored the primitive stages of the Internet, and I thought we should at least use it to connect our alumni. Plus, I could envision teaching classes over this *phone-line thing.* But no one grabbed the hook, and I was assured that the accrediting people would never approve of such a crazy idea.

Eighteen years later, all of our classes are available in a distance-learning format, and I am retracting some of the glowing possibilities I espoused

---

4. You might want to review the "Ministry Role Model" section in chapter 6, "Mentoring: The Opportunity to Leave a Legacy," concerning living a transparent ministry life in front of the student.

for Internet use. Too often I have watched the technology gurus drive online education as if it is the final advancement in the evolution of human learning. Nowhere is that more true than in the academy. For a while it was the bandwagon everyone wanted to jump on.

Now we are discovering across the teaching/educational spectrum that we cannot achieve, in most subjects, the same level of quality through distance learning that we can face-to-face. I do not want my surgeon or counselor getting their degrees through an online computer class. I want my surgeon to have experienced a real scalpel and an operating room and my counselor to have actually practiced face-to-face with another human. I want the students who graduate from our seminary to have wrestled through their ministry struggles and theological questions in a small-group encounter with other students and mentors.

Let me hasten to add that distance learning (and the Internet, or whatever comes next) is here to stay, so we must find a way to make it work to its fullest. And I am committed to using it as a tool, when it fits both the learning style and needs of my students. Our culture is filled with lonely people. The Internet perpetuates aloneness. I can sit behind my screen and never let you into who I really am or see my body language or look deep into my eyes to touch my soul. Our student-pastors must learn to live in the Internet world—using it for all it is worth—while also connecting deeply with people face-to-face. That is a fine line to walk but one we all must walk in this generation.

The key—and we must be persistently intentional to pull it off, when it seems everyone wants to go totally online—is to always *think face-to-face first*. Whether we are training mentors or teaching students, look for ways to include face-to-face interaction. Whether working on campus or online, always look for ways to include face-to-face interaction. Depending on your training setting, face-to-face may seem difficult to do, but think radically about how you might integrate it before too easily buying into the electronic substitute.

At the Association for Theological Field Education Biennial Consultation in 2007, one session discussed the topic of equipping students and mentors using online models. As the discussion worked its way around the room, almost everyone (these were professional, mostly out-of-box-thinking field educators) agreed that we will continue using online instructional methods into the foreseeable future. However, we are discovering that some form of face-to-face interaction must be included (if at all possible) for the online classes to be the most effective. For some this meant bringing students to campus for a weekend retreat or weeklong intensive during the time they were enrolled in the field education classes. For others it meant periodically gathering online students from a regional area, at a local church or coffee shop, to work on case studies or reflect theologically on their experiences in the field. Each person worked in a different setting but was attempting to make face-to-face interaction a reality in their context. High tech–high touch is now reality.

On-Campus Students and Local Mentors

If possible, train mentors in person. I would suggest (since this is what we do, it is my favorite) doing a one-day seminar on campus so that mentors are together as a group and can connect to your physical campus. Mentors who spend a day together often build relationships with other mentors or reconnect with persons they have known in the past. It builds a sense of team for them to share the day together. In addition, many mentors, even our graduates from the Kentucky campus, have never been to the Florida campus. Seeing the facility and experiencing the atmosphere always yields long-term results beyond the mentor training they receive. It builds long-term relationships between the seminary and the mentors' ministry setting.

Our Orlando campus is a drive-in campus with students arriving throughout the week from as far away as Georgia, Alabama, and south Florida. The students take classes in person and online, depending on what they need and how far away they live. Since we have discovered that the online classes do not achieve the same results, particularly in mentored ministry, we do not allow students who live within 150 miles of campus to take the classes online.

Thus we consider our mentors within that 150-mile radius to be local. We offer the mentored ministry training on campus twice a year for the mentors of the students who take our on-campus mentored ministry classes. All mentors are required to attend the one-day training session before they are allowed to mentor students. We have found that it has taken time to build a reputation of seriousness about our mentor training, but we now achieve nearly 100 percent attendance.

For those mentors who think they do not need training to mentor or who experience actual conflicts, we offer a makeup session. Sometimes, we bring the absent mentors to campus on a second date or one of us on the mentored ministry team will meet the mentor at another location for an abbreviated version of the daylong event. As mentioned above, absences are rare since most people will come to the scheduled date when they realize that they cannot get out of the training and still be a mentor. The on-campus training is better than two or three hours at a table in a McDonald's restaurant, sitting with me and my laptop.

Off-Campus Students and Distance Mentors

Despite all that has been said previously about the downside of distance learning, there are students who cannot attend campus classes and mentors who will not attend on-campus training. For most, distance is the issue. For those students and mentors, something else must be created.

If an institutional budget will pay for the travel and lodging expenses of a mentor to attend on-campus training, the benefits are worth it. The couple of times we have worked this into our budget, the mentors have found the training effective and loved the retreat away from the office.

For several years, we could not find an answer to the dilemma of training mentors whom we could not meet in person. Our first attempts were feeble. We set up a video camera in our on-campus training room and recorded all the sessions. (Some sessions came out better than others.) We talked a friend into volunteering his time to transfer the videotape to a DVD, we wrote up a few notes, and sent a packet to each off-campus mentor. We still have no idea if anyone watched them.

In our second attempt (and subsequent attempts as we keep practicing), we planned for what was to be said with a watching audience in mind. We even staged some of the teaching directly for the mentors who would be watching, using a studio on campus and a park downtown. We sought professional help in duplicating and recording. We then translated all our on-campus materials to a note-taking guide to match what was said on the DVD. Finally, we added a brief response sheet with open-ended questions to discover if the mentors actually watched the material and took notes. The recent results, both in forms returned and in student responses about mentors, are promising.

Keep Equipping, Keep Appreciating

Equipping mentors is not a onetime event unless you never plan to use the same mentor twice. It is an ongoing ministry partnership. As we create new materials, the mentors must be kept current with what we are doing. As new mentoring research becomes available, it must be shared with mentors. As mentors give themselves to our students, we must continue to give the mentors our appreciation and support.

With the growing capability of Web sites, newsletters, videos, and Internet, resource links are readily available. Most every field educator can drop an encouraging word or the "latest tip" to each mentor on a regular basis. We can increase the effectiveness of a mentor if we will sift through the many possible mentoring resources and grab a gem or two and send it to the mentors. They will probably not have or take the time to do their own improvement research, but we can keep them motivated with a key thought now and then.

A Sample Equipping Session

When I came as a rookie field educator to Asbury Seminary, I interviewed several of our graduates to see if they would be our "start-up mentors." Most went into a raving (actually, some were kind but said the same thing) explanation of how their seminary supervised ministry experience was the worst class they had had in seminary and they wanted no part of it now. (Actually, they told story after story of lousy relationships with supervisors.) It became apparent that we needed a new model—even to the point of changing the name from *supervisor* to *mentor*.

Since I was new and did not have a mentor-training model, I browsed around at what some other schools were doing, borrowed some ideas, and created my own. I wish there had been someone to give me a packaged mentor training kit; it would not have taken so much experimentation to get to where we are today.

You may be where I was, or you may want some fresh ideas. Either way, the sample mentor training in figure 18.1 is offered as a tool or as an idea starter. I find that looking at what others are doing usually sparks new ideas in me, even if I do not directly use what they have done. Some teaching quotes are included (in *italics*) in the outline to give you a starting point for comments. You will want to rewrite or add to them, to make them your own. This outline is used at both the Orlando and Kentucky campuses of Asbury Theological Seminary in a one-day, 9 A.M. to 2:30 P.M. seminar.

Figure 18.1. Sample Mentor Training

SETUP CHECKLIST
The Facility
- ❏ Direction signs in lobby and hallway
- ❏ Name tags and larger markers (on table at door)
- ❏ Sign-in sheet
- ❏ Water pitcher and glasses on each table

Food
- ❏ Tablecloths, napkins, paper coffee cups
- ❏ Beverages (coffee, juice, water) and snack (cheese, crackers, grapes)

Mentor Supplies (at each chair)
- ❏ Mentored Ministry Handbook with Note-Taking Guide
- ❏ Parish Advisory Handbook
- ❏ Seminary promo packet and D.Min. DVD
- ❏ Mentored Ministry brochures
- ❏ Mentor Profile Sheet
- ❏ Seminary pen and paper pad

Teaching Supplies
- ❏ Computer and PowerPoint
- ❏ Overhead projector
- ❏ White board markers
- ❏ Philippians 4:8–9 on transparency
- ❏ Blank transparencies and markers
- ❏ Stool and music stand/podium

Communion Elements
- ❏ Bread
- ❏ Grape juice/Wine
- ❏ 2 Chalices
- ❏ 2 Plates

Lunch (to be delivered)
- ❏ Sub sandwiches
- ❏ Soup
- ❏ Cookies
- ❏ Chips
- ❏ Beverages

TEACHING OUTLINE

9:30 A.M.
Greeting and Refreshments

- ❏ Greet each mentor and direct to the sign-in table.
- ❏ Make sure that each mentor creates a name tag.
- ❏ Introduce mentors to one another and direct to snack table.

9:45 A.M.
A. Welcome to Mentor Training and Introduction to the Role of Mentor
1. Introduce self, including brief ministry background.
2. Welcome Mentors
   "Welcome to Mentor Training _____. We are delighted that you are here today. You are our special guests. We are grateful that you have chosen to serve in this vital role of mentoring one of our students during the upcoming semester."
3. Introduce staff/faculty team and guests.
4. Mentors meet one another (Allow 5 minutes)
   "Please get into pairs with someone near you. If you don't already know your partner at the table, introduce yourself. Then, I'd like you to interview each other. Ask two things:
   a. Where are you ministering, and
   b. What ONE thing should we know about you that we don't already know but must know to know you better?
5. Pairs introduce one another, answering the two questions.

6. Importance of Mentoring
   In a 1968 sermon, Dr. Martin Luther King Jr. made a statement like this: Every person has the potential for greatness; not fame, but for greatness . . . because greatness is determined by service.* *We believe that about our students. We believe that about you as a mentor. Mentoring is the key to birthing greatness in another.*
7. Modeling a life of servant-leadership is a key to mentoring.
8. Leaving a legacy
   "You as a mentor have the opportunity to leave a powerful, positive legacy on the life of another ministry person. Think about whose legacy has impacted you."

10:10 A.M.

B. Overview of the Day and Getting Focused
1. Review of the schedule for the day
2. Get mentors into groups of four people. Read Philippians 4:8–9, and discuss what it says about thinking like a mentor. Have each group share.
3. Tell coaching story.
4. Pray.

10:25 A.M.

C. The "Nuts and Bolts" of Our Mentored Ministry Program
1. Demonstrate Mentored Ministry Web page and where to find mentoring materials.
2. Look into Handbook and Note-Taking Guide and go over:
   a. Basic assumptions of mentored ministry
   b. The goals of mentored ministry
      i. The spiritual formation of students for life and ministry. Done in Campus Reflection Group, mentoring, and Dialogical Journal.

---

* From a sermon preached by Martin Luther King Jr. in 1968. The entire statement follows: "Jesus gave us a new norm of greatness. If you want to be important—wonderful. If you want to be recognized—wonderful. If you want to be great—wonderful. But recognize that he who is greatest among you shall be your servant. That's a new definition of greatness. And this morning, the thing that I like about it: by giving that definition of greatness, it means that everybody can be great, because everybody can serve. You don't have to have a college degree to serve. You don't have to make your subject and your verb agree to serve. You don't have to know about Plato and Aristotle to serve. You don't have to know Einstein's theory of relativity to serve. You don't have to know the second theory of thermodynamics in physics to serve. You only need a heart full of grace, a soul generated by love. And you can be that servant" (http://www.stanford.edu/group/King/publications/sermons/680204.000_Drum_Major_Instinct.html).

  ii. The students create intentional relationships for accountability and enhance relational ministry skills. Done in mentoring, Parish Advisory Group, and congregation.

  iii. The personal and professional development of the students. Done in active ministry in the parish setting, case studies, and Dialogical Journal.

3. Go over student requirements.
   a. Experience broad exposure to ministry in the parish, working eight hours per week in the ministry setting.
   b. Experience cross-cultural extension ministry of the parish, working eight hours per week in the ministry setting.
   c. Work toward three or four meaningful and measurable Growth Goals:
      i. Personal spiritual growth
      ii. Family life
      iii. Ministry growth area
      iv. Optional ministry growth area
   d. Meet weekly with Campus Reflection Group for case study discussion, spiritual formation, ministry skills instruction, and accountability with the group.
   e. Meet monthly with Parish Advisory Group.
   f. Complete the weekly Dialogical Journal assignments.
   g. Meet with the mentor for a minimum of one hour per week.
4. Go over mentor expectations.
   a. Guide the student in an increasingly comprehensive experience in ministry practice.
      i. Help student set appropriate Growth Goals.
      ii. Help the student set up the Parish Advisory Group.
      iii. Provide the student with opportunity (and hold accountable) for eight hours of ministry work per week (inside the parish walls; outside the parish walls/cross-cultural).
      iv. Meet with the student for a minimum of one hour for consultation/interview each week.
   b. Encourage the student to maintain integration of study that informs ministry—to intentionally think theologically in daily life; to diligently complete Dialogical Journal.
   c. Model ministry and Christian living, within the life of ministry, for the student.
   d. Actively reflect with the student on ministry issues.
      i. Using quality questions (not just facts): open-ended, non-judgmental
      ii. Use right attitude: positive and helpful
      iii. Use right audience: one-on-one

iv. Offer right alternatives: What went well? Where got stuck? What would you do differently?

11:05 A.M.
Break

11:20 A.M.
D. Living as a Mentor, Like Jesus
Note: The content for this section can all be found in chapter 6 of this text and the corresponding resources; thus it is not duplicated here except in outline form.
1. Mentoring has direction: vertical, horizontal, mentoring up
2. Nine Types of Mentors from Bobby Clinton
3. Essentials of Mentoring from Keith Anderson and Randy Reese
4. Jesus' Model of Mentoring

12:30 P.M.
Lunch Break

1 P.M.
E. Talk at the Table
1. Brief interviews of previous mentors
2. Questions and answers
3. Introduce cross-cultural requirements so mentors are thinking ahead with students about a future cross-cultural location.
4. Remind mentors that this is a required seminary class, just like others. The *practice of ministry* is its content.
5. Go through remainder of Mentored Ministry Handbook.
a. Talk through the various forms that must be filled out.
b. Emphasize Confidentiality page.
6. Make any final announcements.
7. Explain mentor resources available on campus and online.

1:45 P.M.
Break

2 P.M.
F. Holy Communion and Commissioning

2:25 P.M.
G. Thanks and Benediction

Final Thoughts and Comments

Make Any Training/Equipping Model Relational

There is nothing quite as crazy as lecturing people about how to build relationships. While the preceding outline only demonstrates a couple of break-out sessions for the mentors, it is important for the mentors to regularly offer feedback and discuss matters among themselves. They can easily move back and forth between listening to teaching from the front and processing in groups of two or four. Despite what adults usually say when asked, they actually learn more with a few good questions and a small group than through lecture.[5]

Do not be afraid to experiment with multiple ways of relationship building between the mentors. Often adults attend a training session, expecting to sit and absorb. What we know is that they do sit but little gets absorbed. I have found that using humorous (some would call them silly) games can raise the positive endorphin level so the students relax and actually enjoy their time together. When introducing a silly game—for example, "Simon Says"—I expect to hear groans and see people looking at one another as if to say, "Why am I wasting my time here?" So I tell them right up front that I am not too bright and as they get to know me, they will discover I am just plain crazy. But I want them to try a silly game for me, just to see what happens. Once they have started laughing together, I have won the day.

Another key is to give time for sharing around a Bible passage. Use a few questions that let the mentors talk about the struggles they are facing in ministry and what they expect to happen through the mentoring they will do.

Always Commission the Mentors

Even with limited time, at least pray over the mentors and bless them for the vital ministry that you and God have asked them to do. Since you are committed to raising the bar for your field education program, mentors must know how important they are to you, to your program, and to God's work on earth. You and I are dependent upon their success. So are our students.

In addition to the prayer time, you might include a brief responsive liturgy and other portions of a worship service. You will note from the outline section of this chapter that we plan a combined Holy Communion and commissioning service to last about thirty minutes.

Find Ways to Encourage and Cheer

Do not be afraid to be a cheerleader. Giving small gifts and communicating

---

5. Daryl L. Smith, "The Effects of Cooperative Learning in a Short-Term, Intensive, Adult, Religious Education Seminary" (Ed.D. dissertation, University of Kentucky, 1995), 107–21.

regularly can keep mentors connected to you and your ministry.[6] We have found that a periodic e-newsletter helps us stay in touch with mentors. It includes tips on mentoring, reminders of what they are to do, a schedule of coming events, and encouraging words of thanksgiving for what they have done.

Hit a Home Run: Visit the Ministry Campus

Due to budget restrictions, I have had to temporarily curtail the most effective part of my field education ministry—visiting every mentor and student on-site at their ministry location. When I was able to visit every student every year, the rewards were outstanding.

You can design all sorts of plans. Most of my trips were out and back, connecting to as many students as possible between my home and the farthest student. I booked my time to spend about ninety minutes with each student, and then leave drive time to the next. My most rewarding but difficult trip was a loop around the state of Florida. Over the two days I visited eight or nine students, from Orlando west to Tampa, south to Naples, east to Miami, up the east coast, and back. My cell phone helped make adjustments as traffic or a prolonged stay at one site changed my schedule.

For me, it was too complicated to see every student working in a public ministry event. To find any time to connect at their site was the best I could do. In fact, if a student was leading an event, I had less time to spend in depth with the student. Thus, I have grown to prefer a drop-in during the office day.

When I first arrive at each ministry setting, usually a church, I hunt down the student. Often the student is looking for me in the parking lot. I always hope that the student has remembered to arrange for the mentor to be available for a visit as well, although the bulk of my time is spent with the student. The mentor visit is often in private, to catch up on how the relationship and student work is progressing. Most mentors are willing to give only a few minutes (maybe ten) of their time. I then move back to the student.

Over the years, I have found the facility to be the best tool for learning the ministry story—better than sitting in an office, asking the student to tell me what is happening in the internship. As we walk around the facility, I ask questions about what happens in various rooms, gardens, and worship spots. Students quickly begin telling the story of the congregation. They describe struggles they have had in "this room" or the transformation that happened while "we were praying in this corner." After an hour, I have a quite thorough understanding, both from the mentor interview and the student's story, of how the field education experience is going.

---

6. We have discovered that the size of gift does not really matter. We have also discovered that most mentors have more labeled pens than a drawer can hold. We have turned to designing mouse pads in our office (with our office name on them) to keep mentored ministry in front of the mentors. You will need to find out what your mentors can use and create it.

Before I leave, I always pray with the student (and mentor, if she or he is still available) and ask God to bless the mentor, the student, and the ministry in general. When prayer has ended and hugs are completed, I jump into the car and charge to my next visit.

Let me repeat, these visits have been the most effective part of our field experience. They are literally home runs. The mentors are appreciative of the personal care. Students are astounded that a professor actually visited them. The relationship between the student and me has grown, and I have a better understanding when students report (for example, in case studies) from their sites.

The Payoff

When I look back on my field education work to check for success, I always start by evaluating transformed student lives. If I see a difference in the ministry effectiveness of students, I know that the mentor and I have done our work in partnership with the Holy Spirit. Judy (not her real name) is one of those stories.

Judy started in my fall semester mentored ministry group, just after her mentor had completed training. Judy is passionate about people, particularly people with pain-filled lives. Years earlier she had been active in ministry until it all flatlined with a broken relationship and a lost marriage. As recovery slowly came, so did her desire to help people who have walked her same painful road.

As the semester moved along, I began to hear stories of Judy and her new husband hanging out with homeless people. In reality, they hung out with both the homeless and the East Coast "bar crowd." The more time they spent with these needful people, the more they realized it was their task to make a difference. What developed was a Sunday afternoon feeding program at the church and a rockin' street-people worship event to follow. The worship band was recruited from bar performers who lived on the fringes of life. Judy's mentor, though not always comfortable with this new ministry invasion of a "seniors only" congregation, was as supportive as possible.

A year into the project, the ministry was running on its own—no longer related to a seminary credit. Judy came to me one day and said, "You've got to hear this! Last Sunday night a man stayed after our worship, demanding to meet with the entire staff team, including the pastor (my mentor), who had already gone home across the backyard. When we could not dissuade him—since we were all so tired—we joined him in the church sanctuary. Once the staff team arrived, he began to weep. We thought we had an addict on our hands. When he could finally talk, he said, 'One year ago, I was sitting in a bar listening to the band. I'd lost my family, my job, my home. Two of the band members, who play in your worship band, came to my table during the break and said that I needed to come to this church for help. Tonight my life is changed. My family has returned, I have a job, and tomorrow we close on our new home. I want you to pray a blessing on it for us.'"

But the story doesn't end there; it goes on like the ripples in the nearby ocean. In the last two years, the bar band (also the worship band) has created a powerful ministry CD of their original music—telling the stories of their transforming lives. Judy and her husband met an AIDS mother living with her son in a car. After befriending her for only a few months, the AIDS mother died, so Judy and her husband (now empty nesters) took the fifteen-year-old son in as their own.

Judy's story, while miraculous, is not an exception. When mentors and those of us who equip them partner together to help a ministry student catch a vision of God's best dream, amazing miracles begin. And that's when our "paycheck," greater than any money, arrives.

What a privilege! What a responsibility!

Prayer of Transformation

What an amazing privilege it is to partner with you, God—to watch as your dream unfolds in the lives of students and as you use us in the unfolding. What a joy it is to see mentors take seriously their role in your work, touching lives and leaving the imprint of their (and your) ministry legacy. Thank you for this privilege. Bless each of our mentors in their ministries. And continue to empower us who equip them for the serious and awesome task to which you've called us. All this we pray in Jesus' name. Amen.

Reflection Questions

1. If you were a news photographer viewing your last mentor training session, what would you have photographed? Why? How would you have labeled the picture for a newspaper story?

2. What is the biggest joy you face in preparing mentors for their role with your students? What is the greatest challenge?

3. As you think back across the students you have known, which one or two stories were the biggest miracles for you?

4. If money and time were not issues, what *one* thing would you love to do with the mentors that you cannot do right now? Is there something that could be changed so you could do it? Are there resources you need to tap into?

Further Reading

Anderson, Keith, and Randy Reese. *Spiritual Mentoring: A Guide for Seeking and Giving Direction.* Downers Grove, IL: InterVarsity Press, 1999.

Biehl, Bobb. *Mentoring: Confidence in Finding a Mentor and Becoming One.* Nashville: Broadman & Holman, 1996.

Daloz, Laurent. *Effective Teaching and Mentoring: Realizing the Transformational Power of Adult Learning Experiences.* San Francisco: Jossey-Bass, 1986.

Stanley, Paul, and J. Robert Clinton. *Connecting: The Mentoring Relationships You Need to Succeed in Life.* Colorado Springs: NavPress, 1992.

Zachary, Lois. *The Mentor's Guide: Facilitating Effective Learning Relationships.* San Francisco: Jossey-Bass, 2000.

Bibliography

Aburdene, Patricia, and John Naisbitt. *Megatrends for Women*. Rev. and updated ed. New York: Fawcett Columbine, 1993.

Adsit, Christopher. *Personal Disciple-Making: A Step-by-Step Guide for Leading a New Christian from New Birth to Maturity*. 2nd ed. Orlando: Integrated Resources, 1996.

Alexander, Archibald. *The Log College*. London: Banner of Truth Trust, 1968.

Anderson, Keith, and Randy Reese. *Spiritual Mentoring: A Guide for Seeking and Giving Direction*. Downers Grove, IL: InterVarsity Press, 1999.

Anderson, Leith. *A Church for the Twenty-First Century*. Minneapolis: Bethany House, 1992.

Anderson, Ray. *The Shape of Practical Theology: Empowering Ministry with Theological Praxis*. Downers Grove, IL: InterVarsity Press, 2001.

Anthony, Michael. *The Effective Church Board: A Handbook for Mentoring and Training Servant Leaders*. Grand Rapids: Baker, 1993.

———, ed. *Introducing Christian Education: Foundations for the Twenty-First Century*. Grand Rapids: Baker, 2001.

———. "Working with Boards and Committees." In *Management Essentials for Christian Ministries*, edited by Michael J. Anthony and James Estep Jr. Nashville: Broadman & Holman, 2005.

Association of Theological Schools. "Degree Program Standards." http://www.ats .edu/accrediting/standards/DegreeStandards.pdf.

———. *Fact Book on Theological Education, 1972–1999*. Vandalia, OH: Association of Theological Schools, 2000.

———. "Fact Books/Annual Data Tables, 1999–2007." www.ats.edu.

Atkinson, Harley. *The Power of Small Groups in Christian Education*. Nappanee, IN: Evangel, 2002.

Augsburger, David. *Caring Enough to Confront: How to Understand and Express Your Deepest Feelings Toward Others*. Rev. ed. Glendale, CA: Regal, 1980.

Baker, Joye. "An Analysis of the Leadership Challenges Facing the Dallas Theological Seminary Women Alumnae." D.Min. dissertation, Dallas Theological Seminary, 2005.

Baker, Julie. *A Pebble in the Pond: The Ripple Effect: Leadership Skills Every Woman Can Achieve*. Colorado Springs: Cook, 2001.

Banks, Robert. *Reenvisioning Theological Education: Exploring a Missional Alternative to Current Models*. Grand Rapids: Eerdmans, 1999.

Barclay, Oliver. *Evangelicalism in Britain, 1935–1995: A Personal Sketch*. Leicester: InterVarsity Press, 1997.

Barclay, William. *The Gospel of Matthew, Volume 1.* Philadelphia: Westminster, 1958.

Bebbington, David. *Evangelicalism in Modern Britain: A History from the 1730s to the 1980s.* London: Unwin Hyman, 1989.

Becker, Carol. *Leading Women: How Church Women Can Avoid Leadership Traps and Negotiate the Gender Maze.* Nashville: Abingdon, 1996.

Belenky, Mary, Blythe Clinchy, Nancy Goldberger, and Jill Tarule. *Women's Ways of Knowing: The Development of Self, Voice, and Mind.* 10th anniversary ed. New York: Basic Books, 1986.

Bell, Rob. *Velvet Elvis: Repainting the Christian Faith.* Grand Rapids: Zondervan, 2005.

Biehl, Bobb. *Mentoring: Confidence in Finding a Mentor and Becoming One.* Nashville: Broadman & Holman, 1996.

Bloom, Myra. "Multiple Roles of the Mentor: Supporting Women's Adult Development." In *Learning Environments for Women's Adult Development: Bridges Toward Change,* edited by Kathleen Taylor and Catherine Marienau. New Directions for Adult and Continuing Education. San Francisco: Jossey-Bass, 1995.

Bonhoeffer, Dietrich. *Life Together.* Translated by John W. Doberstein. New York: Harper & Row, 1954.

Bradley, John, and Jay Carty. *Discovering Your Natural Talents.* Colorado Springs: NavPress, 1994.

Bridston, Keith, ed. *Casebook on Church and Society.* Nashville: Abingdon, 1974.

Bromiley, Geoffrey, ed. *The New International Standard Bible Encyclopedia.* Rev. ed. 4 vols. Grand Rapids: Eerdmans, 1986.

Brookfield, Stephen. *The Skilled Teacher.* San Francisco: Jossey-Bass, 1990.

Buckingham, Marcus, and Donald Clifton. *Now, Discover Your Strengths.* New York: Free Press, 2001.

Buechner, Frederick. *Wishful Thinking: A Theological ABC.* New York: Harper & Row, 1973.

Bystrom, Raymond. *Slices of Ministry: The Case Study Method of Teaching and Learning.* Fresno: Pacific Seminary, 2005.

Calvin, John. *Institutes of the Christian Religion.* Translated by Ford Lewis Battles. Philadelphia: Westminster, 1960.

Charlton, Joy. "Women in Seminary: A Review of Current Social Science Research." *Review of Religious Review* 28, no. 4 (1987): 305–19.

Chliwniak, Luba. "Leadership in Higher Education: Influences on Perceptions of Women and Men Leaders." Ph.D. dissertation, University of Arizona, 1996.

Clifton, Donald, and Edward Anderson. *StrengthsQuest: Discover and Develop Your Strengths in Academics, Career, and Beyond.* Washington, DC: Gallup, 2002.

Clinton, J. Robert. "Constellation Model." http://www.bobbyclinton.com/articles/downloads/ConstellationModel.pd.pdf.

——. *Leadership Emergence Theory.* Altadena, CA: Barnabas Resources, 1989.

——. *The Making of a Leader.* Colorado Springs: NavPress, 1988.

Clinton, J. Robert, and Richard Clinton. *The Mentor Handbook: Detailed Guidelines and Helps for Christian Mentors and Mentorees.* Altadena, CA: Barnabas, 1991.

Cloud, Henry. *Integrity: The Courage to Meet the Demands of Reality*. New York: Collins, 2006.

Cohen, Norman, and Michael Galbraith. "Mentoring in the Learning Society." In *Mentoring: New Strategies and Challenges*, edited by Norman Cohen and Michael Galbraith, 5–14. New Directions in Adult and Continuing Education. San Francisco: Jossey-Bass, 1995.

Conde-Frazier, Elizabeth, S. Steve Kang, and Gary A. Parrett. *A Many Colored Kingdom: Multicultural Dynamics for Spiritual Formation*. Grand Rapids: Baker, 2004.

Cowart, D. Keith. "The Role of Mentoring in the Preparation of Church Planters of Reproducing Churches." D.Min. dissertation, Asbury Theological Seminary, 2002.

Daloz, Laurent. *Effective Teaching and Mentoring: Realizing the Transformational Power of Adult Learning Experiences*. San Francisco: Jossey-Bass, 1986.

———. *Mentor: Guiding the Journey of Adult Learners*. San Francisco: Jossey-Bass, 1999.

De Young, Curtiss Paul. *United by Faith: The Multiracial Congregation as an Answer to the Problem of Race*. New York: Oxford University Press, 2003.

Donovan, Craig, and Jim Garnett. *Internships for Dummies*. New York: Hungry Minds, 2001.

Duff, Carolyn. *Learning from Other Women: How to Benefit from the Knowledge, Wisdom, and Experience of Female Mentors*. New York: American Management Association, 1999.

Edwards, Sue, and Kelley Mathews. *New Doors to Ministry to Women: A Fresh Model for Transforming Your Church, Campus, or Mission Field*. Grand Rapids: Kregel, 2002.

Engstrom, Ted. *The Fine Art of Mentoring*. Brentwood, TN: Wolgemuth & Hyatt, 1989.

Evans, Tony. *Let's Get to Know Each Other: What White Christians Should Know About Black Christians*. Nashville: Thomas Nelson, 1995.

Farrel, Bill, and Pam Farrel. *Men Are Like Waffles, Women Are Like Spaghetti*. Eugene, OR: Harvest House, 2001.

Fenwick, Tara, and Jim Parsons. *The Art of Evaluation*. Toronto: Thompson, 2000.

Gallup Organization. *Strengths Performance Coach for Faith*. Princeton, NJ: Gallup, 2005.

Gangel, Kenneth. *Team Leadership in Christian Ministry: Using Multiple Gifts to Build a Unified Vision*. Chicago: Moody, 1997.

Garner, Howard. *Frames of Mind: The Theory of Multiple Intelligences*. 2nd ed. New York: Basic Books, 2004.

Gilligan, Carol. *In a Different Voice: Psychological Theory and Women's Development*. Cambridge, MA: Harvard University Press, 1982.

Goleman, Daniel. *Working with Emotional Intelligence*. New York: Bantam, 1998.

Goleman, Daniel, Richard Boyatzis, and Annie McKee. *Primal Leadership: Realizing the Power of Emotional Intelligence*. Boston: Harvard Business School Press, 2002.

Graves, Stephen, and Thomas Addington. *A Case for Character: Authentic Living in Your Workplace*. Nashville: Broadman & Holman, 1998.

Green, Michele. "The Preparation of Women for Ministry: An Exploratory Study of the Traditional Curriculum in Evangelical Seminaries." Ph.D. dissertation, Loyola University, 2002.

Gross, Lynn Schafer. *The Internship Experience*. Prospect Heights, IL: Waveland, 1987.

Harris, Philip, and Robert Moran. *Managing Cultural Differences*. 3rd ed. Houston: Gulf, 1991.

Heatherly, Joyce Landorf. *Balcony People*. Austin, TX: Balcony, 1984.

Helgesen, Sally. *The Female Advantage: Women's Ways of Leadership*. 1st ed. New York: Doubleday Currency, 1990.

Hendricks, Howard, and William Hendricks. *As Iron Sharpens Iron: Building Character in a Mentoring Relationship*. Chicago: Moody, 1995.

Hightower, James E., Jr., and W. Craig Gilliam. *A Time for Change? Revisioning Your Call*. Bethesda, MD: Alban, 2000.

Hillman, George M., Jr. *Ministry Greenhouse: Cultivating Environments for Practical Learning*. Herndon, VA: Alban, 2008.

Hoefer, Herbert. "Rooted or Uprooted: The Necessity of Contextualization in Missions." *International Journal of Frontier Mission* 24, no. 3 (2007): 131–38.

Hoekema, Anthony. *Created in God's Image*. Grand Rapids: Eerdmans, 1986.

Hornecker, Ronald. "Choosing a Ministry Placement and Field Supervisor." In *Experiencing Ministry Supervision: A Field-Based Approach*, edited by William T. Pyle and Mary Alice Seals, 19–32. Nashville: Broadman & Holman, 1995.

Hsu, Albert. *Singles at the Crossroads: A Fresh Perspective on Christian Singleness*. Downers Grove, IL: InterVarsity Press, 1997.

Hybels, Bill. *Courageous Leadership*. Grand Rapids: Zondervan, 2002.

Inrig, Elizabeth. *Release Your Potential: Using Your Gifts in a Thriving Women's Ministry*. Chicago: Moody, 2001.

Jackson, Walter. "An Introduction to Theological Field Education." In *Experiencing Ministry Supervision: A Field-Based Approach*, edited by William T. Pyle and Mary Alice Seals, 1–18. Nashville: Broadman & Holman, 1995.

Johnson, Ben Campbell. *Hearing Gods Call: Ways of Discernment for Laity and Clergy*. Grand Rapids: Eerdmans, 2002.

Johnson, David, and Frank Johnson. *Joining Together*. Englewood Cliffs, NJ: Prentice-Hall, 1975.

Johnson, Gregg. "Biological Basis for Gender-Specific Behavior." In *Recovering Biblical Manhood and Womanhood*, edited by John Piper and Wayne A. Grudem. Wheaton, IL: Crossway, 1991.

Killen, Patricia O'Connell, and John DeBeer. *The Art of Theological Reflection*. New York: Crossroad, 1995.

Kim, Young-Il. *Knowledge, Attitude and Experience: Ministry in the Cross-Cultural Context*. Nashville: Abingdon, 1992.

King Jr., Martin Luther. "The Drum Major Instinct." In *The Essential Writings and*

Speeches of Martin Luther King Jr., edited by James M. Washington, 259–67. New York: Harper Collins, 1986.

Knowles, Malcolm. *The Modern Practice of Adult Education: From Pedagogy to Andragogy*. River Grove, IL: Follett, 1980.

——. *Self-Directed Learning: A Guide for Learners and Teachers*. New York: Association Press, 1975.

Kouzes, James, and Barry Posner. *The Leadership Challenge*. 2nd ed. San Francisco: Jossey-Bass, 1995.

Lane, Patty. *A Beginner's Guide to Crossing Cultures: Making Friends in a Multicultural World*. Downers Grove, IL: InterVarsity Press, 2002.

Levinson, Daniel. *The Seasons of a Man's Life*. New York: Ballantine, 1978.

Liesveld, Roseanne, Jo Ann Miller, and Jennifer Robinson. *Teach with Your Strengths*. New York: Gallup, 2006.

Lingenfelter, Sherwood G. *Transforming Culture: A Challenge for Christian Mission*. 2nd ed. Grand Rapids: Baker, 1998.

Luecke, David, and Samuel Southard. *Pastoral Administration: Integrating Ministry and Management in the Church*. Waco, TX: Word, 1986.

Martin, Ralph P., and Peter Davids, eds. *Dictionary of the Later New Testament and Its Developments*. Downers Grove, IL: InterVarsity Press, 1997.

McCarty, Doran. *Supervising Ministry Students*. Atlanta: Home Mission Board of the Southern Baptist Convention, 1986.

——. *Working with People*. Nashville: Broadman & Holman, 1986.

Moe, Kenneth Alan. *The Pastor's Survival Manual*. Bethesda, MD: Alban, 1995.

Moir, Anne, and David Jessel. *Brain Sex: The Real Difference Between Men and Women*. New York: Carol, 1991.

Moore, Ralph. *Starting a New Church*. Ventura, CA: Regal, 2002.

Morgan, Timothy. "Re-Engineering the Seminary: Crisis of Credibility Forces Change." *Christianity Today*, 24 October 1994, 74–79.

Mulholland, M. Robert, Jr. *Invitation to a Journey: A Road Map for Spiritual Formation*. Downers Grove, IL: InterVarsity Press, 1993.

Osborne, Grant. *The Hermeneutical Spiral: A Comprehensive Introduction to Biblical Interpretation*. Downers Grove, IL: InterVarsity Press, 2006.

Oswald, Roy. *Clergy Self Care: Finding a Balance for Effective Ministry*. Herndon, VA: Alban, 1991.

——. *New Beginnings: A Pastorate Start Up Workbook*. Bethesda, MD: Alban, 1993.

Outler, Albert. "Introduction." In *The Works of John Wesley*, edited by Albert C. Outler. Nashville: Abingdon, 1984.

Palloff, Rena, and Keith Pratt. *Building Learning Communities in Cyberspace: Effective Strategies for the Online Classroom*. San Francisco: Jossey-Bass, 1999.

Patton, John. *From Ministry to Theology: Pastoral Action and Reflection*. Decatur, GA: Journal of Pastoral Care Publications, 1995.

Paul, Richard. *Critical Thinking*. 2nd ed. Santa Rosa, CA: Foundation for Critical Thinking, 1992.

Peterson, Brooks. *Cultural Intelligence: A Guide to Working with People from Other Cultures*. Yarmouth, ME: Intercultural, 2004.

Peterson, Eugene. *A Long Obedience in the Same Direction: Discipleship in an Instant Society*. 20th anniversary ed. Downers Grove, IL: InterVarsity Press, 2000.

——. *Working the Angles: The Shape of Pastoral Integrity*. Grand Rapids: Eerdmans, 1987.

Petrie, Alistair. *Releasing Heaven on Earth: God's Principles for Restoring the Land*. Grand Rapids: Chosen, 2000.

Phillips, Harold, and Robert Firth. *Cases in Denominational Administration: A Management Casebook for Decision-Making*. Berrien Springs, MI: Andrews University Press, 1978.

Pocock, Michael, Gailyn Van Rheenen, and Douglas McConnell. *The Changing Face of World Missions: Engaging Contemporary Issues and Trends*. Grand Rapids: Baker, 2002.

Polanyi, Michael. *The Tacit Dimension*. Gloucester, MA: Peter Smith, 1983.

Polhill, John. "Toward a Biblical View of Call." In *Preparing for Christian Ministry: An Evangelical Approach*, edited by David P. Gushee and Walter C. Jackson, 65–79. Grand Rapids: Baker, 1996.

Purves, Andrew. *Reconstructing Pastoral Theology: A Christological Foundation*. Louisville: Westminster, 2004.

Pyle, William T. "Theological Reflection." In *Experiencing Ministry Supervision: A Field-Based Approach*, edited by William T. Pyle and Mary Alice Seals, 109–24. Nashville: Broadman & Holman, 1995.

Pyle, William T., and Mary Alice Seals. "Tools for Data Gathering." In *Experiencing Ministry Supervision: A Field-Based Approach*, edited by William T. Pyle and Mary Alice Seals, 99–108. Nashville: Broadman & Holman, 1995.

Rath, Tom. *StrenghtsFinder 2.0*. New York: Gallup, 2007.

Rhoads, Steven. *Taking Sex Differences Seriously*. San Francisco: Encounter, 2004.

Rodriguez, Jeanette, and Sharon Callahan. "Creating a Space in Oneself for the Other." Paper presented at the 27th Biennial Consultation of the Association for Theological Field Education, Chicago, January 2003.

Romanowski, William. *Eyes Wide Open*. Grand Rapids: Brazos, 2001.

Rosenthal, Cindy Simon, ed. *Women Transforming Congress*. Norman, OK: University of Oklahoma Press, 2002.

Ruderman, Marian. "Leader Development Across Gender." In *The Center for Creative Leadership Handbook of Leadership Development*, edited by Cynthia McCauley and Ellen Van Velsor, 271–303. San Francisco: Jossey-Bass, 2004.

Saucy, Robert L., and Judith K. TenElshof. *Women and Men in Ministry: A Complementary Perspective*. Chicago: Moody, 2001.

Sax, Leonard. *Why Gender Matters: What Parents and Teachers Need to Know About the Emerging Science of Sex Differences*. New York: Broadway, 2005.

Scarf, Maggie. *Unfinished Business: Pressure Points in the Lives of Women*. New York: Ballantine, 1980.

Schon, Donald. *The Reflective Practitioner: How Professionals Think in Action*. New York: Basic Books, 1983.

Schutz, William. *FIRO: A Three-Dimensional Theory of Interpersonal Behavior*. 3rd ed. Muir Beach, CA: Will Schutz Associates, 1998.

Seals, Mary Alice. "Evaluation in the Supervisory Experience." In *Experiencing Ministry Supervision: A Field-Based Approach*, edited by William T. Pyle and Mary Alice Seals, 125–37. Nashville: Broadman & Holman, 1995.

Seymour, Jack L. "Perspectives on Diversity: Addressing and Embodying Diversity in Theological Education." In *Diversity in Theological Education*, edited by the Association of Theological Schools, 5–8. Pittsburgh: Association of Theological Schools, n.d.

Sheehy, Gail. *New Passages: Mapping Your Life Across Time*. New York: Random House, 1995.

———. *Passages: Predictable Crises of Adult Life*. New York: Ballantine, 2006.

Shuler, Clarence. *Winning the Race to Unity: Is Racial Reconciliation Really Working?* Chicago: Moody, 2003.

Smith, Daryl L. "The Effects of Cooperative Learning in a Short-Term, Intensive, Adult, Religious Education Seminary." Ed.D. dissertation, University of Kentucky, 1995.

Snarey, John, and George Vaillant. "How Lower- and Working-Class Youth Become Middle-Class Adults: The Association Between Ego Defense Mechanisms and Upward Social Mobility." *Child Development* 56, no. 4 (1985): 889–910.

Southerland, James. "African American Underrepresentation in Intercultural Missions: Perceptions of Black Missionaries and the Theology of Survival/Security." Ph.D. dissertation, Trinity Evangelical Divinity School, 1988.

Sparks, Barbara. "A Sociocultural Approach to Planning Programs for Immigrant Learners." *Adult Learning* 12, no. 4 (2001): 22–25.

Sprague, William. *Annals of the American Pulpit*. Vol. 1. New York: Carter and Brothers, 1859.

Spring, Beth, and Kelsey Menehan. "Women in Seminary: Preparing for What?" *Christianity Today*, September 5, 1986, 18–23.

Stanley, Paul, and J. Robert Clinton. *Connecting: The Mentoring Relationships You Need to Succeed in Life*. Colorado Springs: NavPress, 1992.

Stevens, Paul. "The Supervisory Conference." In *Experiencing Ministry Supervision: A Field-Based Approach*, edited by William T. Pyle and Mary Alice Seals, 85–98. Nashville: Broadman & Holman, 1995.

Stone, Howard, and James Duke. *How to Think Theologically*. 2nd ed. Minneapolis: Fortress, 2006.

Swetland, Kenneth. *Facing Messy Stuff in the Church: Case Studies for Pastors and Congregations*. Grand Rapids: Kregel, 2005.

———. *The Hidden World of the Pastor: Case Studies on Personal Issues of Real Pastors*. Grand Rapids: Baker, 1995.

Tannen, Deborah. *You Just Don't Understand: Women and Men in Conversation*. New York: Morrow, 1990.

Trent, John. *Life Mapping*. Colorado Springs: WaterBrook, 1998.

United States Census Bureau. "Projected Population of the United States, by Race and Hispanic Origin: 2000 to 2050." http://www.census.gov/ipc/www/usinterimproj/.

———. "Summary of Fertility, Mortality, and Migration Assumptions by Race and

Hispanic Origin: Lowest, Middle, and Highest Series, 1999 to 2100." http://www.census.gov/population/www/projections/natsum.html.

Walling, Terry. "Perspective Time Line." In *Focused Living Resource Kit*, edited by Terry B. Walling. Anaheim, CA: ChurchSmart Resources, 1996.

Warner, Fara. "Inside Intel's Mentoring Movement." *Fast Company*, March 2002, 116.

Westminster Theological Seminary. "Teaching Churches Network." http://www.wts.edu/mentor/tcnetwork.html.

Whitehead, James, and Evelyn Eaton Whitehead. *Method in Ministry: Theological Reflection and Christian Ministry*. Rev. ed. Lanham, MD: Sheed & Ward, 1995.

Winseman, Albert L., Donald Clifton, and Curt Liesveld. *Living Your Strengths: Discover Your God-Given Talents and Inspire Your Community*. New York: Gallup, 2003–2004.

Wolvin, Andrew, and Carolyn Gwynn Coakly. *Listening*. 4th ed. Dubuque, IA: Brown, 1992.

Wu, Esther. "Asians Finding a Place in the Political Process." *Dallas Morning News*, August 2, 2007.